THEY INSPIRED ME

THEY INSPIRED ME

My Life Journey from Gardi to Tomahawk Mountain

An Autobiography by:

Jimmy L. Hill

For more information contact:
The Hill Group Inc.
1217 Eagle Ridge Road, Dawsonville, GA 30534
Call 404-372-8680 or visit www.Jimmy-Hill.com

Printing by The Hill Group Inc., Dawsonville, Georgia, founded in 1996

Library of Congress Control Number – 2020911174
Print ISBN - 978-1-7352407-0-1
Ebook ISBN - 978-1-7352407-1-8

Jacket design by Gail H. Hill
Jacket photos by Jimmy L. Hill
Author photo by John Seibel

DEDICATION

To my wife and partner in life, Gail

ACKNOWLEDGMENTS

As I was thinking about writing my autobiography, I imagined that I would sit down at my computer and write. What a novice I was. I ultimately spent numerous hours researching how to write a book. That led to many additional hours researching facts, figures, events, and timelines. One thing that I did not realize I had was forty-four years of personal calendars. Who has that? I knew that I had some, but they were scattered everywhere in my files. I do admit that this book project was harder than I thought it would be. I have spent over 18 months working to complete it.

My wife, Gail, has been a great partner in writing this book, as she has in life. I am an engineer and love details, and she is the one who pulls me out of the weeds and helps me communicate more effectively. Both of our children, Chris and Miranda, have provided valuable input.

My mother wrote a draft manuscript of her partial life story that I found in her files after her death. I was not aware that she had started writing her life story, but I am so thankful that she did. I learned so much from her writings that I did not know. I have shared much of that information in Chapter 1.

My siblings, Jerry Hill Sr. and Linda Hill Day, contributed valuable information for this book. Two of my first cousins, Margaret Campbell and Winona Cameron, provided details of events that helped me immensely. Another first cousin, Deborah Latham, encouraged me to share this story, and Exley Hill, also a first cousin, was enthusiastic about the book and shared a story about our growing up. My second cousins, Stephanie Hopkins DeMilio and Florrie Hopkins, provided input and encouraged me to write this book.

Richard Jackson, Gus Shanklin, and Troy Fore Jr., all from Gardi, spent a considerable amount of time helping me recall names, locations, and events. Melba Bennett Murphy shared information about her dad, Fred Bennett, and the Lambert Bennett place. My Internet searches produced valuable information to add richness to details and events. I have listed those and other informational sources in the Appendix.

Several of my Georgia Power co-workers have provided names and additional information that have been extremely valuable. These include Martha Ruth Whatley, Emma Henry, Linda Smith, Bantes Hodges, Shannon Brown, Marcel Wildes, and Mary Alice Caldwell.

I owe a big thank you to several organizations for providing information for the book. They include the Georgia Agribusiness Council, AgriTrust of Georgia, and the ABAC Alumni Association.

Numerous individuals contributed information for this book, including Kevin Reeves, Mrs. Jimmie Nell Tate, Jim Girtman, Van McCall, Vann Wooten, Kay Harrell, Tim Callaway, Tommy Purser, Anne Young, Lynn Pitts, Mitch Head, Dr. Gary Burtle, Chip Blalock, Donnie Smith, Spencer Black, the late Delane Borron, Michele Creamer, Robert Howell, Jimmy Grimes, Cindy Theiler, Georgia Agriculture Commissioner Gary Black, Heather Hardy Leo, Judy Ricketson Carter, Hanna and Johnny Rogers, Reverend Dewitt R. Corbin, Reverend Keith Yawn, Reverend Donnie Brown, Reverend Charles Morgan, Fran Ricketson, JaLayne Coleman, Jimmie and Arlene Ryles, Louise Hill, and Sharon Baldwin.

Friends Emory Jones, Jim Barber, and Dink NeSmith Jr., all authors, were extremely helpful for inspiration and technical questions and as a valuable resource of writing knowledge and expertise. Emory Jones has written several books, including *The Valley Where They Danced* and *Memories Etched in Pott'ry*. Jim Barber has written two books: *Plowed Fields* and *They Made Good Great*. Dink NeSmith wrote a book about his family and his dad entitled *The Last Man To Let You Down*. Thanks, Emory, Jim, and Dink, for your valuable assistance and encouragement.

A representative with a New York publishing house sent me an e-mail with the following comments after reading the first five chapters of my book: "Your life is a truly remarkable one. I read your chapters with tremendous interest; your family is incredible. It really illustrates how a loving family can make even tough circumstances feel luxurious to a child. You also have a real knack for setting scenes and atmosphere for a vivid reading experience." Thank you for your kind words and immense encouragement!

I owe a huge debt of gratitude to the thirty-three individuals listed in Chapter 29, who truly inspired me on my life journey. Almost half of them have passed. They made a huge, positive difference in my life. I hope and pray that I can inspire those who are behind me to be the best that they can be and to serve others.

I called Ann Willis, my editor, after she had completed two chapters. As she answered the phone, my first words were, "You are awesome!" She has been a pleasure to work with and is a consummate professional. Ann made my book shine with the best of them. Ann, thank you so much for your assistance in creating a treasure for me, my family, and friends.

PREFACE

My inspiration for this book came from several sources. One of those was Garland Thompson, who wrote a book for his grandchildren chronicling their early life experiences. I knew very little about my grandparents, and this book will make sure that my grandkids and future great-grandkids know about their grandparents—Gail and me. It has been said that everyone has a book in them. I tend to believe that, and this is my book.

I felt that I had a story to tell as I shared my life experiences. This book starts in the 1940s with a mule and my parents. Gardi, Georgia, is where I was brought home from the hospital as an infant to our tar paper shack home. I spent sixteen years in Gardi and have shared my experiences growing up in rural Georgia. My family moved to Snipesville, Georgia, in the early 1960s. My dad was a Baptist preacher, and my mother was a homemaker and dietary supervisor. In 1970, an unthinkable tragedy happened to our family, and it shook us to the core. This tragedy also had a silver lining.

I left home in the mid-1960s to start my formal education and ultimately spent twenty-eight years at a Fortune 500 company. My life after the corporate world was exciting and impactful. I am in retirement now on Tomahawk Mountain and reflecting on my life, family, and career.

This book takes you through my years of meeting inspiring people, my educational experiences, my career path, and ultimately my reflections of what shaped me. You will shed tears, laugh, learn, reflect, and meet some awesome and inspiring individuals.

Black pepper—or the lack thereof—may be responsible for my coming into this world.

My life's mission is based on the belief that we are put on this earth to serve others. I have always strived to do so. A lot of individuals have inspired me along my life journey, and you will meet them. I hope by sharing my life story, I might inspire others to look for opportunities to serve, inspire, and share their stories.

Man's greatest goal is that his life will make a difference in the world … man's greatest realization is knowing that every day he does make a difference in the world.
Author Unknown

PRAISE FOR THEY INSPIRED ME

"From humble beginnings in a tarpaper shack to a high-level management job at Georgia Power, Jimmy Hill has lived an extraordinary life. Now he's captured it in a riveting autobiography, which is no easy feat. I know; I've tried! I had the pleasure of meeting Jimmy when we both worked for Georgia Power. I was a newbie to the company and dumbstruck to discover Georgia Power knew what agriculture was—much less had a department dedicated to making it better. Jimmy led those efforts, including the technology that enabled Georgia-grown Vidalia Onions to become a year-round treat. Jimmy may have written this autobiography for his family but it's a fascinating story for anyone who loves a good tale about a South Georgia farm boy making the most of the life given to him by God. Along the way, you'll read about the cousin who convinced Jimmy sucking out the insides of raw chicken eggs was a delicacy, the bow and arrow that rivaled the Red-Rider BB Gun in "A Christmas Story," two summers spent picking green beans for Green Giant, and his mama who created the Cadillac of dumplings. All in all, this is an intriguing story of a life well lived by a man I'm honored to call my friend."

— **Jim Barber, author of PLOWED FIELDS**

"Jimmy Hill's book is so very much more than a narrative of his family's history. It's the story of Southern life as it truly existed not so long ago. This is a chronicle any American, especially those lucky enough to have been born Southerners, can hold dear. Read this once, and you'll keep it around for the rest of your days."

— **Emory Jones, author of *The Valley Where They Danced***

PRAISE FOR THEY INSPIRED ME

"Jimmy Hill had a huge impact on my life, both personally and professionally. I was lucky to be selected for the Agri-Leaders program where Jimmy helped us all become better versions of ourselves. This wonderful collection of memories gives even more people the opportunity to learn from his life."

— April Sorrow, Vice President of Communication, Jackson EMC

"Dad writes a great perspective covering our family, a slice of life from his career, and Georgia agriculture spanning decades. The latter alone is worth the read as he illustrates and bridges the gap from some early days of technological developments to their implementation. On a personal level, I learned a lot of new things and relearned others (I've never known someone to keep so many calendars/journals) that I had either forgotten or had always thought were different."

— Chris Hill (Son)

CONTENTS

FOREWARD

Maybe it's from being thirty years in close proximity to the Capitol? Maybe it's from forty years of listening to stories while traveling most of Georgia's backroads? Maybe it's from the internal barometer of age? I am not sure, but frequently I find myself identifying important tidbits and admonishing others to "write that down!" Knowing how and why certain things happened as they did is a valuable contribution one generation can provide the next.

The "someone should write a book about that" challenge is easy to administer. Those who take up that mantle in service to others—past, present, and future—are heroes. The sorting and filtering required for such a cerebral voyage take time, likely produce as many tears as smiles, and most certainly become a ball and chain before the work is completed.

I am thankful for a number of friends who, through their keystrokes, have fed my mind and soul with their personal experiences. These accounts range from historical to hysterical. Great Georgians like The Honorable Larry Walker Sr., Editor Extraordinaire Dink NeSmith, and Harris Blackwood, the Grizzard of Our Time, know how to cram more of the Georgia Experience into one sentence than I could into an entire chapter. Emory Jones and Bobby Rowan also top the list. Recording treasured stories, circumstances, and facts through the skillful use of the English language—and yes, our dialect—is a gift for the ages.

In the following pages, my friend Jimmy Hill blesses us with another volume for our collective enjoyment. *They Inspired Me* takes the reader on a wonderful life journey ranging from very humble beginnings to the Olympic Games. Time and time again, the book demonstrates how the values of family love and support, a willingness to dream the impossible, and a tireless work ethic are still alive and well.

Jimmy credits his parents, his high school agriculture teacher Mr. B. H. Claxton, his beloved wife, Gail, and many others with inspiring him to greatness along the path of life. He has stepped up, yet again, to be the leader we all know and love, to be that "somebody should write a book about that" servant. Expect tugs at the heart, a number of "aha" moments, and other forms of fuel for your personal benefit as you dive into this rewarding timeline of a life well spent.

Jimmy, thank you for your book. But you should know, my friend, many of us—and I seek to be first on that list—owe you a debt that we will never be able to repay. You have poured your life into us. You have inspired us. We are grateful for you beyond all measure. God bless you, and Gail, and all who read *They Inspired Me*.

— **Gary Black, Georgia Commissioner of Agriculture**

1

Spring 1944 – Gardi, Georgia

Clip-clop, clip-clop … the sound was coming from Old Bethlehem Road that ran by Ben and Mattie Hill's residence. Their twenty-year-old son, Jasper, was in the front yard and heard the sound. He strained to see down the road as a small mule rounded the curve in a cloud of dust. As it got closer, Jasper noticed the rider, a beautiful brunette who straddled the mule bareback, and his face lit up like a 100-watt light bulb. She seemed very young. He found out later that she was twelve years old.

Mary Louise Ryals Hill, the mule rider, was asked about this meeting many years later. "I do remember the mule," she said. "But I don't remember meeting Jasper."

One of Mary's teachers had taken her to the Hills' home a few years earlier. They were checking on one of the Hill boys who had taken ill. Mary had stayed outside of the home near the front gate and did not meet the boy. She found out later that it was Jasper. The unknown infectious disease in his leg that he suffered from then would trouble him intermittently his entire life.

Mary was a slender young woman with soft, white skin, and gorgeous lips. Jasper was completely mesmerized by her beauty and poise. He began to hang around the Ryalses' home with the excuse that he was visiting with her two older brothers, Robert and Donald. The Ryals family only lived a few miles away.

Mary said that she remembered boys and girls from the surrounding area would sometimes gather at the Ryalses' home to play a game called "Post Office." The boys would line up and put on blindfolds. The girls would go by and kiss each boy. Mary said that she did not remember the names of most of the boys that she kissed, but she did remember kissing Jasper. That must have been some kiss!

About six months after their first meeting, Jasper asked Mary to be his steady. Their dating consisted primarily of Jasper going to her house, where they would sit on the porch and talk.

Then, a few months after Mary turned thirteen, Jasper asked her to marry him. Back in those days, some girls married at an early age. When Jasper told Mrs. Ryals that he wanted to marry her daughter, she gave the following response: "If Mary will cook breakfast for our family for one week and she still wants to marry, I will give my consent."

Mary cooked biscuits, bacon, black-peppered eggs, and grits on the old wood stove for her family's breakfast for one week. She passed the test and received her mother's blessing for the marriage.

The young couple did not want to tell anyone, other than Mary's mother, about their marriage plans. They came up with a plan to get married by the County Ordinary in Jesup without any family present and concocted a story for family and friends that they were going to a movie that evening in Jesup.

On Wednesday, June 13, 1945, Jasper went to Mary's house to get her. Her sister Edna had fixed Mary's hair for the evening but did not know about their secret wedding plans. The bus service ran twice daily from Brunswick to Jesup and back. Jasper and Mary took the bus to Jesup as if they were going to the movies. Then they right away caught a taxi back to Gardi. The seven-mile taxi ride was exciting and scary at the same time. They were going to Jasper's home for him to get dressed for the wedding. By the time they got to the house, it was dark. Jasper had to go through his parents' bedroom to get to his room to change clothes. Ben and Mattie had already gone to bed. At that time there was no electricity in the home, so Jasper had to light a kerosene lantern to see how to dress. Mary was left sitting in the parents' bedroom, in the dark, and was startled when Jasper's mother suddenly spoke up. Mattie Hill was a very inquisitive and bold woman. When she started asking questions, Jasper came back into the room and informed his parents that he was marrying Mary Ryals.

"Married, shit. I've heard that till it makes me sick," said Mattie.

And Ben added, "Son, if you make your bed hard, you will have to sleep in it."

Mary was scared to death. She and Jasper left immediately.

The taxi had been waiting and carried them to the home of Gordon Bishop, Wayne County's Ordinary. Mr. Bishop, who was half asleep, had to wake up his wife to be a witness to the marriage. He said a few words and ended with, "I pronounce you man and wife." They left quickly!

Mary and Jasper Hill

Mary and Jasper went to the movie for a few minutes but realized they had to catch the last bus home. The bus stopped in Gardi at the railroad crossing to let them off. They went to the home of a friend of Jasper's and woke up the friend and his wife to tell them what had just happened. The couple decided to let the newlyweds have their bed for the night while they slept in the spare room.

The next morning, Jasper went to tell his boss that he had married and needed time off to work on his housing situation. He also asked the boss for a loan of one hundred dollars to put a down payment on their first furniture. Jasper's friend had agreed to rent them a room to live in temporarily.

While Jasper was gone, Mary's dad, Frank, sent word to her that he needed to talk with her. He wanted her to write a letter for him, which was something she did frequently. Mary went to her dad's house, and they sat on the front porch as Frank dictated the letter to her. Frank Ryals always used his arms and hands very expressively and was doing so during the dictation. Jasper came up the road and saw him seemingly lecturing Mary about the marriage. The new groom stopped for a minute, trying to assess the situation. "Well, am I a man or a mouse?" he thought. Taking a deep breath, he headed to the porch to confront Frank, who by then had gone inside the house. Jasper stepped on the porch and asked Mary what was going on. She quickly told him that her daddy was okay with the marriage, that she was just writing a letter for him. Jasper breathed a sigh of relief.

Jasper and Mary went to Jesup shortly thereafter and picked out their new furniture: a bedroom suite, a cardboard chest, a dining set, and a kerosene stove. The store delivered the merchandise the same day, and they spent the night on the new bed.

The next morning, young Mary cooked her new husband a breakfast of fried eggs, bacon, grits, and biscuits. Mary's family loved black pepper, and her mother always coated the eggs with plenty of it, so Mary did the same. That was when she discovered Jasper did not like pepper. He would not even taste the eggs. To the day that he died, Jasper hated pepper.

Ben H. (no middle name, only initial) Hill and Mattie Crosby Hill were both born in Mount Pleasant, Georgia. Ben was born on February 13, 1877, and Mattie was born on September 15, 1879. Mount Pleasant was an unincorporated community in Wayne County, Georgia, located on US Highway 341 about twenty-eight miles northeast of Brunswick. It had a US Post Office, established in 1855, that ceased operation in 1948. Only a few homes remain in Mount Pleasant now.

The 1940 United States Census reports that the Hill family lived in Gardi, on Old Bethlehem Road. Ben and Mattie had four children—Willie, Minnie, Jim, and Jasper. Ben was a sharecropper farmer, and his sons helped him farm. Sharecroppers rented farmland and would plant, till, and harvest the crop. At harvest time, they would share the crop harvest with the landowner as payment for use of the land. Ben spent most of his working life as a sharecropper.

Jasper was born on September 25, 1924, at 9:00 p.m. in Mount Pleasant. A midwife named Mrs. W. H. May assisted with the birth. The certified birth certificate indicates that Ben Hill was a farmer and Mattie Crosby Hill was a housewife.

Jasper attended Gardi School through the third grade, then had to quit because of a seriously infected leg. He helped his father farm when he was able, but never returned to school. He spent time in the Old University Hospital—Talmadge Memorial Hospital in Augusta, Georgia.

Mattie and Ben Hill after day of gathering tobacco

During one of Jasper's extended hospital stays in Augusta, Mattie received a letter from Dr. Charles Goodrich Henry. It was dated January 24, 1939:

Dear Mrs. Ben Hill,

Your letter of January 23rd has just been received. I notified the General Office in Atlanta to have you send for Jasper last Saturday, January 21st. Jasper told me that he had written to you as well. Jasper seems to be making good progress. I shall expect you to send for him just as soon as possible.

Yours Very Truly, C. G. Henry, M.D.

Jasper also spent time at the Georgia Warm Springs Foundation's rehabilitation facility in Warm Springs, Georgia. This facility was legendarily visited by President Franklin Delano Roosevelt over forty times. President Roosevelt had ultimately bought the facility and the 1,700-acre farm surrounding it in 1927 and created the Foundation.

The Ben Hill family lived in a three-bedroom house with a front porch and a back porch. The house was made of wood, with unpainted clapboard siding. It had windows with glass panes and a tin roof with gables. There was no running water indoors, but there was a well with a hand pump on the back porch. An outhouse was located about one hundred feet behind the house in a weed patch.

Surrounding the house and yard was a thirty-inch-high steel wire fence, which was topped along the front of the property with a white board that ran between the wooden fence posts. Located in the back corner of the fence was a chicken coop. Mattie always kept chickens for their eggs and as a meat protein source. She had Rhode Island Reds, Dominiques, and the smaller Bantams, among other breeds.

Every Sunday, Mattie would cook a chicken for dinner. On Saturday, she would select the one for the table and proceed to kill it. She used a method called "wringing." She would grab the chicken by the head and spin it clockwise while holding on firmly to the head. The spinning broke the chicken's neck, and it died. This is not the most humane way to kill a chicken, but it was the way that Mattie did it.

Frank Ryals was born on August 1, 1885, in McIntosh County, Georgia, on the coast north of Brunswick. Willow Horton Ryals was born on April 19, 1898, in Glynn County, which is also on the coast of Georgia and includes the City of Brunswick. They were married on December 20, 1911.

Frank and Willow moved to the old Shedd place on Little Creek Road in the Little Creek community, about five miles southwest of Gardi. Their house was built in the 1920s. It was an unpainted wood frame house with clapboard siding and a tin roof. A porch ran across the front. The windows had no glass panes but did have wood shutters that could be closed. The floor consisted of wooden boards that shrank after they were installed. Mary was able to see the chickens scratching for food under the floor and the dogs that slept under the house. The house had three bedrooms. Frank and Willow had one bedroom, the boys had a bedroom, and the girls had the other one. Heating was provided by two brick fireplaces. There was no electricity or running water and no indoor bathroom. An outdoor privy was even farther behind the house in the woods. A well, with a hand pump, was located behind the kitchen, which was a separate room on the rear of the house. Cooking was done with a Sears and Roebuck stove that could run on coal or wood. They did not have access to coal, so wood was the source of fuel.

Frank and Willow Ryals

Mary was born on February 4, 1932. She was born at home with no attending physician. A midwife assisted Willow with the birth.

Years later, Mary needed her birth certificate and realized she had never seen or possessed a copy. She requested one in June of 1970, at the age of forty-six. She was informed that there was no record of her birth. Willow and Mary were able to locate or create unofficial records of her birth. One was dated shortly after her birth and was listed in an old family Bible. The second, dated September 1940, was a Wayne County Gardi Public School Record showing her birthdate and the names of her parents. The third one, dated June 1970, was an affidavit by her mother, notarized by Gordon Bishop, Ordinary for Wayne County, Jesup, Georgia. This is the same Gordon Bishop who married Jasper and Mary in 1945. These records allowed Mary to obtain a copy of her Delayed Certificate of Birth.

The Ryalses had nine surviving children—five boys and four girls. The order of birth was Ruth, Robert, Edna, Donald, Infant baby boy died at birth, Leroy, Mary, Earl, Lorraine, and Gene. This was enough kids to complete a baseball team or to play any sort of game where you needed several players. Mary said that they would hold dances in their yard. The music was from an old battery-powered radio tuned to WSM and the Grand Old Opry in Nashville, Tennessee. WSM had a one-hour radio barn dance show. The Ryals kids would invite boys and girls from the surrounding area and have, as they called it, a "shindig."

Frank owned a pulpwood harvesting company. His company, consisting of him and his boys, would cut down six- to nine-inch diameter pine trees, saw them into logs, and haul them to a wood-processing mill or load them onto railroad cars for transportation to the mill. Pulpwood from loblolly and slash pines was then used for making paper, as well as other products. Also, Frank did some farming and had milk cows. He even planted a rice crop in an area of wetland on the property. The family had a large garden each year.

One issue that bothered Mary, as she grew up, was the obsession the family had with drinking alcohol. Almost every member of the family, male and female, drank alcohol to excess. Mary was the exception. She did not drink and did not approve of it. She saw how negatively it affected her family. Several of her siblings, later in life, would abuse alcohol to the point that it ultimately impacted their families severely. Some family members died at a relatively early age, and their deaths were related to alcohol abuse.

After experiencing the toll that alcohol had on her family, Mary knew that she did not ever want to allow it to pass her lips—and she didn't.

Mary attended the Gardi School, located in Gardi at the corner of Bethlehem Road and Morning Glory Circle. Started in 1896, it was a one-room school with grades one through eight. It initially did not have a lunchroom. She had to take her lunch in a tin bucket. There was an outdoor privy, and the school's water source was a hand-dug well with a manual pump. Mary graduated from the eighth grade in 1945. No other educational opportunities were available to her at that time.

Before her passing, Mary shared with us kids a frightening childhood experience that she was put through regularly when she was ten and eleven years old. An old man driving a Model T Ford would come to the Shedd place on Saturday afternoons and take Mary for a ride with him. Whenever she heard his car coming, she would hide. However, Willow would make her come out of hiding and get in the car with the old man. He would take Mary in the woods and touch her in her private places. These assaults took place over an extended period of time. He would also bring her candy. Mary hated him but never shared his name. She said, "I have lived with the horror of that old man touching me all my life." She did write these words in her life story: "I hope he got right with God and got forgiveness before he died."

Once they were married, Jasper and Mary knew they had to figure out a permanent living arrangement. Jasper found a one-half acre of land on Morning Glory Circle in Gardi that was for sale, and he bought it. They cleared the land by removing the trees and underbrush. Together, the two of them cut down the pine trees with a crosscut saw.

They decided to use the removed trees to build a structure on the land. Using a debarking tool, they stripped the bark from the trees. The logs were then used to build the frame of the structure. It had asphalt rolled siding as well as some rolled tar paper siding for the outside wall covering. Jasper used whatever he could find in building the structure, a shack that was approximately thirty feet deep and twelve feet wide. The heating system was an old steel barrel made into a heater. Jasper created a door in the side of the drum where they could put wood in the barrel for fuel. He also cut a round hole in the top of the barrel and inserted a stove pipe. The pipe then turned ninety degrees and went out the side of the structure for venting. Mary told us that it would get so hot at times that the barrel would turn red. It was a wonder that the shack did not catch on fire. There was no running water or inside bathroom.

Next to the closed-in back porch, they had a shallow well that Jasper had dug by hand and fitted with a hand pump. The outhouse was located several yards from the house to the rear of the property. It was a two-holer. Two years after Jasper and Mary married, they welcomed a new baby boy.

Jasper sitting behind Tar Paper Shack

His name was Jimmy Leroy Hill; of course, that was me. I was born on Thursday, July 10, 1947, at the Ritch-Leaphart Hospital in downtown Jesup, Georgia. The hospital had been started by two local doctors—Dr. T. G. Ritch and Dr. J. A. Leaphart. My mother, Mary, was hospitalized from Tuesday, July 8, until Sunday, July 13. I was her firstborn, and she was only fifteen years old. A copy of the bill from the hospital shows that I cost a grand total of $109.00.

I was taken home to the tar paper shack, which my mother called a "log cabin" and "home sweet home." With my being the firstborn, my mama and daddy did not know how to take care of me. One night I started crying and did not stop. Daddy went up the road and woke his mother, Mattie, to see if she could tell them what to do.

"I will be down there in a few minutes," she said.

"I need you now," he insisted.

To which she said: "GO BACK HOME, AND I WILL BE THERE SHORTLY."

Little Jimmy Hill

When she arrived, she told him to warm a blanket and put it in my bed. He did, and I went right to sleep. When he asked what to do if it happened again, Mattie replied, "Repeat the process." She was a woman of few words.

Daddy hired a local black woman the next day to assist Mama in taking care of me.

My earliest memory of the "log cabin" was when I was about five years old. I remember spending a lot of time in the yard and in the small stream that flowed next to the property.

Two years after I was born, another child was added to the family. My brother, Jerry Woodrow Hill, was born on August 27, 1949, at the Ritch-Leaphart Hospital.

Two years later, another sibling was added to the family. Linda Jean Hill was born on July 29, 1951, also in the Ritch-Leaphart Hospital in Jesup. At that time, it became very obvious that the family had outgrown the tar paper shack. Daddy and Mama started planning for a new home on the same property.

In the summer of 1952, Daddy started building a new house adjacent to the log cabin. This was to be a conventional stick-built home. He bought the materials as he could afford them, and he and his brother Jim built the house. Constructed with factory lumber using two-by-fours, two-by-sixes, and two-by-eights, the house was approximately twenty feet by forty feet with a crawl space. A porch that ran across the front of the house was added a few years later. Daddy used white asbestos siding on the house (back in those days, asbestos had not been determined to be a health hazard). The roof was covered using tin sheets.

Our family occupied the new house in late 1952. It was much bigger than the tar paper shack and was insulated and had running water. It was not until a couple of years later that Daddy finished the installation of the new indoor bathroom. The two-hole privy was finally eliminated. Daddy also installed a large kerosene heater to heat the house. He and his brother, Jim, both had awesome building skills. Jim Hill served in the US Army during World War II. Then he came back to Gardi and spent most of his

Young Mary and Jasper Hill

career as a carpenter, with a few years serving as a Wayne County deputy sheriff.

The new house was only one hundred yards from my grandparents, Ben and Mattie Hill. Ben died on August 3, 1952, at the age of seventy-five. He was buried in the Union Baptist Church Cemetery near Akin, Georgia, which is only a few miles from Gardi. Ben's father and mother, James H. Hill and Julia Ann Arnett Hill, are both buried there as well.

Hill family new house

Jasper and Jim Hill

2

Boyhood Days in Gardi

* Photo Courtesy of Florie Hopkins

Gardi is a small, unincorporated area in the middle of Wayne County, just south of Jesup, Georgia. Wayne County was created in three separate actions between 1805 and 1822 out of neighboring Glynn County, which is just to its southeast on the Georgia coast. Glynn County's most prominent town is Brunswick, Georgia.

Gardi was once known as Sallytown, but the name did not last long. The name Gardi may have come from several sources. One report said the name came from a person by the name of Gardner and that the "ner" was dropped and an "i" added to get Gardi. Another source said that when passing through a nearby swamp, one had to "guard one's eyes." We may never know, for sure, where the name Gardi came from.

Gardi had a population of over eight hundred at one time in the 1920s. The population today is around two hundred. The area's economy was based on the naval stores (turpentine) industry, the growing and harvesting of timber, primarily pine, and some limited agriculture.

The turpentine industry needed a pine tree to be a minimum of eight to nine inches in diameter, with no less than 25 percent crown length. Each crop (ten thousand trees) could produce between thirty-five and forty barrels of turpentine per year. The tree bark was removed in sections of twelve inches across the diameter of the tree with a total of fourteen to sixteen inches vertical per season. Turpentine cups were nailed to the tree along with gutters and aprons. The tree wood under the bark would extrude the turpentine, and gravity would cause it to flow to the cups nailed at the bottom of the tree. This is a simplified version of what happens to create the face (or catface) of the tree. It is a labor-intensive job, and one person could work fifteen hundred faces per day. There were thirteen grades of rosin that had a multiplicity of uses, including in the food industry and medicine.

The turpentine industry was most fascinating. Many people around Gardi who had timberland harvested turpentine from their pine trees before felling the trees for pulpwood or saw timber. This was an economic boost for the area.

The pine tree, with its many uses, was a staple for the industry in the Gardi area. This was spurred on by the location of a new cellulose plant in Doctortown, just east of Jesup. The Rayonier plant was built in 1954 and nowadays employs over eight hundred people. Now known as Rayonier Advanced Materials (RYAM), it is the largest cellulose specialty plant in the world. It manufactures approximately 330,000 metric tons of hardwood and softwood cellulose specialties each year, according to the Rayonier Advanced Materials Jesup Plant web page.

As a boy, I loved riding my bicycle, so I thought that I would narrate a bicycle tour of Gardi and describe what I saw in the 1950s and 1960s.

As I traveled along US Highway 341 going south into Gardi, I passed over the Gardi Bridge. This was where Wayne County Sheriff Clarence Reddish hit the bridge in November 1962. Sheriff Reddish and two other occupants of the car died at the scene. The fiery crash was the talk of the town for many years.

Jimmy and his bicycle

Traveling on south, I passed Little Creek Road on the right, which went to the Little Creek community, Little Creek Baptist Church, and to the house where my mother was born.

The next building on my right was the store owned by Troy Fore Sr. The drink machine was cooled by ice and cold water. My choice of soft drinks was Royal Crown (RC) Colas and Orange Crush. Of course, many food items were also available for purchase. The building was a painted, brick structure and had gasoline pumps in the front. Mr. Fore also owned the Honey House, which I would be passing by in a little while.

Traveling on past the Fore store, on the right, was the Westbury store, which was leased by my Aunt Minnie Hill O'Neal Williams. She sold grocery items and gasoline as well. This building was of wood construction and painted white. It had a Sunbeam Bread sign in front. She also sold kerosene for heating in the winter. Aunt Minnie lived in the back of the store along with her daughter Carolyn. I had to stop for a minute and say hello to Aunt Minnie. She sure was happy to see me.

Continuing, I came up to the last store on the right, also of wood construction, and painted white. This was owned by Tiny and Von Carter.

They, too, lived in the back of their store. My family shopped at all these stores at various times.

Making a 180-degree turn and heading north, the next road I came to on the right was Morning Glory Circle, a road that ran in a large, rectangular loop around Gardi. I turned right and crossed the Norfolk Southern Railway track. The railroad carried passengers and freight traffic. On the right was a side rail where pulpwood was loaded onto freight cars to be shipped to the Rayonier plant in Doctortown.

Morning Glory Circle Circa 2018

Continuing down Morning Glory Circle, and about one hundred feet on the right, I came to Mr. Caryl Shanklin's grocery store and the US Post Office. I had to stop and see if Mr. Shanklin would give me a piece of candy this morning. He did not disappoint. His was the best candy that I had ever tasted.

After biking past Mr. Shanklin's store, the next road to the right that I passed was River Road. That road ultimately led to the Altamaha River by way of Paradise Park Road. Fishermen launched their boats at Paradise Park Landing to fish the Altamaha River.

Traveling further along Morning Glory Circle, and just past River Road, was the home of Lonnie and Mary Elizabeth Jackson. Mr. Jackson was in the front yard and waved to me. Of course, I waved back.

Mary Brown Murphy lived in the next house on the left. Everett and Nell Jackson lived in the next house on the right. Nell waved through the kitchen window, and I waved back.

Next on the right, on the corner of Jackson Road and Morning Glory Circle, was the home of Willie "Peg" and Oma "Queechy" Jackson. Their sons were Richard and Bill. Queechy was the last postmaster in Gardi. They closed the post office in the late 1950s or early 1960s, and the postal addresses for Gardi changed to Route One, Jesup, Georgia. Our address before the closing of the Post Office was PO Box 35, Gardi, Georgia.

Past Jackson Road, and across the street from the Jacksons, was the Ben Milliken home. Behind the Milliken home was a small housing complex where some African American families lived.

Continuing biking down Morning Glory Circle past a large wooded area, I came to the Mal Harper home. A small road in front of the Harper home led to John and Nell Tyre's house.

At this point, Morning Glory Circle turned left, and just ahead on the left was my Uncle Jim and Aunt Joann Hill's home. My cousins Exley, Jay, and Jan lived there. A short distance beyond Uncle Jim's home, on the left, was a vacant area where Grandpa and Grandma Hill's house had stood a few years earlier.

Morning Glory Circle again turned left. Past a broom sedge field, and about 425 feet on the left from the last turn, was my home. Across from it was a large, plowed field.

Cycling on past my house on Morning Glory Circle for about 1,250 feet, I came to the Gardi School, which was on the right side, at the corner of Bethlehem Road. Jackson Road was on the left and connected back with Morning Glory Circle, but with no homes or structures along it. Straight ahead of the intersection, on the left, was the Gardi Baptist Church. This was the first church that my family attended.

As I biked ahead, Teston Road was on the left, past the church. Claude Teston's house was on the left side of his namesake road. He had three sons—Bully, Chubby, and Billy. Teston Road also cut across to other portion of Morning Glory Circle.

Returning from the Teston house to resume my tour of Morning Glory Circle again, I passed the Med and Ruby Odum home, located on the right just as Morning Glory Circle turned left. As I biked around the curve, the Troy Fore Sr. home was on the left. On the right side of the road was the Norfolk Southern Railway track, which ran parallel with Morning Glory Circle.

I had now almost completed the full loop of Morning Glory Circle back to where it started. This was the last leg of my bicycle tour, with one more building to see: the "Fancy Honey–The Altamaha Apiaries" building, standing on the left. It was locally called the Honey House. With this, I had concluded the bicycle tour of my hometown and community.

The Honey House

The building now locally known as the Honey House was constructed by a Mr. Harper about 1905–1906 and served as a general store and Gardi's first post office for the first half of its life. The building was twenty-six feet by sixty-two feet and had a twelve-foot ceiling of beadboard. The walls were solid brick and were finished with plaster inside. The bricks were fairly soft and made at the Garbutt Brick Yard in Odessa, just two miles away. The roof was tiled with Ludowici clay tiles made by the Ludowici Tile Company, which opened a plant in Ludowici, Georgia, in 1905. Close by the brickyard was a similar building, constructed from the same brick and roofed with Ludowici tiles. The bricks and the tiles are the color of native Georgia red clay.

Sometime before World War II, the Harper store was closed, and the community was served by a newer store. The empty building attracted T. H. Fore Sr., who was searching for a suitable place to locate his fledgling beekeeping and honey business. He purchased the store building and the neighboring residence and moved into both in 1941. In the years he, and then his son, operated the honey business, they employed dozens of local people, particularly in the busy summer months. This building, now owned by Troy Fore Jr. and his wife, Mary, was used as storage for beekeeping and honey equipment for years. The structure has suffered from the ravages of time and nature. Some of the mortar has loosened from the bricks. The soffits have deteriorated in places. The roof has been pierced by two tree limbs, and the leaks have damaged the ceiling.

The oldest building in the community, it was at one time Gardi's center of commerce. A neighbor stated that, in the past, he had seen families with their mules and wagons queued up in a line a quarter-mile long on Saturdays, waiting for their turn to shop in Mr. Harper's store.

In July 1982, the Honey House was selected for inclusion in a collection of Wayne County historic buildings by the Altamaha Georgia Southern Area Planning and Development Commission in their survey of Georgia Architectural and Historic Buildings. In the front windowsill, the US Coast and Geodetic Survey installed a benchmark that is dated 1917.

The Honey House is in a highly visible location on a major highway to the coast used by many from upstate Georgia. Before the advent of interstate highways, almost all traffic from Atlanta and environs to the coast passed through Gardi. The Norfolk Southern Railway separates the building from US Highway 341, also known as the Golden Isles Parkway. That visibility has attracted myriad photographers and even some artists. People stopping to take photographs are a common sight—even engagement and wedding parties have used the building as a photo backdrop. An Atlanta artist created a painting of the Honey House that was subsequently used as the cover illustration for the now-defunct magazine, *Brown's Guide to Georgia*. Photographs of the Honey House have been used in several local calendars and on a picture postcard distributed by the Wayne County Board of Tourism. Jesup artist Lita Morales drew the building that has been reproduced on Christmas tree ornaments, coffee cups, a Wayne County afghan, and even on the walls of a local restaurant.

My life was interesting and busy as I sharpened my wilderness training and explored the wilds. Next to our house, on the right side, was a small stream that went from a trickle to a torrent, depending on when it rained. It was perfect for exploring and taking my dog, Rocks, hunting. Rocks was a mutt with black coloring and small amounts of brown scattered about. He and I chased many squirrels, rabbits, and assorted varmints. I started each day with a walk around the large, one-half-acre lot and other extended properties, always making sure that everything was as it should be.

On March 23, 1956, my brother Ricky was born. This brought our family to a total of six. My brother Jerry and sister, Linda, played outside as much as possible. We did not have air conditioning, but we did have a couple of fans that did a great job of circulating hot air in the summertime. Looking back though, I don't remember the hot weather being a problem, and maybe that was because we didn't know about air conditioning. Dad had installed a kerosene heater. As I recall, it did a great job of keeping our family warm in the winter.

The first store-bought toy that I remember was a yellow Caterpillar bulldozer. It sent sparks out of the exhaust pipe as I moved it. I thought that was the most amazing toy that I had ever seen. Dad was working in road construction at that time, and he drove a Caterpillar bulldozer at work. He also had a Caterpillar medallion chain attached to his pocket watch. I remember how proud I was of my dad and how sharp he looked. He had to be seven feet tall and looked very muscular. It was later in life that I learned he was only five feet, eleven inches tall, but he was muscular.

Jasper, wearing the Caterpillar medallion, and Mary

My first gun was a wooden toy rifle. It was the most accurate gun that I ever owned. It never missed its target. My second gun was a cap-shooting pistol made by Roy Rogers. He was the King of Cowboys and had a great TV show. I graduated finally to a Red Ryder BB gun. Now, that was a masterpiece. That gun and I had many hours of shooting time. Life was very good.

Recently, I was reminded by my cousin Exley of an incident with the Red Ryder. He recalled that our neighbor JP and I were shooting at birds that flew over my house. Exley wanted to shoot the Red Ryder. JP and I were not having it, and the gun went off and accidentally shot Exley in the hand. Exley remembers seeing blood. However, it was just a scrape with no entry wound. He survived!

I remember getting up one morning in our home and hearing a noise in the outside wall of my bedroom. It was a buzzing sound. I yelled for my dad to come listen and see if he could figure it out. Dad went outside and found honeybees entering a hole in the wall. He called local beekeeper Mr. Troy Fore Sr. to come and investigate. Mr. Fore located where he thought the bees were inside the wall and cut a hole in the Sheetrock. He found them, along with a large amount of honey. He captured the bees and took them to his bee operation, and we had honey to enjoy for a whole year. Dad patched the hole in my bedroom wall, and everything was back to normal.

One day I heard my daddy say the words "deer tongue," and it caught my attention. He was saying something to Mama about going into the woods and harvesting deer tongue to make some extra money. I asked Daddy what deer tongue was. He told me that it grew wild in the woods and was very valuable. Deer tongue leaves are shaped like a deer's tongue or a dog's tongue. They have a vanilla-like flavor and are used in witchcraft, soaps, and cosmetics, as a flavoring for tobacco, and much more. He and Mama talked about it and agreed he would harvest some from the woods around Gardi. When he brought it home, Daddy spread it on the ground and the shed roof so that it could dry out. It needed to be dried to be sold. Our closest buyer was in Brunswick, Georgia. I don't know what it sold for back in the late 1950s or 1960s, but today it could bring up to $70 per pound. As I recall, we harvested the deer tongue for about three weeks before the season ended.

Our first structure on this property was the tar paper shack, and the second was a two-holer outdoor privy. We continued to use the outdoor privy for some time, even after Dad built the new house. I remember that our toilet paper was the previous year's Sears, Roebuck and Co. catalog. If the Sears catalog was used up, we used corn cobs. I preferred the Sears catalog.

Sometime in the mid to late 1950s, I started to smell an odor in the air, particularly early in the morning. I noticed it even more on the mornings with a dense fog. It had a pungent smell, unlike anything that I had ever smelled. I learned that it was the new Rayonier plant that had been built at Doctortown, which was about eight miles from Gardi as the crow flies. Later, I learned that some people said the smell reminded them of money. It was good wages to hundreds of people from Wayne County, including many Gardi residents. Rayonier is still operating today. I have been told the odor was eliminated.

My mama was an amazing woman. I did not know all of the details about her growing up until I found her notes after her death in 2012. Can you imagine marrying at age thirteen and having three children before you were twenty years old?

Being her firstborn, I am sure that I got extra love and care as she was learning to be a mother. She would take me in the yard and play with me when I learned to walk and tote a gun. She made me behave but did it with kindness.

My dad was a strict disciplinarian. He would bring the belt out or use his hand if we kids misbehaved. I always dreaded him handling the discipline, but he wanted us raised to respect others and to do the right thing. Did he administer corporal punishment to me? Yes, he did! Did I deserve it? In most cases—and it helped me to become the man I am today. As I think back, my dad had a way of looking at us. We called it the "Hill

Jerry, Linda and Jimmy

look." This look struck the fear of God in you. If you misbehaved, it caused you right away to correct your behavior.

Mama made our clothes in the early days. She put our initials on our shirts. We thought that we were special, and we were. Very few of our friends had shirts with initials on them. Money was in short supply in our house. My dad was a hard worker, but his job opportunities were not great. He kept a steady job, but usually at a lower wage scale. He did not go far in school. Mama was one of the thriftiest women that I ever knew, and she continued that way until her death.

Mama raised chickens for meat and eggs. She raised Rhode Island Reds, Dominiques, and Bantams, among other breeds. We had a chicken coop that Daddy built on the rear of our property. The chickens were allowed to roam during the day and would roost in the coop at night. We fed them chicken scratch feed, which was 8–9 percent protein along with other nutrients. The scratch feed required the chickens to scratch the ground, and they would find other food like insects, worms, and seeds. We bought our feed supplies from Strickland's Feed and Seed on southwest Broad Street in Jesup. Part of my responsibility was to protect the chickens.

As you read this book and learn about my family, you might conclude that we were poor. Looking back on it now, maybe we were. However, I sure did not know it or feel it; we had what we needed and the awesome love of a great mother. The first time that I remember thinking we might be poor was when I got a reduced-price lunch at school. My parents never mentioned to us kids about being poor or disadvantaged in any way. I believe that with our loving parents and their positive attitudes, we thought that we had the world by the tail.

Mama was also the one who would take us to church on Sundays. She was the spiritual leader of our family at that time. Dad was not a churchgoer early in their marriage and very rarely entered the door of a church. I would consider Dad, at this point in his life, as a good provider for the family but not spiritual in any way. He, however, would not prevent Mama or us kids from going to church. Gardi was a very church-going community, and the church played a great role in most people's lives at that time.

Mama had to go to the Crawford W. Long Hospital in Atlanta, Georgia, in the fall of 1958. Unfortunately, I do not know what the medical issue was, but I assume it was serious since she was not sent to the Ritch-Leaphart Hospital in Jesup. Daddy suggested that we all write a separate letter to Mama and mail them to her in the hospital. You will find a copy of the letter from my Dad in the Appendix.

Hardi, Georgia
November 6, 1958

Dear Mother,
Just a few lines to tell you how we are
doing, I made ninety-four on my monthly
report at traing union, Ricky has been good.
Except for ~~his~~ nights he wakes me up to
change his, wet ~~diaper~~ panties. Tony and Lonnie
are good too. Jerry and I are sleeping with daddy
Lonnie is crying so I will go see what is wrong.
Right me soon

Your Son,
Jimmy

Jimmy guarding the chickens (Grandpa Hill's home in background)

As far as I can determine, my dad's first job off the farm was working for the J. A. Jones Construction Company in Brunswick, Georgia. J. A. Jones was a builder of ships that were used to transport cargo for the war effort during World War II. I found a J. A. Jones ID card with my father's name and photograph in his records following his death.

Dad started work at the company on April 3, 1943. He never mentioned to me that he had worked at J. A. Jones. He had a severe infection in his leg that kept him from being drafted and from serving his country in the military during World War II.

The company employed over sixteen thousand people during the Second World War. They built over one hundred cargo ships that were immediately commissioned to the war effort. The ships had a ten-thousand-ton capacity and transported troops, armaments, and supplies overseas to the front lines. My Aunt Minnie, Dad's sister, also worked at the company. It was reported that workers earned up to $1.20 per hour.

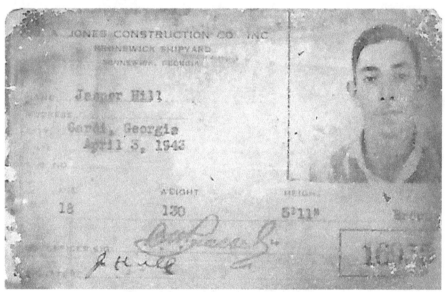

Jasper Hill's ID card for J. A. Jones Construction Company

In my research, I learned that three sisters from Wayne County were employed by the company as welders. They were Nanelle, Carobeth, and Lauree Surrency and were known as the Three Welding Sisters. The World War II Home Front Museum, located on St. Simons Island, Georgia, has a video interview of the three women. My junior high school teacher was none other than Nanelle Surrency Bacon. Nanelle and my mama were close friends. Mama called me one day in the spring of 2012 and said that Nanelle wanted to see me. When I asked Mama what she wanted, she didn't know. I went to visit Nanelle in Jesup that summer of 2012. As I walked into her home, I asked her if I had done something wrong, missed a test, or forgotten to turn in a paper on time. She laughed and said, "I have been keeping up with you all these years, and I wanted to see you." We had a great visit. Unfortunately, Nanelle passed away on February 27, 2014, at the age of ninety. I did not learn of her wartime job until after her death.

I had the pleasure of speaking with Nanelle's sisters, Carobeth and Lauree , recently. It was an awesome experience to listen to them talk about their work experience in Brunswick. Carobeth worked there for about two and a half years, Lauree for about eighteen months. Lauree invited me to come to see her in Jesup when I was in the area. She told me that she was ninety-seven years old. There were so many heroes on the World War II home front in our communities, and we are losing them rapidly. Thanks, to all of our men and women who served our nation, either at home or abroad.

My dad and my uncle, Jim Exley Hill, created a fishing venture in the 1940s. They fished the Altamaha River for sturgeon. Sturgeon is one of the oldest known species of fish. The shortnose sturgeon grows to nearly fifty-three pounds and can live up to sixty years. It is harvested for its meat and its eggs. The eggs are made into a flavorful delicacy similar to caviar.

Dad and Uncle Jim built a cabin on the bank of the Altamaha River, down below Paradise Park. The cabin was used for lodging when they were doing night or extended day fishing. It had one door and two windows and was built of rough sawn timber. Inside was one double bed and a wood stove. One night, they had gone to bed and were trying to go to sleep. Uncle Jim was cold, so he pulled the cover toward him and pulled it off Dad. Dad pulled the cover back. Uncle Jim again pulled the cover to his side of the bed. Dad pulled it back. All heck broke loose. Neither one admits to having thrown the first punch. However, they punched, tossed, and tumbled on the bed until the bed railing broke and they landed on the floor. They stopped the fight to fix the bed. Dad went outside and cut down a small tree and brought it into the cabin. Both being carpenters, they measured the exact center of the bed and the cover. They then nailed the de-limbed tree down the middle of the bed and nailed the cover to the tree. There were no more fights that night over the cover.

Dad had a variety of handyman jobs over the years. He worked harvesting turpentine from pine trees. Later, he started a residential plumbing and wiring business. My work with him started as soon as I could tote a wrench or a pipe or pull electrical wire. I learned a lot from my dad as we worked together. I probably could have wired a house by the time I was twelve years old. I could have done most of the plumbing as well. As I was the oldest boy, Dad had me working with him whenever I was not in school.

Back in those days, the only pipe used for residential water service inside the home was galvanized steel pipe. It came in sticks, twenty feet long. We had to cut it to length and thread each end as we plumbed each house. In addition to me and my brother Jerry, Dad had another worker, by the name of John, who helped him occasionally. I discovered quickly that John had trouble reading a tape measure or rather, the foldable six-foot wooden measuring device that we called a ruler. One day, John was under a house measuring a pipe section, and Dad asked him for the measurement. John was quiet for what seemed like a couple of minutes. He then hollered out, "It is as long as the six-foot ruler and a ten-penny nail."

"That will work," my dad said.

My job many times was to crawl under houses, pull electrical wire, or carry pipes. I was in some tight places as a kid and remember being stuck under a floor joist in a crawl space one day. I did not know what claustrophobia was at that time, but I think that I experienced it as my chest was against the floor joist and my back was tightly forced on the ground. I shudder today as I remember those tight places.

Another job I had, while helping him install plumbing pipe, was to thread the galvanized pipe. This required a special threading tool with several sizes of dies based on pipe size and threads per inch. The pipe would be held in a pipe vise, and the threader would be started on the pipe and rotated clockwise for a minimum of one or one and one-quarter inches. The threader would then be reversed and removed from the pipe. Each end of the pipe had to be threaded. This was hard work for a young person.

Dad built me an extension on the pipe threader so that I could get more leverage, as it was difficult to turn. I still have that extension and the entire set of pipe threading tools we used back in the 1950s and 1960s.

Daddy worked for Fred Wedincamp Construction Company in Jesup for several years. The company cleared land and provided construction of building sites and drainage lines. Fred also operated Fred's Service Station, which was a full-service Gulf station on US Highway 301 South.

The Wayne County Commissioners of Road and Revenues called Daddy about a job running a dragline in 1956. A dragline is a piece of heavy, dirt-moving equipment with a boom, cable, and bucket that can move large amounts of soil. That was his last public job before moving to Snipesville, Georgia.

Dad was a jack-of-all-trades and could build or repair anything that had to do with wood, metal, wiring, plumbing, or almost anything else. He was an amazing, self-taught man, who I revered and learned so much from as I grew up.

It wasn't just the practical skills I learned from my dad. There were also his "Jasperisms," sayings or ideas that he shared with me and my siblings frequently. Whenever he sent me to get a tool, pipe, wood, or wire, he would always say, "Turn your hat around to make me think you are coming back." He was not a man with a lot of patience. When a board was too short, he would send me to get the "lumber stretcher." I learned after many trips that lumber stretchers do not exist.

He hated all peppers, but especially black pepper, and would tell everyone at mealtime about his dislike of pepper. You may remember the story earlier about when he and Mama were newlyweds, and she cooked him fried eggs with black pepper, which he refused to eat. He said, and I quote: "If I ever become president of the United States of America, I am going to ban black pepper." I am glad he never became president because I love black pepper and sprinkle it on almost everything; I must take after my mother's side of the family.

I had a habit, when working with Daddy, of tightening bolts to the point that they would break. In other words, I would ruin the bolt and nut and sometimes twist the bolt off in something like an engine block. The engine block one was always bad news; he would have to remove the remaining bolts from the block, and that was not an easy job. When I was about to tighten a bolt, one of the well-remembered comments to me, which I heard often, was, "DON'T TIGHTEN IT TOO TIGHT!"

Another expression that my dad often used was "layover to catch meddlers," which was his standard response to questions like "Where do babies come from?" When he gave that answer, I would say, "What?"

"Layover to catch meddlers," he would say again.

I would repeat the question, and still, he would give the same answer. After a while, I would give up.

After I was grown, I asked Daddy what the words meant. He didn't know. His mother would use that expression with him and his siblings when they asked questions that she did not want to answer. One time I asked former governor Zell Miller what those words meant since he was sort of an expert on Southern language. He had no idea either.

According to the *Morris Dictionary of Word and Phrase Origins*, "layover to catch meddlers" is a dialect variant of a very common answer used by adults to evade a direct answer to children's questions, another way of saying to the child, It's none of your business. So, what is a layover? It is a trap for bears or other unwary animals, made of a pit covered with boughs. And a meddler, of course, is a person who interferes in other people's business. The phrase was recorded in Eastern and Southern states as long ago as 1890. It also appears as "larovers for meddlers," "layos to catch meddlers," and even as a single word, "larofamedlers."

Daddy had another saying that I heard maybe a thousand times: He would say that he was "so mad" that he "could throw his hat in the fire." I saw him mad many times, but I also knew he was a hat lover and would never throw his hat in the fire. He would make you think he would, though. Years later, I had an experience that made me feel the same way. Only then did I understand how he must have felt when he said it.

Daddy never ate oranges as a child or as an adult after an orange episode as a young boy. He told us that he went to help (or play) as his father and his brothers Willie and Jim installed a drainage pipe across the road near their home. The county government would allow citizens to do work for the county in place of paying property taxes. The county road department brought the pipe to the location, and Grandpa Hill and the boys proceeded to dig a trench across the road, put the pipe in the ditch and cover it up. As they were about halfway through the installation, a neighbor close by invited them to come over to his house and have an orange for a snack. Grandpa accepted, and they all went over to the house. Everybody took an orange from the neighbor except my daddy. The neighbor and Grandpa tried to persuade him, but he refused. About an hour later, Daddy decided he wanted to have one of those oranges. He sneaked over to the neighbor's porch and took one without asking permission, then went back to the site, sat down, and started to eat it. Grandpa caught a glimpse of the orange and asked Daddy where he got it. When he told him, Grandpa was mad and upset that he had taken the orange without asking. He made Daddy go with him over to the house, tell the neighbor he had stolen the orange, and apologize. Daddy did apologize but never ever, after that day, ate another orange. We would get fresh fruit for Christmas every year, but there never was an orange in the mix.

Daddy was a smoker for many years. He quit when he was in his sixties. But throughout the years that we kids were growing up, he always had his Camels with him. I wanted to try smoking, and one day I had my chance. Dad got the contract to reroof a public-school building in Odum, which was in Wayne County, about nine miles west-northwest of Jesup, on US Highway 341. It was a two-story building with a hip roof. He was installing tar shingles, and he allowed me to help him that day. My job was to climb the ladder to the second-floor roof and make sure he had a supply of shingles near him all the time as he worked. When I got caught up, I stepped over to the other side of the roof and spied his cigarettes and matches. I took out one of his Camel cigarettes, struck a match, and lit it up. Then I took a long deep draw and almost choked to death. I started coughing and spat the cigarette out. Daddy must have heard me but never mentioned that incident, and nor did I. That was the day that I decided that smoking cigarettes was not in my future.

Mr. Caryl Shanklin was one of the first men that I remember in Gardi. He owned a general store, which hosted the Gardi Post Office. Mr. Shanklin was born in 1896 in Grangerville, Georgia, and moved to Gardi in 1938.

The Shanklin family consisted of his wife, Winnie, and four children. Gus, Caryl's son, now resides in his father's original home on Bethlehem Road, near where the old Gardi School was located. Gus had three siblings—all girls.

Mr. Shanklin originally opened the general store and post office in a rented brick building on the west side of US Highway 341, going into Gardi from Jesup. It was across from Morning Glory Circle, which leads into the residential part of Gardi.

In the 1950s, he moved to another building, which was on the other side of US Highway 341, on Morning Glory Circle. It also hosted the general store, as well as the second ever US Post Office in Gardi, and stood across the street from the Honey House. Mr. Shanklin closed the store and post office after a few years. The post office's third and final location was in the remodeled carport of Peg and Queechy Jackson's home, located on the corner of Jackson Road and Morning Glory Circle until it closed in the 1950s or early 1960s.

One night, I overheard my mother tell my father that we only had enough food in the house for one more meal. The meal would be homemade biscuits and canned, homemade pear preserves. I know that I was not supposed to hear that conversation, as neither of my parents would openly share our dire situation. I could not hear all of what was said between them, but I went to bed and could only think about not having food to eat.

The next day, Mr. Shanklin showed up at our house with two sacks of groceries from his store. My mother credited God and Mr. Shanklin with providing us with the meal fixings for several days. I am told that Daddy was out of work due to a cataract surgery that ultimately required his eyelids to be sewn together for a time. I am sure that if you didn't work back then, you didn't get paid. Other community members also brought groceries to us during that time.

Mr. Shanklin was a godly man, who attended the Gardi Baptist Church. When he delivered the *Savannah Morning News* newspaper on a Sunday, he would always invite our family to attend the church. My dad would deflect the offer and finally got to the point of not going to the door. He would send one of us kids to get the paper when it was delivered. Mr.

Shanklin would still ask my dad to attend the church every time he saw him around town.

I think that God started working on my father, and several things happened that changed his mind about attending church. Dad was known to be very stubborn and hardheaded and could be very confrontational.

My brother Jerry had developed Bell's Palsy, and that had a great impact on my dad. Bell's Palsy could cause facial pain and droop on one side of the face. It rarely was a long-term issue, and many people were able to overcome it and return to normal over time. I think, though, that things were not going well in Daddy's life, and he saw Jerry's condition as a warning that he needed to change. I am sure that God was working on him to change his life and to serve the Lord. Jerry made a full recovery.

My dad started attending the Gardi Baptist Church and ultimately accepted Jesus Christ as his personal savior. Our life as a family improved greatly as a result. He was more attentive and loving as a father, husband, and friend.

I give Mr. Shanklin a lot of credit for his effort in encouraging Daddy to attend church and to make sure we kids were in church as well. I never heard anybody say a bad word about Mr. Shanklin. Thank you, Mr. Shanklin, for your efforts on behalf of our family. I wish I had been able to thank him in person. Unfortunately, he passed away in 1962. He is buried in the Gardi Cemetery.

Grandma Hill had one Rhode Island Red rooster that hated me. He tried to spur me every time I went to see her and Grandpa. That rooster and I tussled many times, and he always got the better of me. I was glad the day that he showed up on the Sunday dinner table.

One Saturday afternoon, Grandma asked me if I wanted to kill a chicken for Sunday dinner. I said yes. She pointed out the one for me, and I caught it. I had never done this before, so I was apprehensive, to say the least. I grabbed the chicken by the neck and applied the "wringing method." I swung the chicken around and around, holding its neck, and then let the chicken loose as I had seen Grandma do many times. It took the bird a few seconds to get her bearings after the wringing procedure. She jumped up and flew over the fence, and we never saw her again. Grandma never let me do the wringing again.

Grandma Hill's yard was always clean, with no grass or limbs anywhere. She swept it daily with a broom-sedge broom. Broom sedge is a native plant that is a clump-forming, warm-season perennial grass. It grew wild in pastures and fields around Gardi. I asked her one day why she kept the sandy yard swept so clean. She said it was to see any snakes that might come after her chicken eggs. Also, to sweep up chicken manure; the chickens roamed the yard and left their valuable manure that was used as fertilizer in her garden.

Grandma loved to sit on her front porch and watch people travel by, primarily in their cars. The house was located on Morning Glory Circle, just up the road from our house. I always enjoyed listening to her yell at those who traveled by her house speeding and raising dust off the dirt road. The dust would end up on her porch. Speeding on that road in those days was probably running thirty miles per hour. She would yell, "There they go again with a high head and windy tail! They didn't have manners enough to slow down or at least wave."

Grandma had a collection of silver dimes that she kept in a Prince Albert tobacco can. The can originally held crimp-cut, long-burning pipe-and-cigarette tobacco. I do not know if she smoked tobacco, but she did use snuff. She collected silver dimes and had nearly a can full. My cousin Bill Hill, son of Uncle Willie Hill, stole the can one day and brought it down the road to my house. He shared a story of finding these dimes with my brother Jerry and me. We knew immediately that they belonged to Grandma. She had shown them to us many times. We wanted nothing to do with the dimes and told Bill that he needed to return them to Grandma. He didn't. Grandma let everyone know about the missing dimes, and all-knowing Daddy figured out it was Bill. However, he called Jerry and me to the front porch of our house for interrogation. Daddy said, "I am calling the Georgia Bureau of Investigation to investigate who stole Grandma's dimes. Stealing is a state crime and punishable by a year in jail. However, if you stole the dimes or know who did and share that name, I will not involve the GBI." Jerry and I both blurted out Bill's name. He said, "I knew it was not you boys and that it was Bill." Bill returned the dimes in the Prince Albert tobacco can to Grandma. I am not sure of his punishment, but that was Uncle Willie's responsibility.

Cousin Bill was about two years older than I was. He was always getting Jerry and me in trouble. He convinced us that sucking raw eggs was a delicacy and led us up to Grandma Hill's house and into her chicken coop. Bill reached into a nest and got a fresh egg. He punched a hole in it and began sucking out the yolk and the clear egg-white substance. He persuaded us that it was good. Jerry and I each found an egg and proceeded to punch a hole in it and suck. To my surprise, it was good. However, two eggs were about my limit. Bill said that snakes also loved to suck eggs, so we left the empty, whole shells in the coop so that Grandma would think that a snake had done the egg-sucking.

Grandma found the eggshells on her next trip to the coop. She knew well that some animals and snakes would suck eggs. In the past, she had found a snake that had eaten some eggs. She also knew that snakes swallowed the egg and that the spines at the back of their neck cracked it. The egg contents would travel to the snake's stomach, and he would regurgitate the crushed shell. She searched for snake tracks and animal tracks and found none. She did find three sets of footprints. Grandma was also all-knowing, and she immediately knew who the culprits were—Bill, Jimmy, and Jerry. That concluded our egg-sucking adventure.

Grandpa was always teasing me and calling me "pretty boy." I was his favorite grandson, per my recollection. I would leave our house and go through the broom sedge field to Grandpa's house. He always had time for me. One of the things that he would let me do was help him with his crop of sweet potatoes. He would harvest them from the ground and place them in a bed of straw next to his outbuilding, then cover them with more straw and sand. This would preserve them for use all year long.

I was only five when he passed. I missed him. He was tall and skinny. One of my memories of him is a photograph taken of him on his return trip from a visit to the outdoor privy.

Grandma was short and rotund. She always seemed mad to me. I heard her say many times, and I quote, "I don't know if I will live to tomorrow or not." I thought that she was ill and about to die. She repeated that state-

Grandpa Hill returning from the outdoor privy

ment for another eleven years before she did pass. Grandpa was seventy-five years old when he passed, in 1952. Both he and Grandma are buried at the Union Baptist Church Cemetery near Akin, Georgia.

I do not have as many memories of my Ryals grandparents from when I was a boy. We did see them now and again, but unlike my dad's parents, who lived on the same road as we did when I was small, my mother's parents lived several miles away. My grandfather Frank Bartow Ryals died in 1954, aged sixty-nine. Willow Beauford Horton Ryals, my grandmother, who, like my mother, had married very young, was thirteen years his junior. Willow remained a widow for more than ten years after Frank passed. She married L. W. Strickland on June 1, 1965, and she passed on in 1977. Her father was William (Bill) Horton, and her mother was Lula Franklin Horton.

Growing up in Gardi, we did not have sports fields or organized sports. We did not have a movie theater in our community or a skating rink. If we were lucky, we had a bicycle and maybe a baseball, a bat, and sometimes a glove.

There were nevertheless lots of things to do in Gardi in those days. On some Saturdays, we would go to Gardi Creek to play and swim. I remember vividly one Saturday when the creek was running very swiftly following a gully washer of rain, and my sister almost drowned. My dad got to her and saved her from going under the water.

We also went to the Penholoway Creek on US Highway 341 between Gardi and Jesup to play and swim. We would take corn cobs, wet them, and use them to throw at each other. Sunday afternoons would involve a pickup baseball game with neighbor kids. Several kids would show up to give us enough players for a game. I got my first baseball mitt, which meant I did not have to catch the balls with my bare hands.

I do not remember how I got it, but I had a crystal radio. This was the precursor to our later battery-powered radios. It had a tiny speaker. If you listened intently, particularly at night, you could pick up far-off radio stations with strong signals. I would lie in bed at night and listen to these stations. One that I enjoyed was WSM radio station in Nashville, Tennessee. Ralph Emery was the late night and early morning host of a country music show. I thought that I was very special to have one of these awesome radios.

Daddy purchased our first black-and-white television in the early 1950s. I remember Mama inviting over our cousins to watch the Ed Sullivan show when Elvis Presley was on the TV for the first time. Sunday, September 9, 1956, will live in infamy, as it was a national event with over 80 percent of those watching TV that night tuned in to the show. He sang "Don't Be Cruel," "Love Me Tender," "Ready Teddy," and two verses of "Hound Dog." We had never seen anybody sing and move as he did.

The television set would only pick up three channels at that time: ABC, CBS, and NBC. However, we were able to watch lots of cowboy shows. We watched *Gunsmoke*, *Wagon Train*, *The Rifleman*, *The Lone Ranger*, *The Cisco Kid*, *The Roy Rogers Show*, and many others.

We would hardly ever go to see a movie in the theater in Jesup. One day, the elementary school bused us to the Strand Theater to see *Gone with the Wind*. That well-known movie, adapted from Georgia novelist

Margaret Mitchell's book, was released in 1939, but I saw it in the late 1950s. I went to see a few other movies, but I don't remember their titles.

I do remember one summer capturing hornworms from the tobacco field and taking them with me to the movie theater. I sat in the balcony, and every few minutes I would throw one down to the first floor into the seating area. Girls would freak out when the hornworms crawled on them. After a few minutes of their screaming, I decided that was not a good idea. I left the sack full of worms in the balcony following the movie. My story is that "the devil made me do it."

My favorite sport as a young child was riding my horse—a stick horse. We would use a tobacco stick or just cut a stick from the woods and add a rope for a harness. I would grab the harness, mount the horse, and ride off at a gallop. This horse did not require feeding or watering and was always ready for the next adventure. We played cowboys and Indians. I had a cap pistol that belonged to Roy Rogers as signified by his signature on the gun. It had a fancy holster too. What better fun could be had anywhere?

When I later got a Red Ryder BB gun, Daddy taught me how to use it and all about gun safety. I thought I was a real hunter with that gun.

On my trips to the creek and other swampy areas, I collected frogs, crawfish, and other marine specimens. I spent many hours being wet and dirty but having the time of my life.

When we kids were older, Dad started taking us fishing in the Altamaha River in a johnboat. He had a device called a "telephone fish-shocking machine." We would place the probes in the water, turn the crank, and the fish would be shocked and come to the surface. We then used nets to grab them. The fish were not dead, just in a state of shock. We learned later in life that this was called electrofishing. I did not know that it was illegal until one day when Daddy heard the game warden coming down the river just as I was turning the telephone crank. "Drop it in the river! Drop it in the river!" said Daddy. I did. The game warden stopped to check our licenses and see what we had caught. We had our licenses and had caught a few fish. Daddy never found the device. That ended our electrofishing adventures.

As a young boy, I had a few factory-made toys, but mostly we played in the sandy South Georgia soil with blocks of wood, sticks, bricks, and other assorted items from around the yard and the woods and thought it was awesome.

One sport that was hot when I was a boy and consumed us for hours was marbles. Someone would draw a circle in the dirt, and each player would put his or her marbles in the center. Players would take turns in trying to hit the opposing players' marbles out of the circle. If you were able to knock out all of the other players' marbles, you were the winner. If we played keeps, you got to keep the marbles you knocked out. However, each player had certain marbles that were collectibles, and a fight could develop over losing them. We had to declare at the beginning of the game what the rules were. We would take the marbles to school and play at recess. I wish that I still had some of those beautiful marbles. We collected them as well as traded them. I particularly remember a cat's-eye blue marble that I once owned. She was a beauty!

Another memory from my childhood was seeing the Goat Man. His real name was Charles McCartney, and he used to travel all over the eastern United States. He came through Gardi at least one time that I remember. He traveled in a wagon pulled by goats. He stopped outside of Gardi on US Highway 341 and spent the night. Daddy took us out to see him that night. You could smell him and his entourage before you got there. Goats can have a strong smell, and the Goat Man did too. He had a dozen or so goats around that evening. They were eating grass and playing. He was an oddity, and we just stood there and watched him. We had never seen such a sight. Goat Man later became a legend, traveling around the whole country until 1987.

A summertime ritual of ours was capturing lightning bugs. I learned years later that they were called fireflies in the West and New England. They would start appearing at dusk and were very visible in the dark. We would catch them by hand or with a net and put them in quart Mason jars to serve as a flashlight. With enough of them in the jar, you could see in the dark. When Mama called us in for supper, we would turn them loose to be caught another night.

One of my very favorite pastimes was our Gardi equivalent to the Olympics. Of course, back then we didn't call them Olympics. They were called fun and were competitive, with no medals awarded. We held them almost every day during the summer, with similar events to those being practiced today.

As I am writing this book and thinking back to our Gardi Olympics, I have become overwhelmed with a surge of excitement and a longing for the past. Some of the events we held that you would recognize were the one-hundred-yard dash, long jump, high jump, pole vault, basketball, baseball, and volleyball. We had no modern equipment and no distinguished judges from various states or countries. There was no need for judges—we could tell who won. Come to think of it, we didn't have much equipment at all. But what a great time we had with little equipment and lots of imagination and fun.

We held other races as well, such as putting someone on your back and racing another piggyback team. Did our backs hurt? Not that I remember. I do remember how when we ended the day and went home for supper, we were dirty, exhausted, and exhilarated, and we didn't need anyone to sing us to sleep at night. We did not win gold, silver, or bronze medals, but we did have a great time and learned a lot about life in the Gardi Olympics.

When I was eleven years old, comic books were all the rage. I loved reading them and trading them. To support my comic book purchases, I needed some money. As I was reading a comic book one day, I found an advertisement for the *Grit* newspaper. It promised you could earn thousands of dollars selling copies of their newspaper. I got excited and read further. It said that 30,000 kids were earning thousands of dollars and hundreds of prizes selling the *Grit*. I knew newspaper selling was in my future. So, I mailed off the ad and waited for a reply. Sure enough, I was accepted and became the Gardi *Grit* newspaper salesman. I placed my order for twenty weekly papers and received them, along with a *Grit* salesman's bag that could be put on your bike or carried across your shoulder to deliver the papers. The cloth bag had the words "America's Greatest Family Newspaper" printed across the front. I knew that I was about to be in the money.

I connected the bag to my bike, loaded it up with the twenty papers, and headed out to start selling them in my hometown of Gardi. The first day I sold five papers. I was somewhat discouraged but was not giving up. I kept calling on the residents of Gardi, and the next day I sold another five papers. I was now getting into the money. The ten papers sold for fifteen cents each, and I got to keep five cents for each paper sold. I had made fifty cents in two days. That was a lot of money for an eleven-year-old boy. There was only one problem: I had to pay Grit ten cents for each paper that I ordered, which came to two dollars. I knew that I needed to become a better salesman, not just to make ends meet but to create some profit for me. I sold the papers for about three years and was able to buy some comic books with a little extra leftover. All in all, it was a great lesson in the free enterprise system.

Another job that I had was harvesting tobacco. The tobacco plants were set out in rows in the spring and harvested mid to late summer. My Aunt Minnie and her husband had a field of tobacco near our house.

Harvesting jobs included suckering, topping, cropping, handing, stringing, and hanging the tobacco, then removing it from the barn after it was cured.

Suckering was the removal of the suckers from the tobacco plant. These were newly formed stems or leaves that came on after the original leaves were formed. The suckers took away nutrients from the plant that could be used more productively in the growth of the original leaves. At one point before harvesting, the tobacco plant would produce a seed topper that was of no value to the plant. This needed to be removed, a process that was called topping.

Harvest time came when the lower leaves started to ripen and turn a yellow color. Ripening began at the bottom of the plant and continued up to the top. The tobacco harvest, at that time, required a lot of hand labor. The harvesting process was called cropping. Each tobacco cropper was assigned a row. He or she would first remove two to three bottom leaves (called sand lugs) from each plant. The sand lugs were called that because they generally had a lot of sand on them as they were close to the ground. Each week, further cropping of two to three more leaves took place until the entire plant was harvested. The cropping crew would bend over and go from plant to plant, cropping two to three leaves and putting them under their arm. When they could not carry any more, the croppers would load the leaves onto a wooden sled that was being pulled by a mule between every four rows of tobacco. When full, the sled was pulled to the tobacco barn, where the leaves were unloaded and placed on tables under the shed area. From there, they were handed by a "hander" to be strung onto a tobacco stick by a "stringer." The stringer wrapped twine around the leaves and attached the leaf bundles to the stick, filling each stick by rotating the bundles from side to side. After the sticks were full, they were hung inside the barn by workers called "hangers." The hangers would start at the top of the barn and work their way to the bottom. These processes continued until all the tobacco leaves were harvested, transported, unloaded, handed, strung, and placed in the barn.

The tobacco was called "flue-cured," as it was placed in a barn with a heat source, fueled by either wood or propane gas, to cure it. The barn was typically, twenty feet by twenty feet square and about twenty feet tall. Attached to it there would generally be a shed with tables built underneath. Inside the barn, a system of wooden poles would run side to side and from head-height to the ceiling, the vertical poles about four feet apart, and the horizontal poles set at about three-foot intervals. After the tobacco was placed in the barn, the heat would be turned on for up to six or seven days to cure it.

The largest city close to Gardi was Jesup, Georgia, which in 1960 had about nine thousand residents. Jesup was where my family went every Saturday, rain or shine, for shopping and other services. We would go to the grocery store, and while Mama shopped, my siblings and I would people-watch. On haircut Saturdays, we went to Jack's Barber Shop, and Herbert Dent cut my hair. We occasionally went to Strickland's Feed and Seed for chicken feed (chicken scratch). Knight's Drug Store was our destination for medicine and drugs. Our medical doctors were Dr. Lanier Harrell and Dr. Ollie McGahee. For clothing, we went to S & R Clothing,

Photo Courtesy of Florie Hopkins

Sullivan's, Maxwell's, and Mooney's. Our hardware supplies came from Hodges Hardware.

We rarely ate in restaurants, but The Pig restaurant was a favorite, along with Candy Land and the Dairy Ranch. The movie theatres in Jesup were the Strand Theater and the Jesup Drive-In. Both theatres are still open today.

Christmas was always very special in Gardi, as we knew there would be presents, new clothes (PJs, for sure), and fresh fruit, minus oranges.

We wrote letters to Santa Claus, and some of them were read over the radio in the days before Christmas. We spent a considerable amount of time studying the Sears, Roebuck and Co. catalog and other sales papers, searching for the right gift. We only usually got one major gift each year. Toys that I received over the years included toy guns, cap pistols, a wooden rifle, a BB gun, and numerous others such as trucks, bulldozers, cowboy outfits, and a bow and arrow set. I even once got a bicycle.

Our stockings were always hung on the fireplace mantle. These stockings usually had candy in them on Christmas morning. We had a very specific ritual we practiced on Christmas morning: we did not go into the room where the Christmas tree and Santa Claus presents were without our parents being there.

Christmas Eve was always the longest day of the year. We had to be asleep for Santa Claus to come. It was so hard to fall asleep knowing that in just a few hours we would get to open our presents.

The Christmas I asked Santa Claus for a bow and arrow set, I had wanted that set for the longest time. I was so excited that I got up at 3:00 a.m. and sneaked into the living room. Santa, at that time, did not wrap our Christmas presents. Each of us siblings had a small pile of gifts. I found my pile, and there was the bow and arrow set. My wish had finally come true. I could not wait to try it out. I opened the box and proceeded to attach the string to each end of the bow. In my excitement, I decided to shoot one arrow to see how it worked. I pulled back on the string, and as I was about to release the arrow, the bow broke. I had put the string on backward, and the bow had splintered in my hand. My heart was pounding, and I could not tell my parents about the broken bow, because I was not supposed to see it until Christmas morning. I boxed everything back up and went back to bed.

Of course, I could not sleep, and I lay there awake until daylight. When I heard some voices, I went back into the living room. Everybody was ready to open their presents. I acted excited and opened my bow and arrow box. Taking out the bow, I attached the string correctly and, holding the bow at the broken part, was able to pull the string so that it would pitch the arrow out, but not far. I never told my parents about that incident. Later, I found some black electrical tape (we did not have duct tape back then) and wrapped the broken section of the bow. I continued to use it for a couple of years.

⁓

My dad did not believe in taking vacations. He was a workaholic and saw absolutely no reason or justification for leisure breaks. The first and only time that my family went to the beach when I was a kid was in 1961. We drove to Jekyll Island, which was about thirty miles from Gardi, on a Saturday afternoon. We had had the 1950 Buick Power Glide straight-eight-engine car for about two months by then. The Buick was long and black and had a turtle shell look to the body. It was an awesome vehicle.

Dad drove straight to the public beach and parked. We kids had only seen pictures of the ocean before that day. We jumped out of the car and raced to the beach as hard as we could run. We didn't stop at the water's edge but ran right in, up to our shoulders, with our clothes on. That was the saltiest water that I had ever tasted. However, the taste did not matter. We had been to the beach and conquered it. At the time, we considered this trip a vacation. Many years later, I won a real vacation. More on the Callaway Gardens vacation later.

Most of our relatives lived in or near Gardi except Uncle Willie. Aunt Minnie lived on a farm near us before moving to the grocery store in downtown Gardi. Her children were Rita, Mary Lee, Margaret, Winona, and Carolyn. Carolyn was two years older than I was and probably the one I knew best in the early years. My favorite memory of Carolyn was when I lived with Aunt Minnie and her family during the summer of 1963. She loved to aggravate me and kid me about my girlfriend. I did also spend time with Margaret and Winona then and as an adult. Rita and Mary Lee were much older, and I did not have much contact with them until later in life.

Uncle Willie and his family lived the farthest away from Gardi, and we did not see much of him or his family. They would appear at our doorstep in an old panel wagon vehicle with all of his children in the back. They would unload and stay a few hours, or a day or two, and then disappear again. I did get to know his children better later in life.

Uncle Jim and Aunt Joann Hill lived just down the road from us. Their children, Exley, Jan, and Jay, were my frequent playmates.

A great-uncle and great-aunt I remember from when I was a boy were Mack and Alice Herrin, who were on my dad's side of the family. They lived out toward Akin, not far from Gardi, in an old log cabin that had been somewhat updated. The house was set off the road and had a kitchen on the back, slightly separated from the main house. This was common in the early days in case a fire started in the kitchen. I do remember the kitchen. Aunt Alice cooked on a wood stove. She made the best-smelling, best-tasting biscuits that I have ever eaten. They were slightly smoky, with a firm crust, and tender inside. As I write this, I can close my eyes and still see the kitchen and smell those cathead biscuits.

Aunt Alice and Uncle Mack loved to eat squirrel. Aunt Alice told me about their squirrel hunting adventures. Uncle Mack would ask her to carry the .22 rifle into the woods until they reached the hunting area. Once a squirrel was located, Uncle Mack would take the rifle and shoot the creature. It was then Aunt Alice's responsibility to locate it and carry it back to their home. I never tried Aunt Alice's squirrel recipe, but Mama cooked squirrel and rabbit occasionally. I remember that they tasted like chicken. I always enjoyed our visits with Uncle Mack and Aunt Alice. They both passed years ago and are buried in the Union Baptist Church graveyard.

Another great-uncle was my grandfather's brother Oscar Hill. He would come and visit Grandpa Hill and my family from time to time. The one thing that I remember about him was that he was terrified of cemeteries. I never found out why he was so scared of the dead. One day, my brother Jerry and I decided to take Uncle Oscar for a ride in our car. I didn't tell him where we were going. I headed to the Midway Baptist Church Cemetery. As I drove on Midway Church Road next to the cemetery, we were so close to the headstones that you could almost touch them. I stopped and switched off the engine. I acted as if it had shut off on its own and then pretended it would not restart. I kept turning loose the ignition key just before the car could kick into start. After I had made a few "attempts," Uncle Oscar was about to have a conniption fit. He said some words that I cannot print in this book. "You get this lovely car started and get me out of here, and I mean right now," he said. Jerry and I were about to bust with laughter but did not want to give away our prank. I tried several more times to start the car and was not able to hear the engine due to Uncle Oscar's ranting and raving. I think that he was also afraid of getting out of the car and walking home. I decided, finally, after about five minutes, that we probably should end the prank. I cranked the car and headed home. As I recall, he never rode in a car with me after that incident.

Brothers Benjamin and Oscar Hill

3

The Lambert Bennett Place

Sometime in the late 1950s, Daddy sold our house on Morning Glory Circle. I never knew why he sold the house until I asked an older cousin not long ago.

Uncle Willie Hill was an interesting character and was known to find ways to interact with law enforcement. As the story goes, he wrote some checks that the bank said were not appropriate due to a lack of funds in the account. He was arrested and taken to jail. Then, he requested that Daddy and Uncle Jim co-sign on his bond so that he could get out of jail. They each posted a five-hundred-dollar bond on his behalf, with him agreeing to go to trial when the case came to court.

When the case came to court, Uncle Willie disappeared and was nowhere to be found. The court required the bonds to be paid in cash. I assume that Uncle Jim paid his bond, but as best I can determine, Daddy did not have the cash to pay. Mama tried to get him to borrow the money, but Daddy refused to do so. He sold the house to the McDuffie family, and we moved.

It was about eighteen months later that the Wayne County sheriff got a call from a sheriff in Florida. He had arrested a man named Willie Hill and wanted to know if it was the same Willie Hill that Wayne County wanted for skipping bond. Our local sheriff called Daddy and Uncle Jim and told them about the phone call. They agreed to go to Florida and pick up Uncle Willie.

The two of them traveled down to Florida. When they arrived, the sheriff said that Willie Hill had convinced them that he was not the Willie Hill wanted in Wayne County, Georgia, so he was about to be released. As Daddy and Uncle Jim walked into the cell, Willie said, "Hello, Jasper and Jim." Willie was known as a slick and smooth talker and could talk his way out of any situation.

⚬❧⚬

Willie, Jim and Jasper Hill

My brother Jerry and I had the responsibility of securing firewood for the three fireplaces. Our only tools were an ax and a bow saw, and a Wheelbarrow to transport the wood back to the house. On the southeast side of the house was timberland that had been farmed for turpentine. Following the turpentine harvest, the pine trees had been harvested. The area of the tree where the turpentine was collected, the catface, was removed from the trunk during pine tree harvesting and left in the woods. The remainder of the tree was sold for pulpwood. We cut the catface in small pieces and carried it home in the wheelbarrow to burn in our fireplaces. Jerry was a good salesman and talker. He would talk to me and distract me as I rolled the wheelbarrow, and we would be home before I realized it. These catfaces provided wood for our home for over two years.

The house was in bad repair. You could see the chickens through the floorboards as they wandered under the house. It was the coldest house that I recall ever living in.

I had my first wreck on Lambert Bennett Road. I was driving my dad's old Studebaker pickup truck. The Studebaker truck did not have an ignition switch, and you had to connect two wires to start the engine. It was fun to drive. The road was so sandy that ruts had developed in it, and you had to stay in the ruts, or you would lose control of the vehicle. My brother was

*Aunt Minnie Hill O'Neal Williams (in white blouse and seated)
at a Hill Family Reunion*

with me, and I was showing off (age twelve). I lost control and hit the ditch. My brother ran home and told Daddy about the wreck. I thought that I was sure to get a whipping, but Dad asked me if I was hurt, and when I said no, he told me we would go get the truck in a few minutes. Whew!

After my dad sold our house on Morning Glory Circle, we moved to a rental house on the Lambert Bennett place. We rented from Fred Bennett. Fred's father was Lambert Bennett; the house and land had been passed on to Fred. I later worked for Fred Bennett on the land surrounding the Lambert Bennett place. Mainly I helped him mow fields. I got to operate a Ford 8N tractor. I am sure that I got my love of tractors from this experience. I have the replica of this tractor in my scale model tractor collection.

The Lambert Bennett house was the only house on Lambert Bennett Road. The road was about one and a half miles long and primarily made of soft sand.

The house was a rustic farmhouse with a wraparound porch about eight feet wide on three sides. It had three fireplaces that burned wood for fuel. There was no running water, and we used an outhouse for the bathroom. The kitchen was off on the left side, at the rear of the house, as most kitchens were in the older farmhouses. There was a huge scuppernong vine that had been trellised behind the house. The vine covered approximately six hundred square feet, and the top was about five feet from the ground. The scuppernongs were sweet and flavorful in late August and September. We would just walk out back and eat them off the vine. Great memories.

As kids, we would get under the front porch and play in the sand. It was cooler under there during the hot summer days. You could build farms, cities, and other structures in the sand for all-day enjoyment. We had a few toys, but pieces of wood and rocks worked just as well as store-bought toys.

Another fun game to play was doodlebug hunting. Doodlebugs dug an inverted cone-like hole in the sand about two inches in diameter at the top and about one and a half inches deep. They would wait in the bottom, under the sand, for a bug, ant, or another insect to come by. The prey would fall in the hole, and the doodlebug would grab them, pull them under the sand, and the rest is history. We would take a pine needle and scratch the bottom of the hole so that the doodlebug came out, and we would catch it.

Dad told me a story when I was older, and we were reminiscing about his cars over the years. One of our neighbors needed to borrow a car to take his wife to the doctor in nearby Douglas, Georgia. We owned a 1950 Buick that was built like a tank. The only thing wrong with the car was that the park gear and parking brake did not work. Dad warned our neighbor about that and told him not to park on a hill, as the car might roll away.

The neighbor brought the car back around 5:00 p.m. and told Daddy that the car had been involved in a wreck. Dad looked at the car and could find no damage.

"Well, I have already repaired it," said the neighbor. He went on to tell Dad that he had to park on a street that had a substantial grade to it. While he was in the doctor's office, somebody came running into the office and said that a black Buick had rolled backward down the street and into the Chevrolet dealership, hitting three new cars and totaling them.

Dad was about to flip out. Looking at the car again, he said, "But, I don't see any damage to the Buick!"

"The only damage was a broken taillight," said the neighbor. "And I have already fixed that."

The first vehicle that I remember was a 1949 Ford convertible when we were living on Morning Glory Circle. My brother Jerry figured out a way to destroy the convertible top. We were at Grandma Ryalses' home in Jesup, and Jerry climbed a chinaberry tree. He went out on a limb that was over the 1949 Ford and took a fall. Miraculously, his fall was broken by the canvas roof, but he went through it and into the car. Jerry was scared about what was going to happen to him, as was I as a bystander. Mother had to drive home to Gardi with the top flapping. We knew Daddy would not be happy, and he was not. However, Jerry survived the ordeal, and that was what was important. That is my story, and I am sticking to it.

One afternoon, my brother Jerry and I decided to go down Lambert Bennett Road about five hundred feet, get in the bushes, and throw rocks at passing cars. With no other houses on the road and nobody around, we felt very comfortable that no one would know who we were. Not many cars came by, but those that did had rocks thrown at them. It was fun until Daddy came down the road and confronted us. We could not figure out how he found out. He always had the uncanny ability to know all things about what we were doing or had done. He stopped our rock-throwing for good.

Daddy, as mentioned earlier, was a jack-of-all-trades, and auto mechanic was one of them. It seemed that there was always something that needed repairing on our old cars. We did not have a garage or carport from which to work. However, we did have a large Southern Live Oak tree across the Lambert Bennett Road from our house. It had huge branches

that reached horizontally over twenty-five feet. Daddy attached a chain hoist to one of the limbs, which was perfect for pulling engines and lifting vehicles. We did a lot of repairs during the time we lived there.

One time, Daddy and I were working on our 1952 Chevrolet two-door sedan. As I remember, it was the car that replaced the convertible, before he got the Buick. We had to pull the engine head to replace the head gasket. The head was replaced, and Daddy reinstalled the carburetor. He tried to start the engine. It would not start. He poured a small amount of gasoline into the carburetor. It started this time, but a flame about two feet high came out of the carburetor. I had always heard that you could put out a fire with dirt, so I grabbed a handful and tossed it in the carburetor. The flame went out, and Daddy went berserk. He, in no uncertain terms, explained that he would have to remove the carburetor and clean out the dirt before the engine would ever start again. I never made that mistake again.

About one hundred feet behind that Southern Live Oak tree was a clear piece of land of approximately one acre where Daddy planted a garden. His parents always had a garden, and Daddy continued that tradition. The only problem with this garden was that deer and rabbits loved it, and they would almost destroy it before we were able to harvest the fruits of our labor. We tried several things to obstruct these critters, but they always outsmarted us. The only thing that worked was a bullet.

I always enjoyed hunting rabbits. Dad had an old .22 single-shot rifle, and I would borrow it (without permission) to go hunting. There was a period when mumps was going around at school, and I caught it. While I was recuperating at home, I saw a rabbit in the front yard. Even though I should have been in bed, resting, I got the rifle and stepped onto the front porch and started shooting. I did not hit the rabbit and did not even scare him. He slowly hopped from the front of the house around the right side while I kept shooting at him. I must have shot twenty times without hitting him. I even went into the yard to see if I could get closer. I learned later that the sights on the gun had been damaged and that it would not have hit the side of the barn. I got close enough to the rabbit that I could have swung the barrel and hit him. But by then, I was exhausted and had to call an end to the hunt. I suffered a major setback in my recovery from the mumps. The rabbit hunt was not worth the resulting pain that I experienced after it.

The Gardi Creek in front of the Lambert Bennett place was one of my favorite fishing spots for catching redfin pike. The creek was very small, only a few feet wide at its widest point. We would enter it from the Lambert Bennett Road. The underbrush was thick and plentiful. It was so dense that you never went in and out of the creek the same way. We would fish with short cane poles or just cut a slender branch from a tree for a pole. We used short pieces of fishing line and tied red flannel cloth to the ends. The trick was to move the red flannel up and down the creek to attract the pike. They would grab hold of it, and you could pull them ashore. They would generally be six to ten inches in length, and their meat was white, flakey, and delicious. The pike had lots of bones, but they were manageable. My favorite way to eat them was fried.

We took many trips to the Altamaha River, where we would spend a couple of nights on a sandbar in the river and fish all day. We would carry a tent for sleeping and utensils for cooking our fish, primarily catfish and some bream.

One of my favorite memories is catching catfish on trout lines. These were lines that were tied to a tree limb leaning over the river's edge. There was one hook on the line. We would set a dozen or so lines and fish them several times a day, even sometimes at night.

One afternoon, we caught a large catfish, around seven pounds. Daddy asked me if I could skin and gut it in preparation for cooking. I eagerly said yes. This was the first time that he had asked me to do this job alone. I was so excited to get to prove my ability to him. I grabbed the catfish and went to the river's edge. Cutting right behind its head with a circular motion to free the skin, I then pulled the skin toward the tail to remove it from the body. I got about one half of the skin removed when I dropped the fish into the water, and off it swam. I had not killed it before starting my cleaning. I knew that I was in trouble because that was one of two catfish that were to be our dinner. I panicked and ran into the river and started looking for the fish. Fortunately, the water was only inches deep on the sand bar, and I found the catfish swimming around and finished cleaning it. I never told Daddy about losing the fish.

Grandma Hill became bedridden and came to live with us. I remember her bed in the living room as we helped her with her daily activities. However, Mother was her major caregiver. It was my first experience in seeing how people, as they get older, may require significant assistance. The most distinct thing that I remember about her over the years was that she was not a very positive person. She would always make statements like, "I don't know how much longer I can make it. I am not going to last long." She passed away in 1963.

When the family closed Grandpa and Grandma's old home place on Morning Glory Circle, Dad got their dining room table and bench. The table was made by my great-grandfather James H. Hill in 1877. It had a very distinctive mark on it, which came about when it was being moved one time by horse and wagon. The table scrubbed against a wagon wheel, which left its round mark permanently on the tabletop. My brother Jerry now has the table and the bench that went with it.

In addition to living in Fred Bennett's rental house, I worked for him. As was my custom, I was always looking for ways to earn money. Next to our house was a field that Fred planted every year with corn. In the fall, after the corn harvest, he would allow me to cut the corn stalks with his 1949 8N Ford tractor and a Bush Hog mower. I fell in love with tractors at that point. I was not sure what I wanted to do in life, but I knew it would involve agriculture in some form.

One beautiful fall day, I was mowing the cornfield when, all of a sudden, I was surrounded by yellow jackets. I had to leave the tractor hurriedly but was able to switch off the engine. The yellow jackets had nested in the ground, which is their normal habitat. I estimate that over a thousand, or maybe a million of them, chased after me. A few were successful in leaving me with their venom. It was later that day before I could go back to check on the tractor. I was able to mount the tractor and leave that location quickly. Unfortunately, the only sign of a yellow jacket nest is seeing a swarm of them.

Fred Bennett also operated a land surveying business and a full-service gas station in Jesup. He hired me to work for him in both of those businesses. I was just fourteen when I went to work for him. I started in the surveying business. Fred had also employed a Wayne County High School senior by the name of Art Nolan to work there. Art and I, along with other employees, surveyed land all over Wayne County.

Our equipment consisted of a transit level, a marked surveying rod, surveying steel tape, stakes, a magnetic compass, and machetes. My job involved using the marked surveying rod, surveying steel tape, stakes, and a machete, the last of which we used to cut our way through the underbrush to open the trail for measuring and locating.

I was cutting a path through sagebrush one day and hit something that forced me to let go of the machete. I felt a shock as I let go. After looking around, I found an electric fence wire that was connected to a power source. The shock will not kill you, but it will make you hurt yourself trying to get away from it.

Another time, I was cutting through the underbrush, and my partner was coming from the opposite direction. We met when his machete blade landed on top of my blade. His blade continued down my blade and hit my right thumb. The pain was so intense, and there was so much blood, that I first thought that I had severed my thumb; however, it was only a deep cut. We were in the middle of the woods, miles away from medical help, so we taped it up with electrical tape and went on working. I still have a scar on my thumb to this day. It healed but did not go back in place as it should have.

One day, we were surveying land north of Jesup, in a swamp. We had to measure the property line, which ran down the middle of a small creek. The creek was about chin-deep on me. As we were moving the steel surveying tape (chain) along in the water, something caught my attention.

On the bank was a water moccasin, who decided to take a dip in the creek right next to me. I saw my life flash before me as he went underwater. I just knew he was heading for me. Swiftly, I headed back upstream and out of the creek. We discovered that there was another way to measure the property line, by running horizontally to the creek. That experience almost ended my surveying career.

When we were not surveying, I worked at Fred's full-service Gulf station in downtown Jesup. Based on my mechanic experience with my dad, I was able to do quite a few things to help fuel and repair vehicles. Full service meant that when you pulled into the station, I would come out and fill your gas tank, wash your windshield, check your oil level, and sweep out your floorboards if needed. I could also change your oil and repair flat tires. That awesome service went by the wayside many years ago.

Fred was a superb businessman. He owned and ran many businesses over the years, managed his land and forest resources in Gardi, and was a railroad engineer. He was a mentor to me, and I appreciated his taking an interest in me. I never got to visit with him later in life to thank him in person for his mentorship. Fred passed away on January 23, 2002, at the age of eighty-three.

In 1961, we moved into downtown Gardi. I am still not sure why we left the Lambert Bennett house. We moved next door to Lonnie Calvin Jackson and his wife, Mary Elizabeth, on River Road. The house was of wood-frame construction with a high crawl space underneath. It was old and in need of repairs. Since my dad was a carpenter, a plumber, and an electrician, he immediately began working on some of those repairs. He installed an indoor bathroom and updated the wiring. I enjoyed the location. It was about one hundred and fifty feet from the railroad. We got to hear the train up close and personal as it came by. We were close to the three stores with lots of treats for us kids. We were across the street from the Honey House. I could ride all over downtown Gardi on my bike and explore the area.

This new house was short on bedrooms and space, so Grandma Hill went to live with her daughter, my Aunt Minnie, at her store just across

US Highway 341. Unfortunately, Grandma died two years later, on June 16, 1963.

In May 1963, Daddy was called to pastor the Mount Pleasant Baptist Church in Snipesville, Georgia. Snipesville is in Jeff Davis County, some sixty-six miles west-northwest of Gardi. The family moved to Snipesville in June of 1963. Everybody, except me, moved. I had already committed to work for Fred Bennett during the summer of 1963 in his surveying and service station businesses. I made plans to stay with Aunt Minnie for the summer at her residence in the rear of her store. When I asked Daddy to allow me to stay and work in Gardi and Jesup through the summer, he reluctantly agreed.

That summer, Fred allowed me to use his surveying vehicle to drive from Gardi to Jesup every day for work. The vehicle was an old Chevy station wagon that was just about worn out. I did not have a driver's license, since I was only fifteen years old, but this did not stop me from driving. I had several years of experience, having started driving at the age of eleven. Fortunately, I never got stopped by law enforcement. I had a great summer and earned money.

When fall came and it was time to head back to school, Daddy phoned and said, "Son, it is time to come home." With all summer to plan my strategy of staying in Gardi, I had worked it out with Aunt Minnie to continue living with her while I finished my last two years of high school. I had already gotten approval from Fred Bennett to continue working for him.

My next words to Daddy were as follows: "Daddy, I have worked out a plan for me to stay in Gardi, live with Aunt Minnie, finish high school, and work for Fred Bennett." There was a time of silence on the phone after I shared those words. It seemed like five minutes, but I am sure it was only seconds.

"Son, you obviously didn't hear what I said," was his reply.

I knew then that my plan was not Daddy-approved. He told me he had bought me a train ticket from Jesup to Hazlehurst, my first ride on a passenger train, and that he would be there to pick me up at the train depot in Hazlehurst.

The Hill family

4

Faith Brings a Turning Point

After Daddy accepted Christ as his savior in February of 1956, he was a changed man. He turned his life around, and his focus was on God, his family, and his work. Daddy became the spiritual head of our family. Mama had already accepted Christ as her savior many years earlier. The change in Daddy was obvious to everyone in the Gardi community.

Was Daddy a perfect man? No, but who is? Daddy's faith was not just a Sunday event. His mission became to serve Christ, minister to others, and serve others. He lived his faith every day as best he could and shared the good news of Christ.

Gardi Baptist Church

Daddy joined the Gardi Baptist Church and attended every time the doors were open. He took our family, and we got involved in church activities. I joined the Royal Ambassadors program. The RA program was named after 2 Corinthians 5:20, "Now then we are ambassadors for Christ, as though God did beseech you by us: we pray you in Christ's stead, be ye reconciled to God." The RA motto is: We are Ambassadors for Christ. RA programs helped boys develop Christian character through mission involvement and virtue commitments. They also helped boys to grow spiritually, mentally, and physically, and to build good relationships with others. The RAs, along with helping me listen to and internalize the gospel of Christ, led me to commit my life to Jesus Christ and to be baptized.

One obstacle that Daddy had to overcome was his lack of reading skills to read and understand the Bible. He had only attended school through the third grade. Mama and the Bible became his reading teachers. I remember the many times that he had to struggle to read and comprehend the Bible. He amazed me and many others on how fast his reading skills improved. He was a very talented man but lacked the basics taught in school. However, he overcame his weaknesses and became a good reader, and he was able to explain the Bible in a way that anyone could understand it.

I found a notecard in Daddy's Bible after he passed that was headed in bold letters and read as follows:

SOUL WINNING BIBLE REFERENCES
1. God Loves all sinners – John 3:16
2. Call upon him – Romans 10:13
3. Turn away from sin – Luke 13:3
4. Believe on Jesus as Savior – Acts 16:31
5. Confess him – Romans 10:9
6. Assurance of Salvation – John 1:12

This is what he used to lead people to accept Jesus Christ as their personal savior.

Daddy started teaching a Junior Boys Sunday School class. He was later ordained as a deacon of the church and served in that capacity for several years. He shared his call from the Holy Spirit to preach the gospel with the church pastor and the members of the Gardi Baptist Church on Homecoming Day in 1959. The church voted to license Daddy to preach on June 10, 1959.

Daddy filled in as a lay speaker at several churches in Gardi and the surrounding area. In the late fall of 1959, he was called to be the pastor of the Union Baptist Church in Akin, Georgia. Union Baptist Church requested that Gardi Baptist Church ordain Daddy to the ministry. The church ordained him on January 3, 1960. He then accepted the call to be the pastor of Union Baptist Church. It was a part-time position as the church held services twice a month.

Union Baptist Church

TENTATIVE PROGRAM
For
O R D I N A T I O N   S E R V I C E

of
JASPER HILL
At
GARDI BAPTIST CHURCH

SUNDAY 3:00 P. ..,, JANUARY 3RD 1960

HYMN NO. 254 "Have Thine Own Way, Lord!" . . . . . Stebbins

PRAYER . . . . Rev. A. T. Arnette

HYMN NO. 417 "Breathe On Me" . . . . McKinney

CHARGE TO CHURCH . . . . Rev. E. A. Rozier

CHARGE TO CANDIDATE . . . . Rev. C. N. Mills

SERMON . . . . Rev. Stetson Bennett

PRESENTATION OF BIBLE . . . . Rev. R. Mills

ORDINATION PRAYER . . . . Rev. Marcus Rushin

HYMN NO. 273 "Near To The Heart of God" . . . . McAfee

RIGHT HAND OF FELLOWSHIP TO CANDIDATE AND WIFE . . Congregation

BENEDICTION . . . . Rev. Jasper Hill

EXAMINATION OF CANDIDATE

Will be held on the same day January 3rd, at 2:30 P. M. at the

Gardi Baptist Church, preceeding the Ordination Service. The

Examining Council will be composed of the above listed ministers

and other ministers who will be present.

Rance Richardson, Pastor

Gardi Baptist Church

Altamaha Baptist Association

Jasper Hill Ordination Service Program

Midway Baptist Church

About a year later, Midway Baptist Church in Gardi called Daddy to pastor their church. They, also, held services part-time, but on opposite Sundays from Union Baptist Church. This allowed Daddy to pastor both churches at the same time.

My parents always instructed us to never, never ever steal—not even the dust off the floor. I was certainly well aware that stealing was very wrong. However, it did not stop me from stealing from the Midway Baptist Church.

I don't know what happened that made me walk up to the bulletin board and steal all of the paperwork thumbtacked to the board. I couldn't be happy with just the paperwork; I stole the thumbtacks as well.

Daddy had been the pastor for about two years when this incident happened. The church was about eleven hundred feet down Midway Church Road from our house.

I put the papers in my pants pocket and took them home with me. I then made the serious mistake of forgetting to empty my pockets before Mama washed my pants. She found the paperwork. All I heard was, "Jimmy Leroy Hill, come here right this minute." I knew I was in trouble as soon as I saw the papers in her hand.

When Mama asked me why I had stolen the paperwork from the church, I told her I didn't know why. As she pointed out to me, the papers I had taken were notices about upcoming events at the church and a list of committees. "They have no useful value to you, do they?"

"No, ma'am," I answered. "I am so sorry for taking them."

Mama told me she was sure that Daddy would want to talk to me about stealing the paperwork. I knew then that I was in deep trouble. She only mentioned Daddy when she felt it was a most serious offense.

That evening, Daddy got home, and after supper, he asked me about the stolen papers. He said, "You knew it was wrong to steal that paperwork, didn't you?" I assured him I did and said I would never do it again. I just knew that he was going to administer corporal punishment for this great error in my judgment. Daddy gave me the "Hill look" and lectured me on why stealing was wrong and how I could damage the Hill reputation. I made him and God a solemn promise never to steal again. And I never did.

Little Creek Baptist Church called Daddy to pastor their church the next year. It met part-time, on the same Sundays as Union Baptist Church. Daddy felt the Holy Spirit calling him to go to Little Creek Baptist Church, and therefore he resigned from the Union Baptist Church.
He was now pastoring Midway and Little Creek churches at the same time, and he continued with both until May of 1963.

Before Daddy's time at Little Creek, one of their previous pastors was Stetson Bennett Sr. He was one of the first pastors that I remember. The reason he made such a lasting impression on me was his booming voice. Had I not known otherwise, I would have thought that it was God speaking instead of Pastor Bennett. I still remember that unique voice as if I had heard him speak only yesterday.

Little Creek Baptist Church

While Daddy pastored the churches in the Gardi area, he also conducted revival services in other churches in Wayne County. He had a tremendous, positive impact on many people's lives in his early pastoral career. Many were brought to a personal relationship with Christ during his preaching and ministry.

Mama was a tremendous helpmate to Dad in his pastoral duties. She was a servant leader in her own right and was loved by everyone; she had an amazing ability to make everyone feel good about themselves. Mama was an encourager and a dedicated servant of the Lord. She also participated in the Woman's Missionary Union. The WMU assisted churches in developing and implementing strategies for mission work.

Daddy was asked to accept the pastorate at the Mount Pleasant Baptist Church in Snipesville, Georgia, in June of 1963. As Daddy and Mom always did, they prayed over the decision. Feeling the Holy Spirit's presence, Dad accepted the call, and our family moved to Snipesville and into the church-owned pastorium.

5

School Days

Starting school can be a very traumatic time for children. I know it was for me. Gardi had a three-room community school, Gardi School, which had been around since the 1800s. My father and mother had both attended this school. It was my dream, as a four-year-old boy, to start my pursuit of education at this fine facility.

Gardi School
*Painting commissioned by Mary Hill - artist Mack Donald Oswalt 2002

We lived close to the school grounds, and I could hear children playing outside every day. I learned later that this playing was called recess. I would time my arrival at school to be during recess. No, I was not enrolled in school—I just attended recess. I learned that this was the best thing about school. Of course, it was the only thing that I knew about school at that point.

My dog Rocks and I would leave home in time to do some hunting on the way to school. Going through the woods, we would see wild squirrels, rabbits, and an occasional possum. Rock's bark would cause them to race away.

Jimmy with his dog Rocks

Following my arrival at the school grounds, I would look up my friend Ronnie. Ronnie was two years older than I was and had enrolled in the first grade. He told me exciting things about the school and how he hated the girls. (He might have hated girls back then, but he was a womanizer later in life.) Ronnie and I would play and explore the school grounds. These visits became part of my daily routine, and I looked forward to the day when I would be allowed to attend school officially when I was six years old. Yes, six years old. We were smart enough back then that we didn't have to attend pre-kindergarten or kindergarten before going to the first grade. Of course, we didn't see those "-gartens" until a few years later.

Finally, my body caught up in years with my mind. I turned six. However, during the summer before I was due to start there, they closed the Gardi School. The closing had something to do with better educational opportunities being offered in a larger school in Jesup, the county seat. Hogwash! My school had educated thousands of kids for many years. All the kids that I knew who had studied there turned out okay. Many turned out to be successful in our community and beyond.

I was upset. No, I was mad! How dare they close my school? I was determined that, since they had closed my school of preference, I would not attend school at all. No, sir. That was it. I was through with education.

My mother had other ideas. She explained that I was going to school and that I would love the new school. Besides, I would get to ride a school bus. Her plan did not appeal to me at all. I came up with my own.

We lived in a house without running water, in other words with no flushable toilet or faucets. We had to use an outdoor privy, which was a small, stand-alone building, usually located a fair distance from the house, with one door, no windows, and either one or two holes cut in a board that sort of resembled a bench. Our privy had two holes, one larger than the other.

My plan that Monday, August 31, 1953, the day my education was officially due to begin, was to be in the privy at the time that the school bus arrived to take me to school. My mother had explained that the bus would not wait for me and that I had to be ready when it rolled up to our house. I reckoned that if I could stay in the privy long enough, the bus would leave without me. I would then have a justifiable excuse for missing school. I lowered my pants and seated myself over the smaller hole, then started to look through the Sears and Roebuck catalog, which, as I have mentioned before, served more than one purpose in the privy back then.

The plan almost worked. I didn't count on my mother coming into the privy and taking control of the situation. She did not explain anything about how I was missing a great educational experience. I found myself with my drawers up and going out the door in an instant. I would not have had time to flush the toilet, even if we had a flusher. My mother dragged me onto the bus and sent me off on my educational journey. Mr. Tom Howard, the bus driver, was related to our family, as my mother explained to me. I liked him, but he was part of the evil empire that was trying to get me to go to school.

As I entered the bus, I went to the very back and crawled under the seat. My mother may have won the first round, but she had not considered the wise old saying: you can take a horse to water, but you can't make him drink. I was determined not to participate in school. No one seemed to notice that I had disappeared on the bus. It was a long, winding trip over bumpy dirt roads to reach the school. Everyone then exited the bus. Everyone, that is, but for me. I stayed under the seat and did not move a muscle.

When they noticed I was missing, the school called my mother to see where I was. She explained that I had boarded the bus. My soon-to-be teacher, Mrs. Lois Thornton, came and looked under every seat until she found me. She tried in a nice way to get me to come out. No, sir. I was not going to this school. She finally gave up and sent in a young, pretty, blonde girl named Nell Rose Sears, who had candy to bribe me to come out. I gave in and agreed to get off the bus. As I reached the walkway going into the school, having consumed the candy—which was as delicious as Nell Rose was beautiful—I changed my mind. One of the support poles holding the roof over the walkway became my latching-on point. I had gone as far as I was going. Nothing they could do would get me to turn loose of that pole and go inside the school.

Unbeknownst to me, my teacher had called my mother. She came, and I knew then that I was in big trouble. She did not try to pry me from the pole or cajole me. She whipped my britches and me until the last thing that I thought about was holding onto the pole. I let go and went to find my desk in the first-grade room. No, sir, I did not start school of my own free will, but under duress. I chose to stay that day, but I immediately started hatching a new plan; however, that is a story for another day.

I did survive my first day at Orange Street Elementary School. I received a First Day Diploma to prove it. I am not sure how I received a score of Good for Behavior, Observation, Group Action, and Appetite.

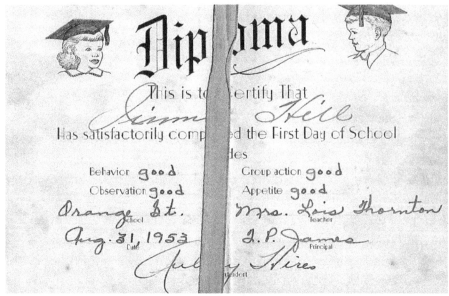

Jimmy's Diploma for first day of school

Well, maybe I do understand the appetite score. I was hungry after my escapade.

The school was on the north side of Jesup, in a residential neighborhood. They had recess time, but it was not nearly as much fun as at the Gardi School. The bathroom was located between two classrooms, and you could enter from either classroom. I learned that you had to raise your hand when you needed to go to the bathroom, so I raised my hand on the morning of the first day and was given permission to go. As I walked into the bathroom, I found a little boy crying. I asked him why he was crying, and he said, "I got my wiener hung on my zipper, and I can't get it loose."

I knew that addressing this issue was out of my wheelhouse. I ran back into the classroom and shouted out, "There's a boy in the bathroom, and he has his wiener caught in his zipper!" Mrs. Thornton rushed to his aid.

I attended the Orange Street School for four years. I made all Ss in the first grade, which I found out was Satisfactory. I even missed twenty-one days of school that year. I don't remember why I missed that many days—unless it was part of my plan.

In second grade, I only missed two days of school for the entire year and again made all Ss. We were getting into the hard stuff like reading, writing, and arithmetic. I started the school year at 49.5 inches tall and weighed 55 pounds. I ended the year at 51 inches tall and weighed 63 pounds. By the way, we did have two other grade scores: Poor and Failure. I thought you might want to know that so you could gauge my progress.

Grades, or marking system, changed in the third grade to include five ratings, from E for Excellent to U for Unsatisfactory. Classes were getting harder, and I was not able to get any Es. I did get lots of Ss and S minuses. I got a few Ps, very few. The Ps were in things like Arithmetic and English. My teacher, Mrs. Eason, wrote on my report that I had improved in general, but needed "to work on English grammar and Arithmetic borrowing."

My fourth-grade teacher was Ms. Susan Jones. I still have her picture. I think that I was in love with her. Our scoring method changed again. I think the scoring changes got me confused and were directly attributable to my grade scores not being where I wanted them to be. Let's put it this way, I had scores that ran the gamut from A to F, with mostly As and Bs. My attendance record was 100 percent. I did so well that I was promoted to the fifth grade, which meant moving to the T. G. Ritch Elementary School, which was across town.

I joined the 4-H club in the fall of 1958 at T. G. Ritch Elementary. I entered local and district competitions and learned a lot through 4-H. I particularly liked their motto, To Make the Best Better. Their pledge was: "I pledge My Head to clearer thinking, My Heart to greater loyalty, My Hands to larger service, and My Health to better living for my club, my community, my country, and my world." It was my first experience with youth clubs, and I enjoyed it.

After two years at T. G. Ritch, I moved up to junior high school. I must have liked it at Jesup Junior High School, as I did well and did not miss a day of class. My deportment score year-end average was 91—I was extremely proud of that—and I was presented with a Merit Award for perfect attendance.

In September 1961, I transferred to the Wayne County High School. I had finally made it to high school. This was a major change, with tougher classes and teachers. My homeroom teacher was Mr. R. E. Harrison. He also was an agricultural education, FFA, and shop teacher. Mr. Charles E. Bacon was the principal.

The second year in high school, my tenth-grade homeroom teacher was Mrs. Vera Flowers. I remember as she called the roll every morning, she would call out "James Hill."

Since my name was officially Jimmy, I would answer, "Jimmy is here."

She would say, "No, your name is James."

That exchange took place every day for 180 days. She would never call me Jimmy. It got to the point that my classmates would laugh every day when she called me James.

One of my favorite classes, when I started high school, was Shop I. My dad knew carpentry skills, and I had learned some from him. In shop class, we were taught how to use hand tools and power tools with an emphasis on safety, as well as how to measure, cut, and handle lumber. My first project was to build a wooden shoeshine kit with a storage area and a rack on top for shining shoes. I still have that shoeshine kit.

My other classes at Wayne County High included English, world history, algebra, biology, and agriculture. I also worked with Mrs. Bruce in the guidance council office.

I was struggling with English II. It looked like I might have to retake it. Our family was moving to Jeff Davis County, and I would be in a new school in the eleventh grade. I dreaded the thought of having to take tenth-grade English in the eleventh grade. I went to see my English II teacher, Mrs. Merle Cockfield, to plead my case for a passing grade. I promised to study harder and not to disappoint her if she would allow me to enter the eleventh grade taking English III. I don't know exactly how it worked out, but I received a passing grade (rounded off to reach 70). Thank you, Mrs. Cockfield, for believing in me. You made my day, year, and career on that special day.

I spoke with Mrs. Merle Cockfield in the fall of 2019, and I reminded her about my pleading with her all those years ago. She said that she remembered it. She also asked me for a copy of this book when it was completed, which I promised to send. Unfortunately, she passed away on January 5, 2020, at the age of 93. However, I did not disappoint her for having believed in me. At my new high school, Jeff Davis High School in Hazlehurst, Georgia, my English III final grade was 87 and my English IV final grade was 90.

Mr. Jim Collins was my algebra teacher at Wayne County High. He was slightly hard of hearing. When announcements came over the intercom system, Mr. Collins would cup his hand around his ear to hear the announcement. One day, a student brought a reel-to-reel tape recorder to school. He had pre-recorded a message on it. About halfway through our algebra class period, the student (who will remain nameless, and it was not me) hit the Play button on the hidden recorder. The message started, and Mr. Collins cupped his ear to listen to it: "Mr. Collins, please come to the principal's office," said the recording. Mr. Collins had been explaining an algebraic equation on the blackboard. He told us to continue to work on the problem and that he would be back shortly. As soon as he left the room, you could have heard the laughter two blocks away. As you know, algebra is not fun or funny, but this prank was. After about five minutes, Mr. Collins came back into the room. He never mentioned the message or his trip to the principal's office. However, we did receive double homework for that night.

Agriculture was one class that I took to and excelled in. Spending my youth in the rural Gardi area and working in the fields had already given me a love and respect for the land. The agricultural education course that I took under Mr. Harrison and Mr. Joe Davis opened my eyes and inspired in me an even greater interest in agriculture. I joined the FFA organization in the fall of 1962. The Jesup FFA Chapter awarded me the FFA Greenhand degree that October and the Degree of Junior Farmer in February 1963. I also won third place in the Soil Conservation District Essay Contest in December 1962 and was named Outstanding FFA Student in Soil and Water Conservation on May 16, 1963. After receiving all those awards, I felt as if my studying and hard work was paying off.

I knew that I was going to continue to be a member of FFA in my new school in Hazlehurst, Georgia, when we moved. This area of interest was very exciting, and it could lead to a career.

FFA Green Hand Degree

FFA Junior Farmer Degree

6

New Beginnings and Marching Orders

It was 10:15 p.m. on August 20, 1963, when the train whistle blew and I arrived in Hazlehurst, Georgia, on the passenger train from Gardi. My first train ride ever. I was sixteen years old, and it was a great adventure for me. I was one of only six people on the train that night. I exited the train at the Hazlehurst Railroad Depot and looked around for my dad. Sure enough, he was there to pick me up as promised.

We left the depot immediately and traveled to our new home in Snipesville. Snipesville is southwest of Hazlehurst, in Jeff Davis County. Our mailing address was Route One, Denton, Georgia, even though we lived about eight miles from Snipesville and thirteen miles from Denton. My family had moved to Snipesville back in June. I had stayed in Gardi and spent the summer working with Fred Bennett.

Photo Courtesy of Vann Wooten

We arrived at the home around 10:45 p.m. Our home was located about one mile off Broxton Highway, on Mount Pleasant Church Road. My mother and my siblings were waiting for me. We had not seen each other since early June. Mother fixed me a snack to welcome me home. I spent a few minutes catching up with my family.

Finally, at about 11:30 p.m., we went to bed. I was exhausted and wanted to get some sleep so that I could check out the house and the area the next morning. I woke up early, and Mother fixed me a great breakfast of eggs, grits, bacon, and toast. I sure had missed Mother's cooking while I was living in Gardi.

Our new home was a pastorium, which was provided by the Mount Pleasant Baptist Church as part of my dad's compensation for pastoring the church. This home was new and modern; it had been completed a year earlier. With three bedrooms and one bathroom, it was adequate for all six of us. As you entered the home, the living room was on the right and the dining room on the left. Dad and Mom slept in the master bedroom down the hallway, adjacent to the living room. Continuing down the hall, the next and last room on the right was the boys' bedroom, where Jerry, Ricky, and I slept. Across the hall was the third bedroom, which belonged to Linda. Next to Linda's room, and opening off the hallway, was the one bathroom. Adjacent to the bathroom was the kitchen, which opened into the dining room.

The home did not have an air conditioning system, which was not a problem because we had never had air conditioning. However, it did have a whole-house exhaust fan for cooling. I thought we had died and gone to heaven. It was almost like having air conditioning. At least, I thought that until I experienced real air conditioning during my freshman year in college. There was a one-car carport attached to the left side of the house, with a utility room for the washer and dryer.

Mount Pleasant Baptist Church was formed in 1820 and was initially known as the Byrd Church. The Byrd family donated the land, and several family members were original members of the church. It still stands and has been remodeled and added on to over the years. Dad helped to remodel the church while he was pastor.

Mt. Pleasant Baptist Church

Mt. Pleasant Baptist Church Pastorium

The property around the house included the church and over ten acres of pine trees. The church was about seven hundred feet west of the pastorium, on Mount Pleasant Church Road. Near the pastorium was a location for a large garden. Dad, following the tradition he had grown up with, always had a large garden for our family and extra to share with the community. Its benefits were twofold: having access to fresh fruits and vegetables and saving money on groceries.

The day after I arrived home, Mother took me school shopping as school was due to start the following Tuesday, the day after Labor Day. We went to Victor's Department Store and B & R Clothing to get outfitted. I was ready for my first day of school at Jeff Davis High School.

My junior year started in September 1963 with a full load of classes: agriculture, history, geometry, English, and typing. I also served as a teacher assistant to Mrs. McBride in the counseling office. This was a challenging year, being at a new high school and making new friends. However, it went well, and I felt right at home. We lived about thirty minutes from the high school and rode the school bus there and back each day. Dad took a part-time job driving the school bus to supplement his pastor's salary.

Having the opportunity to take an agriculture class again was just up my alley. I was not sure at that point what I wanted to do in life, but I knew it had to be something connected to that field. I immediately joined the FFA organization and began my agriculture classes. This is where I met Mr. B. H. Claxton, my Agriculture II teacher, who became a major influence on my life and career.

I decided that I would participate in a Supervised Agricultural Experience (SAE) project in FFA. My chosen project was to raise two pigs. I named them Hazle and Hurst. Dad and I built them a pen behind the house, on church property. I took care of the pigs daily, including feeding and medicating them when needed, and recorded it all in my SAE record book. After my project was over, we further enjoyed the pigs on the dinner table.

Dad enjoyed his gardens. He loved sharing his bounty with his friends and with widows and older people in the community who could not grow a garden anymore. He grew snap beans, peas, squash, okra, potatoes, sweet corn, cucumbers, watermelons, and other seasonal items.

As his gardens grew larger each year, he needed to find a better way to till the soil and plant the garden. Though he did not have a college education or a high school diploma, my dad was a mechanical genius, a gifted man with mechanical expertise and lots of common sense. He could build a house, wire a house, install plumbing, and work on engines or most anything else. He now needed a tractor to tend to the garden, so he decided to build one.

As a family, we did not have any extra resources for a tractor or indeed for most modern technologies of that time. He found a rear end from an old car, a transmission from an old truck, a front end of a trailer, and a

Dad on the tractor that he made

lawnmower engine. He fabricated the parts, along with a steering wheel from an old truck, into a garden tractor. He even built a three-point hitch on the rear. He used this tractor for many years and grew great gardens. My nephew Jerry Hill Jr. now has the tractor.

Shortly after we arrived in Snipesville, Mom got a job as the food service director at the Clyde Duncan Memorial Hospital, now known as the Jeff Davis Hospital, in Hazlehurst. The hospital was new at the time, and she started the kitchen facility and remained there for twenty-two years. Mom joined a national association of dietitians and won several awards for her work. She traveled to numerous places across the country in support of the national organization. All of this she achieved with only an eighth-grade education. Later, she received her GED at age forty.

Mother with her staff at the Jeff Davis Hospital Kitchen

The Mount Pleasant Baptist Church welcomed our family as one of their own. It was a great experience to get to know the families in the church. Waymon and Francis Ricketson and their children were one of the first families we became friendly with. They owned Ricketson Farm and grew primarily tobacco. I worked for them cropping tobacco in the summer of 1964 and 1965. Of course, I had prior experience working for my Aunt Minnie in Gardi. Mr. Ricketson harvested his tobacco just like Aunt Minnie did, so I was trained and ready to go on the first day.

Cropping tobacco was a hard job. It required getting up, eating an early breakfast, and being ready to hit the field around 7:00 a.m. At that time of the morning, the dew was still on the tobacco leaves, and I would get soaking wet after a few minutes of cropping. Also, the black tobacco tar would cover my arms and clothes. The mule pulling the sled would not always be where he was supposed to be, and that required quite a bit of extra walking. In early June, when we started cropping tobacco, the temperature would rise to over 100 degrees in the field. I don't think that I have ever been any hotter, wetter, or more exhausted than I was in the tobacco patch. As I was told at the time, it would make a man out of you. I guess it did; I survived and thrived.

My favorite store in Hazlehurst was the Western Auto Associate Store. I had always wanted a set of mechanic's tools like my dad's, and I was able to purchase my first set at the Western Auto. It came with a set of sockets and ratchets, adjustable wrenches, pliers, screwdrivers, a hammer, a hex wrench set, and various other small tools. I thought that I had arrived in mechanic heaven with these new tools. I still have them to this day, though since then, I have added many more specialized tools. I have been called a hoarder of small tools. I plead guilty to the charge.

I held various other jobs during my junior year. I worked for the Rish Poultry Farm, peeling poles for use in building chicken houses on the farm. Mr. Rish paid me four dollars a day. Peeling poles is hard work, and that is the hardest work that I have ever done for four dollars a day.

Mr. Rish had several chicken houses at the time, full of baby chickens that he was raising for a poultry processing company. The processing plants only wanted female birds for processing. At that time, determining the sex of the baby chickens was not easy or reliable. As the chicks got older, it was easier to determine their sex. I helped him remove the roosters from his chicken houses. We slaughtered the roosters during the morning and placed them in his freezer. The slaughtering involved killing the roosters, de-feathering them, removing their entrails, and cleaning them for freezing. This process has a certain odor to it. Mr. Rish asked me if I wanted to stay for lunch; they were having fried chicken. After smelling raw chicken all morning long, I said no, thank you. Fried chicken was the last thing that I would want for lunch. I went home and had a bologna sandwich.

During the fall of 1965, Dad, my brother Jerry, and I planted pine trees on the church land surrounding the church and the pastorium to replace those that had been harvested years earlier for use in building the new pastorium. The trees we planted were then harvested about twenty years later, and the land again replanted with young pine seedlings.

Another job I had was working part-time at the Piggly Wiggly grocery store in Hazlehurst as a meat cutter. Mr. Ralph Edwards was the store manager. I graduated high school with his daughter, Patricia. The meat market was full-service; the meat was cut up daily, and special orders were available at any time. I learned how to cut up hogs, cows, and chickens. However, my primary job was to wait on customers at the meat counter. I wore a Piggly Wiggly butcher hat and a white apron. I worked after school and on Saturdays during the spring and summer of 1964 until the end of August, when I went back to school for my senior year. Based on my State of Georgia tax form for that year, I earned $514.20 and paid in $18.66 in Social Security taxes and $72.40 in federal income taxes.

My senior year started again with a full load of classes: forestry (agriculture), algebra, and chemistry, in addition to English and typing. I also continued with my teacher assistant role.

Up to my senior year in high school, I had not thought much about college, or about a career for that matter. One day, in my agriculture class, Mr. Claxton asked me and my friend Stanley Hutchinson a question: "Boys, what are you going to do after graduation?" We looked at each other, stunned; no one had ever asked us that question so bluntly. We stuttered and mumbled a few unintelligible words.

"Here is a brochure that I want you to read," Mr. Claxton continued. "I think it is something you boys might be interested in."

The brochure described an engineering degree offered at the University of Georgia. It was in agricultural engineering. We read it through, and, thinking he was presenting us with our marching orders, we both followed his counsel and never looked back. Stanley and I would end up attending the University of Georgia, by way of Abraham Baldwin Agricultural College (ABAC), and both got our undergraduate degrees in agricultural engineering.

I knew that I had to get another math course under my belt in high school to prepare me for college, so I dropped typing and replaced it with Algebra II.

I was inducted into the National Beta Club on March 5, 1965. The Beta Club promotes the ideals of academic achievement, character, leadership, and service. To be confirmed as a member, I had to go through an initiation, which was to wear a toga all day at school and after school when visiting various businesses downtown. I wore a white sheet wrapped around me as the toga. I think they might call this hazing now.

The US Air Force offered me an opportunity to take their aptitude test. I took it and was informed that I had qualified for enlistment in the United States Air Force after graduation from high school. The letter requested a few minutes of my time to discuss what the Air Force could offer me. I decided that I was going to college, so I did not pursue this request.

Writing was always something that I was interested in. I decided to join the high school newspaper staff. *The Jacket Racket* was published once a month and sold for ten cents. My job was to write stories and updates about the Jeff Davis FFA Chapter. I had articles in all but one issue of *The Jacket Racket* in my senior year.

In the spring of 1965, I decided to enter the Jeff Davis High School Math and Science Fair. Searching for a project, I went to the school library and found a book entitled *The Boys' Book of Science and Construction* by Alfred Powell Morgan. The first edition was published in 1922. There were many ideas and projects outlined in the book. The first potential project that I found was a sundial. However, the one that I found most interesting was a mechanical telautograph. What excited me was the challenge of building something complicated and seeing it work. I studied all the information on the telautograph and decided this would be my project. It was a perfect fit for using the skills learned in my Algebra II class. The mechanical telautograph was used to copy and transmit words or pictures, using wires and geometric shapes, to a distant station and there to reproduce the same image as the original. I won first prize in the Algebra Division and was second place overall winner in the Math and Science Fair. As you can imagine, I was extremely proud. I didn't know at the time that this type of project was leading me toward an engineering career. *The Boys' Book of Science and Construction* is still available today but is extremely rare and costs upwards of $250 for a first edition and $150 for a second edition.

Victor's Department Store in Hazlehurst hired me part-time to sell men's clothing in 1965. Based on my W-2 form for that year, I earned a total of $18.50, with $0.67 paid in Social Security tax. I must have only worked a few hours before I concluded—or Victor's Department Store concluded—my career. I was not cut out to be a clothing salesman.

I made many friends at Jeff Davis High School even though I only attended the eleventh and twelfth grades. Several are still my closest friends today. I ran into one recently, who, after I mentioned having attended Wayne County High School in Jesup, said, "I thought you had attended all twelve grades in Jeff Davis County." I had been concerned about leaving Gardi and had wanted to finish high school in Jesup. However, I flourished at Jeff Davis High, with grades in the 90s and near-perfect attendance. I now know that it was not the end of the world to change high schools as an upcoming junior. Life is about change, and I learned that valuable lesson as a teenager. I think it served me well.

The Baccalaureate Sermon was held on Sunday, May 30, 1965. The Graduation Exercise was held the following evening, Monday, May 31. There were 125 in my graduating class. We closed out our graduation ceremony singing our alma mater, which goes like this:

Hail, Dear old J. D. H.
We'll always heed thy call
We'll true and faithful be
Here in thy walls

When we are gone from thee
Our hearts will always be
Loyal and true to thee
Dear J. D. H.

Jimmy and his family at 1965 Jeff Davis High School Graduation

Following graduation, my parents and siblings went home, and I rode around town for a while with a couple of friends in my dad's car. We traveled our usual circular route from downtown to the Tastee Freeze and back downtown. We visited with several members of our class at the Tastee Freeze. Then I headed home.

I spent part of the summer after graduation working for Waymon Ricketson in the tobacco fields. Another job I found myself was at the tobacco warehouse in Hazlehurst. After the tobacco was cured and packed in croker sack (burlap) sheets, it was brought to the tobacco house for sale. Buyers from the cigarette manufacturers came to Hazlehurst to buy the tobacco. Before the sale took place, each tobacco sheet had to be flipped 180 degrees to reveal any foreign objects inside the tobacco and to make sure that the best tobacco was not just on top. The tobacco was sold by weight and quality of the leaves. My job, along with a partner, was to flip the tobacco sheets. Their weight was not allowed to exceed three hundred pounds. Almost every sheet that I flipped weighed three hundred pounds. I built up my arm and shoulder muscles during that job. The buyers would compete against each other in a live auction as they were led down the rows of tobacco sheets in the warehouse. Free enterprise at its best.

In July, I attended the Georgia FFA Convention in Covington, Georgia, at the State FFA–FHA Camp. I had applied to become a state FFA officer for the 1965–66 school year. The competition was fierce, and the convention delegates were the ones who elected the state officers. I had to go through several rounds of interviews conducted by the 1964–65 state officer team before being elected a state FFA vice president. I assumed my duties immediately. All the other officers were high school seniors; I was the only one who had already graduated from high school. This allowed me to participate in many activities that those who were still in high school were not able to enjoy.

As a result of becoming a state FFA officer, I postponed attending college for a year. I had been accepted at Abraham Baldwin Agriculture College (ABAC) in Tifton, Georgia, to start in the fall of 1965. The registrar at ABAC agreed to allow me to be the first enrollee for the fall 1966 class. I was extremely grateful.

With state FFA officer duties being part-time, I realized I needed a part-time job that would provide me income for my college expenses starting in the fall of 1966. I learned about an opening at McLendon Grocery, located on Tallahassee Street in Hazlehurst. The store proudly shared that it was home-owned and home-operated and advertised that it had reasonable prices and was reliable. McLendon's motto was: A Square Deal or No Deal and We Deliver. I went for an interview and met with the store manager, Mr. Oris McLendon. He hired me with the understanding that I would have to do some traveling in my capacity as a state FFA officer. My duties would include working in the meat department, stocking the store, cashiering, and delivering groceries. The store was open Monday to Saturday, all day every day, except for Wednesdays, when we closed at 1:00 p.m., as did most stores in downtown Hazlehurst. I worked every hour the store was open.

My first responsibility was in the meat department. The store cut fresh meat daily, such as beef steaks, pork chops, bacon, chickens, and various sandwich meats. The meat companies delivered quarters of beef and half hogs that were then cut into consumer cuts by the store. Mr. Oris taught me how to cut up these large pieces. With the beef, we started with the hindquarter, which produced ground beef, top round, bottom round, T-bones, top sirloins, tenderloins, flank steaks, sirloin tip, and rump roasts. We used a meat band saw to cut the carcass into the various steaks and the components. We then cut the front quarter into chuck steaks, pot roasts, rib steaks, short ribs, and soup bones.

Mr. Oris also taught me how to cut up the one-half hog into butts, picnics, jowls, chops, loin roasts, tenderloin, ham, spareribs, pork steak, and the most important pork product—bacon. These meat skills later helped to pay my way through the University of Georgia.

The process of stocking the shelves with canned goods and other items was my least favorite. I enjoyed running the cash register and meeting the customers. Delivery of the groceries was a great way to get out of the store for a while and travel to customer homes. We primarily delivered to the elderly and shut-ins, who could not come to the store and shop. This was a great service that the store provided, and we received a lot of compliments for it.

Mr. Oris was a good man, who took the time to train me well, and I appreciated his mentoring. His brother Otto, I learned later, actually owned the store, as well as owning the Jeff Davis Abattoir, McLendon Tractor Company, Hazlehurst Livestock Market, and Hazlehurst Ice Company. Another brother, Devoy, was also involved in the businesses.

When I first started with McLendon Grocery, my parents were taking me back and forth, and it got to be a burden on them. I eventually realized that I needed a vehicle to get to and from work. I bought my first car during the summer of 1966. It was a 1960 light-blue Dodge Dart Pioneer and was from the first year of production of the Dodge Dart. It had a 316-cubic-inch engine (5.2L) V8 and three-speed TorqueFlite transmission. I bought it for six hundred dollars from a local Snipesville man, J. M. Newman. The Jeff Davis Bank loaned me the money, and my dad and Mr. Newman were co-signers on the banknote. My payments were $68.23 per month for one year. I paid the bank a total of $818.76, including interest, and on time.

About a month before entering college, I noticed the engine was using oil, so I decided to give it an overhaul. Before I removed the engine, I took my Dodge out for a final spin to Snipesville, which was about eight miles

1960 Dodge Dart Pioneer

away. I turned around at Wooten's store and headed back home. It was a fairly straight road, so I put the pedal to the metal. Before I knew it, I was doing over one hundred miles per hour. It was fun, but I knew that I had to slow down and make sure that I did not blow the engine or have a wreck. What an experience—it was the fastest that I have ever driven.

I had assisted my dad for many years as he worked on and rebuilt engines in most of our family vehicles. I asked for his help this time, and he agreed, on the condition that I did most of the work. I hung a crossbeam adjacent to the carport and proceeded to remove the engine. I then disassembled it so that I could take the engine block and get it enlarged for new pistons and oil rings.

This was the biggest mechanic job that I had ever undertaken. I was very apprehensive about the project but was able, with Dad's help, to get the engine reassembled and installed back in the car. I got everything back together, and it ran like a new engine. I only had a few bolts left over. I never needed them, and I still have them.

I worked at McLendon Grocery until the fall of 1966 when I started my studies at Abraham Baldwin Agricultural College in Tifton. As I submitted my resignation, Mr. Oris offered me a fifty-cents-an-hour raise to stay on. I politely declined. I did thank him for his mentorship and for allowing me to conduct my duties as a state FFA officer. From the fall of 1965 to the fall of 1966, I made $2,803. It was a great help in paying my college expenses.

7

Selective Service and the Vietnam War

According to the US Department of Defense, the Vietnam War officially started on November 1, 1955, and concluded on April 30, 1975. I recall hearing about it more frequently on the news around 1963. It was a growing war that created many controversies. Some opposed the war on moral grounds, and others did not think it was winnable. All I knew for sure was that many of my friends had already enlisted, been drafted, or were scheduled to go into the military.

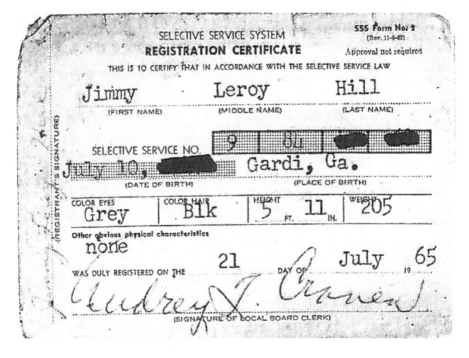

Upon reaching eighteen years of age, all males were required to register for the draft. I registered on July 21, 1965, at the local Selective Service Office #84 in Hazlehurst. On August 11, 1965, I received a classification questionnaire and returned it on August 23, 1965. I received a letter from the Selective Service Office on September 25, 1965, telling me that I was classified 1-A. This meant that I was available for military service. Had I not postponed my first year of college, they would have classified me as 1-S. That would have allowed me deferment for being a student in college.

Selective Service sent me a letter in early February 1966, stating that I had been scheduled for an army medical exam at Naval Air Station Jacksonville in Florida.

On March 17, 1966, I, along with about twenty other Jeff Davis residents, traveled by bus to the naval air station. As I recall, they paraded us through several medical buildings, including some Quonset huts. Doctors and nurses examined us from one end to the other. About halfway through the examination, I was called aside and told to gather up my clothes and report to the main building. This is where they told me that I was going home. Being an eighteen-year-old, I did not question them on any details. I caught the bus and headed home to Hazlehurst. I received a letter on April 9, 1966, notifying me that my classification had been changed from 1-A to 1-Y. This new classification was based on the fact that I was found not acceptable for induction under current standards. However, I could be drafted in the case of a national emergency.

As the years went by, and after much thought, I wanted to know why they did not take me into the military. I did some research, found that the records were stored at the National Personnel Records Center in St. Louis, Missouri, and wrote them a letter. The response came back that all records before 1970 had been destroyed under normal retention schedules. I therefore never learned why I was not accepted into the military.

I have had a deep void in my life because I did not serve my country. Many of my friends and neighbors did serve and were on the bus that March day in 1966. I shared my feelings with a friend and neighbor who did serve in Vietnam—Wayne Watkins. As I told Wayne of my feelings of inadequacy for not being able to serve my country, he said, "Jimmy, get over it. The Lord must have had a different mission in life for you." I understood that, but it does not make it any easier to live with. I have a deep and abiding respect for those who have served and are serving our country in the military.

On October 29, 2019, my good friend and neighbor, Wayne Watkins, passed from this life. He had retired as a sergeant first class from the US Army, where he served for twenty years. He served two tours in Vietnam as a combat infantryman and was awarded twenty-one medals, including the Bronze Star and the Silver Star. Wayne was very active in the Vietnam Veterans of America and first joined the VVA Savannah Chapter #671 in 1992. He helped organize the Liberty Chapter #789 in Hinesville and, in 2005, the Dawson County Chapter #970. Wayne served in leadership positions in each chapter where he was a member. He was always concerned about the Vietnam veterans and the way they were treated upon returning home, and he looked for ways to be involved. Wayne served two terms as president of the Georgia State Council and on the Conference of State Presidents at the national level.

I was honored to speak at his memorial service on November 1, 2019, in Dawsonville, Georgia. I shared the story of my discussion with him about my regrets for not serving my country. After the service, a man spoke to me and said that he had the same discussion with Wayne. He thanked me for sharing my story. About sixty veterans, mostly of the Vietnam War, attended the service and participated in the flag ceremony, standing the watch. He was buried in the Georgia National Cemetery in Canton, Georgia. Rest in peace, my friend. You are continually missed.

During my 50th Jeff Davis High School Class Reunion, I visited with Phil Merritt, an old friend from my last two years in high school. I found out that Phil was drafted into the army and went to Vietnam. He wrote a book about his Vietnam experiences: *A Soldier's "Blues": My Personal Story*, by Phillip W. Merritt. It is a very personal story of the war, his girlfriend, who is now his wife, his family, and his recovery from a fall from a helicopter.

Phil Merritt and Jimmy Hill

I shared with Phil my concerns about not being able to serve. He gave me some sage advice: "Jimmy, you registered and went when they called you for your medical exam, and they sent you home. You don't have anything to apologize for. You did everything right. You don't need to feel bad about not getting to serve in the military." Thanks, Phil, for your kind words and your service and sacrifice.

To this day, whenever I see retired or active members of the military, I thank them for their service and sacrifice. I have had the great opportunity to thank an estimated five hundred men and women who have served. Several times, I have had veterans from the Vietnam, Korean War and World War II eras shed tears and thank me. Many others have simply said thank you; others have nodded or said nothing and moved on quickly. Many spouses have shared with me how much they appreciated my comments. Since I did not serve my country, the least that I can do is thank those who did. I encourage you to do the same. You will bless them and be blessed yourself.

My brother Jerry and my brother-in-law, Jerry Day, served our country in Vietnam. I thank them for their service and sacrifice. Jerry has been recognized by the Jeff Davis County Veterans Association. His name, along

Mother at Jeff Davis Veteran's Square Park

with all others who served in Vietnam, is inscribed on a monument on the courthouse square in Hazlehurst. My mother handled the arrangements for Jerry's name to be added. Almost one thousand people attended the dedication of this monument.

My uncle Jim served in World War II, and I appreciate his service and sacrifice as well. Ashlee South, my second cousin, is now serving in the US Navy. Thank you, Ashlee, for your service and sacrifice. Thank you to the veterans of all wars who served and sacrificed for our freedom. I hope we never lose the memory of these great Americans.

8

FFA and Its Transformative Impact

According to the FFA website, "FFA is the premier youth organization preparing members for leadership and careers in the science, business, and technology of agriculture," https://www.ffa.org. Founded in 1928, the program is administered through the agricultural education curriculum in public and private schools.

When I was a member, it was called the Future Farmers of America. It is now known as FFA and is affiliated with the National FFA Organization. It became more than just future farmers because so many other careers are involved in agriculture. For example, I earned my undergraduate degree in agricultural engineering. Agricultural engineers, along with a host of other careers, provide services to and products for agriculture. The program needed to expand its scope to encompass the more than three hundred jobs and careers that impact agriculture.

FFA makes a positive difference in the lives of students by developing their potential for premier leadership, personal growth, and career success through agricultural education. The FFA motto is: Learning to Do, Doing to Learn, Earning to Live, Living to Serve.

The FFA emblem is very distinctive and features a cross-section of an ear of corn as its centerpiece. The words *Agricultural Education* and *FFA* appear in the emblem as well.

A student is required to take agricultural education courses to be a member of FFA. A variety of these courses are taught in middle schools and high schools on subjects such as general agriculture, forestry, animal agriculture, food and natural resources, and many others. All the courses include classroom or laboratory instruction, experiential learning, and leadership education (through FFA). In 2018, Georgia implemented a three-year pilot program for agricultural education programs to be taught in elementary schools.

I took agricultural education classes in all four years of high school after joining FFA immediately in my freshman year. My first class, Shop I, prepared me to work with hand tools and to learn about measurement techniques and safety issues. My first hands-on project, building a shoeshine kit, was a great learning experience, as it involved measuring, sawing, cutting angles into the wood, nailing, gluing, and sanding—almost all the techniques that are needed to build anything from lumber.

Shoe shine box made by Jimmy in 1962

Not only did Shop I teach me to work with wood, but it taught me mathematics for use in measuring and cutting wood curves. Throughout my time in high school, my agriculture classes involved using skills not only from mathematics but from science, writing, chemistry, and other courses. It was a great way to reinforce what I had learned in those academic subjects.

The sophomore Agriculture I class was a general introduction to various areas of agriculture and helped improve my "agriculture literacy." It helped me see how agriculture interfaces with all of life: I eat three times a day, and that involves agriculture and the growing of food; I wear cotton clothing, which involves agriculture and growing cotton; I live in a house made primarily of wood, the construction of which depends on the wood from trees; I drive a vehicle that uses fuel that can be made from corn or other agricultural products. In the end, our lives depend on agriculture.

In my sophomore year, I earned my FFA Greenhand degree. This was the first of several recognitions I received in high school. The Greenhand degree symbolizes a first step in taking agricultural science courses, having satisfactory plans for a supervised agricultural experience, and understanding the history and purpose of FFA.

This was the year that I learned about the upcoming 34th Annual Convention of the Georgia FFA Association to be held in July 1962. I was fascinated by the blue FFA jackets and the leadership demonstrated by the FFA officers and wanted to attend the convention. I got approval from my parents and started planning the trip. It would be during the summer, so I would have to take off from work to attend. At that time, it meant fewer days cropping tobacco in the middle of the hot summer, and that was fine with me.

I was told that I had to keep detailed notes on the convention and present them back to my agriculture teacher, Mr. Harrison. I still have those notes today. The most impressive part of the convention was seeing the state FFA officers in action as they demonstrated their leadership and organizational skills. It blew me away. They looked super sharp in their blue jackets with the FFA emblem. They were able to lead meetings and communicate effectively and were extremely excited about what they were doing. As they presided over the convention, they were dressed in black pants, a white shirt, and the famous blue and gold FFA jacket. They had a gold-colored chain clipped to their belt and looped into their front pocket. The chain was for attaching the awards they had won in various contests. The officers were well-spoken, thoroughly trained, and presided over the meetings with professionalism. I was in awe of them. I thought to myself, I am going to be one of those officers someday.

My junior year Agriculture II was an advanced class on production agriculture and included public speaking. This started my speaking career. I earned the Jeff Davis FFA Chapter Public Speaking Award, which was my first public-speaking prize. Public speaking was very difficult for me.

Every time I stood up to speak, my knees were wobbly, my stomach was churning, and I felt sick. My teacher, Mr. B. H. Claxton, became my mentor and helped me to overcome those feelings. He told me many times that the way you overcome your fears is by facing them every chance you get. That meant to me that I had to stand up and speak at every opportunity. It also meant entering the FFA speaking contests.

As a senior, I took another Agriculture II course, this one specializing in forestry. I continued to enter FFA speaking contests, winning at the chapter level and in a sub-district contest in Lyons, Georgia. I took second place in the district speaking contest, competing against students from forty-two counties. My speech was entitled "Soil Conservation: The Key to Better Farming." That same year, I also ran successfully for the office of the secretary of the Jeff Davis FFA Chapter, and I applied for and received the FFA Planter Degree from the Georgia FFA Association.

It was in the senior year that I encountered Robert's Rules of Order. I was part of a team that spent many hours learning the rules set out in this oldest and most widely used authority on parliamentary procedures. This knowledge would enable me, later on, to manage meetings as the presiding officer of the five statewide organizations that I eventually headed during my career.

The Georgia FFA Association put out a bimonthly publication that was sent to all Georgia members. It covered the achievements of FFA members and other related news. I was asked to write a story about how our Jeff Davis FFA Chapter learned and practiced parliamentary law. The article was published in the April–May issue in 1965. Our FFA Parliamentary Team members were David Miller, Ralph Pace, Albert Wildes, Jerry Hill (my brother), Kenny Durden, and me. We also, as one of our projects, made team presentations on the twelve abilities of Robert's Rules of Order to the local Lions Club, the First Baptist Church of Hazlehurst Brotherhood group, and the student body of our high school.

In the February–March 1966 issue of the Georgia FFA magazine, Mr. Claxton, my brother Jerry, and I are mentioned in an article on building layer cages for hens. This project combined community service, shop skills, and fundraising into one activity. The layer cages were bought by FFA students or their parents for use on egg-laying farms. Mr. Claxton taught us how to build the cages in the classroom, but the actual work of putting them together was done outside of classroom time.

Another practical endeavor that taught me a lot about planning, managing, and recording a hands-on project was my FFA Supervised Agricultural Experience of raising a couple of pigs. These types of skills served me well later on in my career.

Mr. B. H. Claxton was a teacher, mentor, and major influencer in my life. He was a native of Jeff Davis County, Georgia, and received his associate degree from ABAC and his bachelor's, master's, and specialist degrees from the University of Georgia (UGA). He enlisted in the Army in 1950. Following his military service, he taught vocational agriculture for thirty-eight years and retired in 1989. Along with teaching, he supervised apprentice teachers from UGA for seventeen years. Some of his apprentice teachers included: Dennis Clarke, Chuck Ellington, Preston Dees, James Thompson, James Woodard, John Lindsey, John Allen Bailey, Edwin Avery, Virgil Rainey, David Burton, Frank Flanders, Richard Wheeler, Danny Carter, Larry Moore, Charles Anderson, and others.

Mr. Claxton was an awesome teacher, who led from a position of positive personal power and influence. His classroom created an atmosphere of learning and mentoring that was different from anything I had ever experienced. Mr. Claxton acted as if I was his only student, and he was focused on my learning and progression.

With his encouragement, I became involved in FFA activities such as public speaking, Robert's Rules of Order, and leadership activities. I also, at his urging, became a staff writer on the high school newspaper, covering primarily FFA program updates on activities, contests, and awards.

Mr. Claxton was a mentor to me during college and into my career at Georgia Power Company. I would call him occasionally and seek his wisdom as I was facing decisions or career changes. He was always helpful and mentored me as if I was still his student. In a way, I guess that I was a lifelong student of his.

Mr. Claxton was inducted into the Georgia Agricultural Education Hall of Fame on August 28, 2015, at the Georgia FFA-FCCLA Center in

Covington, Georgia. I was there that night to express my appreciation to him and to honor him.

Of note is that his son, Dr. Argene Claxton, was also inducted into the Hall of Fame later. They are the only father-son members of the Hall of Fame. Dr. Claxton taught at Perry High School in Perry, Georgia, for thirty-seven years. He was nationally recognized for his teaching efforts, and many of his FFA members earned local, regional, state, and national honors. He was a three-time Star Teacher of the Year at Perry High School and was named Teacher of the Year by school faculty.

Mr. B. H. Claxton and Jimmy Hill

During my senior year, it was Mr. Claxton who encouraged me to run for state office in the Georgia FFA Association at the 37th Annual Convention, due to take place in the summer of 1965. I was so excited that he saw such potential in me. He tutored and mentored me in preparation for the questioning that candidates would have to go through at the convention. I had to learn everything that I could about FFA and agricultural education.

The state officer process involved going before several committees of the 1964-65 officers. They asked questions about me, about FFA and agricultural education, and about how I would handle various scenarios. The process was very intimidating, daunting, and nerve-wracking. Negotiating all the steps to become an officer was demanding. It involved presentations, answering tough questions, and being able to speak on your feet. It was a challenging experience, but I was determined to do my best and hoped that I could do well enough to be in the final group of potential officers. At the closing of the convention, the 1964-65 officer team made their recommendations of candidates to be voted on. The votes were taken, and I was elected a state vice president of the Georgia FFA Association. One of my first goals in life had come true. I decided then and there that if I committed the time and effort, I could be or do whatever I chose. I was on a tremendous high that day.

The 1965–66 Georgia State FFA Association officer team included: Gerald Spencer, president; Tommy Norman, vice president; Jimmy Hill, vice president; Tryon Reynolds Jr., vice president; Jackie Barrett, vice president; William Woodruff, vice president; Mike Callaway, vice president; Edward Miller Jr., vice president; William Sellers, vice president; Moses Wilcox, vice president; Samuel Hawkins, vice president; Jim Mayweather, vice president; Carlis Philpot, vice president; Donald Dotson, vice president; Terry Floyd, student secretary; J. G. Bryant, state advisor; and J. E. Dunn, executive secretary.

I committed at that moment to be the best officer that I could be and to encourage other FFA members to work toward reaching their goals. I knew if I could do it, so could others.

One of my greatest experiences in life was serving as a state FFA officer. I traveled across the state of Georgia and visited with students and teachers who were involved in FFA. I was able to get a lot of practical experience giving speeches and appearing on radio and TV as I promoted FFA and agriculture.

It was my pleasure to attend many FFA annual school banquets and other functions all over Georgia. A list of the functions that I attended or spoke at during my year as a state FFA officer can be found in the Appendix.

Jimmy's State FFA Vice President Jacket

Another highlight of my time of serving as a state FFA officer was attending the National FFA Convention held on October 13–15, 1965, in Kansas City, Missouri. We traveled by bus to Kansas City, with one overnight stay along the way. Thousands of FFA members from across the United States attended the convention. It was an awesome experience to be a part of this great event. Attending the convention inspired me to continue finding opportunities for leadership experience and to seek a career in some aspect of agriculture.

During the convention, I had lunch with Romaine Smith, editor of *Progressive Farmer* magazine. This is notable because now, fifty-five years later, my son, Chris Hill, is the managing editor of that very publication.

One of the highlights of our trip back to Georgia was a stop to attend a Saturday night show at the Grand Ole Opry in Nashville, Tennessee.

I must share my thoughts about Mr. J. E. Dunn, who was the executive secretary of the Georgia FFA Association. He was our main contact with the organization, and he kept a tight rein on us all year. Mr. Dunn was a pleasure to work with, offering us all types of advice as we learned our roles as state officers. Here is an example from a letter he wrote on February 8, 1966:

> I have had an opportunity to talk with a number of teachers to inquire as to their impression of you fellows. They have related some very favorable reports for which we are proud. It has been mentioned that some of you have adopted styles of haircuts that, although far from being Beatles or beatnik, do not give a well-groomed look that is accepted by teachers.... I trust this can be corrected immediately.

It was!

One of my fellow state vice presidents who became a good friend was Tyron Reynolds from Millen, Georgia. He started his senior year in high school shortly after he was elected. I had of course already finished high school. I wanted to surprise Tyron and attend his graduation, so I enlisted two friends of mine to go with me to Millen that early June afternoon in 1966. I drove my 1960 Dodge Dart, and my friends Larry Sellers and Stan Hutchinson accompanied me.

After the ceremony, we visited with Tyron for only a few minutes, as he had plans with his fellow seniors. Larry, Stan, and I were not quite ready to go home. Darkness was falling. We decided to ride around for a while. It didn't take us long to figure out the route that the others were making as they circled the Dairy Queen, leaving rubber on the street. Well, in my lack of better judgment, I circled the Dairy Queen and left some Jeff Davis County tire rubber on the street. My Dodge had a V-8 engine and the power to peel rubber. As I left, I noticed a police vehicle behind me. He turned on his blue lights. By this time, I was traveling over the speed limit in downtown Millen. I knew that I was headed for trouble. I had seen in movies how you could turn your headlamps off, turn down a side road, and get away from the police. That is exactly what I did—and it worked. The police vehicle, a truck, went past the road. I told Larry and Stan that we had better head back to Jeff Davis County while we had the chance. I turned around, and we headed out of town in the opposite direction from the route the police truck had taken.

We were almost out of the city when I saw blue lights in my rearview mirror. We were pulled over by a police car this time. He asked me for my license and insurance card. I politely handed them to him. He then said, "You boys were speeding and squealing tires near the Dairy Queen, and you ran several traffic lights downtown." Realizing we were in trouble, I fessed up and told him that it was not us that ran the traffic lights, because we had turned off the main road and switched off our headlamps. He told us that the officer who had seen us was on his way and would decide what to do. In a short while, the original officer in the police truck arrived. He went through the same scenario again about running the traffic lights. I told him the same story about how we had lost him. He wasn't too happy. I had never been in jail but thought that this might be the night. The officers told us to wait while they went off to consider our situation.

When they came back, they said that they were charging me with running two red lights and speeding. They said that I could just pay the fine and be on my way. The fine was $17.50. I knew that I didn't have that kind of money on me, but I had my checkbook. I told them that I could write a check. "We don't accept checks," was the reply.

I looked at Larry and Stan: "How much money do you-all have?" Adding it all up, we had only $8.00. On being told this, the officers huddled again and returned with a lower fine. This time it was $12.50. I said again, "We only have eight dollars."

The officers huddled again. They came back and said, "I tell you what we are going to do: we are reducing this incident to a warning ticket if you boys will promise never to come back to Millen again." Of course, we promised. Larry named this incident "The Great Millen, Georgia, Police Chase."

I traveled back to Millen on business twenty years later and was in a community meeting with the police chief. When I told him the story, he laughed and laughed. Fortunately, he was not one of the officers from that night. He did ask me if I had this time obeyed all traffic laws coming into town. I assured him that I had.

The state officer team conducts a Goodwill Tour each year. In 1966, it was held June 13–17 in Atlanta and was sponsored by the Georgia Society of Association Executives. Our team toured or met with the following Georgia-FFA-sponsoring businesses and organizations: Georgia Motor Trucking Association and the Georgia Highway Express Company; Georgia State Farmers Market; Georgia Hatchery Association; Georgia Municipal Association; Atlanta Police and Fire Departments; Atlantic Steel Company; J.D. Jewell Inc in Gainesville; C & S Bank; General Motors Assembly Plant; Associated Industries of Georgia; WAGA-TV Atlanta; Georgia Textile Manufacturers Association; First Federal Savings and Loan Association; and Colonial Stores Inc. Our state officer team attended a June 15 Atlanta Braves v. New York Mets game at the Atlanta–Fulton County Stadium. The Braves lost 4–5. This was my first time attending a major league baseball game, and the 1966 season was the first for the Braves franchise in Atlanta.

My last official function was attending and presiding over the 38th Annual Convention of the Georgia Association Future Farmers of America on July 11–15, 1966, at the Atlanta Biltmore Hotel. Our officer team was responsible for managing the convention program and for serving on various committees, including a candidate selection committee for the next state officer team. I presided over the Fourth General Session, held on Friday, July 15. This session included reports from three state officers and committees, a business segment, and the election of new state officers. State FFA President Gerald Spencer presided over the Fifth General Session, at which the parents of state officers, including my parents, present that evening, were recognized.

As the State FFA Convention was short, I submitted my State Officer Annual Report in writing. My letter expressed that the year was one of the most educational and rewarding years of my life and that I had gained confidence in myself, extended my leadership ability, and gained more experience in public speaking. I thanked my parents for their support during the year of my service. I mentioned my gratitude to Mr. B. H. Claxton, my agriculture teacher, whose encouragement, advice and

Family vacation that I won at Callaway Gardens for a week

inspiration had been invaluable. He had lifted me and inspired me in periods of discouragement and had pushed me onward in times of smooth sailing. Finally, I thanked the twenty-five thousand members of the Georgia FFA Association for electing me as their state vice president.

I traveled a total of 6,118 miles serving FFA during 1965–66. Following my year as a state vice president, the Ida Cason Callaway Foundation awarded me the Callaway Leadership Award, given in recognition of outstanding leadership in the Georgia FFA Association. The award entitled me and my family to a 1966 vacation week at the family cottages at Callaway Gardens in Pine Mountain, Georgia. Our family traveled to Pine Mountain during the week of July 31–August 6, 1966. We left home on that Sunday afternoon, July 31, and arrived at Pine Mountain later in the day. This was our first-ever family vacation. My dad was a workaholic and only took Sundays off work, as that was a day of worship. We enjoyed the time away and all the activities at Callaway Gardens. By Wednesday afternoon, however, Dad announced that he had had all the vacation experience he could handle. The vacation was over, and we headed home.

In 1990, I was selected to receive the Honorary American FFA Degree at that year's National FFA Convention. Unfortunately, I was unable to attend the event, but I was, and am still, very honored by and grateful for this award.

My brother, Jerry, and I in our FFA Jackets

9

ABAC Days and Bean-Harvesting Summers

Abraham Baldwin Agricultural College (ABAC) started as the Second District Agricultural and Mechanical School in 1908. The college was renamed the South Georgia Agricultural and Mechanical College in 1924. It was again renamed, in 1929, as the Georgia State College for Men. In 1933, when the University System of Georgia (USG) was formed, the college was renamed ABAC and became part of USG as a two-year college. In 2006, ABAC was granted state college status, offering junior- and senior-level classes. ABAC now offers bachelor's degrees in four schools: agricultural and natural resources; arts and sciences; nursing and health sciences; and business.

I was due to begin studies at ABAC in the fall of 1966, having postponed my attendance by a year. During the summer of 1966, I received a call from Mr. Paul Gaines, ABAC registrar, asking if I would agree to room with a student from Norway. I asked if the student could speak English, and Mr. Gaines responded in the affirmative. I realized that it would be awesome to meet someone from Norway and to learn more about his country, and I gave my consent.

One of my best friends from high school, Stanley Hutchinson, had also been accepted at ABAC. Stan had ridden with me to the ABAC campus in Tifton for our first visit. We had got lost on the way and traveled through Tifton and were on our way to Ty Ty, Georgia, before we realized it. We had finally stopped and asked for directions, which was not an easy thing for eighteen- and nineteen-year-olds who had their act together.

September 18th finally came, and I made the trip to ABAC to start my collegiate career. I found the college without any trouble this time. As I registered, I learned that I was going to be living in the New Men's Dormitory. The dorm was completed just before the start of the quarter. My dorm room number was 108, and I was glad it was on the first floor because I did not have experience with anything above two floors. The most amazing thing about the room was the air conditioning. This was my first experience living in an air-conditioned environment. It was great, except at night, when it would get very cool. The control for the air conditioning was located somewhere other than in my room. I finally lifted the removable panels in the ceiling to try to let the cold air dissipate and maybe raise the temperature in my room. It didn't work.

ABAC Photo of Jimmy

About two weeks after I arrived, there was a knock at my door around two o'clock in the morning. I opened it to find Campus Security Officer James Dearman and Sverre Stub, my new roommate from Norway, standing there. Sverre and I immediately became good friends. He went home with me several times and attended my church where my dad was pastor.

I took him to his first drive-in theater experience in my 1960 Dodge Dart. We double-dated, and he sat in the back seat with his date. Of course, with a rearview mirror in my line of sight, I inadvertently caught all of the action. Needless to say, he had a good time. After we returned to the dorm, he wanted to know when we were going again.

We went out to eat one night at a local restaurant. As we exited the vehicle, a crowd was gathering in the parking lot. We went over to see what the excitement was about, and it appeared to be two guys arguing. Someone mentioned a knife. I looked around, and Sverre was nowhere to be seen. I searched the parking lot and the restaurant and could not find him. When I returned to the dorm, I found him in our room. Sverre was an experienced runner, and he had run about one and a half miles back to ABAC. He did not want to be involved in any violence, and nor did I.

Sverre could speak English as well as his native Norwegian. If fact, he spoke better English than I did. However, my South Georgia phraseology was a whole new language to him. I told him one day that I was fixing to go to the store. He asked what "fixing" meant, and I explained.

Other words also required explanation, like *y'all*; *hankering*; *cattywampus*, *bless your heart*; *well, I'll be*; *thingamajigger*, *happy as a dead pig in the sunshine*; *madder than a wet, setting hen*; and *over yonder*. These are just a few examples, but there were many, many more words and phrases that he learned over the year.

The New Men's Dorm had one large bathroom with community showers on each floor. A large gathering room was on the first floor, on the front of the dorm. Our dorm mother was Mrs. Hilda Goodman. She was more like a grandmother to us boys. She took us under her wing and made us feel at home. I became close to her during my year in the dorm. Mrs. Goodman didn't take any crap from us boys, and we had to obey the rules. In other words, she was an excellent dorm mother.

The dining hall was a great place to eat, obviously, but was also a gathering place after a long day of classes and work. The food was excellent, and the college did a great job of meeting our nutritional needs. Many friendships were created in the dining hall as we met and engaged in conversation.

The college had many organizations and clubs in which we could participate. I became a member of the Vespers organization, which was non-denominational and focused on religious activities. I also immediately joined the agricultural engineering organization, as that was my major study area. The Agriculture Club was about promoting farmers and all things agriculture, and I believed that agriculture was in my DNA; I, therefore, joined that, too. I was very interested in mathematics since my career choice was engineering, and Mu Alpha Theta was the next organization that I joined.

The Baptist Student Union (BSU) created links between ABAC and local Baptist churches, and I became deeply involved with them, serving on outreach teams that attended local churches and conducted morning and evening services. Our adult leader, Reverend John D. Wortham, became a close friend of mine. He inspired all of our team members as we participated in BSU activities.

Baptist Student Union Mission Team visits Mt. Pleasant Baptist Church

In addition to my club activities, I ran for and was elected as vice president of the student government organization during my sophomore year. One of my friends, Nada Fincher, was elected president. Other friends elected were Loma Young, as secretary, and Donald Stodghill, as treasurer.

My parents were unable to help me financially to attend ABAC. However, I was able to use the funds that I had saved from working for McLendon Grocery in Hazlehurst to help pay for my first year of college. Also, I took a job with ABAC, working for the physical plant. The job involved light maintenance work, such as replacing light bulbs in dorms, lawn maintenance, painting, moving furniture, working special events, and helping with many other chores. My W-2 from ABAC for 1967 showed that I earned $228.75 and I paid $0.89 in federal income tax. In my sophomore year, I took on an additional on-campus job, as dorm monitor, and my W-2 from ABAC for 1968 showed that I earned $386.25 and paid $5.70 in federal income tax. I also added a third job, at Roses Department Store in Tifton. At Roses, my W-2 showed that I made $287.28 in 1968, with $20.11 in federal income tax and $12.64 in Social Security taxes. That doesn't sound like much, but that, along with my other jobs, paid almost all of my college expenses for two years. I only had to borrow $300 from the National Defense Student Loan Program to finish paying for my two years at ABAC.

One job that I volunteered for was driving the ABAC bus to events. In the fall of 1967, I drove the bus to Chipola College in Marianna, Florida, for a basketball game between ABAC and Chipola. The trip was about two and a half hours, 135 miles, each way. On the way there, the engine-cooling light came on. I stopped beside the road and crawled under the bus and found the fan belt had come off the crankshaft pulley. Fortunately, I had brought my trusty Western Auto toolbox. I was able to loosen the tightening pulley and re-install the fan belt. We drove another thirty miles, and it came off again. I thought maybe I had not tightened the belt enough. I re-installed it again, and we were able to make it to Marianna and attend the game.

ABAC Bus that Jimmy drove

It was late when we started back to ABAC, and once again, the fan belt came off. I got under the bus and discovered why it had kept happening. The pulley on the crankshaft had a crack, causing it to tilt slightly and sling the fan belt off. I knew that I would not be able to fix the crankshaft pulley, and we had to get back to ABAC. I took a hammer to the pulley and was able to straighten it. We headed toward ABAC, praying that we would make it back.

Just east of Cairo, Georgia, at about 11:30 p.m., the right front tire blew out just before a narrow bridge on Highway 111. As the tire blew, we were heading down a slope and entering a curve about two hundred feet from the bridge. Most students were asleep before the blowout, but the sudden swaying of the bus woke them up. They were screaming while I was trying to get across the bridge and avoid a semi-truck coming from the opposite direction. Thank the Lord, we made it across the bridge and were able to stop at a pull-over area. This was long before cell phone days, so we had no way to call for help. Fortunately, there was a house close by, and we called ABAC from there. We were told it might be morning before a bus could come and pick us up. We finally got back to ABAC the next morning.

ABAC friends L to R - Neil Eunice, Charles Rossman and Donald Stodghill

My experience at ABAC was awesome. I met friends there who are still my friends today, and we keep in touch. The professors at ABAC were very friendly and helpful to me as a freshman starting my college life. After being out of school for a year, serving as a state FFA officer, I had trouble getting my studying skills back. The professors helped me to learn how to study again. They were outstanding teachers and did a great job of shaping this young country boy into a focused student.

My classmates and friends in the two-year agricultural engineering program were Daniel Campbell, Ralph Carlysle, James Dean, Andra Dickens, Tom Dickerson, Harold Gillespie, Butch Goff, Stan Hutchinson, Don Mott, Leroy Pearman, Lewis (Rufus) Powell, Charles Rossman, Phillip Walsh, William Wheeler, and Ben Williams. Most of this group went on to attend the University of Georgia and earn their Bachelor of Science in agricultural engineering. I am still friends with many of them.

I became friends with many other people during my two years at ABAC. Some were already friends from high school or through other connections. You can find their names in the Appendix.

Certain campus activities I remember from when I was at ABAC fall into the category of "may or may not have occurred—no witnesses came forward." Note that during this time, young men and women at ABAC had separate dorms, and the men were not allowed to enter women's rooms. They had to go to the women's dorm reception area and request to speak to a girl or to pick her up to go on a date.

An event that took place on campus (of course, after all these years, my memory may be a little fuzzy) was panty raids. As I remember (or was told after the fact), an announcement would travel unofficially through campus that on a certain weekday night, at a certain time, a panty raid would commence. I recall one that occurred as I was returning to my dorm after studying in the library. I was in the wrong place at the wrong time and got caught up in the event as it was taking place. There was a lot of shouting, with windows being raised in the women's dorm and panties flying out the windows. I also remember the campus security officers screaming at the boys to go back to their dorms, and the girls screaming for the boys to come and get the panties that were floating in the wind. I remember seeing boys hiding in the shrubbery surrounding the women's dorm. Other boys were zooming across campus to avoid the security officers. I was almost swept up in the chaos surrounding this event. As I recall (or was told), several of these events took place during my two years at ABAC.

A panty raid was written about in the editorial section of *The Stallion*, ABAC's school newspaper, on Friday, April 5, 1968. It appeared that some damage occurred at the two women's dorms—Lewis and Creswell Halls. The Tifton Police Department was called, out of an abundance of caution. However, the campus security department handled everything appropriately. It was reported that the event was first characterized as a student riot. It was also learned that the downstairs window screens at Creswell Hall were permanently nailed shut. It was not determined if this was done to keep the young men out or the young women in.

I remember one night, after supper at the dining hall, an idea arose among a group of boys regarding a beautiful, dark-blue 1965 Mustang owned by a fellow student. Again, this is hearsay, and I have no direct knowledge of this incident or others like it. The group decided to take the

Jimmy's study desk in his dorm room at ABAC

Mustang from the parking lot and place it on the raised concrete porch (several steps off the ground) in front of the dining hall. When I say take it, they did not have the keys to the car, so they had to lift it and carry it there. The owner of the Mustang, Tom Dickerson, came out a few minutes later to find his car on the porch. He was visibly shaken for a moment but quickly realized it was a prank and got it moved back with the help of several boys who just happened to be hanging around the front of the dining hall.

In my role as a dorm monitor, I experienced many events that could be written about, but I chose then, and choose now, to protect the innocent and the guilty. Let's just say that I earned every penny of my salary monitoring and working out issues on the second floor of Weltner Annex during my sophomore year.

I received two recognitions while attending ABAC: being named in *Who's Who at ABAC* and in *Who's Who Among Students in American Junior Colleges* in 1968.

My sophomore year roommate was Neil Eunice, who was from Bristol, Georgia. Neil and I became fast friends during our freshman year, and that relationship continues to this day. Neil was majoring in agricultural economics, and we had a lot of agricultural issues to discuss in the evenings.

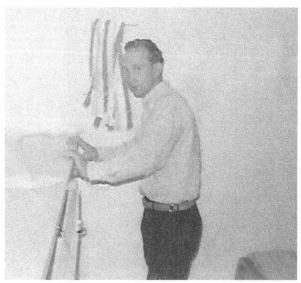

Neil Eunice my sophomore year roommate

I am pretty sure that we solved a number of them during our year together. We had several mutual friends and attended vespers together every night.

Neil and I were fortunate enough over the years to see each other several times a year at agricultural events. I have appreciated his friendship and camaraderie over these many years. However, the two of us have agreed, should there be any question, that what happened at ABAC stayed at ABAC. End of the subject!

Neil married his best friend Kay in June 1969. I was the best man at his wedding, and he at mine. Gail and I were present at their fiftieth wedding anniversary celebration in June 2019. It was great to reminisce about our ABAC days with them and with other ABAC friends in attendance.

Dr. J. Clyde Driggers, ABAC's president, proposed to build a new religious structure on the ABAC campus and to call it the Chapel of All Faiths. The reasoning behind the chapel was: to help an unchurched student find God; to create an atmosphere conducive to religious thinking; to serve as a constant reminder of the Supreme Being and Master Teacher; to provide easy access to a place of prayerful worship as the personal need arose and to establish a definite place for services of all religious faiths.

I got to know Dr. Driggers and visited with him many times while on campus, as he was very approachable. The chapel had to be built with private donations. The idea had started in 1964, and there were spurts of activity over the following years, but it was the 1967–68 Baldwin Alumni Association that got the project back on track. Dr. Driggers wrote a book about the challenges that were faced in building the chapel and how it finally came about: *It Took A Miracle! ABAC's Lecture Hall, God's Chapel of all Faiths*. And it was a miracle! I urge you to read the book, as it describes how the project overcame great difficulties and finally came to fruition with dedication on November 21, 1974. You can find it on Amazon.

The plans for this chapel, and ideas for financing it, were being discussed during my time at ABAC. I remember speaking to several groups regarding the project and being invited to speak about the chapel on Albany's WALB TV station.

On February 10, 1968, the Honorable Lester Maddox, Governor of Georgia, spoke at the General Assembly homecoming at noon. This was the first time I had seen Governor Maddox in person, or any governor, for that matter. I had read about him and seen him on TV news and in newspapers. He demonstrated his skill of riding a bicycle backward during the homecoming parade at 2:00 p.m. that day. The event theme was "Parade of Progress."

Other speakers at homecoming included Alumni President Rufus Adams, State Senator Ford Spinks, President of the ABAC Student Body Nada Fincher, Lieutenant Governor Georgia T. Smith, and ABAC President J. Clyde Driggers.

My two years at ABAC flew by, and it was time to say goodbye to the college and many of my friends. Two of my friends and fellow graduates spoke at the graduation ceremony: Miss Virginia Thomas, Second Honor Graduate, presented the invocation, and Wendell Cannon, First Honor Graduate, introduced the graduation speaker, Dr. Felix Robb. Dr. J. Clyde Driggers, president of ABAC, conferred our degrees upon us. Dr. Driggers had become a close friend to me during my two years at ABAC. He was a great mentor and inspired me to continue my educational pursuits after earning my associate degree. I did continue my education at the University of Georgia and earned a bachelor's degree in agricultural engineering.

My connections with ABAC have continued in different ways throughout my life:

- I served as president of the ABAC Alumni Association in 1991 and served on the Alumni Board for several years prior.
- Chris Hill, my son, attended ABAC in 1992–93. Also, Chris's future wife, Rachel Manley, attended ABAC in 1993.

- Chris and I each wrote articles for the *ABAC Today* publication without the collaboration of the other. The articles are similar and can be found in the Appendix.
- I was nominated for and received the 1991 J. Lamar Branch Outstanding Agriculture Leader Award.

Jimmy, President of the ABAC Alumni Association, speaking at 1991 Graduation
* Photo Courtesy of ABAC Alumni Association

- As president of the ABAC Alumni Association, I spoke at the 1991 ABAC graduation.
- My oldest grandson (Chris and Rachel's son), William has attended ABAC since 2018. He plans to graduate with his bachelor's degree in natural resource management (forestry) at ABAC in 2022.
- I was a featured alumnus (Spotlight on Excellence) at the ABAC exhibit at the Sunbelt Agricultural Expo in the fall of 2018. I was also featured under the Family Legacy category of the 2017–18 ABAC Foundation Annual Report.

Gail and Jimmy Attending an ABAC Reunion with Nada Kerr and Sandra Kelley

Grandson, William Hill and Jimmy at Sunbelt Expo in ABAC Exhibit
* Photo Courtesy of ABAC Alumni Association

Have you ever eaten Green Giant Cut Green Beans from a can? Well, I have eaten them and harvested them. I am talking about harvesting tons of them in South Carolina, North Carolina, Virginia, Delaware, and Pennsylvania. I was working for the Green Giant company; remember the giant standing in a green field? I worked under contract with Flint Farms Inc., who had a harvesting contract with Green Giant.

How did I get involved in picking green beans? It started when Flint Farms sent a representative to ABAC, seeking young men who had relevant farm experience. They had had a disastrous experience previously in hiring summer employees with no farm background or farm equipment operational experience. They concluded that they needed employees who already knew how to operate tractors and harvesting equipment, and who understood farm operations. They went to the right place, as ABAC had many young men with practical experience on their family farms.

Flint Farms offered full summer employment from the date ABAC let out for the summer until students started back in the fall. This appealed to me for several reasons: I needed a job to pay college expenses; I liked working outdoors, and it would be fun to travel to all the states where the beans were grown. I had only traveled out of Georgia a couple of times in my life.

I had one issue to work out before I committed to picking beans. I had already accepted an engineering summer job with Lilliston Corporation in Albany, Georgia. I had met Mr. John Phillips, president of Lilliston, and was looking forward to working for him. He had an agricultural engineering degree from the University of Georgia, and that was the degree that I was working towards. However, this new job with Green Giant was very enticing, and I felt that I would make more money doing it.

Should I resign from Lilliston Corporation and take the Green Giant job? I could not make up my mind what to do. I decided to call my dad. We had a phone booth on campus, and I placed the call after 7:00 p.m. to make sure he was home. He answered the phone, and I explained my dilemma to him.

Dad thought for second and said, "Son, you are nineteen years old, and it is time for you to make your own decisions." That was not what I wanted to hear. I was silent for a moment.

He continued: "Jimmy, you will face many decisions in your life, and it is now time for you to accept the responsibility to make and live with your decisions."

I said, "Okay Dad, but it is hard."

"You will do fine, and I trust your judgment," he said.

That day I became closer to being an adult and responsible for making my own decisions.

I talked to my manager at Lilliston and asked to be released from my summer job with them, and he agreed.

I accepted the job with Green Giant/Flint Farms and hit the road as soon as the quarter was over at ABAC. Our remuneration was two dollars per hour worked and thirty-five dollars per week for food, and lodging costs were covered by the company.

My first assignment was in South Carolina. A group of us from ABAC traveled together in several vehicles.

The crew that worked together included Stan Hutchinson, Jerry Hill (my brother), Oscar Dean, Eldon Deal, Tom Dickerson, Alvin Manning, Robert Bishop, Ronnie Coleman, Milton Kellam, and others.

Jimmy standing in a field of green beans before harvesting begins

Stan Hutchinson and Jimmy at the Rainbow Motor Court in Melfa, VA

We lodged in motor courts. We stayed at: Laurinburg, North Carolina; Whistling Pines Motel in Elizabeth City, North Carolina; Habit Motel in Edenton, North Carolina; Rainbow Motor Court, Melfa, Virginia; Hanover Motor Court in Hanover, Pennsylvania; Clearview Motel in Hanover, Pennsylvania; Exmore, Virginia; and there were others that I can't recall. We lodged two people in each room. Many of these locations had small restaurants attached to them, where we ate breakfast and sometimes supper. We would eat at local restaurants for lunch, depending on our location.

The crews had five or more harvesters and five or more operators; one mechanic was assigned to each crew. Our day started with a 5:45 a.m. wake-up, then breakfast, and travel to the field that we would be harvesting. We would lubricate the tractor and harvester (lots of moving parts, gears, and bearings) and start harvest at 7:00 a.m. We would have lunch at a local restaurant and most days would keep working until 6:00 p.m. We worked six or seven days per week, depending on whether the field of beans was ripe and ready to harvest. At one point, we worked for thirty days without a day off. I do not think that I have ever been as tired as I was at the end of those thirty days. Our work schedule was dependent on the maturity of the beans. Those long workdays were a blessing to us, as our goal was to earn as much money as possible to help pay for our educational expenses.

The equipment harvested two rows at a time. Each harvester had drum rollers with steel fingers attached, which rotated and knocked the beans from the bush onto a conveyor belt that carried them to the final bin. One type of harvester had the bin located on top of the tractor, and the other type pulled a bin from behind the tractor.

As soon as the bin was full, the operator drove to the edge of the field, and the bin was dumped into a semi-trailer. The trailer, when full, was taken to the Green Giant plant for processing and canning.

I worked for Green Giant/Flint Farms during the summers of 1967 and 1968. My remuneration for the summer of 1967 was $1,325.00 with $58.30 in FICA taxes. In 1968, my remuneration was $1417.50 with $68.37 in FICA taxes. I was able to save a considerable amount of these funds for my college education. My expenses were very minimal during the harvesting season.

Two types of bean harvesting equipment

As you can imagine, several stories came out of these two summers of picking green beans. We were lodging at the Laurinburg Motel in Laurinburg, North Carolina, and one afternoon, Stan Hutchinson and I were throwing a baseball. Stan threw way over my head, and the ball disappeared behind the Laurinburg Restaurant. I ran behind the restaurant, and all of sudden my feet went out from under me. I hit the ground, slid, and landed on top of a sink drain. Not just an ordinary drain, but the restaurant kitchen drain, which had deposited grease all over the ground. I tried to get up but slipped again and landed hard. After several attempts, I was able to stand. And then I noticed the smell: it was putrid and unlike anything that I had ever smelled. The stench was in my clothes and on my body. I came back around to the front and found Stan laughing so hard he was almost crying about my grease landing. I went to the room to take a soaking bath. Then I took another bath; the smell would not go away. I had to get rid of my clothes. It was about a week before that smell was completely gone. Stan told me recently that it was the funniest thing that he had witnessed in the last fifty-three years. It was surely not funny to me then, or now. It was all Stan's fault for throwing the ball way over my head and into the cooking grease. I just want to get that on the official record. Thanks so much, Stan.

During the harvesting process, the weeds, dirt, sticks, green-bean leaves, and other debris were vacuumed out and expelled from the harvester on the right side of the equipment. The clean beans traveled to the hopper for later unloading. Where the debris came out of the harvester, there was a shield mounted to divert it to the ground. One Saturday afternoon, my shield got damaged and was removed for repair. This meant the chaff was expelled horizontally out of the equipment, which is no problem in the middle of a field.

We had to work on the next day, a Sunday. It was a beautiful morning, the birds were singing, and I was starting my harvesting of the field of beans. I started at the right side of the field in the first two rows. To my right was a pine thicket. I was about two hundred feet down the row and was looking backward, checking to make sure the equipment was working properly. All of a sudden, a man appeared in front of my tractor; he was jumping up and down and screaming. I could not hear what he was saying, due to the noise of the tractor and harvester. I stopped the equipment and dismounted. It was at that point I saw a building that was next to the two rows that I was picking. I had not noticed that the pine thicket had ended and that I was now behind a subdivision. I had sprayed the man's beautiful white building with the green debris from my harvester. The man was mad as a wet, setting hen. He was yelling at me and told me how I had ruined the backside of his building, that I was going to have to clean and paint the building. I finally got a word in to the conversation and told him that I would get my boss over to talk to him. My boss came over and looked at the building. He sent me to town to get two five-gallon buckets, liquid soap, brushes, and sponges. I was going to get the pleasure of cleaning the building. Fortunately, the green debris came off fairly easily, and we were able to bring the building back to its white color. I learned a good lesson about watching on both sides of the equipment while harvesting the beans.

If the tractor and equipment were working properly, the job could be monotonous. Our team was always looking for something that would be interesting and different to break the boredom. One day, we saw an old car at the end of a field we were working on. It appeared to have been abandoned for years. Stan Hutchinson found it still had a horn, so he mounted the horn on his tractor. It was a new toy. I found a horn for my tractor from another abandoned vehicle. We could honk at each other as we passed in the field.

The tractors and equipment were driven from field to field as we moved up the east coast. It was too difficult and expensive to break the equipment down and load it onto a flatbed trailer. Hence, there were boring journeys between fields at a top speed of fifteen miles per hour. I recall one incident on an interstate in Virginia when I noticed something on the side of the road. I eased closer to the side of the road to see what it was. As I got near, I realized it was a portable radar system mounted on a three-legged tripod. I nearly ran over it but was able to miss it by inches. A little further down the road, I saw the state trooper parked in the woods. I could have wound up in jail!

One Sunday morning, we were moving our vehicles to a new lodging location. I was driving Tom Dickerson's 1965 dark-blue Mustang. Five cars were being moved, and I was the third vehicle. The first vehicle came to a stop sign and made a rolling stop and turned right. Each of the cars following the first car made the same move. What we could not see, due to heavy brush and trees at the stop sign, was a state trooper pulling us over, each in turn. After he got all of us stopped, he requested that we follow him to the courthouse. I knew that I was in trouble. My Georgia driver's license had expired on July 10, and this was August 15.

At the courthouse, the trooper ushered us to the jail; we could see the cell-area bars. He started writing tickets for not stopping at a stop sign. I waited till last, hoping that he would not see my license had expired. The tickets were for eight dollars, and my fervent hope was that he would give me my ticket and we could leave. When he got to me, he said, "Mr. Hill, did you realize that your license has expired?" I looked at him, shocked and surprised, and asked to see the license. "Mr. Hill, your license is expired!" he said again.

I apologized and explained that I had left Georgia around the first of June and had not thought about my license expiring. He asked me how much longer I was planning to be in Maryland. "Probably another three weeks," I answered.

"Mr. Hill, you will need to get a Maryland driver's license, and I don't want to catch you driving without a license again, because that is an arrestable offense." "Yes, sir," was my reply.

We each got our eight-dollar ticket for running the stop sign and left the courthouse. I was not driving the dark-blue Mustang this time. We saw the state trooper get into his vehicle and pull away. As he did so, he hit a steel pole and nearly tore off his front bumper. That is all I am going to say about that.

We only transported the harvesting equipment one time, and that was to travel through the Chesapeake Bay Bridge-Tunnel in Virginia. They would not allow us to drive the tractors and harvesters through the tunnel. The bridge-tunnel is 17.6 miles long and crosses the mouth of the Chesapeake Bay, the Hampton Roads Harbor, and the nearby mouths of the James River and the Elizabeth River in Virginia.

We drove our equipment to near the entrance of the bridge-tunnel. Green Giant company had arranged for a semi-truck and flatbed trailer to transport us one at a time with our equipment through the tunnel. Our mechanic broke down the machines and loaded them on the flatbed trailer. We rode in the cab of the semi-truck with the driver and unloaded on the other side; our next farm was close by.

As I got in the truck and settled in, the driver was starting her up and getting ready to enter the bridge-tunnel. I noticed several small, square pieces of paper taped to the dash. Each had a number and an arrow on it. I was interested in what these might be, so I asked him. He said that he was unable to read and that his wife laid out each trip for him on these square papers, showing the road or highway number and the direction he would need to travel. I was fascinated by this system, never having seen anything like it, but he said it worked for him.

During 1967, which was my first summer working for Green Giant, we had an incident on a farm where we could not harvest the beans on time. We arrived at the farm when the beans were mature, but several days of rain prevented us from harvesting. The field was so muddy and unstable that the equipment could not stay on the rows and pick the beans. We tried several times the first day and got stuck so many times in the mud that we could only get a handful of beans from two rows. We came back a week later, and it had continued to rain. We tried again and still could not harvest the beans. We finally got back about two weeks later and were able to proceed with the harvesting. The semi-truck and trailer from the Green Giant plant arrived, and we filled the trailer with beans. About an hour later, the truck came back and unloaded the beans from the trailer in the farmer's field. I was shocked and did not know what was happening. It turned out that the crop had too much mold, and the plant could not process the beans. The contract called for dumping them back into the field. I felt sorry for the farmer, but we had done everything we could to harvest the beans.

On February 14, 1968, I received a letter from the Green Giant legal department. The letter said that the farmer whose moldy crop had been rejected had disputed the processing of the green beans from his farm. He felt that Green Giant should have processed his beans and paid him accordingly. Since I was one of the harvest operators, I was asked to provide details about the day in question and the issues surrounding his beans. I responded in a letter to Green Giant dated February 27, 1968. More than a year later, I received another letter from Green Giant, dated August 1, 1969, requesting that I make myself available for a deposition due to be scheduled in Maryland. I have got to be honest, this letter scared me to death. I had started on the cooperative learning program and was working in Albany, Georgia. I asked my Georgia Power manager if I could get some legal advice. He contacted the company attorney, who advised me that I could request that they come to Georgia to do the deposition. I informed Green Giant of my decision not to travel to Maryland but indicating I would do the deposition in Georgia. Green Giant lawyers came to Georgia and took my deposition, and I have not heard anything since that time. Whew!

In the first week of September 1968, after finishing my second summer of bean harvesting, I entered the University of Georgia to continue pursuing my agricultural engineering degree.

10

The University of Georgia and Cooperative Learning Plan

During the spring of my sophomore year at ABAC, I was accepted to the University of Georgia School of Engineering in the College of Agricultural and Environmental Sciences. My first UGA experience started in September and ran through early December 1968.

I did not have a place to live when I arrived in Athens, Georgia. Most of my engineering classes were in the Driftmier Engineering Center on the campus, and I found a note about possible lodging on the bulletin board in the Center. The house was only a few blocks from the University of Georgia campus at 144 Harden Drive. A dairy farmer and his wife were offering two bedrooms, each with two beds, for rent by the academic quarter. I went to the house and met the farmer's wife. She gave me the grand tour of the bedroom and bathroom. She only had one bed left. With no other option, I took it. I roomed with a senior agricultural engineering student. I don't recall the rent amount, but it must have been very reasonable since I could afford it. The rent included one bed, limited closet space, access to a bathroom shared by four students, and no laundry or kitchen privileges. I had to furnish my sheets and towels.

Being on a very limited budget, I became intimately familiar with the nearby Burger King for my nutritional needs for supper. I could afford the Whopper. The Whopper was my nightly meal for the entire quarter. I read where Elvis Presley would eat the same meal for months at a time. I figured if he could do it, so could I.

Dr. Robert Brown was the chair and head of the Department of Agricultural Engineering. Professors in the department who I had classes with included: Dr. Jim Allison, Dr. Jerry Chesness, Dr. Rex Clark, Mr. Carlisle Cobb, Dr. Derrell McLendon, Dr. John Perry, Dr. Wilbur Ratterree, Dr. P. D. Rodgers, and Dr. Ralph Smith.

My first classes were statics of engineering, calculus, and physics. I had to get my big boy britches on to handle these courses.

Dr. Ratterree taught the statics of engineering class. He was tough, thorough, and demanding. He called the roll every day by name, and you had to respond by saying the number of homework problems you had worked. If you didn't work all of the problems, he gave you another opportunity at that time. For example, he would say, "Mr. Hill, which problem did you not work?" If I responded with problem number three, he would say, "Go to the board and show us how to work problem number three, Mr. Hill!"

Driftmier Engineering Center

* Photo Courtesy of Kyle Haney

Of course, since I had not been able to solve it overnight, how could I do it the next morning? The assignments were difficult and required a diagram of each problem. I would go to the board and spend a lot of time diagramming the problem in front of the class. After a while, he would tell me to go and sit down. He would then work the problem and show the solution in a matter of a couple of minutes. I dreaded the class if I had not worked all of the problems and was too scared to find out what would happen if you didn't tell the truth about the number of problems you had worked.

Dr. Ratterree and I became good friends after graduation and later in my career. We were both members of the Georgia Section of the American Society of Agricultural Engineers (ASAE). He was a different person outside the classroom. In class, I had thought he was mad all the time, but he was a very effective teacher, and he taught me a lot.

My first quarter at UGA was very challenging. I thought that I knew how to study, but I had to take it to the next level. I had taken the first two courses of Calculus (MAT 253 and 254) at ABAC, and so I enrolled in Calculus MAT 255 at UGA. After about a week into the course, I was lost. I could not find any connection between my last calculus class at ABAC and this class at UGA, which was taught from a different textbook. I set up an appointment with the instructor to see if he could help me figure out what I needed to do to catch up. His response: "Son, I am doing a research project this quarter, and I don't have time to help you." I was shocked and frustrated. Every one of my professors at ABAC would have taken time to help me, and he was refusing. Welcome to UGA, was the response from my friends. I dropped the course and passed it later.

Physics class was taught by a graduate student with little ability to speak English. I again was lost. Lectures were held in a large auditorium with about three hundred people in the class. There was no way to ask questions. I dropped the class and took it later and passed.

As you can see, my first quarter at UGA was a disaster. This experience led me to think about changing to another course of study. I considered becoming a lawyer or anything but engineering. As I was pondering my life choices, I also realized that I had to earn money to stay at UGA, no matter which career I chose.

One day, while in the Driftmier Engineering Center, I saw a notice on the bulletin board about a program sponsored by Georgia Power Company, in which a student could alternate between work and academics. It was called the Cooperative Learning Plan (co-op plan). The requirement for participation was that the student engineer must have completed five quarters of academic study before applying. I was completing my fifth quarter and would be eligible. I talked to Mr. Cobb, my advisor, about the program. He indicated that several engineering students participated in the co-op plan and that it had two positive features: you were able to earn money for college and, at the same time, get a lot of practical experience. The downside was that it would take longer to complete the engineering degree. My need for college dollars outweighed the delay in finishing college. I asked Mr. Cobb if I could apply. He provided me with the paperwork, and I sent in my application. After my disastrous first-quarter experience, I felt that maybe a quarter away from academics might be helpful.

I received notification from Georgia Power that I had been accepted into the co-op plan and I would start the winter quarter 1969. The letter came from Mr. Jim Prather, Columbus Division sales manager, telling me that I would be assigned to the district office in Americus, Georgia. He further shared that I was to report to the Columbus Division office first, for training and acclimation, on January 2, 1969. I would report to Americus two weeks later. I was so excited to be given this opportunity, and so in need of income, that I showed up on December 26, 1968. I was told that I was a week early, but they let me start anyway. Thank God and Georgia Power!

Mr. Marshall Timberlake, Columbus District marketing supervisor, was a big man with a gentle personality and a great laugh. He helped me find a place to stay for the two weeks that I was assigned to Columbus. My accommodations were at the John P. Thayer YMCA on 14th Street. The rooms were clean and nice, and it was close to the Columbus office.

Mr. Timberlake coordinated my training with his staff. The training included topics like Georgia Power Company's corporate, divisional, and district structures, and background on its marketing programs and the priority of customer service. I had a chance to visit the Columbus District operating headquarters, where the line crews worked to build and maintain power lines. I also spent some time with the Accounting Department, learning about customer records, and meter reading. The Columbus office played a great part in my career a year and a half later.

After the two-week training program, I traveled to Americus to meet with Americus district manager John Roberts. He introduced me to his marketing staff, which included: Terry Duncan, residential marketing; Jimmy Ford, agricultural marketing; and Richard Hill, heat pump coordinator.

My first job, again, was to find a place to live. For the first week, I stayed at the Windsor Hotel in downtown Americus, on the same block as the Georgia Power office. The Windsor was built in 1892 to attract visitors from the north. It was designed as a Victorian masterpiece, with a turret, balconies, and a tower with one hundred rooms. It is now known as the Best Western Plus Windsor Hotel.

After my stay at the Windsor, I found a room to rent in a home at 106 West Furlow Street, a few blocks from work. The homeowner was Mrs. John (Lita) Morgan, a retired educator. She rented two rooms on one end of the white-painted, brick home. The two rooms shared a Jack-and-Jill bathroom. As it turned out, another Georgia Power employee was renting the other room. He and I worked in the same Georgia Power building. His name was Randy Murchison, and he was in accounting.

Mrs. Morgan was a very nice lady, who loved having us in her house. My arrangement did not include her providing any meals, but she did so at least a couple of times a week. She cleaned my room and made the bed. She was well-educated and a pleasure to talk with on multiple subjects. I thoroughly enjoyed my stay with her.

The first couple of weeks were spent traveling with Terry, Richard, and Jim, learning about their jobs as well as Georgia Power sales and marketing programs. Terry Duncan was my immediate supervisor. He was a pleasant man and always had a smile and a great attitude. Terry taught me a lot in a short time frame. About a month after I arrived, he turned in his resignation and went to work for Parker's Heating and Air Conditioning Company.

My work involved helping customers who had electrical issues or complaints about high billing, or who required an energy efficiency audit. I also assisted customers who needed to replace their existing heating and cooling system (HVAC) units or add a new system to their home. With Terry's resignation, my workload increased dramatically. I was assigned Terry's company vehicle and traveled extensively across the Americus district addressing customer needs and solving problems.

The district included the following towns: Americus, Plains, Pitts, Ellaville, Preston, Richland, Smithville, Andersonville, Oglethorpe,

Montezuma, Vienna, Pinehurst, Unadilla, Rochelle, and other small communities in between.

One of the most memorable people that I met in Americus during my time there was Mr. Roy Parker III. He was the founder and president of Parker's Heating and Air Conditioning Company (PHAC). Parker started the company in 1949 as a one-man operation. Working in cooperation with this company is where I got my first practical experience in the HVAC industry. Roy Parker's vision was "to be the most trusted and reliable heating and air conditioning provider in Southwest Georgia." His mission statement was "to provide our customers with comfortable, healthy, energy-efficient homes and businesses." PHAC was an outstanding contractor that used sound business principles and engineered solutions with a "do it right the first time" philosophy and operated on Christian principles. Mr. Parker passed on July 4, 2006, but the business is still family-owned and is located on Thomas Drive in Americus.

My later inspiration for developing a corporate heat-pump-marketing program for Georgia Power was based, in part, on Parker's philosophy, which included expert craftsmanship, engineered solutions, honesty, and integrity.

Observing Roy's work, I polished my skills in sizing HVAC equipment and designing air duct systems and learned proper installation practices. He and his crew did HVAC jobs correctly and efficiently.

Being single and having lots of evenings open, I tutored high schoolers in math during my three months in Americus. I also served on an engineering advisory board at the South Georgia Technical College.

One day in February, I got a call from Mrs. Lillian Carter, who lived in Plains; she needed to change out her HVAC system. It was broken, and the old coal furnace had seen better days. Mrs. Lillian was Jimmy Carter's mother. I set up an appointment and traveled to Plains to Mrs. Lillian's house. I knocked on the door, and Jimmy Carter opened it and welcomed me into his mother's home. Georgia Power was able to assist in getting Mrs. Lillian a new HVAC system.

Mr. Carter served in the Georgia Senate from 1963 to 1967. He was governor of Georgia from 1971 to 1975. On January 20, 1977, he became the 39th president of the United States.

I ended my first co-op experience in late March and returned to the University of Georgia. Soon after arriving back in Athens, I received a letter from Jim Prather, Columbus Division sales manager, part of which reads as follows:

> I had hoped to have an opportunity to see you before you left Americus and express my sincere appreciation for the contribution you made while working for our company. I was in Americus recently and everyone gave you a great deal of praise for the manner in which you received instructions and discharged the duties assigned to you. We look forward to having you back in the summer months, and I am confident that we can expect even bigger things from you. Thanks again for the fine effort and the desire to get involved that you so well demonstrated while being with us.

On March 20, 1969, I received a letter from Marshall Timberlake, Columbus Division residential sales supervisor, who was responsible for Americus District residential sales. He said in the letter:

> I would like to thank and commend you for the fine job you have done while working in the Americus District. The way you accepted the responsibility of the Residential Sales job when Terry Duncan left the company proves to us that if a man has the desire and the right attitude, he can do the job with very little experience. Your good nature and hard work have been an inspiration to all of us. I assure you, you will be greatly missed, and we will be looking forward to your hasty return. Electrically yours, Marshall Timberlake.

After returning to UGA, I had to secure lodging again. As it happened, my former roommate at ABAC, Neil Eunice, was looking for a roommate, and we decided to room together during that spring quarter. Neil found a mobile home located at 800 Gaines School Road that we were able to rent. The Bill Thompson Trailer Court rented trailers and had some spaces for rent. The park was fairly close to campus and was clean and well maintained. It had approximately thirty sites. Several UGA students lived there. Stan Hutchinson and Ted McMillian, fellow agricultural engineering students, lived in separate trailers at the rear of the park.

Neil and I shared the responsibility of preparing meals. Neil's future wife, Kay, would prepare a meal occasionally when she was over visiting.

I guess one of my worst cooking disasters occurred when I decided to bake a cake. This was my first cake-baking experience. I had a rough idea of what ingredients I thought the cake should contain. I whipped it up and put it in the gas oven. Everything was fine for about twenty minutes, and then it happened: there was this loud boom—more like a blast of dynamite. I was studying at the time, and it nearly knocked me out of my chair. I knew it was the range since the oven door blew open. My cake had blown to smithereens. Not only that, but the entire oven interior—walls, ceiling, and floor—was covered with cake. I tried to clean the oven with a scraper and got some of the cake out. When I moved out of the mobile home, you could still see remnants of cake inside the oven. I am sure that wherever the oven is now, it still has cake inside. I shared my cake disaster with my future wife, Gail, and she told me that I must have gotten the ingredients wrong. I agreed with her.

I had enjoyed my first work experience in the co-op program, but now it was time to settle down and get serious about my academic program. I registered for my classes in the Stegeman Hall Coliseum, where UGA played basketball. This was quite an experience, with thousands of students trying to register at the same time. It seemed to take several hours. After registering for a class, I had to take the paperwork to another location to get it verified. If for some reason the class was full, I would have to start the process all over. I did have to change one class. What a mess! However, I finally got all my classes scheduled.

My classes for the spring quarter of 1969 included the dynamics of engineering, as well as the physics and calculus classes that I had previously dropped. It was off to the races in attending class, doing homework, and studying. I had a great quarter, and my grades were moving up. It increased my confidence and elevated my attitude toward accomplishing my goal of becoming an agricultural engineer.

My rotation of moving back into the cooperative learning plan was coming up in the summer quarter of 1969. I had been in touch with Georgia Power, trying to work out my next location. I wanted to be stationed in Albany, Georgia, as that was closer to my girlfriend, Gail Hobbs, who lived in Tifton. Georgia Power eventually informed me that I would be assigned to the Columbus Division, but based in the district office that was located in Albany, Georgia. My girlfriend and I were very happy that this worked out so well.

I traveled to Albany and met with Mr. Temp Davis, who was the district manager. He was a Georgia Tech graduate, and I knew that I would get some flack from him since I was studying to be an agricultural engineer from UGA. The marketing staff included: Ray Baurband, commercial sales engineer (also an agricultural engineer); Dennis Loper, residential sales representative; Sarah Ray (Sloan), district home economist; along with other office staff. I would be working for Dennis Loper and helping him in residential sales.

My biggest hurdle was finding a place to live. I searched for several days, and the only thing that I could find was an old, furnished, duplex apartment built in the 1940s. It was located in an older part of Albany. I rented the apartment on the left side of the building, and an older man and woman lived on the right side. It did not seem to be a safe area, but it was all I could find and afford.

My side of the duplex had four rooms, including a living room, bedroom with a bath, and a small kitchen with a dining space. I moved in, and that was easy, as I had only one suitcase, hang-up clothes, and a few boxes. I bought kitchen utensils, which included a pot, a frying pan, a plate, one each of fork, knife, and spoon, a cooking spoon, and a glass. That served my needs for the three months that I lived there.

The place had mice. I had set traps and caught a few. However, they multiplied by the dozens, and I could not keep up. Yes, under normal circumstances, I would have left. However, I was on a limited salary, and this place was all I could afford. I almost did leave one night when a mouse got into the bed with me. I was praying that the three months would pass quickly. I went to bed late and got up early and did not spend much time at the duplex. I survived!

My job responsibilities were similar to my work in Americus, except that Dennis and I split up the territory between us. The towns in the district included Albany, Arlington, Dawson, Sasser, Shellman, Parrott, Smithville, Bronwood, Edison, Leary, Cuthbert, Newton, Camilla, Pelham, Damascus, and other small communities in between.

I enjoyed my work in Albany and learned about Georgia Power's involvement in the communities it served. The slogan of Georgia Power was "A Citizen Wherever We Serve." The company lived and breathed that slogan every day. I was blessed to be able to work for a great company. They treated me extremely well. I asked them if I could continue the cooperative learning plan for the next consecutive quarter, which would be the fall of 1969. UGA and Georgia Power agreed, and I made plans accordingly.

In December 1968, just before Christmas, I proposed to Gail, and she accepted. We decided to get married the following August.

Since Gail lived in Tifton, which is only an hour from Albany, I spent a considerable amount of time at her house when I was not working. We started planning how to survive financially after the wedding, as I would be continuing my studies at UGA.

Gail's dad, Wendell Hobbs, was a very practical man. He made us an offer regarding the wedding: either they would pay for a large church wedding or they would buy us a trailer, and we could have a smaller wedding at Gail's parents' home. Gail and I prayed over it and decided that having housing paid for with just rent for a space to park the trailer seemed like a great deal.

We accepted his alternative offer. Mr. Hobbs had already found a trailer not far from the farm. He took Gail to see it, and she thought it would work fine, so he bought it for us. The trailer had some major repair issues, but Gail and I were willing to tackle them. We worked on weekends during the summer getting it ready to move to Albany, so that I could finish my co-op program at Georgia Power.

Once it was ready, we found a location to park it in Albany. The site was in a grove of pecan trees, several miles east of downtown and just off Highway 82, between Albany and Tifton. The trailer did not have air conditioning, and that would be a challenge with the hot weather continuing into the fall.

Our wedding took place on August 29, 1969, at Gail's parents' home, outside Tifton. After our short honeymoon, we moved the trailer to Albany and settled into our new life.

Gail put the finishing touches on our trailer home while I was at work. One advantage that I did have was that I could go home for lunch some days. Gail was an excellent cook, and she made some awesome meals. She ironed my dress shirts and pressed my pants every day. I had to wear a suit and tie every day to work.

We realized, with the upcoming move to UGA in December, that we would need more income. Gail found a job working for Orkin Exterminating Company in Albany. Her office was not far from mine. We rode together to work on days when I was not traveling. It was a godsend for her to get the job and contribute to our financial resources.

We made the decision that I would end my participation in the cooperative learning plan once my time in Albany expired, and that I would continue straight through to finish my degree. We were moving to the same trailer park in Athens where I had roomed with Neil in the spring quarter of 1969, and to the same lot. Our rent and electricity would run about thirty-five dollars per month. We hired a trucking company to move our trailer to Athens.

We were able to spend Christmas with Gail's family and mine before heading to Athens. We arrived in Athens after Christmas, just as the trucking company was parking our trailer in Lot 6. Our new address was 800 Gaines School Road, Space 6, Athens, Georgia.

Setting up the trailer turned out to be a bigger job than we had anticipated, due to preparing it for winter living. This meant closing in the area under the trailer to keep the cold air out. It meant insulating the water lines to withstand below-freezing temperatures. Even the wastewater line had to be

Our first home - Rocket Trailer

insulated. We discovered air leaks around windows and doors that had to be sealed. Finally, we got it all done and ready for the cold weather. I had installed a wall-mounted electric heater that provided adequate comfort in the cold.

A few weeks after our move, the water heater died. It was an electric water heater with a five-gallon capacity. I was able to find one at Sears that had a seven-gallon capacity. We had to tear out almost all of the kitchen sink cabinet to remove the old heater and install the new one. The trailer was eight feet wide and thirty feet long. It had a combined living and dining room, a kitchen, closet area, small pantry, bedroom with a three-quarter mattress, and a storage area in the rear, next to the bathroom. The bathroom was super small, with a toilet, a sink, and a shower area. You could sit on the toilet and brush your teeth over the sink at the same time (I could shave as well). The shower area was about four feet by two feet with a showerhead on the wall. Needless to say, it was an experience in small-space living. As I look back, we were in love, and all we needed was a place to study, sleep, and eat; and we were happy.

Classes started on January 6, 1970. My course load increased for winter quarter, with four classes: computer application engineering, electric circuits, strength of materials, and thermodynamics. My grades were surging upward—I was looking forward to graduating after winter quarter of 1971.

Dr. Ed Law, one of my professors, asked me to write a summary of my experiences in the Cooperative Learning Plan. It follows here:

> My first assignment was in Georgia Power's Americus District where I was assigned to work with Terry Duncan in residential sales. I was assigned a vehicle as well as an expense account. My job involved calculating heat losses and gains on residential structures to determine HVAC requirements. Also, I handled customer complaints and general questions on energy usage. I worked with HVAC dealers in meeting the heating and cooling needs of customers. My territory was a 75-mile radius of Americus and I traveled 1,800 miles per month. After six weeks of my arriving, Terry Duncan left the company, and I was assigned his responsibilities. I was carrying the load of a full-time employee and received an exemplary rating for my work.
>
> My second and third assignments were in Georgia Power's Albany District. I was assigned to work with Dennis Loper, who was the district residential sales representative. My duties were similar to those in the Americus District. However, my duties and responsibilities increased as my experience broadened. I was again assigned a company vehicle and an expense account. I traveled an area of 90 miles radius of Albany, which resulted in traveling 2,000 miles a month. I became more experienced in company operations and was even more valuable to the company. My expertise increased in handling customer complaints. I was assigned more difficult cases of complaints because I was handling them in a manner that customers were thanking me and Georgia Power for my assistance.
>
> I used my engineering skills in sizing and designing electric heat and air conditioning applications including heat pumps. Also, I dealt

with residential wiring issues. I became the go-to person in these areas. I developed my people skills in dealing with all of the various issues. I wanted to participate in the Cooperative Learning Plan for two reasons. Number one was to earn money to be able to complete my engineering degree. Number two was to gain on-the-job experience. I achieved both of these in this program. I can say, without a doubt, this has been a great learning experience for me and this program is first class all the way. I appreciate UGA and Georgia Power for allowing me to be a part of this plan.

Since I had been six months without doing any academic work, I had to refresh my studying skills. I was spending more and more time with my head in books as the courses were progressively getting harder. The only study area available in the trailer was our dining room table.

My academic schedule and Gail's work schedule prevented us from going back to South Georgia to see our families as frequently as we would like. One weekend during February 1970, we left on a Friday and drove to Tifton to visit with Gail's family on Friday night and Saturday until noon. Saturday afternoon, we traveled to my parents' home in Snipesville, which was about an hour east of Tifton. We stayed overnight with my family, then attended church at Mount Pleasant Baptist Church, where Dad was the pastor, and traveled back to Athens late on Sunday afternoon.

We got back to our trailer home after dark. Gail unlocked the door to the trailer. Crouching just inside the doorway, staring at her, was the largest rat that she had ever seen. She screamed, and he turned and scurried toward the back of the trailer. Very few things in life scare Gail, but rats are on the top of the list. She informed me that she was not going into the trailer, and certainly not sleeping there until that rat was removed. I spent the next two hours trying to find the rat. He was gone, although I had a hard time convincing her of that fact. I did find his entrance-and-exit point, which was under the drain line to the shower. I got some flat metal and created a barrier around the drainpipe so he could not come back in. After an hour of my pleading with Gail that I had taken care of the rat, she agreed to stay in the trailer. We had a puppy at the time and had stored dry dog food on the pantry floor. The rat had found it and had moved the entire bag contents up to the front of the trailer, under our couch. Gail found that and again threatened to move out. I convinced her that the rat was gone for good, and everything would be okay. Fortunately, we never saw that rat again.

Several nights later, I heard two gunshots coming from across the street. Two female students lived there. I ran over to see what was wrong. One female answered the door, and I saw the other one with a .22 rifle aimed at the closet. I asked what was going on. "A rat," they said, in unison. I convinced them to lower the rifle and let me hold it. I was afraid they would shoot themselves, hit a gas line in the trailer, or shoot someone outside the trailer. I knew, based on their ability to shoot, that they would probably not ever kill the rat. I searched for the location of the rat entrance, found it, and stopped it up. We found out that the rat problem came about because the owners had mowed a field across from our space, and that had forced the rats to find a new home. Exciting times!

As soon as I got settled in my classes, I began to look for part-time work. I found a note on the bulletin board in the Driftmier Engineering Building that Tenderland Foods was looking for part-time help. I researched Tenderland Foods and found it was an independent wholesale and retail meat market. I quickly called them and set up an appointment for the job interview.

At Tenderland, I met the owner and his wife. They were looking for someone who had experience and was willing to work afternoons from Tuesday through Friday, and all day on Saturday. I convinced them that I was the person they wanted. I outlined my experience of working in the meat markets at Piggly Wiggly and McLendon Grocery in Hazlehurst. The owner handed me a white coat and told me to put it on, go into the meat cooler, bring out a hind quarter of beef, and cut it up. I did exactly that. He watched me cut up the hindquarter into T-bone, porterhouse, tenderloin, flank, and ribeye steaks. He hired me on the spot, and I worked there during the rest of my time at UGA.

Gail was looking for a job, and she contacted Orkin Pest Control Company as she had worked for them in Albany. They did not have any openings, but one of their employees suggested that Gail contact CIT Finance Company in downtown Athens. She did, and they hired her, also on the spot. It was a godsend that she got the job, as it allowed us to begin to feel better about our finances. She worked there until we left Athens.

The cold weather presented many problems for our old trailer home. We had to keep the water running at the kitchen tap to prevent the water line from freezing. I had insulated the line from the connection outside the trailer up to where it entered the trailer floor. I thought that I had the problem solved, but one night we forgot to leave the tap on. The pipe froze, and we were without water. I spent all day trying to thaw the line. Gail's hairdryer was the most useful tool for that job. The weather did not get above freezing for several days. Once I got the line thawed, we did not forget to leave the water tap running again.

The trailer, which was built in the 1950s, was not well-insulated. It would get rather cold inside, but our electric wall-mounted heater did a great job. Also, Gail's mom made beautiful, insulated curtains to help keep the cold out. We survived.

I completed winter quarter and was finally getting in the groove of studying. My grades reflected my renewed commitment to complete my engineering degree.

Spring quarter started on March 24, 1970. I was taking five classes: strength materials laboratory, designing electrical wiring systems, engineering electronics, differential equations, and controls. These classes were challenging my intellect and my previous class learning experiences; in other words, they were difficult.

I continued working at Tenderland Foods. It was a good job but tiring, and I had to work in a cooler, with a temperature of around forty-one to forty-five degrees. However, I found if I kept busy, I did not notice the cold as much.

Employees were able to buy meat at a 20 percent discount. As I was cutting up meat, I could save us a great steak or roast. Gail was always happy when I brought home some protein. I learned to cut up a whole chicken into eight parts in about eight seconds. This required experience, a sharp boning knife, and quick movements. Don't try this at home; it is best done by a professional. Back in the 1970s, we sold mostly whole chickens but would cut them up upon customer request.

The wholesale side of Tenderland's business was primarily with the local school systems and restaurants. We would cut up chickens into their parts, prepare ground beef, and cut pork chops.

As you can imagine, using sharp knives, meat band saws, and hamburger patty machines could be very dangerous. Safety was emphasized to all employees all the time. I was very lucky, in that I had only a few cuts and bruises during my fifteen months of employment at Tenderland Foods. One of my co-workers was not so lucky when we were making hamburger patties one time. The patty machine packed ground beef into a steel chamber and then knocked it out of the patty mold. This was a very fast process. The next patty would be ready in seconds. Occasionally, the mold would not release the entire patty. If you were quick enough, you could use a finger or your thumb to clean the patty mold before the next patty. Bill was not fast enough, and he lost the end of his thumb. We rushed to his aid. I gave him a clean apron to wrap up the bleeding thumb. One of my co-workers rushed him to the hospital. After they left, we thought about the tip of his thumb—could it be reattached? We found it, iced it, and put it in a plastic bag. I jumped into my vehicle and traveled to St. Mary's hospital, just down the road. He was not there. He was at the other hospital in Athens. By the time I got there, they had already stitched up his thumb and had completed the medical procedure. He was back at work the next day—minus the tip of his right thumb.

Driving old cars gave me a lot of mechanical experience, particularly when I had to do all of the maintenance and repair work myself. I became a regular at the local auto parts stores in Athens. One day, I needed a new car battery. I went to the auto parts store to buy one and asked for the wholesale price. The salesman looked at me as if I had lost my mind. "What makes you qualified to get a wholesale price?" he asked. I gave him my poor college student speech and told him I had always gotten a discount back home. He looked at me for what seemed like five minutes and finally said, "Alright, just this one time." I got the battery at the wholesale price.

We were able to keep my first vehicle, the 1960 Dodge Dart Pioneer, in working order until the spring of 1970. My daily schedule was to take Gail to work at CIT Finance Company in downtown Athens, and then go on to the Driftmier Engineering Center on the south campus to attend my classes. One morning, I dropped Gail at her office and attempted to leave. The car would not go into any gear except reverse. The shift control was a push-button on the left side of the steering column, and it would not engage the transmission to move forward. I had to park the car and leave it in front of Gail's office and head to class. This issue would have to be dealt with later in the afternoon.

That afternoon, I got one of my friends to take me downtown to my car. I had a solution to get the car back home. I thought, since the car would not go forward, I would just back it all the way home. I asked my friend to go in front of me and lead the way. He did, and I followed him, driving backward. I don't know how we avoided the police, but we made it home unchallenged.

I called my dad and told him what had happened. He had seen the same model car as mine parked in a field near his home and suggested that maybe the transmission would fit in my car. He called me the next day to say that the engine was bad, but the transmission was good. He bought the car for twenty-five dollars and removed the transmission. He came up to Athens with it the next day. We removed the transmission from my Dodge and installed the one he had brought. We were nearly completed with the installation when we discovered a problem. The original transmission was cooled by running the oil through the radiator and returning it to the transmission. The newly installed transmission was air-cooled. It had air scoops that cooled the transmission fluid. We could not finish the install because the air scoops would not fit in the hole where the transmission was located. A major problem develops if you cannot cool the transmission fluid! The fluid will overheat and ruin the transmission.

Dad asked me how far I drove the car each day. My round trip was about seven miles. His solution to this issue was either to find another transmission or to take a hammer to the air scoops and close them. The transmission would work fine, but after about thirty minutes, the oil would begin to get very hot. After an hour or two, the oil would cool down for a return trip. We hammered the air scoops closed and declared victory.

In preparation for the eventual failure of the Dodge, I bought a Simca 1000 for $125 from a UGA student who had damaged the rear, driver's side wheel and frame during an Athens ice storm. I went to my favorite junkyard, C. P. Alewine Junkyard on the Athens–Monroe Highway, and found the wheel and frame needed to repair the vehicle. The cost was $25.75. Removing the wheel and frame from the wrecked vehicle, I installed them on the Simca. The repair was made quickly, and we had a second vehicle.

The Simca was made by a French automaker founded by Fiat. This was a small, red vehicle, and Gail nicknamed it the Red Tomato. It had a rear, water-cooled engine and a manual 4-speed transmission and would run about 55 mph at top speed. The one saving grace was its gas mileage, which was around 40 mpg average.

"Red Tomato" Simca 1000

The Simca had issues from time to time. One of those was keeping the carburetor tuned. I would work on it almost every week. I finally went to C. P. Alewine Junkyard and found an old wrecked Simca with a carburetor. My existing carburetor was in such bad shape that I bought the used one from Alewine and installed it on the car in the Alewine parking lot. I paid $15.45 for the carburetor. As I was removing and installing the new carburetor, I discovered the problem with the existing one was a hairline crack at its base. The car would run very smoothly when it was cold. After it warmed up, it would start to skip. As the engine heated up, the crack would open and give too much air to the fuel mixture in the carburetor. Problem solved.

Summer quarter kicked off with a bang in June 1970. I was scheduled to take four engineering courses: fluid mechanics, electrical design machine lab, agriculture structure design, and heat transfer.

Things were going pretty well for Gail and me. She had just received a promotion to Assistant Loan Manager at CIT Finance Company, and I was at Tenderland Foods. Our finances were improving, and it was summertime.

Summer in our old trailer home was barely comfortable. It could have been much worse. I had anticipated the effect of spring and summer heat in Athens, knowing we would need some sort of air conditioning. The only applicable system would be a window unit. While I was still working with HVAC contractors in the Albany district, I had mentioned that I needed a window unit AC. One of the contractors was removing a suitable unit from a home that was adding central air conditioning. I bought it from him and installed it in the early spring. As a result, we were at least somewhat prepared when the hot weather came.

We were able to take some time off and visit our folks in South Georgia during this time. Due to both of us working and my classes, time to travel back home was limited.

One of the highlights of our summer was Karl Wallenda's high wire walk across Tallulah Gorge on July 18, 1970. Gail and I had never visited Tallulah Gorge, which was in the northeast Georgia Mountains, near the town of Tallulah Falls. I saw a notice on the Driftmier Engineering Center bulletin board about a company needing workers for the Wallenda event. I inquired and found that Economark Inc. needed student workers to man concession stands. Gail and I signed up. We were fortunate to be located right near where Wallenda would end his walk. We could see his entire walk across the gorge. Gail and I served soft drinks and hot dogs from a wooden concession stand brought onto the site for this event. There were not any facilities nearby, so everything had to be brought in, such as water and portable bathrooms.

About 300,000 people, along with Governor Lester Maddox, attended the event that day. Wallenda walked across a steel cable about 1,000 feet long and 750 feet above the ground. He spent eighteen minutes on his walk and did two handstands in the middle. I can't find my records, but I remember that we were paid very well for our day's work.

My mother and my sister, Linda, came to visit us in late July. Mother brought us some fresh vegetables that she had grown, processed, and frozen. Not only did she bring the vegetables, but she also brought a brand new twelve-cubic-foot freezer to put them in. The freezer was a total surprise. Gail and I looked at each other. Where were we going to put the freezer? This was a small trailer home, and we had just about used every available spot. Of course, when your mother delivers such a great gift, you must accommodate it. After considering several options, we decided on placing it next to the front door. Also, we received the payment book for the freezer: fifteen payments of $12.15, starting the following month. The freezer came in handy because the small freezer section at the top of our little refrigerator would not hold very much. We used that freezer for many years, and then my son took it, and he retired it many years later.

Spring quarter went well, and I passed all my classes with my grades surging upward, even with hard coursework. I think that I was finally in the groove. It didn't hurt that I was inching closer to graduation.

Fall quarter started on September 24, 1970. I again signed up for four engineering classes: engineer math, physical properties, management of plant environment, and unit processing.

Things were going well at work and UGA, but I was still having mechanical problems with our vehicles. If it wasn't the Dodge with an issue, it was the Simca. It seemed like I was spending all my free time keeping the vehicles running.

As we were reviewing our finances, Gail totaled up what we were spending on monthly repairs for our cars. She felt that we were paying more for repairs than we would for the monthly payment on a new vehicle. Gail had connections with a local bank since she was working in the finance industry. She checked with Clarke County Motors, the Volkswagen dealership, and with C & S Bank in Athens. She was able to get us a brand new, shiny, 1970 Volkswagen Beetle for $76.32 per month for thirty-six months. Volkswagen Beetles were selling like hotcakes at that time.

Our new 1979 Volkswagen Beetle

We were able to get the last one on the upcoming shipment. That was a no-brainer, and we bought the new, baby-blue Volkswagen and took possession on September 9, 1970. The thought of not having to spend my weekends working on vehicles was a great relief, and we were saving money. What a deal!

Since we had the new Volkswagen, we decided to sell the 1960 Dodge. I took the Dodge to a car lot where I left it on consignment. I told the car lot owner that I wanted one hundred dollars for the car. He said that he would try to sell it, and he would keep anything over the one hundred. I received a call from him about a month later: he had sold the car. He asked me to come by and sign the title. The new owner was buying the car for parts and was in immediate need of a transmission. I could not get to the car lot and get my check quick enough, praying that the new owner needed a transmission with bent air scoops.

I also decided to sell the Simca. I was asking one hundred dollars for it. I put it on the bulletin board at the Driftmier Engineering Center. About a week later, I got a call from a student who needed cheap transportation. We met, completed the deal, and he left with the Red Tomato. And after selling the cars, I could afford to buy my 1971 John Roberts UGA class ring for $56.14.

I knew that I was getting close to having enough credits to get my degree, so I set up a meeting with my advisor, Mr. Cobb. He checked all of my records and credits for accuracy. He then told me that I should be able to complete the needed requirements by the end of the winter quarter of 1971. I was excited that I was only one more quarter away from earning my bachelor's degree in agricultural engineering.

I told Gail the good news, and we celebrated that night by having a steak from Tenderland Foods—at a discount, of course. We started thinking about our plans and what we were going to do. I immediately notified Georgia Power, hoping that they would offer me a job since they felt that I had done a great job for them during my time in the co-op program.

I finished the quarter with passing grades and was looking forward to completing my last quarter.

Winter quarter started on January 5, 1971, with the scheduling of my final course load: management of agriculture environment, soil and water engineering, introduction to systems analysis, agricultural power, and design of hydraulic structures.

Georgia Power called me several times in January as we were discussing my going to work for them. I verbally committed to them that I would accept the job offer and received a letter from them, dated January 21, 1971, confirming their offer and my acceptance of a position as a residential sales engineer in Columbus Division, Columbus District, reporting to Marshall Timberlake. I was to start work on March 29, 1971. Gail and I were ecstatic that I had gotten the job, and the salary was awesome at a little under $10,000 a year. We thought we were rich!

Georgia Power sent me a letter in early February, asking me if I would consider another job which was located in Rome, Georgia. It would pay the same, and I would be released from the Columbus position. They needed an agricultural engineer in the Rome Division, and the job had been vacant for over a year. The job was enticing because it was a perfect fit for my engineering degree. Gail and I prayed over it and decided that we wanted to take the job in Columbus. I found out later that Olin Ginn, agricultural affairs manager at Georgia Power corporate, wanted me for that job. He was rather upset that I didn't take it. Many years later, I would take Olin's place at the corporate office as manager of the Agricultural Affairs Department.

GEORGIA POWER COMPANY

W. R. WORLEY
PERSONNEL MANAGER
R. W. FAGLIER
ASSISTANT PERSONNEL MANAGER
D. B. BOWLES
EMPLOYMENT COORDINATOR

270 PEACHTREE STREET

P. O. BOX 4Ϩ
ATLANTA, GA. Ϩ
(404) 521-34

ATLANTA

January 21, 1971

Mr. James L. Hill
800 Gaines School Road
Space 6
Athens, Georgia   30601

Dear Mr. Hill:

This letter will confirm our offer and your acceptance of the position of Residential Sales Engineer for assignment in the Columbus Division at the starting salary of $810 per month.

May I suggest that you contact Mr. Marshall Timberlake, Division Residential Sales Supervisor, Columbus Division, to confirm a definite starting date. We expect this will be around March 15.

When you report for work please bring a copy of your birth certificate with you as it will be needed in your initial employment process.

We are looking forward to having you as an employee of our Company, and we feel that you will find many satisfying and rewarding experiences with us. Please let us know if we can be of any assistance to you in the future.

Very truly yours,

W. R. Worley

cc: Mr. Marshall Timberlake

I shared the news with my boss at Tenderland Foods that I was leaving Athens following my final exams in mid-March. He was not happy. I also had to tell him that I needed to take one weekend off before that to look for a place to live in Columbus. He refused me the time off, saying he needed me on weekends. When I told him that I had to go to Columbus to find a place to live, he said, "If you take off a weekend, you are fired." I took the weekend off, and we went to Columbus. When I showed up for work on Monday afternoon, he met me at the door and told me I was fired and to pick up my check and leave.

His wife overheard the conversation, and said, "What? You are not going to fire Jimmy. He's one of our best employees!" I was re-hired by his wife and continued working until we moved. I found out who was the boss of that outfit!

Finally, Gail and I could move forward with planning for the move. On our trip to Columbus to find somewhere to live, we had identified a furnished apartment to rent, since we did not have any furniture. It was in the Hilton Arms Apartments on Hilton Avenue in Columbus, apartment number A-4, located on the second floor. We had paid a deposit and the first month's rent to make sure we had a place to live. The rental cost was $172 per month.

My last exam was on March 15, and UGA did not have a March graduation ceremony. I was therefore scheduled to graduate at the end of the spring quarter on June 5, 1971.

The agricultural engineering degree required earning 205 hours of credit, exclusive of physical education. This was about ten more hours than other bachelor's degrees at UGA. An agricultural engineering degree provides well-balanced training in basic sciences, engineering sciences, engineering design, and analysis in humanistic and social sciences. The agricultural engineering curriculum was accredited by the Engineer's Council for Professional Development.

Agricultural engineers take the same basic degree courses in engineering as all other engineers. They tend to specialize in their senior year, depending on what field they chose to enter. One of my supervisors, a Georgia Tech engineer, told me that I did not have an engineering degree like a Georgia Tech engineer. We compared the required engineering courses, and he changed his mind.

Jimmy and Gail going to Graduation from UGA, June 1971

11

My Brother Ricky Hill

I was nine years old when Jasper Ricky Hill was born on March 23, 1956. He and I became great buddies. I left for college when he was ten years old, and we didn't get to spend much time together after that.

Ricky started at T. G. Ritch Elementary School in Jesup as a first grader in the 1962–63 school year. That summer, our family moved to Jeff Davis County, so Ricky began second grade at the Excelsior School in Snipesville in the fall. He continued there through the fifth grade and excelled in school, with A grades in almost every subject. In 1967, Excelsior School closed, and all local children traveled by bus to Jeff Davis Middle School in Hazlehurst starting that fall. My brother continued to be an outstanding student. In the fall of 1969, he was promoted into eighth grade and started at Jeff Davis County Junior High School. Unfortunately, he did not complete the final six weeks of school.

Ricky - 3rd Grade
Photo Courtesy of Mrs. Jimmie Nell Tate

Ricky Loved Fishing

Late in the afternoon of Monday, May 11, 1970, my dad sent Ricky to deliver some fresh red potatoes to our neighbors, the Coxes. Ricky was fourteen and was already driving, as was very common in rural South Georgia.

Ricky was gone for quite a while. Dad became concerned when over an hour had gone by, so he decided to go look for him. He traversed the roads that Ricky would have taken, looking for signs of the black Volkswagen Beetle he had been driving. Just off Highway 268, the Broxton Highway, near Mount Pleasant Church Road, he discovered the Volkswagen on a trail that led to a bar pit. The pit, formed where clay had been dug for the construction of Highway 268, was full of water and covered about an acre. These bar pit water holes are common across South Georgia. The car was unoccupied, and there was no sign of Ricky except for his clothes lying near the water's edge. Fear gripped Dad as he tried to find Ricky. He concluded that he must have gone into the water. Dad immediately went back home and called for help. Emergency crews arrived shortly afterward, and they found Ricky's body in about sixteen feet of water, forty feet from the bank.

Why did Ricky go into the water, particularly since he was by himself? Why did he remove all of his clothes? How did he drown? We still do not know the answers to these questions. Several of his friends speculated that he went into the water hole because he had been teased about not knowing how to swim.

Losing a child is one of the most horrendous events that can happen to a family. My dad and mom were in shock, as you can imagine. My brother Jerry was in Vietnam, and I was in my senior year at UGA in Athens, Georgia. My sister, Linda, was attending college at ABAC in Tifton.

I received a call from my dad that evening with the horrific news. Gail and I were heartbroken and in shock. We immediately packed our suitcases and headed to Snipesville.

We got about thirty miles south of Athens, near Madison, Georgia, when we realized that we didn't have any cash for gas. Nor did we have any credit or gas cards. All we had was our checkbook. As we pulled into Madison, we knew that we needed to purchase fuel. It was after dark, and

Ricky at a picnic just prior to his death

not many service stations were open at night. The fuel gauge in the Simca
was unreliable, and we were afraid that we would run out of gas before we
got to my family's home. I stopped at the first place we could find, a Texaco
station in the downtown area. After I explained to the manager why we
were traveling, he took my check for $1.20, which bought us just under
four gallons at thirty-six cents per gallon. If he had not taken my check, I
don't know what we would have done. The Simca got 40 mpg, and the
distance from Madison to Snipesville was about 168 miles or just over four
gallons of fuel.

We arrived at my parents' parsonage home in Snipesville around
midnight. None of us slept that night. We were all still in shock. Dad had
contacted the army to get word to Jerry in Vietnam about coming home
as soon as he could. He was going to be home in about three days. My
sister had already arrived from Tifton.

The funeral was delayed so that Jerry could get home. In the meantime, Ricky's body was brought to our home to await Jerry's arrival. The casket was open for viewing by family, friends, and neighbors during this time.

For the next few days, we felt as if we were in a fog. Many of our friends and family were coming and going, trying to comfort us as we faced an unspeakable tragedy. Many of Ricky's friends came to our home and shared their grief.

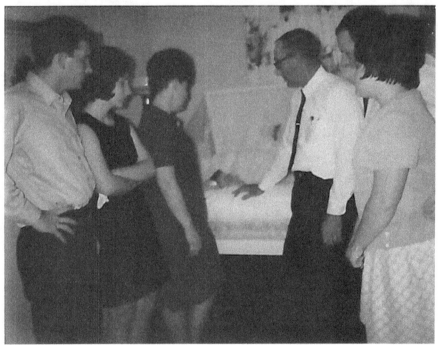

Our family gathered at Ricky's casket

Making all of the arrangements for the funeral was a great burden in this time of extreme stress. I don't know how Dad and Mom were able to cope, except by the grace of God.

The funeral service at Mount Pleasant Baptist Church was held on Thursday, May 14, 1970, at 5:00 p.m., and was conducted by Reverends Paul Curl, Stetson Bennett Sr., and Ray Freeman. Ricky was buried in the church cemetery, adjacent to the church. Active pallbearers were Gene

Ryals, Leroy Ryals, Rhonwyn Dawson, Waymon Ricketson, J. W. Sapp, and Larry Smith. Honorary pallbearers were Carlos Graham, Jim Girtman, Buck Caves, Edward Dyal, Carroll Walker, C. A. Smith Sr., C. A. Smith Jr., Buddy Hutto, A. R. Mills, John Tyre, Sam Wooten, Clyde Wooten, J. M. Ricketson, Marcus Ricketson, Kenneth Drawdy, Exley Hill, D. L. Brantley, Keith Hutchinson, Harry Hurley, Rev. T. L. McConnel, Rev. Bill Burkett, Rev. Frank Meeks, Murrell Wooten, Johnny Caves, Tommy Beasley, Wendell Hobbs, Mike Dallas, Dr. Sidney Johnson, Donnie Ricketson, Randall Ursery, Wiley Caves, and Thomas E. Padgett. Miles Funeral Home handled the arrangements. I don't remember many details of the service because I was in shock. I do remember having never been to a funeral where there was so much crying and anguish.

Ricky lived his life in service to his Lord Jesus Christ and others around him. He was extremely well-liked in the church and at school. Ricky was an amazing young man. He was a talented singer and piano player, as well

Ricky just prior to his death   *Ricky playing the piano and singing with his friends*

as being an inspiration to many. He was a Christian and was very active in Mount Pleasant Baptist Church. Everybody admired his kindness and the way he treated people. He was one of those people who lit up the room when he entered. His impact on people was even more evident as the weeks, months, and years unfolded. His influence continues to this day.

Ricky's friends and fellow students at school responded in shock, disbelief, and sadness. The school newspaper, *Jacket Junk*, dedicated the issue that was printed on the Friday after he died to Ricky's memory. Please see the Appendix to see the Newspaper. The headline read:

STUDENTS SADDENED ...

The students and faculty of Jeff Davis Junior High School were saddened at the death of an eighth-grade friend. Jasper Ricky Hill, 14, of Route 1, Denton, drowned Monday while swimming at a water hole near his home. Surviving are his parents, The Rev. and Mrs. Jasper Hill of Denton; a sister, Miss Linda Hill of Denton; two brothers, Jimmy Hill of Athens and Spec. 4 Jerry Hill, US Army, Vietnam; his grandmother, Mrs. L. W. Strickland of Jesup; and several aunts and uncles. Ricky is at Miles Funeral Home.

Listed below are two poems that were written by Ricky's friends in the newspaper:

HE WON NO MEDALS,
BUT WINNING HEARTS IS BETTER ... TO RICKY HILL

He is gone, we know not where,
Probably to that place up there.

His tone was soft, his way was kind,
People like him are hard to find.

His soul was pure, his heart was true,
Each day he lived was adventure new.

He went swimming we know not why,
But it won't help anything if we cry.

His friends were few, his admirers many,
People envied him quite a plenty.

In time his memory will grow dim,
But I think we'll always remember him.

By Melina Farris

FINAL TRIBUTE TO RICKY HILL

He lived a life of happiness as everyone could see,
He never said an unkind word to you, his friends, or me.

He always tried to do his best at everything he'd do,
His laughter touched the hearts of all, especially me and you.

Everyone respected him as he respected them,
His heart reached out to everyone, he truly was a gem.

By Raylene Morris

The next church service was on the morning of Sunday, May 17, at Mount Pleasant Baptist Church. Dad preached the morning sermon to a full house. At the close of the service, a dozen or more people came down the aisle and confessed their sins and accepted Jesus Christ as their Lord and Savior. There were more people saved that morning than at any time in the church's recorded history. Ricky Hill had touched so many lives in his short time on this earth.

The church experienced its greatest ever revival over the following two weeks. God blessed the church with new members and with others who recommitted their lives to Jesus Christ.

Preacher Hill conducting baptisms on Sunday following Ricky's death

I found the following in my mother's files after she passed. It is a written exchange of questions and answers that took place between Ricky and his best friend, Jim Girtman.

Ricky: I have to talk with you Jim about this again, so please don't get mad at me. I had planned on doing this yesterday, but I guess you put a stop to that. Let's put it in a question and answer form.

Why won't you become a Christian? I have talked and talked and talked and still, you won't?

Jim: Let me decide (please).

Ricky: O.K. but when are you going to do it? I don't mean to make you mad or aggravate you with it but do you know why I keep on and on? It is because I love you as much or more as I do my brothers and sister. Sometimes I get to thinking what if the world ended tomorrow and I think about you not being a Christian. Then is when I beg God to give you a little more time. A day doesn't go by that I don't ask God several times to burden your heart and show you that you need to accept him before it is too late. Do you understand what you have to do to be saved? Or is it that you're afraid somebody is going to laugh at you?

Jim: Why do you say you had to call me before Friday?

Ricky: Because I asked God to burden your heart every day this week. So I promised him I would talk to you one day or every day this week, whichever one is more convenient. But if you don't accept him sometime this week, it doesn't mean I am going to stop talking, because I ain't. I'm going to keep on until you do. You didn't answer my question. Do you understand what you have to do?

Jim: Have got to get up there and say, "I want to accept Jesus Christ as my personal savior"?

Ricky: Yes, but do you want to?

Jim: That's my decision.

Ricky: I know it Jim, but I would like to know if you want to. Why is it that you won't talk to me about it?

Jim: It's my decision.

Ricky: Jim, please do you want to or not? PLEASE ANSWER ME.

Jim: I don't want to talk about it now.

After I read the above questions and answers, I asked Jim Girtman if he would share some comments regarding his friendship and spiritual experience with Ricky. He agreed that I could publish his comments in this book. The following are excerpts from his comments:

Hi, my name is really of little consequence. I am 28 days shy of 63 years old. I have been asked by Jimmy Hill to share some things about my friendship with his younger brother, and what he meant to me. Ricky, during our childhood, was my best friend and classmate from the second grade to the eighth grade.

As I recall the events of some 55 years ago, I will do so with as much accuracy as plausible. Into my life and Mrs. Austin's second-grade classroom came a young man who would soon become a special friend and classmate. Our next four years would be at Excelsior School, an old rural school in our community of Snipesville, in Jeff Davis County; Hazlehurst, being the county seat, was 12 miles away.

Ricky's dad, Preacher Jasper Hill, a Baptist minister, had come to Mount Pleasant Baptist Church as the new church leader. We just called him "The Preacher." The church was the church that my mother faithfully attended, along with my three siblings. I was the oldest of the four Girtmans.

There were many similarities in our family dynamics. Except my dad was neither a preacher nor a Christian during my childhood. I had three siblings, and he had three siblings. I was the oldest of my siblings, and he was the youngest of his. But all this would change and in great part because of my friend Ricky. We both took piano lessons. He thrived at it, and I cried about it.

I was anxious about being in Preacher Hill's presence. He had not been rude in any way to me. He was and had been our bus driver for the sixth grade through the eighth grade. When I would spend the night with Ricky, I would avoid at all cost any eye contact with his dad. Upon arrival at Ricky's house, I would head straight to Ricky's bedroom and would only speak to Mrs. Mary, Ricky's mother. Mrs. Mary was a calming and caring lady and had a smile that dissolved barriers and invited love to come in. She was a friend and encourager. Her warmth was always welcomed and her advice always wise.

Mrs. Mary was also my Sunday School teacher and our youth group leader. Every day there were "Hills" surrounding me, with Saturday being the exception. As time moved on, I became less anxious around Preacher Hill and more appreciative of him in his many roles in my life.

In the eighth grade, we were about two weeks from completing school and we were facing a social studies/history test. In preparation, Ricky and I planned to get together that very evening to study. Our plan came together on the bus ride home. He was to call me with a time. I had been at home for a while and had not heard from Ricky. I called his home and Preacher Hill answered and said, "Ricky is not here right now but should have already returned." Ricky had taken the Coxes some garden-fresh potatoes. Preacher Hill said that he would have Ricky call me when he got back. That call never came!

My sister got a call from Teresa Carver saying something about "Have you all heard about Ricky Hill? His daddy had gone to look for him because he was late in returning from taking some potatoes to the neighbors. On the way to look for Ricky, he saw the car at the water hole very near the Coxes."

A red flag had been raised in our small community, and with each subsequent phone call, our alarm increased. What had really happened? Had Ricky drowned?

I was increasingly fearful as the phone calls continued to come in. From the very first call about his drowning, I was in another world—a world in which I had never been. Fear gripped my heart! And now the reality of death I could no longer ignore.

As fear was wreaking havoc in my head and heart, I made my way outside to my motorcycle. I began riding it aimlessly in our yard. Questions were racing through my mind and pain was tearing at my heart as I rode in looping circles. Question after question and no answers.

As I numbly rode my motorcycle in aimless patterns, there was one recurring question that haunted me! Death! How could this be?

I remember Ricky mentioning death over and over in the many times he witnessed to me. It was always "What if you died, Jim?" Now his words rang loud. I could not escape this truth … the reality of life. What if "death" had come to me? Where would I be?

The many, many conversations and communications (letters, notes galore) that Ricky had directed to me were now piercing my heart. A brutal and painful truth in life came in the death of my best friend. Only now I could see the truth that it could happen to me.

Ricky had told me time and time again, death could intervene, but I had always imagined it to be a long time away. Years away … maybe 50, 60, or 70 years away, but NEVER now and NEVER him.

Ricky's death was the first death of anyone close, and because of Ricky's love, tenacity, and hush nudges from Mrs. Mary, I gave my life to Christ.

The first Sunday after Ricky's funeral, I think it was 13 young people who came forward that morning and accepted Christ as their savior. And in the weeks to follow, many parents also surrendered their hearts to Jesus.

It is a strange twist in life for such a tragedy to turn into glorious triumph. One last thought that I would like to leave fresh in your heart.

I was so shy in school and church and especially in the presence of the Hill family. And during that first church service following Ricky's death, my fear was stopping me in my tracks from following others to the altar. It was a miserable, miserable battle for me. My heart was saying "Go ..." but my brain was saying "NO." I was so torn between what I knew I should do but did not have the courage to do. As I clutched the pew in front of me as the altar call continued, I was so fearful that I would not be able to do what I knew I should.

Then an angel came right up to my seat. Amazingly she looked just like Mrs. Mary Hill. She wrapped her arms around the young boy she knew was struggling with a big decision. My heart was racing, my tears flowing, my hands held tight to the pew in front of me. Here is what she said as best I can remember. "Do it; don't do it, do it, don't do it." Then her voice said, "Jim, Ricky loved you like a brother, and he would be happy if you would ask Jesus into your heart." WOW! She was an angel with a 98.6 temperature and the voice for my best friend. She was now encouraging me to do exactly what Ricky had been asking of me for months and years.

What a relief and what disbelief as I stepped out of my fear into the life of FAITH as I gave my heart to Jesus. I have always asked what would happen if the Hill family from Gardi had not come in my world and into my life.

The lives of the "Hills" literally changed the landscape of our community, the "role" of Heaven, and the hearts of those who knew them. Today the faithfulness of that young man named Ricky Hill continues to be seen in the lives of all who surrendered to Christ following his death.

Well, Jimmy, Ricky meant the world to me and because of his faithfulness, I received the world hereafter.

It is with great gratitude that I can trace my spiritual roots to my best friend Ricky and his family! Ricky sowed only a brief time, but the seeds sown by him are still producing. What a sower, what a son, and what a friend!

Jim Girtman

Jim and Cindy Girtman with Mother and Daddy

In addition to singing and playing the piano, Ricky was a songwriter. He wrote the following song:

He Died But Now He Lives, written in 1969

My God in Heaven gave his son to come
to this world of sin. To save the ones
that he loved, he gave his only son.
He died on the cross just for you
and for me. So why, tell me why, oh tell
me why, you won't believe in him today.

Tomorrow may be too late to trust in
him, so today is the time oh make it right.
He will guard you and keep you for the

rest of your time. Just put your
trust in him he will do the rest.

<u>CHORUS</u>

He died, but now he lives to save
us all from sin and set us free. If we
trust in him now we will live in a city
of pure gold, where no pain can come in,
and no tears will be seen, in that
city up above, that I am going to.

By Ricky Hill. All publishing rights reserved

The Mount Pleasant Baptist Church was a close-knit family of believers. They supported each other in times of need. And this is exactly what they did in the loss of Ricky. I could not ask for any more support, comfort, and prayers than were offered to our family. Also, the church family provided
food for many days for our family as we were struggling to understand and accept Ricky's death. Many cards and letters of support and comfort came rolling in.

The following letter came from the Ricketson family, who were very close to our family. It was dated May 14, 1970, which was the day of Ricky's funeral:

Dear Bro. Hill, Mary, Linda, and Jerry,

I would like to put on paper some of the feelings that are in my heart. They are feelings that I don't know how to express any other way.

Bro. Hill, I would first like to thank you for listening to God and following his directions when he led you and your family to our community. Because if you had not come here, we would never have known it was possible to love someone as much as we love each of you. You have not only been our pastor, but you are like a brother.

Mary, to me you are like a sister, and I love you very much. You have meant so much to me as a Christian. I always feel better after talking to you because your light shines so bright. I hope that I can be the mother, wife, and witness that you are. Ricky was also an inspiration to me. I thank God for letting me know him and love him here on earth. I think today I have a great determination to live closer to God than ever before in my life because I want to be ready when God calls for me. Thanks to God and Ricky for that determination.

Ricky was also someone my boys looked up to. He was someone that Donnie could talk to; he felt that Ricky would tell him the right things to do. It seems that a lot of boys can talk to other boys better than their parents. I just thank Ricky for being there and always willing to listen to Donnie's problems. The way I know this is because Ricky and I had some long talks about it. He will always be special in my heart. I will always remember what a talented Christian he was. He was talented in so many ways.

Linda, you are like a younger sister whom I love and would do anything for. There will always be a special place in my heart for you.

Jerry, you have meant so much to each of us. We will never be able to express our feelings for you. Remember wherever you go our love and prayers will always be with you.

Tell Jimmy and Gail that even though we haven't been around them as much as the rest of you, they have begun to mean so much to me. They will always have our love and prayers.

Bro. Hill and Mary, if there was some way to shield you from the loneliness ahead, believe me I would try. If ever you need me for anything, please let me know because I will do anything to help you.

So remember we love you from the bottom of our hearts. We send you our deepest sympathy at this time.

We are not sending flowers for the funeral, because there are so many. The money enclosed means we want to help in some way.

May God bless and comfort you each day of your life is my prayer.
With Lots of Love,
Fran, Waymon, and boys

On December 4, 2012, Mother passed away at the Tift Regional Medical Center in Tifton. Following her death and burial, I was in Hazlehurst working on her financial affairs. I found a credit card that had Mother's name on it. It was from Big Oak Outdoors Inc., which was a business in Hazlehurst. I looked up the account and it seemed to be an account Mother opened to buy a lawnmower. However, I knew that my mother did not have a new mower, and now I was curious. I went to the Big Oak Outdoors store to see what I could find out. Kay was at the counter, and I asked her about the account. She explained to me that my mother opened the account to buy a lawnmower for the lady who cut Mother's lawn. The lady's lawnmower had died and could not be repaired. Mother bought a new lawnmower, and the two of them reached an agreement where the lady would make the payments, keep the lawnmower, and use it to mow mother's lawn. The account was paid off on time about a year after my mother passed. This was an example of Mother helping others, which she often did.

As I was leaving, Kay asked me, "Are you Ricky's brother?" I replied in the affirmative. She started talking about Ricky and his influence in her life. I was shocked as she started talking about him as if it was yesterday, even though Ricky had died forty-two years earlier. Her voice started breaking, and she began tearing up. She said that Ricky had a tremendous impact on her life. They were good friends in school. Before I left, there were two of us crying. What an impact Ricky had made on her life! I learned later that he had that kind of effect on many others, including on Kay's best friend, Sheila. Kay and Sheila were in the eighth grade with Ricky.

Van McCall of Snipesville shared the following about my brother Ricky:

Ricky was my brother's age, and I don't have many life experiences or memories of him. What I do clearly remember, however, are my thoughts of Ricky as a cornerstone and benchmark of Christian character among other young people our age. He was a living example of the lifestyle that a young person should have as a Christian youth. I have operated a Youth

Christian Character organization, God in the Hunt, in Snipesville, Georgia, for fifteen years. I remember thinking, in the early stages of development, of using the example of Ricky Hill's life in the development of the training platform. The teaching principle is "Character Aware," and it promotes 10 Christian Character principles (Knowledge, Attitude, Truth, Respect, Work Ethic, Humility, Kindness, Purity, Integrity, and Patience). These 10 principles are very reflective of my memories of Ricky's life. Ironically Ricky lived his life within the small community of Snipesville where this ministry is ongoing.

Another stinging memory that has stayed as a permanent and very clear impression was the day we all heard of Ricky's passing from our community. My thought was then and has always been, that serving God in a real Christian relationship is worth the effort as I know that Ricky's reward was sure in God's presence.

I thought that I knew a lot about Ricky and his life, but I have been in awe of what I have learned since I started writing this book. He is still held in high esteem by everyone who came in contact with him. How many of us will be remembered with passion, emotion, and spirituality more than forty years after our death?

12

Love at First Sight

It was cool and cloudy on Sunday, February 18, 1968, in the South Georgia city of Tifton. I was reviewing my notes in preparation for speaking at Zion Hope Baptist Church during the evening service. This was not my first time speaking at a church, as I had spoken in at least a dozen churches during my sophomore year at ABAC. Something about this particular day seemed to be different, and I was not sure what it was.

The Baptist Student Union (BSU) at ABAC, which was affiliated with the Southern Baptist Convention, sponsored students to travel and conduct services at various churches in South Georgia. Reverend John Wortham was the campus advisor of the BSU. I was a member of the team on this particular Sunday and had the speaking role. Loma Young, Nada Fincher, and I arrived at the church and met Reverend Talmadge Wilcox and other church leaders. They welcomed us and mentioned that they were hosting an event with food and beverages in the social hall following the service, which we were invited to attend.

Loma and Nada led the singing and sang a duet. After they finished, I stepped up to the podium and started reading scripture verses. After reading the verses, I shared what the verses meant and how we might apply them in our individual lives—and then it happened.

It was as if a bright light appeared out of nowhere and was concentrated on a beautiful girl toward the back of the church. She was petite with beautiful hair and gorgeous eyes. However, it was her smile and dimples that made my heart flutter. She was the most beautiful girl I had ever seen. I confess that I immediately lost my train of thought. It seemed like five minutes that the light shone, and I was in a trance. My heart was pumping and thumping at near heart-attack rate. I prayed to God that he would help me find my words again, as it felt like an eternity went by without a word coming from my lips. He answered my prayer! I was, finally, able to finish my thoughts. I stepped down and turned the service over to Reverend Wilcox.

I knew that I had to meet this beautiful girl after the service. As I rushed into the social hall, I spotted her. I whispered under my breath, "It was not a dream, there she is!" I introduced myself to her, and she told me her name was Gail Hobbs. I met her dad, Wendell, and her mother, Ruth, as well. Gail and I talked as we enjoyed the spread that the church women had prepared. Before I left, I got her phone number.

As I look back on that night, I knew that she was my true love at that first glimpse in the sanctuary. Before that night, I was not sure about the concept of love at first sight. After my experience that evening, I had no doubt.

Brenda Gail Hobbs
* Photo Courtesy of Tift County High School

I thought about Gail for several days afterward. I wanted to call her and ask her for a date. However, I had one big problem to overcome: I was working three jobs to earn money to pay my way through ABAC. How could I squeeze in the time for a date?

Early one morning, at the beginning of May, I heard a knock on my dorm door. It was 2:00 a.m. I am a light sleeper and woke up immediately. The knock got louder. I opened the door, and it was Security Officer James Dearman. He was Gail's school bus driver during the day and security officer at ABAC on the night shift. "Jimmy, you need to call Gail," he said. "She wants to hear from you."

"Yes sir!" I replied. I don't think that I slept much for the rest of the night.

The next morning, I quit one of my jobs since I was nearing graduation anyway. I called Gail the same day to ask for a date. She already had a date for Friday night as it was her Junior Prom. Her parents did not want her to have more than one date a weekend. Gail talked to her mom, and she agreed that Gail could go on a date with me on Saturday night "since it was Jimmy Hill." On our first date, we went to the drive-in theatre in Tifton.

We went out together a few more times before summer arrived. I got better acquainted with Gail's dad, Wendell, who was a farmer. He grew row crops and tobacco and raised cattle and hogs. He and I hit it off because of my agricultural background. Gail's mother, Ruth, was a beautiful woman and a great cook. I ate many a meal at her table. Gail had two sisters: Kay and Gwen. Kay was four years younger than Gail, and Gwen was thirteen years younger. Gwen and I had the same birthdate, July 10. She would always tell everyone that she and I were twins. She was four years old when I started dating Gail. I teased her from the beginning, and we became best buddies. Gwen loved to interrupt Gail and me when we were alone in the living room. It was a challenge to keep her from getting between us on the couch.

Ruth would always fix extra food just in case I came by, which I did often. She loved to joke with me, and I with her. I complimented her often on the sweet pickles that she canned in glass jars, and I would eat as many as I could, every time she served them. One time, during my birthday celebration, she canned a five-gallon jar of her pickles and gave them to me. She laughed and laughed at me as I was so taken with her gift. It took me a while, but I ate every one of them. Well, to be truthful, Gail ate a few of them.

I would always share stories with Ruth about my adventures, something I read or saw on TV. On the surface, they would appear not to be true, but many were true. I would occasionally throw in some that I had made up. After a while, she would not believe anything that I said. She never knew when I was teasing or being truthful. I relished that role.

Near the driveway of Gail's home, there was a large pine tree where I always parked my car. The tree was leaning and looked like it might fall anytime. However, it had been leaning for years. Every time there was a storm, Ruth would tell me to go move my car. I would tell her that it was fine and remind her that the old tree had been there for years. I would have moved my car, except that I knew it bugged her. I parked there at least a hundred times, and she told me to move it a hundred times. It never fell, but Wendell finally had it removed, just in case.

Wendell's farm had two fishponds on it. I loved to fish, as did Gail. In our spare time, we would fish one, or both, of the ponds. I caught the biggest largemouth bass that I had ever caught in the pond behind the barn one afternoon. It weighed five and a half pounds. I was so proud of it that I had it mounted. I still have it to this day.

Gail asked me late one evening to go frog gigging with her after dark. We went to the pond and got in the johnboat. I paddled, and Gail did the gigging. We captured enough frogs to provide frog legs for dinner the next night.

Gail and I were not going to be able to date during the summer of 1968. I would be traveling all summer long, harvesting string beans for the Green Giant company in the eastern states of the US. That summer we wrote each other fifty-three letters over the course of three months. I would write to tell her that I loved her, what great experiences I was having, and where I was located at that time—our crew stayed in old motor courts and changed lodging every week or so. She would write to me to tell me she loved me and share stories about her family and farm work. She worked for her dad and a cousin stringing tobacco, usually six days a week. I really enjoyed getting those letters. Sometimes, I had already left the motel, and the letter would be forwarded to me. Many times, our letters would cross in the mail. It cost six cents for a first-class stamp in the summer of 1968.

After I returned from working with Green Giant, Gail and I dated a few times in early September. I had to leave in mid-September to enroll at the University of Georgia in Athens. We started writing again, and each of us wrote an average of about fifteen letters a month while I was at UGA that fall. I did telephone her occasionally. Long-distance charges were high, and I charged them to my parents' home phone number. My mother sent me a letter telling me to start writing longer letters and make shorter phone calls. She had just received a phone bill, and my calls were the largest item on the bill at thirty-one dollars.

I was able to get home to see my parents a couple of times in the fall, and I would see Gail during that time as well. My mother invited her to join our family for Thanksgiving in Gardi at Midway Baptist Church. It was a dinner-on-the-grounds gathering that Dad, as a former pastor, and our family always attended. Gail's parents gave their permission, and I picked her up; we spent the day together. As we sat in my car under an old Spanish-moss-covered oak tree, I asked Gail to be my steady girlfriend. I gave her my high school class ring as a symbol of my commitment to her. It was the first time I had taken it off since I had got it. She wore it proudly.

One of the times I drove home from UGA to see Gail, I arrived at about eight o'clock on a Friday evening, and we decided just to stay at her house and enjoy each other's company. I stayed over three hours and then had to drive another hour to get to my parents' home.

As I left Tifton, I was tired, but feeling okay. I had passed through Ocilla and was driving between Ambrose and Broxton on Highway 268 when I dozed off. I ran a stop sign at the intersection of Highway 206 and traveled another thousand feet while asleep. It was well after midnight; fortunately, no other cars were on the road. As my car veered off the right edge of the pavement, it shook violently, waking me up just as it hit the shoulder. My speedometer was registering eighty miles per hour. I saw a roadside sign directly in front of me. It looked nearly as big as my Dodge. I swerved to the left to avoid hitting the sign head-on and struck it with the passenger side of the vehicle. The next thing I remembered was traveling across the road and into the ditch on the other side. I remember seeing pine trees almost horizontal. The car spun around two or three times and stopped in the left-hand lane, facing the direction I had come from. I got out of the car and walked over to pick up the wheel cover that I had lost in the process. I did not want to look at the passenger side of the car, because I knew it had to be destroyed after hitting the road sign. My hood had come unlatched. I slammed it back down, and it stayed latched. I got back into the car and continued to my parents' home, replaying the wreck in my mind over and over as I drove. The amazing thing was that I had not let go of the steering wheel the whole time, even though I was spinning and seeing trees almost sideways. Then it dawned on me: I had been wearing my seat belt—actually, it was just a lap belt. The car had not come with seat belts, so I had installed them as a safety measure. I had started wearing seat belts while working at Georgia Power; it was a company requirement. I am convinced that God and my seat belt saved my life that night.

I got home around 1:00 a.m., slipped into the house, and went to bed. I lay there and did not sleep a wink the rest of the night—at least what was left of it.

Early the next morning, my dad came into my room and said, "Son, what happened to your car?"

"Dad, you are not going to believe it, but someone ran me off the road last night between Ambrose and Broxton," I replied.

"Well, I'm glad you're okay, and your car didn't sustain too much damage."

I got up immediately and went to see my car in the daylight. The right side had some minor damage where the sign had hit the passenger front door at the door handle. Dad looked it over with me. "Son, we can repair the bent metal with a hammer. You might have to purchase a new door handle."

Dad was right. We were able to hammer out the bent metal. I never bought a new door handle. Actually, it looked pretty good. They don't build cars like that anymore. I never told Dad the truth about the wreck, but … he knew … he knew!

I traveled back to Gail's house on Saturday evening and stopped at the accident site. The sign that I had hit was actually a mile-marker sign. It was not nearly as big as it had seemed on Friday night. I am sure the Georgia Department of Transportation had to purchase a new sign because that one was completely destroyed.

The wreck made me rethink my traveling a distance late at night after a long day of classes. I could not afford a motel room, and the Hobbs family did not have an extra bedroom. I had an idea about what I could do: spend the night in my old dorm room at ABAC. My first-floor room had a sliding window. I had hardly ever locked it. I wondered if the current occupant of that room did the same. Maybe he would not be there on the weekends. When I attended ABAC, most kids went home for the weekend.

I know that it was not the right thing to do. However, the next time that I visited Gail, I slid open the window and no one was in the room. I spent the night and left early the next morning.

Gail and I attended services at her home church, Zion Hope Baptist, a week before Christmas, 1968. Santa was unable to attend, and I was called upon to represent Santa Claus at the church Christmas party. The event was held in the social hall where I had first introduced myself to Gail. The lights were low, but the kids' Christmas spirit was high. After I entered the building, the kids went crazy and wanted to sit on Santa's lap and tell him what they wanted for Christmas. I had a lot of fun that evening. The only thing my outfit did not have was Santa's white gloves. When it came to the turn of Gail's younger sister, Gwen, she got in my lap and noticed my hands. She had played with my hands many times when I was on the couch in Gail's living room. She looked puzzled, looking at me and then back at my hands. My white beard and red hat did a good job of covering my identity, but my hands were another story. I got her Christmas list quickly and moved on to the next child. After Santa had finished his duties, he left. I went back to the building after changing, and Gwen came up to me and wanted to look at my hands. I think that I did a pretty good job of convincing her that Santa was not me. It was a close call!

I picked Gail up at her home on Sunday, December 22, 1968, and we traveled to my parents' home in Snipesville to have dinner with my family. After dinner, the two of us went for a walk. While we were out, I got down on one knee and asked Gail to marry me. She said "YES!" What a great Christmas present! I was one happy young man. We shared the good news with my family.

Three days later, on Christmas Day, I went to Tifton to be with Gail. We swapped gifts that morning, and I could tell that Wendell and Ruth seemed a little puzzled. I felt that they thought we would announce our wedding intentions. They knew we were writing to each other almost daily and seeing each other as much as possible. I wanted to ask them on Christmas morning, but I was nervous and did not want to get a negative response.

During the early evening, I finally got up the nerve to ask them if I could marry Gail. We went into the den, where her parents and siblings were on the floor putting a puzzle together. Gail announced to her parents: "Jimmy has something to talk to you about."

Her dad got up and sat in his chair. Her mother stayed on the floor, working on the puzzle.

"Gail and I are requesting your approval to get married," I said.

Ruth started to get up. "Help me up off the floor! You-all shocked me. I thought it would happen this morning."

Wendell said, "I have one condition. Gail has to finish high school first." She was only months from graduating.

Gail and I said in unison, "Of course."

Ruth asked, "When are you-all thinking about getting married?" Gail said we had been considering early or late summer. Wendell pointed out that an early summer wedding would mean having to get extra help to put in the tobacco crop.

"Daddy, we will do it at the end of the summer, so I will be here to help you," said Gail.

We decided to get married on Labor Day weekend. Later, we set the firm date as August 29, 1969.

After New Year's Day 1969, I entered my first quarter of the Cooperative Learning Plan with Georgia Power, based in Americus.

I arranged my schedule so that I could go to Tifton on Friday, February 14—Valentine's Day. Gail and I had a date and went to the movies. After we arrived back at her home, we settled on the living room couch, with

Gwen hanging around. We finally coerced Gwen to leave. I gave Gail the engagement ring, along with a box of chocolate candy. Gail had officially become ring-engaged to me. We were both excited and rushed into the den to show her parents and siblings her ring.

In May, I rented my first tuxedo, bought an orchid, and took Gail to her senior prom. The prom had a beach theme, and that was the beginning of our love of the beach.

Gail and I attended her Senior High School Prom
* Photo Courtesy of Tift County High School

I worked in the Cooperative Learning Plan in the summer of 1969 in Albany with Georgia Power. This allowed me to be around much more often and gave us time to plan our wedding and our future.

Gail finished high school as we had promised her parents. The baccalaureate service and graduation exercises were held on Sunday, June 1, 1969, at the Tift County High School. The next week, Gail went to work on the farm helping as a stringer in the tobacco harvest.

Gail graduates from Tift County High School
* Photo Courtesy of Ray Hancock

Wendell and Gail finalized getting the trailer home that he had offered to give us instead of a large wedding. He paid the seller $995 and brought the trailer to the farm. There he parked it between the house and the pond, adjacent to the farm water well, which had an electrical outlet we could connect to the trailer.

I was able to come over on weekends from Albany to work on cleaning and repairing the trailer home, which had not been occupied for quite a while. The roof and sides were in good condition. The inside needed some work. We replaced the flooring with vinyl, scrubbed the walls, and replaced the three-quarter-size bed. Gail purchased a new couch. She also found a small dining table with two chairs that were exactly what we needed. Gail and Ruth made new curtains for the windows. I enlarged the electrical panel and added an electric wall heater in the living room that would heat the entire trailer. Most of our wedding gifts were things that we needed to set up housekeeping. We were blessed with 117 wedding gifts. These were items that helped us get our trailer furnished. We still have some of those items and use them often.

Gail had several bridal showers. One was hosted by ladies of the Zion Hope Baptist Church in Tifton. Another was hosted by the ladies at the Mount Pleasant Church in Snipesville. The last one was held at Roger and Donna Hobbs's home in Tifton, and guests included Jan Goodwin, Kathy Kelley, Gail Braswell, Patty Marchant, and Gloria Hobbs, among others.

By the middle of August, we had completed the renovation and repairs on the trailer. We were excited to get it moved to Albany after our wedding and honeymoon.

On August 28, I worked until mid-afternoon in Albany and then headed to Tifton for the wedding rehearsal. As I walked out of the office in downtown Albany, a pigeon pooped on my head. Yes, a pigeon! There were power lines going to the building that served as a roosting place. I was already dressed and ready for the wedding rehearsal. I went back into the building and into the bathroom to try to clean up the mess. All evening long, I kept thinking about the pigeon poop on my head. I wondered if anybody could tell.

We had the rehearsal event at Gail's home. It went well, and the preacher got us all trained on our roles and locations for the wedding. Following the rehearsal, we enjoyed ice cream and cake provided by my mother.

I went back to Albany and spent the night, then worked the next day—our wedding day—until noon, when I headed to Tifton to meet my parents and siblings. The ceremony was due to take place at 6:00 p.m.

Reverend Talmadge Wilcox, the pastor of Zion Hope Baptist Church, conducted the marriage ceremony. My best man was my college roommate, Neil Eunice. The maid of honor was my sister, Linda Hill. Kay,

Gail's sister, was the bridesmaid, and the flower girl was Gail's little sister, Gwen. The usher was my younger brother, Ricky. Gail's parents and mine were also in the wedding party.

Wedding guests who signed in included: Mr. and Mrs. Neil Eunice, Mr. and Mrs. Stanley Hutchinson, Mr. and Mrs. Carl Ivey, Rev. and Mrs. Eddie Allen, Iris and Maria Allen, Betty and James Braswell, Mr. and Mrs. Baldwin Davis Jr., Baldwin Davis III, Rev. and Mrs. Talmadge Wilcox, Loma Young, Betsy Harris, Mr. and Mrs. Mike Kerr, Eula Daniels, Mr. and Mrs. Troy Hobbs and family, Mr. and Mrs. Jim Hill and family, Exley Hill, Mr. and Mrs. Waymon Ricketson, Alice Haley, Mrs. E. L. Copeland, Della Scarborough, Donald E. McMillian, Mrs. Catherine Scarborough, Mrs. Eula Myers, Mr. and Mrs. Thomas R. Daniels and Rowell, Linda Hodnett, June Hodnett, Zera Owens, Mr. and Mrs. Wendell Hobbs, Mr. and Mrs. Hinton Goodwin, Mr. and Mrs. Russell Doss, Lynn and Vonda, Kathy Kelley, Jane Young and Carla, Annis Marchant, Nanett Haley, Lucy Haley, Earl, Lloyd, Gerald and Bruce Copeland, Ronnie Braswell, Mr. and Mrs. Harold Ogletree and Joan, Debbie Wilcox, Randy Braswell, Eddie Wilcox, Mrs. Hilda C. Goodman, Linda Hill, Cynthia Cox, Ricky Hill, Kay Hobbs, Gwen Hobbs, Mr. and Mrs. Hendricks Swain, Jan Goodwin, Claude Rosdeutcher, Joan Walker, E. L. Copeland, Mr. and Mrs. Jasper Hill, Gail Braswell, Dixie Scarborough, and Ray Hancock (photographer).

I borrowed my dad's car for the honeymoon. It was a blue Dodge Monaco. It was well decorated for our honeymoon trip, including an old boot and some tin cans that our friends had tied to the rear bumper. We stopped a few miles down the road and removed the cans but did not see the boot until the next morning. The white writing on the car stayed on until the next afternoon.

Our honeymoon trip was to Chattanooga, Tennessee, and Rock City. Our first stop was in Macon to spend the night. We stayed at the Holiday Inn on I-475 in a second-floor, corner room. I have always taken a glass of ice water with me to bed each night. I went to get some ice from the ice machine for my water. As I crawled into bed, I turned off the TV. We were getting comfortable in the bed when the TV came back on. I got up and turned it off again. As I got back into bed, it came on again. I was thinking, somebody is trying to fool us. This time, I got up and unplugged it.

Now, here is what happened next—no, I won't go any further on what you were thinking. However, during the night, I spilled the glass of ice water all over me, Gail, and the bed. We had to put a blanket on the bed to cover the wet spot and reverse our bodies on the bed to find a dry spot.

What a night!

Mr. and Mrs. Jimmy L. Hill
* Photo Courtesy of Ray Hancock

Our parents joining us for a photo
* Photo Courtesy of Ray Hancock

Jimmy and Gail leaving Wedding – Betsy Harris and Nada Kerr throwing rice
* Photo Courtesy of Ray Hancock

We were so excited to get to Chattanooga that we got up early and hit the road. We went first directly to Rock City. We had never been there before and enjoyed the visit. Of course, the Dodge Monaco was still decorated, and we got multiple congratulations as we walked to and from the car. When we arrived at our motel, we were told it was too early to check-in. We found a hamburger joint for lunch and finally checked into the room at 4:00 p.m. We were exhausted and took a nap—and woke up at 9:00 p.m. By this time, we were starving, but when we tried to find somewhere to eat dinner, every restaurant was closed or about to close. We ended up going to a local grocery store to find something to eat and settled on pickled pig feet (yes, we both loved them) and boiled peanuts. Back at the motel, we enjoyed our dinner and left behind pig feet bones and peanut hulls. I can only imagine what the maid thought when she cleaned our room the next day.

Gail pointing out our wedding messages on the car

Jimmy holding up a rock on our Honeymoon

Gail at Rock City on our honeymoon

We left Chattanooga on Sunday morning and headed back to Georgia. Our first stop was Snipesville to trade cars with my dad. I did clean Dad's car on Sunday morning to remove all of the typical Just Married signage. We enjoyed a little time with my parents and siblings and then traveled to Tifton to spend the night at Gail's parents' place. It was my first night in her bedroom.

The next day was Labor Day, September 1. We spent the whole day packing up our wedding presents. They had been displayed inside the trailer home, and the man who was scheduled to move it to Albany was coming bright and early the next morning.

On Tuesday, the man arrived, hooked up to the trailer, and set off for Albany with us following in my Dodge. After he had backed the trailer into our rented site and unhooked it, I spent the rest of the day leveling it up and connecting electricity, water, and sewer, while Gail worked on getting everything ready inside.

That night, in the pecan grove off Highway 82, east of Albany, we spent our first night in our first home as a married couple.

13

Columbus, Georgia – It's a Boy

Gail and I moved to Columbus following the conclusion of the spring quarter of 1971. I had finished my required courses and was approved to graduate that June.

We decided to sell our trailer to a student friend of mine and rent an apartment in Columbus. We had almost no furniture. However, we did have the upright freezer that my mother had bought us, a lot of tools, our clothes, books and a few other items. Our car at the time was the 1970 Volkswagen Beetle. We rented a twelve-foot U-Haul trailer and loaded it with about two thousand pounds for our trip to Columbus. The Beetle was just over thirteen feet long with a fifty-seven-horsepower engine running at a maximum of 4000 rpm. It weighed in at just over 1,700 pounds. In other words, the Beetle was not a good towing vehicle.

We installed a ball hitch on the Beetle to tow the U-Haul trailer. With the trailer loaded, we headed to Columbus. The trip was about three hours and 167 miles. We were only able to achieve 50 mph going downhill, and uphill could drop to 20 mph. This all worked well as we went to Macon and took US Highway 80 toward Columbus. There is one stretch of that highway with a steep incline that runs for a couple of miles. I got her up to about 55 mph and started up the incline. After a half-mile, I was down to 45 mph, and the speed continued to decrease dramatically. As I climbed the last portion and topped the hill, I was running 5 mph. Thanks to Volkswagen and prayer, we made it!

We arrived in Columbus around four o'clock in the afternoon and started unloading. Our apartment was located at 3561 Hilton Avenue, Hilton Arms Apartment, A-4. The only unit available was an upstairs two-bedroom, one-bath. Gail and I were doing the unloading, and everything was going fine until we got to the upright freezer. It just would not make the 180-degree turn on the stairwell. We tried lifting it over the sides of the railing but without success. I was twenty-three years old, in good shape, and could not lift the freezer, even with Gail's efforts, to get it into the apartment. My mother and sister were there to help us, but there is only so much room in the stairwell. Finally, a neighbor, Gary Burkhalter, whose apartment was directly below ours, came to our assistance. As I thanked him, I found out that he was one of my new Georgia Power co-workers. It turned out, after I started work, that our desks were next to each other in the district sales office.

We had to use coin-operated laundry machines while we were in college. Our first purchase, two days after arrival in Columbus, was a new Maytag washing machine and dryer. Six months later, we bought furniture. This was a big help as it lowered our monthly rental cost.

I reported to the Georgia Power office in downtown Columbus at 233 12th Street the following Monday. The building was nine stories, and Georgia Power occupied the first three floors. This was the headquarters of Columbus Division and Columbus District. Columbus Division included the major district towns of Manchester, Albany, Americus, Columbus proper, and other adjacent areas.

Columbus Division management included Andy Speed, vice president; Ben Williams, division manager; and Jim Prather, division sales manager. Columbus District personnel included Marshall Timberlake, district sales manager. Other residential sales personnel in the team I was joining were Larry Walker, residential sales engineer, and Harold Darrah, Gary Burkhalter, Frank Brookins, and Dennis Loper, who were all residential sales representatives. Home economists included Margaret Perry, Kyle Smith, and Martha Ruth Hill (Whatley). Some of the other people that I worked with at the division and district office included Tom Cantrell, John Gay, Bobby Ledford, Melvin Hunt, John Romeo, Ken Hutchinson, Ed Batten, Harry Hughes, Buddy Merrill, Bill Dozier, Richard Ward, Ross McDaniel, Kline Petty, Dot Ward and others.

I worked on the third floor, in the bullpen area. This was an open area with many desks adjacent to each other. It was rather noisy, and there was no privacy for phone calls. However, we were out of the office every day, meeting with customers, HVAC dealers, and other business contacts.

I was working for the Columbus District as a residential sales engineer. It was very similar to the jobs that I had held during my time in the Cooperative Learning Plan. Specifically, I was working with mobile home dealers and helping them provide reliable and economical electricity in their mobile home units. The heat pump was an electrically operated unit that heated and cooled a structure. I assisted the industry in sizing and selecting properly sized units for their homes. During June 18–20, 1971, I helped Roy Browder, Browder Mobile Homes, demonstrate his total electric mobile homes at the Annual Columbus-Phenix City Mobile Home Show at the Columbus Municipal Auditorium. Between twelve and fifteen thousand people attended the three-day event.

My other focus was working directly with customers and HVAC dealers helping to facilitate the installation of high-efficiency electric heating and cooling and promotion of the electric heat pump. If a customer called Georgia Power or the dealer and was interested in installing or upgrading their HVAC unit(s), I would provide the service of visiting the customer's home and conducting a heat-loss and heat-gain calculation. This determined the size of the HVAC system based on the home's insulation values. If the customer needed to upgrade their insulation values, I would assist them in determining what values were needed and how that would affect the size of the HVAC system and the money that could be saved on their electric bill. This process was a win for Georgia Power, as it increased the efficiency of the customer's HVAC system, which meant lowering the amount of generating capacity provided by Georgia Power. It was a win for the customer in lowering their electric bill.

Working on a project with an existing homeowner requires a lot of time and effort. Some of my peers worked with clients who were builders of single-family and multi-family homes, assisting them in their needs for expertise in HVAC and overall structure efficiency. It is much easier and quicker to work with them, as you work on multiple units at the same time. I knew that I was assigned the harder and more time-consuming work because I was the new kid on the block. I relished the challenge and took lemons and made lemonade. Besides, it prepared me for greater challenges later at the corporate office.

The HVAC dealers I worked with included Morris Dean of Dean's Heating and Air Conditioning Company, Ralph Holt of Holt Service Company, and others.

We found out that Gail was three months pregnant around June 1, 1971, just before I formally graduated from UGA. Christopher Jimmy was born on December 28, 1971, at the Columbus Medical Center. Chris weighed nine pounds and was twenty-one inches long. The twenty-two-hour delivery was long and lonely for Gail as I was not allowed in the room with her. I had to ask continually for updates from Gail's nurses. It was a very stressful time for me as well.

In December 1971, as we were awaiting the arrival of Chris, I completed three weeks of residential sales training at the Georgia Power corporate office in Atlanta, Georgia. The course covered HVAC load calculation, HVAC design, duct design, residential wiring and design, competitive equipment, household appliances, lighting, kitchen planning, Georgia Power billing procedures and records, salesmanship, sales tools, and sales programs, and self-improvement, as well as other training needs. To graduate from the class, I also had to pass a correspondence course in basic electricity.

My fellow participants in the course included Bill Blau, Dwayne Hassler, Tony Sammons, John Cooke, Don Wix, Carol Bryan, Phil Meadows, Sarah Ray, Graham Fiveash, Cynthia Hesterly, Lee Hutchens, Fay Simpson, and Frank Brookins. The course was taught by Emily Alexander, Buck Bailie, Bill Blount, Courtenay Bythewood, Robert Carpenter, Jack Carrollton, Ralph Chapman, Warren Faglier, Randy Farlow, J. R. Glass, Jack Murrah, Ralph Odgen, Lillian Pace, Don Sabin, Carl Shaw, Mary E. Smith, and Cornelia Witte.

Shortly afterward, in January 1972, a job opportunity came available at the division level, which sparked my interest. It was a division outdoor lighting coordinator position reporting to Jim Prather, division sales manager. This position would work with all of the district offices in promoting and selling outdoor lighting to Georgia Power customers. I asked to be considered for this position. After interviewing several candidates, Prather transferred John Romeo into the position. I received a letter thanking me for my interest and stating that I would be considered for other jobs in the future. That was the first of several rejections as I was seeking to further my career.

Gail and I joined Beallwood Baptist Church, located on Veterans Parkway in Columbus. Reverend Billy Southerland was the pastor. On October 8, 1972, I was ordained as a deacon in the church. My dad and mom came to my ordination. Dad led the ordination and installation service, which included the deacons from the church. The Deacon Charge was from Acts 6:1–7 and 1 Timothy 3:1–15 in the King James Bible. The deacons participating were James McLendon, Milton Tisdale, Carlton Adams, Fred Barnette, Fred Lewis, Clam Godwin, W. F. Harwick, Buck Smoot, Harvey Moore, Edgar Causley, Wayne Brannon, Julian Reynolds, J. R. Allen, Walter Merritt, Johnny Chandler, Emmett Hale, Lee Railey, Carl Williams, and Jack Hendrix.

Gail and I taught a teenage Training Union class. We also started a bus ministry, where the bus would travel into the community and pick up twenty to thirty children and teenagers. Gail enjoyed using one of her many talents by singing in the choir.

As an opportunity for further involvement in the Columbus community, I was asked by my supervisor to volunteer with the Columbus Junior Achievement organization. In preparation, I attended an Executive Management Development course in 1971–72. This was two hours per week for thirty weeks of training. The course covered the exercise of executive leadership abilities in the overall supervision of an actual mini-business operated by young people. It included all aspects of general business, marketing, production procedure, research and development, and employee supervision.

After completing the training, I was assigned a group of students to assist them in developing a business plan for a hypothetical business and then implementing all phases of the plan. This was not only an exciting opportunity for me to share the free enterprise system with young people but also, for them to see it in action. They developed an idea for a business and took it through design, production, sales, and bookkeeping. Gail joined me in working with them on their business and implementation plans.

Georgia Power encouraged community participation by employees. I joined the East Columbus Lions Club, one of three Lions Clubs located in Columbus. This was my first involvement with a civic organization. As it turned out, my pastor, Billy Southerland, was also a member of the club. Shortly after joining, I was elected a director. I enjoyed my time in the organization and was a member for two years before my promotion and relocation to another city.

I also joined the Columbus Toastmasters Club, which met in downtown Columbus. I really appreciated how much it helped improve my public speaking skills.

From February 9 to February 11, 1973, a huge snowstorm hit southern Alabama and extended northeast into middle Georgia, continuing to north Georgia. It was one of the greatest snowstorms in the history of the southeastern United States. In Columbus, we received about eighteen inches of snow.

The storm shut down the city and surrounding areas. I was called out to work, along with many other employees. We were assigned four-wheel-drive vehicles. One of my jobs was to pick up electrical linemen at their homes and take them to the Georgia Power operating headquarters so that they could start repairing the downed power lines. The snow was so deep that it was hard to determine where the roads might be. I had never experienced snow like this. It took quite a while to get the linemen to their trucks and equipment. Power was out at our apartment, and Gail and our son, Chris, who was just over a year old, were home alone. Fortunately, there was a grocery store nearby, and Gail was able to walk to it to get milk and other essentials. It was my first experience dealing with such significant snowfall and so many electrical outages. It would become one of several storms that I worked during my career.

Gail and Chris in the 18 inches of snow

Southeastern Snowstorm in Columbus, GA

In March 1973, we swapped our 1970 Volkswagen for a family car. It was a light-green 1973 Grand Torino Ford station wagon from Barrington Ford in Columbus. We paid $4,134.32 for our new wheels. We had only had it about a week when we made a trip from Columbus to Tifton to visit Gail's parents. Sunday afternoon, we were on our way home, traveling on Georgia Highway 82 just entering Sylvester, when I heard a loud popping noise. Fortunately, there was a Texaco station just ahead as this happened. I pulled into the station and onto the car lift. The attendant looked underneath and gave me the bad news. Something had come loose inside the transmission and had busted through the case of the transmission leaving a quarter-size hole. All the transmission oil had leaked out. Gail and I and fifteen-month-old Chris were stranded.

I called Barrington Ford in Columbus, and they sent a wrecker to get the car and us. The three of us rode in the wrecker back to Columbus. Of course, Barrington paid for the tow and provided us with a loaner car until our vehicle could be repaired.

In April 1973, we decided to buy a house. We were tired of living in an apartment, and we needed more space for our new son. We found an older home in Columbus, a few miles from our apartment. The house at 3602 15th Avenue needed some work, which Gail and I decided to tackle. We pulled up the carpet and sanded the hardwood floors and repainted most of the inside of the home. I had a new electric heat pump and a 200-amp main electrical service installed. The home was a ranch with a full, unfinished basement. This was a charming home and was just perfect for us.

It took about a month to complete the renovations so that we could move in. Gail would work during the day at the new home, and I would work on it in the evenings after my Georgia Power workday concluded.

We had been living in our new home for about one month when I was offered a promotion. My new job would be as a senior residential marketing engineer, based at the Georgia Power Waycross District office. We agreed I should accept the promotion, and we put our home on the market.

14

Waycross, Georgia – It's a Girl

We moved from Columbus to Waycross in early June 1973, for me to start my next position as a senior residential marketing engineer.

GEORGIA POWER COMPANY

RODNEY E. MOORE
DISTRICT MANAGER

ADDRESS MAIL T:
P. O. BOX 940
WAYCROSS, GA. 3!

WAYCROSS, GEORGIA

June 13, 1973

Division Vice President
Division Manager
Division Department Heads
District Managers
Local Managers

Effective June 23, 1973 Mr. J. L. Hill, Residential Sales Engineer in Columbus, is promoted to Senior Residential Sales Engineer in Waycross.

"Jimmy" is well qualified for the responsibilities of his new position and I know that he will receive your usual help and cooperation.

Sincerely,

R. E. Moore

R. E. MOORE

cc: General Office Sales Department Heads
Vice Presidents in charge of Divisions
Division Managers
Residential Sales Representatives

We looked for a home in Waycross but could not find one. We had to rent for a while and found an apartment at John Kopp Apartments on Darling Avenue, just down the road from the Ware Memorial Hospital. It was a two-story with two bedrooms and one and a half baths. Georgia

Power arranged for a moving company to handle transporting our household items. I was needed immediately in Waycross, so I reported to work before the move. Gail, with seventeen-month-old Chris to look after, handled the moving process in Columbus while I was working in Waycross. I learned a valuable lesson and would never ever leave that responsibility on her shoulders again. However, she did a magnificent job in making the move happen and on time.

Our home in Columbus did not sell immediately. We were making payments both on the Columbus home and on our apartment in Waycross for months. These payments were creating a financial crisis for us. Especially troublesome was that we had a contract on the Columbus home within a matter of days, but for some reason, the buyers' loan approval was not moving forward. I called the realtor to express my concern and found out that a survey of the property had revealed that our driveway was partially on our neighbor's property. A strip of concrete about twenty feet long and a maximum of six inches wide was the problem. I offered to go to Columbus and remove the strip if that was what it took to close the loan. My realtor asked if I could give her a few more days to resolve the situation. I agreed. The purchase was being financed with a Veteran Administration (VA) loan. My realtor finally got the VA to approve the loan with the variance noted, since the driveway had been there for over thirty years. The loan finally closed on August 17, 1974. This made our life a lot easier and allowed us finally to shop for a new home.

We spent every spare moment looking unsuccessfully for the right home. After a few months, we noticed that the land across the street from our apartment was being cleared for a home site. The house was going to be a three-bedroom, two-bath, with a carport and on a one-half-acre lot. It was perfect for us, and we made an offer and it was accepted. We were able to choose colors, flooring, and appliances. We bought the home at 1302 Darling Avenue, Waycross, Georgia for $24,500.

The home was built on a concrete foundation, and the attached carport included a laundry room where the main electrical box was located.

Concerned that the home was not built to the maximum energy efficiency that I wanted, I bought additional blown cellulose fiber to install in the attic. The day that I put in the attic insulation, it was very hot. I began to feel drained and weak and started crawling out of the attic on my hands and knees. I reached the opening for the pull-down-stairs and

1302 Darling Avenue – Our new home

clambered headfirst down the stairs into the carport. I was exhausted and overheated.

After resting, I finished the insulation job later that day. I brought the insulation level in the attic up to an R-30 value for maximum efficiency of cooling and heating the home. I added storm windows over the regular windows, creating a double-pane effect, again for maximum efficiency for heating and cooling. A heat pump had been installed as the home was built and was very efficient. I wrapped the electric water heater with an extra blanket of insulation and installed a timer on the water heater. We created a very energy-efficient home with these additions.

In the Georgia Power Waycross District office, my immediate supervisor was district manager Rodney Moore. I replaced G. A. Nasworthy, who was promoted to local manager of the Jesup office. In my new position, I supervised a staff of two. Harley Morgan was a residential sales representative located in the Jesup, Georgia, local office. Dixie Kieffer, located in the Waycross office, also reported to me; she was a home economist. The only other person in sales was Ralph Brown, a fellow agricultural engineer from the University of Georgia.

In addition to those mentioned above, some of the other people that I worked with were: Marceil Wildes, Addie McMillian, Thelma Hingson, Doris Peterson, Theresa Tanner, Lucy Thigpen, Jack Woodard, J. D. Nix, Carol Lee, Billy Hughes, Billy Carver, Don Caldwell, Bull McClung, Seabron Craven, Buddy Blitch, Stan Meeks, Zack Hancock, Emory Moody, Harold Dixon, Bob Padgett, Ed Brock, Harold Fasnacht, Buddy Martin, R. C. Bell, Gene Pritchard, James Griffin, Pearlie Dorminey, Kenny Parker, Ned Nichols, Ronald Smith, Kemp Dorsett, Jerry DeWeese, Larry Crosby, Don Taylor, and many others.

The Waycross District included the cities of Waycross, Alma, Blackshear, Jesup, Folkston, Homerville, Pearson, and other small towns in those areas. This was a large district and required a lot of travel to meet the needs of our customers. My job duties were similar to my previous job, except for supervising two employees.

After we settled into our new home, we got to know Buddy and Linda Blitch. Buddy was in the Appliance Repair Department at Georgia Power. The Blitches and their two children lived next door to us. Their children were about the same ages as ours and loved to play together. We both had fences around our backyards, and we cut a gate between the properties so that the kids could go back and forth.

Buddy and Linda grew up in Tifton, Georgia, just as Gail did. We had a lot in common with them and spent time together playing card games and dining together occasionally. We even went camping together.

Buddy saved me one Sunday afternoon when my Georgia Power vehicle broke down on Interstate 16 as I was traveling to Atlanta for a week-long training meeting. I had left home right after church and was headed toward Atlanta. Unbeknownst to me, Buddy had a week-long training in Atlanta the same week. I had left a few minutes before him. I got onto I-16 at Dublin, traveling west toward Macon, and had gone about nine miles when, all of a sudden, the engine made a loud noise and died. I pulled over to the side of the interstate just before Exit 42. I tried to restart the engine; it would turn over but not start. The awful feeling of being stranded came over me. On a Sunday afternoon, very few places were open. I did have my CB radio with me, and I placed a shout out to see if a state patrol officer might be close by. All I got was strange voices that asked me where I was located. I was not sure that I wanted to identify my location to a stranger. This was in 1980, before we had access to cell phones. Then a car stopped behind me. I got out of my vehicle, and there was Buddy Blitch. He was in a Georgia Power car and offered to take me on to Atlanta. I called the emergency number of the local Ford dealership in Dublin and arranged for them to pick up my vehicle and transport it temporarily to their dealership. Buddy saved my life that day. We had an enjoyable trip to Atlanta. He dropped me off at my hotel.

The next day, Georgia Power had the car towed to Valdosta, which was our division headquarters. Our mechanics determined the engine had blown up and would have to be completely rebuilt. I returned from Atlanta in a borrowed Georgia Power car, and it took three months before my car was repaired and returned to me.

Georgia Power was promoting energy efficiency in new-home construction through a new program called Good Cents. The program required that a home be built to certain minimum standards of energy efficiency. Our job was to promote the program and inspect the homes as they were built, to make sure they were energy efficient. We took pride in our work and wanted to be sure the buyer of the home would get the value of reduced power bills. We also worked with existing homeowners to assist them in getting efficient HVAC systems and other energy-saving technologies.

Another of my job responsibilities was helping customers who were experiencing high electric bills. This was not always a fun job, because the customer was usually very unhappy when he or she received a higher electric bill than they thought it should be. However, I always tried to be very thorough in my approach to dealing with these complaints.

I worked with several HVAC contractors in the Waycross area, including Billy Day Heating and Air Conditioning Company, Conley Sheet Metal Works Inc., Jim Brown Heating and Air Conditioning, and others.

Duane Dotson, G. A. Nasworthy, Jimmy Hill, District Manager Rodney Moore and Georgia Power President Robert Scherer
* Photo Courtesy of Georgia Power Company

I would evaluate weather patterns because either colder or hotter weather could greatly impact the customer's bill. Data were available to analyze weather changes using a term called "degree days." The increase or decrease in degree days can impact heating and cooling costs. I asked a lot of questions of the customer to determine if something out of the ordinary had happened during the billing period. I would always conduct a meter accuracy check, based on evaluating a known electrical appliance in the home. In my career, I only found one meter to be incorrect, and it was slow. The electric meter is extremely accurate, like a fine watch.

A multiplicity of things can cause higher power bills. It might be additional people staying at the home during the billing period, which creates more energy use for appliances such as ovens, water heating, clothes drying, etc. I have also found water heater pipes that were leaking without the customer being aware of the leak. One customer I investigated had a leaking hot water line inside the concrete slab floor. The way I discovered it was that the customer's dog always lay down at a certain spot on the floor because it was warm.

One of the most interesting complaints that I worked with was with a sweet lady in her eighties. I received her complaint from Marceil Wildes, who worked at our office. I called the lady and set up an appointment. I arrived at Janice's (not her real name) home midafternoon on a cool September day. She complained that her next-door neighbor was stealing her electricity. Her evidence was that every time the neighbor turned on her washing machine, Janice's refrigerator turned off. Janice had a spiral notebook filled with dates and times the refrigerator had cut off when the neighbor's washing machine came on. I went outside and followed the power lines from the pole transformers to each house to make sure that there was no connection between them. The two homes were surrounded by pecan trees, and the nuts were ripe. She watched me the entire time during my investigation.

I asked her if there were other issues regarding her power. She said, "Yes, those switches keep clicking on and off." I asked her to show me where this was occurring. She took me to the hall in the center of the home. She pointed up to the ceiling and said, "They are right up there."

I looked and did not see anything but a plasterboard ceiling. Trying to get further clarification, I asked her, "What color are the switches?"

"Oh, you can't see them," she said. I sure felt a whole lot better about Janice at that point.

I noticed a pull-down stairway to the attic and asked her if I could go up and take a look. In the attic, I found the equivalent of about a gallon bucket of pecans. Most of the nuts were cracked, and the meat was missing.

I had my suspicions and left the attic and went outside again. At the back of the home, I saw it. The vent at the end of the gable roof had a hole about the right size for a squirrel to enter. The squirrels were stealing the pecans and bringing them into Janice's attic for eating and for storing for the winter. I found out that Janice was renting the home, and so I suggested she call her landlord and tell him about the squirrels and the entrance point. She called me the next day to tell me the landlord had gotten rid of the squirrels and had closed up their entrance. As far as the washing machine and the refrigerator—who knows? I do know she had a refrigerator that cut off and on frequently. The final result was that Janice was happy.

Not all of my experiences with customers were that easy to solve. One customer complained that he did not want our meter reader on his property because it was "tearing up" his grass when the reader walked across the yard to check his meter. I explained that our meter readers only came once a month, and I was not clear how that could destroy his grass. In the spirit of making the customer happy, I asked our meter reader if he could read the meter without going onto the property. He said that some meters were not very accessible, and he read them with binoculars. He would try that with this customer. It was determined that the meter reader could get the reading from the street since this customer was on a corner lot.

The next month, I received a call from the customer telling me that the meter reader was reading the meter from the street and was guessing his power usage. I explained what we were doing, and he was unhappy again. He said that the meter reader could not possibly read the meter from the street. I explained how the dials on the meter work. The dials (either four or five dials) rotated clockwise and counterclockwise, and the meter reader could look at the position of the dial and know exactly what the reading was. The meter reader did not have to see the number on the dial to read the meter, only the position of the dial. The customer was still unhappy, even though I pointed out that we were not on his grass and were reading his meter accurately. You can't always satisfy everyone.

A complaint came to my desk about a customer who claimed that he was hardly using any electricity, yet his bill was high. I went to investigate.

I found a large home with two big air conditioning units, a washer, dryer, two refrigerators, and a freezer. There were four bathrooms, and several people lived in the house. By my estimation, the power bill was extremely low instead of high. I asked our meter installer to meet me at the home to check the meter for accuracy. We determined quickly that the meter was accurate, but the electricity usage was extremely low. We went into the attic and discovered the reason. I can't tell you specific facts, because other people might try it. I can say that it was extremely dangerous and could have burned down the home. I billed the customer for the revenue that Georgia Power had lost due to his criminal act. He was turned over to the proper authorities. The takeaway from this experience: don't steal electricity!

Thelma Hingston, who worked in our office, referred Mr. Johnson (not his real name) to me. She said that he always complained about his power bill at the changing of each season. I called Mr. Johnson and made an appointment. He met me at the front door and invited me in. His home was very nicely decorated, and I commented on how beautiful it was. He took me on a tour of the home. The most interesting room was his sunporch. The table and four chairs attached to the ceiling caught my attention. I first thought it was a mirror on the ceiling, because the same table and chairs were right in front of me, on the floor. It was not a mirror. I asked him about it, and he said it was a conversation starter. It certainly was for me!

I did my usual routine of checking the reading on the meter to make sure we had read it correctly, looking at electrical appliances, and asking many questions. I found nothing unusual in my investigation. He continued to tell me about his house and each unique feature. I listened intently. After about thirty minutes, he thanked me for coming and welcomed me to Waycross, and I left. I had many more visits with him in the seven years that I worked there. I concluded that just visiting with him and admiring his unique home was all he wanted.

A call came to me from a customer—we will call him Mr. Smith—who wanted an energy conservation audit. This required me to visit the home and recommend energy conservation technologies that would save the homeowner on his power bill. These recommendations could include such things as more attic insulation, the addition of storm windows, replacing the HVAC system, insulating the water heater, caulking, and other measures. Mr. Smith also asked me to recommend what size a new HVAC system should be. He was currently using window air conditioning and gas space heaters. And he was interested in our total electric rate for homes where all appliances were electric.

I asked him for a convenient time that I might go to conduct the audit. He said that he worked all the time and wanted me to do the audit without him present, that he would leave the back door unlocked for me. I explained that I preferred to have someone home when I conducted an audit so that I could discuss my findings. That would not be possible, he said, and he asked that I please go and do the audit. I agreed, reluctantly and against my better judgment.

As was my usual practice, I looked up his account in our billing system. I printed the account information for his address and went to the home on the appointed day and time. The back door was unlocked, as I had expected, and I went in and started my audit. As I was measuring a window in the dining room, a door opened behind me, and a man's voice said, "What are you doing in my house?" I heard him chamber a round in his shotgun.

Terrified, I quickly explained what I was doing and that the homeowner, Mr. Smith, had asked me to come and do the audit.

"This is my house, and I don't know a Mr. Smith," said the man with the shotgun.

I offered to show him the paperwork with Mr. Smith's name and address. I also showed him my Georgia Power ID. He lowered the gun, and we talked. I apologized for the error and left.

As I went, I checked the meter number; it was not the meter number for his home. When I got back to the office, I determined that I had been at the right street address, but in the wrong town. I was in Blackshear and should have been in Waycross. The street names were the same. I normally checked the meter number to make sure that I was at the correct address, but I had overlooked it that day. I never made that mistake again. I called the gun-toting homeowner and explained to him what had happened. He still was not too happy, and I can't blame him.

We had just received a new company car in our sales department. It was a 1979 Ford LTD II four-door. It was the first air-conditioned vehicle in our fleet. I had the oldest assigned car, and the new car should therefore have been mine. However, there were four of us in sales, and the other three thought that the car should be rotated between us, a week at a time, so that everyone would have air conditioning at least one week a month. Of course, I disagreed, but District Manager Moore agreed with them. At this time, we all had to wear a coat and tie to work, even on the hottest summer days.

On a hot July day, it was my turn to have the air-conditioned new car. I went to visit a homeowner in north Waycross. It was a routine call, and I handled it quickly. I returned to the car and prepared to leave. As I turned the ignition key, there was a loud explosion. It came from under the hood and blew the hood open. I have to be honest: my first thought was that a bomb had been planted in my car. After a momentary delay to collect my thoughts, I got out of the car and lifted the hood. By then the homeowner had joined me. We both said in unison, "The battery blew up." Sure enough, the battery had blown apart. I had heard of that but had never experienced it. I called the office to send a wrecker to get me and the car.

A call came in from a customer regarding whether her electrical panel would handle adding a window air conditioner to her home. An appointment was set up for the next day. I arrived early and went around to the back of the home, where the electric service drop attached to the house. It was clear that she had a very small electrical service that provided only 120 volts. Most homes have a 240-volt service.

The customer saw me in the back yard and invited me to come in, onto the back porch, where her electrical panel was located. I examined the panel and determined that she could not add any more electrical load to the existing panel. She looked very disappointed, then said, "Are you sure there isn't something that you can do for me today?" As she spoke, she reached and touched my face in a sexy sort of way. It caught me completely by surprise. I was shocked and taken back, and though I am sure that I said something, I cannot recall what it was. At that moment, the doorbell rang. "Oh, it's the painter," she said. I quickly excused myself and left by way of the screen door on the back porch.

You never know what you might encounter in a customer home. That is all I am going to say about that.

For many years, Georgia Power Company promoted the electric heat pump as a great, energy-saving technology for heating and cooling homes. The energy savings could be further enhanced with proper sizing, installation, and service. The company offered a service plan on these heat pumps when installed per Georgia Power recommendations. The service plan was for ten years, with a low monthly fee.

I was responsible for managing these plans and the necessary service needs in the Waycross district. Due to some misunderstandings in the plan, I wrote a booklet entitled *Heat Pump Service Contract Guidelines*. This booklet was circulated among my staff, all HVAC dealers associated with the program, and our appliance service personnel. Up to that point, the installing dealers had maintained and serviced the heat pumps that they had installed. As we neared the end of the contract period, we transferred the remaining contract work to our service personnel.

I considered the publication of the *Heat Pump Service Contract Guidelines* just a routine part of my job. My superiors, however, were impressed with my work, and I received several commendations. I guess this was a precursor to my future role with heat pumps, which I describe later in this book.

Just before Christmas 1975, Gail learned that she was pregnant. Our daughter, Miranda, was born on July 15, 1976, at Waycross Memorial Hospital. She weighed in at eight pounds, four ounces, and was twenty and a half inches long. Chris, her four-year-old brother, was excited about getting a new sibling and was so happy that it was a girl. He instantly appointed himself her protector.

When Chris was born in Columbus, fathers were not allowed in the delivery room. However, this time I got to take natural childbirth classes and be involved in every aspect of the pregnancy and Miranda's birth. I was also allowed in the delivery room. It was amazing.

With some experience under our belts raising Chris, we could handle the rigors of caring for and nurturing the little girl we named Miranda Faith Hill.

Unbeknownst to me, Mr. Olin Ginn, manager of Agricultural Affairs at the Georgia Power corporate office in Atlanta, talked to the Valdosta Division vice president, Lamar Wansley, about my being considered for a new job in the Agricultural Affairs Department in Atlanta. Shortly thereafter, I got a letter from Mr. Ginn, requesting that I meet him for an interview for the position.

I accepted the interview and met with Mr. Ginn in Perry, Georgia. Several things about the details of the job concerned me. I was told that I would have to live in a certain part of Atlanta and would not have a company vehicle as I currently had. The job rating would provide me a slight pay increase. However, I would have to move and relocate my family to Atlanta. Gail and I prayed about it and decided to decline the job if it was offered. The offer came in the form of "If we were to offer you this job, would you accept?" I was expecting an offer, not an "If" offer. This gave me further cause for concern, and so I declined.

I was shocked to learn later that I was expected to accept the job and feel lucky that I had got it. I heard from Vice President Wansley, who wanted to know why I had turned it down. So, too, did the divisional sales manager. I learned later that Mr. Ginn had assumed that I would jump at the chance to come to work for him and move to Atlanta. I did get a letter from Mr. Ginn later, thanking me for considering the job and wishing me well in my future endeavors at Georgia Power.

I learned a valuable lesson from this experience, which was that my gut feeling was giving me the necessary feedback that I needed. It has continued to do so throughout my working life. I had no way of knowing that I would eventually assume Mr. Ginn's position, later in my career.

During my time in Waycross, my position, and my interest in being more engaged and taking on more responsibility, led to involvement in many interesting projects.

I was approached by the building trades instructor at the Waycross-Ware County Area Technical School about serving on their advisory board. The instructor felt that my background in engineering and my practical experience in energy efficiency and HVAC would be valuable assets to the building trades curriculum. In addition to serving on the advisory board, I lectured to the classes periodically. I enjoyed the opportunity to participate in this activity.

District Manager Moore asked me to serve as the Georgia Power United Way chairman for the Waycross District. I helped organize an effort to secure voluntary donations from employees to be used to support non-profit organizations in the district. I held this position for several years.

I was approached by County Extension Director Bob Boland to appear on his television show in Jacksonville, Florida. WJXT TV Channel 4 carried The *Farm and Home Show.* I joined Bob on his Saturday show at 6:00 a.m., discussing home insulation while sitting in a rocking chair on the front porch. This was the first time that I had appeared on a television program since serving as a state FFA officer in the mid-1960s.

I was elected to serve as a board member of the Georgia Power Valdosta Federal Credit Union, located at the division headquarters in Valdosta. Ms. Joe Drawdy was the credit union manager. As a board member, I helped set policies and procedures for the credit union as it loaned money to Valdosta Division employees. This was great experience learning about banking and credit unions.

Jimmy as guest instructor at Waycross-Ware County Technical School

For many years, Georgia Power sold electrical appliances to customers. The company provided service for those appliances as well. In the late 1970s, Georgia Power closed out its appliance sales business; however, we continued to be responsible for the servicing of those appliances we had sold. District Manager Moore appointed me to handle the closeout of GPC appliance service contracts, which involved coordinating with local appliance service dealers. I worked with our local Georgia Power managers in securing appliance service agreements for our customers in each local office.

My department provided various energy efficiency studies for projects to evaluate their energy needs and to find the appropriate technologies to address those needs. One example was a study done in Alma, Georgia, entitled "The Energy Efficiency Study of New Housing Projects in Alma, Georgia." We received a letter of commendation for our work with the mayor and his staff.

I made many energy conservation presentations during my time in Waycross. Just a few examples were: a talk at Okefenokee Heritage Center; a Public Energy Workshop in Folkston; a Jesup Kiwanis Club presentation on Three Mile Island Nuclear Plant versus Georgia Power's Plant Hatch; and a presentation to the Wayne County Young Farmers organization on technologies to reduce home energy consumption.

An issue regarding providing electricity to new customers in Georgia in non-assigned areas arose. Several disputes developed, particularly between Georgia Power and the Electric Membership Cooperatives (EMCs) in Georgia. No amicable solution was forthcoming between the utilities, so the General Assembly of Georgia intervened. The Assembly passed a bill in 1973, which set up a procedure regarding the assignment of territory for electric utilities in Georgia. The act required each utility to negotiate with its bordering electric utilities and to define the territorial rights between them.

I was appointed by District Manager Moore to serve on the Waycross District negotiating team. On the team were personnel from our operating and marketing departments and the overall state coordinator from the corporate office. We met with each of our adjacent utilities and negotiated our territories. The negotiation involved territory maps with current utility lines indicated. The two issues we addressed were areas where power lines overlapped and areas with no current power lines, but which had the potential for future growth. We negotiated down to street level and individual structure level. In some places, we served the same street, with Georgia Power serving one side of the street and the EMC serving the other side.

The negotiations were intense, with each side giving and taking territories, but were conducted respectfully. It was an amazing experience to see negotiations leading to decisions that would impact the utilities for the foreseeable future and maybe forever.

Valdosta Division Residential Marketing Team
* Photo Courtesy of Georgia Power Company

Waycross District was under the supervision of the Valdosta Division of Georgia Power, and I reported to I. L. Ridley Jr., the division residential sales supervisor. Mr. Ridley would travel the sixty-two miles from Valdosta to Waycross a couple of times a month to check on our progress and to see how he could help us. He was also a source of answers to issues that would arise in our day-to-day activities. I provided him with weekly updates on our progress and goals. I also indirectly reported to Mr. Ridley's boss, division sales manager Jack Widener Jr., and following Jack was Merrill Dye. I interfaced with other staff across the division, and they included Myrnith Noble, Vicky Biles, Roy Fennell, Luther Joiner, James Hightower, Bob Brewster, Doodle Thomoson, Billy Maxwell, Mike Frassrand, Jay Studstill, Frank O'Quinn, Terry Whigham, Rhett Ward, David Powell, Chris McRae, Horace Hudgins, Larry Stout, Everette Griner, Alan Moore, Clarence Ryan, Cathey Kite King, Bertie Miles, Susan Moss, Ann McDonald, Charlie Lyons, Jack Perry, Garland Anderson, Terry Whigham, and many others.

Gail served two terms as president of the Waycross Chapter, Women of Georgia Power. The Women of Georgia Power's mission was to assist non-profit organizations that served the Waycross area, such as the American Cancer Society. They conducted fundraisers to help these organizations to be more effective in their outreach efforts.

During the spring and summer of 1974, Georgia Power was in negotiations with the International Brotherhood of Electrical Workers (IBEW) union, which represented primarily construction and line-crew employees. In preparation for a possible union strike, Georgia Power trained non-union employees from marketing, accounting, and other areas of the business, who would be called on to keep the power on during a strike. I was assigned to attend a two-week course at the Valdosta, Georgia, power-line training facility. We were taught how to safely operate various pieces of equipment, such as line trucks, bucket trucks, equipment for installing underground lines, and various hand tools.

On July 18, 1974, as part of the training, my crew was assigned to work with a Hi-Ranger bucket truck. We had already done some training with this truck on previous days. The other crew members were: D. E. Miller, safety engineer; C. A. Middlebrooks, commercial sales represent-tative; J. S. Freeman, associate engineer; R. A. Thomas, distribution engineer; and W. G. Maxwell Jr., residential sales engineer.

At approximately 4:15 p.m., Maxwell entered the basket and proceeded to elevate and rotate it up to the top of the power pole next to the truck. Mr. Maxwell elevated the basket to the maximum or near-maximum elevation. At this point, our crew heard a cracking noise. We looked up and saw the aerial basket and boom falling. The basket hit the ground, and Mr. Maxwell was thrown out of the basket; he was still attached to his safety lanyard.

All of our team rushed to his side, and first aid was started while 911 was called. An ambulance arrived, and after Mr. Maxwell was secured on the gurney, the ambulance transported him to the South Georgia Medical Center in Valdosta. He was pronounced dead at 5:15 p.m.

This was a devastating blow to our team, to Georgia Power, and, more importantly, to Mr. Maxwell's family. He was thirty-three years of age and married with three children.

It was determined that the truck had been through numerous safety checks and found to be safe. After an exhaustive investigation, equipment failure was found to be the cause of the accident.

I miss my friend Billy Maxwell and still vividly remember that day, even after forty-six years. His accident taught me to live every day to the fullest because you don't know when it might be your last day on this earth.

Jimmy practicing use of the bucket truck
* Photo Courtesy of Georgia Power Company

Photo Courtesy of Georgia Power Company

Gail and I took our first camping trip during a summer break, while I was attending the University of Georgia. We traveled in our Volkswagen Beetle, which had no air conditioning. We borrowed my dad's tent and traveled to St. Augustine, Florida, and camped at Anastasia State Park, which is right on the Atlantic Ocean. We slept on blankets on the tent floor. To cook food, which consisted mainly of egg and cheese sandwiches, we had borrowed my dad's old soldering pot (blow torch), which he used to heat soldering irons. It was extremely hot, sunny, and miserable on the beach. Nevertheless, we had a great time on that first camping trip, and it was the inspiration, I am sure, for our becoming such keen campers in the years that followed.

While we lived in Columbus, we took a couple of camping trips to the Davis Lake Campground, near Callaway Gardens. We eventually bought a new tent. These were the first camping trips with our son, Chris.

Pop-up camper at Fernandina Beach 1973

When we moved to Waycross, our camping fever was at a high pitch. We had visited Fort Clinch State Park in Fernandina Beach, Florida, and fallen in love with the camping area. I saw an ad in the Waycross newspaper for a small popup camper that required whoever bought it to take up the payments and it would be theirs. Only a few payments remained, so we bought it. It was a homemade camper but was well-designed and solidly built. We used it for a couple of years and outgrew it with the addition of our daughter to the family.

We then sold the popup, and I bought a nineteen-foot camper made by Volunteer. It needed some repairs, such as a new roof and minor touchups. Gail and I were able to replace the roof and get the camper in good shape. We used it for several years, and it moved with us on to my next Georgia Power assignment.

To be able to pull the Volunteer camper, we traded in our Grand Torino Ford station wagon for a 1978 Grand Marquis Mercury car with a 460-cubic-inch engine. The Mercury would be able to pull any size camper we would get in the future.

Grand Marquis Mercury   *19-foot Volunteer travel trailer at Fernandina Beach*

We loved Fort Clinch State Park and spent up to forty days a year there. All of my vacation days, as well as some weekends, were spent at Fort Clinch. In addition to surf fishing, one of our memorable camping activities was clamming on a nearby river. Camping was a great opportunity for me to get away and spend quality time with my family.

We invited Gail's parents to camp with us at Fort Clinch. They bought a slide-in truck camper and joined us. They had such a great time that they invested in a fifth-wheel camper and camped frequently at Fort Clinch, as well as traveling across the country camping.

My parents were interested in camping as well. They borrowed a friend's motor home and joined us one weekend. They had a blast and went camping with us several times after that.

I also bought a used pickup truck from Gail's dad. It was a 1964 Ford F-150 custom cab pickup, with two-tone colors of white and dark blue. I didn't particularly need a pickup, but he was selling it, and I wanted one. I also bought my Georgia Power car when it was retired out of the fleet. It was a 1970 Ford Falcon four-door sedan. It had no air conditioning but was valuable as a second vehicle for our family.

We joined Central Baptist Church (CBC) shortly after we arrived in Waycross and volunteered to help in any way that we could. We were asked to lead the Children's Church, which was held on Sunday mornings at the same time as the regular adult service. Gail and I enjoyed our time with the kids.

A need arose for someone to arrive early on Sunday mornings and turn on all of the HVAC equipment to have the church facilities either warmed up or cooled, depending on the season. I volunteered to take care of this responsibility. I was also in charge of making sure that the HVAC systems were maintained and repaired as needed.

Our pastor, William Young, had a five-day-a-week time slot on the local radio station called *The Sunlight Hour*. It was fifteen minutes of devotion, inspiration, and songs. Pastor Young was not always able to be at the radio station due to other commitments; he asked me if I would fill in, and I was happy to help.

Family photo at Easter 1977

This was my first time being on the radio for an extended period. Fifteen minutes seemed like a long time, but trying to fit in a devotional and a couple of songs was challenging, particularly since I had to watch the clock and the announcer, who had to work within a definite time frame. I helped out with *The Sunlight Hour* for around five years. I enjoyed my time ministering on the radio and heard from many people who said it was a great start to their day.

Reverend Larry Williams was the youth pastor, and Jerry Tyler led the music ministry at CBC. We appreciated their leadership in the church.

Gail was president of the Woman's Missionary Union (WMU) at CBC. The focus of WMU was on missions. She was also responsible for all of the girls' organizations. During that time, Gail also served as an officer in the Waycross Christian Women's Club.

In 1974, I served as vice chairman of membership of the Georgia section, American Society of Agricultural Engineers (ASAE).

The Toastmasters Club was very important to me while in Columbus. I knew that I needed to continue enhancing and strengthening my public speaking skills, so I got a few people together, and we started the first Toastmasters Club in Waycross and affiliated with Toastmasters International.

I also served on the board and as president of the Alice Street Elementary School PTO in 1979–80.

In September 1979, I received a letter from Bill Starrs, a residential services staff representative at the Georgia Power corporate office in Atlanta. He requested that I teach a course in his Residential Services Training Program on Georgia Power's "Rates, Rules, and Regulations." I received approval from District Manager Moore and accepted the invitation. I had taken the course but had never taught it.

The course objective was to familiarize attendees with the electric power rates, rules, and regulations that applied to our residential customers. I knew that it would be difficult to make the course interesting, so I tried making it livelier and more fun by throwing in anecdotes of real interactions with customers on rate issues.

After I taught the course, Mr. Starrs sent me a letter telling me that based on student feedback, I had made the class very interesting and educational. He said in the letter, "I knew you were a good instructor but did not know you were this good."

He provided the participants' comments, some of which are excerpted below:

—Excellent instructor and seemed to enjoy teaching and delivered his material in an organized, direct, and highly professional manner.

—Very good instructor, very thorough, the presentation was excellent, clarifies information so everyone can understand and doesn't rush through and a very pleasing personality.

—Good teacher shows that he sincerely wants everyone to understand his subject, very knowledgeable.

—I think he did a very good job; he was interesting and explained the rates step by step where it was hard not to learn.

—Good speaker, good knowledge of the subject, a boring subject made fairly interesting.

—He did an excellent job of teaching, he knew the material and could convey it to us with clarity, and Mr. Hill could answer all questions to my satisfaction. I enjoyed learning about rates, rules, and regulations.

I taught several other classes in my tenure at Georgia Power and enjoyed teaching. I think that if I had not chosen engineering as my career, I would have become a teacher.

I worked with Mr. Bob Williams in 1979, when he started to construct his home in Homerville, Georgia. I talked with him about Georgia Power's Good Cents home program and explained that we would help him build the most energy-efficient home on the market. Our work involved determining the best efficiency in insulation, thermal windows, HVAC system and appliances, and employing other measures, such as sealing air openings, to lower his monthly power bill.

After submitting all of the changes, I recommended a smaller HVAC system for his home. His builder was skeptical of my calculations. I assured Mr. Williams that Georgia Power would stand behind my calculations if the home was built to our standards.

Mr. Williams built the home as we specified and used Billy Day Heating and Air Conditioning Company from Waycross to install his high-efficiency heat pump system. After a few months of living in the new home, he was extremely happy with our recommendations. He was so pleased that he wrote a letter to Georgia Power president Robert Scherer.

In the letter, Mr. Williams explained in detail all of the energy efficiency recommendations that I had made. He shared with President Scherer about dealing with his builder's recommended HVAC dealer. That dealer had said that a particular high-efficiency heat pump was not available. Mr. Williams had called me, and I had found that seventeen units were available to meet his needs. I had put him in touch with Billy Day's HVAC company, and he was able to secure the unit and install it.

In his letter, he said, "Jimmy Hill has shown me that he is a professional, knowledgeable, and concerned individual who cares about the people he serves. I congratulate Georgia Power on having such an individual as Jimmy Hill to work with customers in the important area of energy conservation."

I received a commendation letter from President Scherer shortly after he received Mr. Williams's letter. I was extremely grateful for Mr. Williams having taken the trouble to write that letter and for the letter from President Scherer. They were career highs for me.

I have included a copy of both letters in the Appendix.

On June 23, 1981, I was selected to interview for a new position in the Georgia Power corporate office in Atlanta. Gail and I left our children with her parents and traveled to Atlanta for the interview. Mr. Jim Manley, manager of Energy Services, interviewed me for a position that would develop an HVAC dealer program and a heat pump marketing program. I was excited about the possibility of advancement but was hesitant about moving to the Atlanta area.

Shortly after the interview, Mr. Manley called me and offered me the position. We had several things that complicated the move. In 1981, interest rates on home loans were around 16 percent and we had an 8 percent mortgage on our home in Waycross. The move would put us further away from both sets of parents. It would also mean that our son, Chris, would have to change schools. It would mean more travel and time away from home in a new job. However, Gail and I thought about it, weighed the pros and cons, prayed about it, and finally decided that I should accept the offer. I called Jim Manley with my acceptance on June 25. My promotion was to field engineer in the Energy Services

Department, and my office would be in the corporate headquarters in Atlanta, on the twentieth floor of the building.

As I mentioned earlier, there was an outside possibility that the IBEW union workers might go on strike at the beginning of July 1981. And in fact, they did—on July 8. I had to postpone my move to Atlanta as I was needed in Waycross to help maintain power to current Georgia Power customers in the district and to serve new customers. My job was as a line-truck and equipment operator. The truck was used to install power poles, maintain power lines, and troubleshoot power outages.

We started work at midnight on July 8, 1981 and worked twelve-hour shifts each day. It was one of the hottest summers on record in South Georgia. I drank Gatorade by the gallon. It was hard work, but our training paid off. We were supervised by a line foreman who was a non-union member. He did a great job of keeping us safe. When we arrived at a site to work, our first responsibility was to review how we would accomplish the job with an emphasis on safety. We worked mostly during the day but occasionally at night if storms or car accidents caused power outages.

We worked for about ten days straight. Gail was getting concerned about finding a home in Atlanta so that we could move after the strike. I finally got approval for a day off for us to go house-hunting. Mr. Manley suggested looking in locations east of Atlanta. We viewed eighteen houses in one day and found the house we wanted to buy. It was located in Gwinnett County, on the outskirts of the city of Grayson.

We traveled back to Waycross, and I resumed line-truck work the next day. About a week later, the strike ended, and we made our final plans to move to Grayson, Georgia.

15

Grayson, Georgia – Corporate Headquarters in Atlanta

The moving company arrived on the morning of August 9, 1981. They loaded our belongings and departed at 5:00 p.m. We left our Waycross home at the same time and headed for Atlanta. Chris and I were in the Grand Marquis Mercury towing our nineteen-foot Volunteer camper, and Gail and Miranda followed us in the 1970 Ford Falcon.

That night, we stayed at a hotel in the Northlake area near Tucker, Georgia. The next morning it took about forty-five minutes to reach our Willow Trace home in Grayson. The movers unloaded and left at about 2:00 p.m. Gail and I had our hands full with unpacking and straightening up the new house.

1193 Willow Trace, Grayson, GA

Our kids were excited that we had bought a two-story home with a basement on a large lot. Each picked a bedroom, and fortunately, they did not pick the same one. The neighborhood had a lot of children who were similar ages to ours. Chris and Miranda spent their growing-up years in Grayson and attended Grayson Elementary School and Snellville Middle School. They both eventually graduated from South Gwinnett High School in Snellville, Georgia. They participated in all kinds of sports and school activities, as well as both being excellent students. The Gwinnett County schools were among the best in Georgia.

Gail was hired as City Clerk by the City of Grayson shortly after we moved there. She and one other part-time employee ran the daily operations of the city government. The city population at that time was about 464 residents. Gail stayed there for four years, then went to work for Gecor Industries in Grayson.

Hill Family Photo

As soon as I arrived in Atlanta, my new role at the corporate office kicked off in high gear. There were several events that I was scheduled to attend immediately, including a course in residential duct design on August 12–14 at the Southern Company corporate headquarters in Atlanta, and on August 16–17, a trip to Kansas City, Missouri, to tour an HVAC plant owned by Coleman Inc. and learn more about heat pump manufacturing.

I immediately started researching information for developing a heat pump marketing plan for Georgia Power. My position was a new one, and there were no guidelines or definitive instructions for me. This was my project to research, develop, secure management approval, and implement across the company.

My office was cubical #065 on the twentieth floor of 333 Piedmont Avenue NE in Atlanta. It was one cubical away from a window in a large, open office area. The building stood on the corner of Piedmont Avenue and Ralph McGill Boulevard NE. This was my first experience working in a large building with several amenities. We had a cafeteria and a parking garage, and in an adjoining annex were a barbershop, a florist, and a dry-cleaning establishment.

My work at the corporate office was both challenging and rewarding. I had the privilege of working with a number of great people in the Marketing and Sales Departments, including: Jim Manley, Bill Davidson, Susan Dyer, Buddy Cromer, Bantes Hodges, Dave Beavin, John Hood, Emma Henry, Jim Brown, Doug Jones, Terry Hodges, Bill Rainwater, Ken Beckworth, Jim Bolton, Carole Clarke, Jim Slaughter, Donna Camp, Jim Smith, Jerry Thomas, Jim Proffitt, Ron Purvis, Arthur Rose, Eddie Carswell, Frank Boyd, Nancy Chastain, Gary Johnson, Russ Demonbreun, David Kee, Dwayne Hassler, Linda Smith, Bill Starrs, Walter Lovett, Kathy Harber, Wayne Dahike, Milton Moore, Ed Fischler, Russ Thrift, David Kay, Pat Sims, Leonard Haynes, Bobby Ledford, Bob Jones, Jim Callahan, Lisa Olens, Jim Doggett, Frank Pucciano, Terry Garber, Gary Birdwell, Rhett Ward, Mike Frassrand, Wendell Carter, Kevin Fletcher, David Bald, Lyman Shivers, Jan Hill, Bruce Holcombe,

Wilber Blackmon, Charles Plunkett, Malcolm Stewart, Carl Shaw, Mark Weaver, Greg Smith, John Casbarro, Ed Ney, Carler Moss, Bobby Dawkins, Lowry Gillespie, Bob Williamson, Debbie Dahlberg, Ronnie Richardson, Bill Craig, Bill Moncrief, and others.

In an attempt to hold down my cost of traveling to and from work, I joined a private carpool. My partners were all Georgia Power employees and included David Norris, Sharon Jones, and Ken Gary. We all lived east of Atlanta and in the general area of Grayson. With the four of us participating, we each drove a week at a time in our personal vehicles. David, Sharon, and Ken were great people to carpool with, and we had many interesting discussions, primarily about Georgia Power. I wish that I could share some of them, but what happens in the carpool stays in the carpool. Carpooling worked for about a year for me, and then I had to drop out due to extensive work-related travel. During the latter part of my time in Residential Marketing, I traveled using a vehicle from our company carpool. After I became a manager, I was assigned a company vehicle.

During this time, I represented Georgia Power on the Georgia Electrification Council. This group had members from all the power suppliers in Georgia, including Georgia Power, Oglethorpe Power Corporation, forty-two Electric Membership Corporations, and Georgia cities that provided electric power to their citizens. The council addressed matters of mutual interest around training and other electrical issues. I served as vice chairman for two terms. I also taught classes for the council on the National Electrical Code as well as HVAC-specific courses on topics such as Manual J Load Calculation and Manual D Duct Design.

I volunteered to have an experimental heat pump system installed in my home for research purposes. Our existing gas furnace and air conditioning unit was removed. The experimental heat pump included a two-stage compressor. The manufacturer was researching whether this compressor would work adequately to heat and cool a home as well as use less energy in the process. To my knowledge, this was the first two-stage heat pump system ever placed in a home environment with a typical family of two adults and two children.

The system had dozens of points where data was recorded as it operated. A computer was installed in my basement to collect the measurements from the monitoring points every thirty seconds, twenty-four hours a day, seven days a week, 365 days a year.

The system worked great, and the data led the manufacturer to proceed with the mass production of these units. The units are available now and are made by several HVAC manufacturers.

Since Gail and I had started camping back in the seventies, we had become passionate campers. We love the outdoors, and there is nothing better than waking up in the fresh air and smelling breakfast cooking on a campfire. We bought a new camper while we lived in Grayson. It was a thirty-foot pull-type camper with a regular bed, large bathroom, three bunk beds, and a large kitchen and dining and den area. We traded in our nineteen-foot Volunteer camper for the larger one to meet the needs of our family of four, and for guests that the kids invited along. We usually had at least one additional child on our camping trips.

We occasionally camped with friends. I remember one trip that we made to Tallulah Gorge Park, which was then owned and maintained by Georgia Power. It is now owned by the state and is known as the Tallulah Gorge State Park. This weekend trip was with Georgia Power employees, including my supervisor, Buddy Cromer, and his wife Cindy, also an employee of Georgia Power. Bantes and Terry Hodges were on the trip as well. Bantes was Buddy's administrative assistant, also assisting me, and Terry worked in the Commercial Marketing Department down the hall from us. It was our first time camping together, and what a great time we had. The food and fellowship were outstanding.

I will always remember those cool mornings with coffee brewing and the smell of bacon and eggs wafting through the campground. Sitting together around a picnic table and sharing stories as we ate was awesome. It does not get much better than that.

We started camping at Yonah Mountain Campground and Resort between Cleveland and Helen, Georgia. We ultimately bought a membership and camped there quite frequently. Later on, we bought a private lot to the rear of the resort. This allowed us to leave our camper parked on the site and not to have to pull it back and forth to our home in Grayson. We sold the site, and our camper, a few years later, when we moved to Tomahawk Mountain.

Our private camping getaway in White County, GA

A major tornado hit our home, subdivision, and the surrounding area at approximately three o'clock in the morning on June 28, 1994. We sustained damage to our home including to the roof, which ultimately required replacement of all of its shingles. The wind and debris destroyed the paint on the home, requiring it to be repainted. The deck was knocked askew from the rear of the home and had to be reattached. A large limb hit the front brick doorsteps, and they had to be replaced. Nearly four acres of trees were leveled and had to be removed. Fortunately, no trees hit our home. Many of our neighbors were not as lucky. Two homes sustained such severe damage from trees that they were split in half and had to be torn down.

Also, our thirty-foot camper was destroyed. The tornado lifted it and spun it on the tongue several times, then tossed it upside down so that it landed on its top. The camper's wall and roof structure were broken up, and the appliances and the inside walls and furnishings were all destroyed.

Aerial photo of the tornado damage around our house
* Photo Courtesy of Miranda Hill Skonie

State Farm Insurance Company did an excellent job of assisting us in repairing our home, deck, and front porch steps, and helped us to secure a replacement camper—a new, thirty-one-footer.

All of our vehicles were in the garage except for my daughter's Chevrolet. However, her car was not damaged, even though several trees fell around it. I was able to remove the trees and limbs with a chainsaw and did not find even a scratch on it.

We were extremely lucky. A young girl was killed in a neighboring subdivision as a result of this tornado.

This was the first tornado that I had ever experienced. Hitting our home in the early morning hours and coming so fast, it was over before we could make it to the basement. I looked out of the basement window, and I could see my neighbor's house about eight hundred feet away. Normally, I could not see his home for the thick woods between us. I have never seen strobe lightning like I did that morning. Many houses were damaged in our subdivision.

It took us months to finish the repairs and remove the trees. I hired a logger to haul away the downed trees from our property and our neighbor's property. The logger did not want the job because the trees were tangled, which would make it extremely hard to harvest the timber. He explained

The Tornado destroyed our camper

that he usually only removed standing trees. I finally persuaded him to take on the challenge. He quit one morning after removing five semi-loads of logs. I quickly found out that my neighbor had fired him for running over a five-foot magnolia tree that was among the downed trees. I told the neighbor that I would have bought him another magnolia tree. However, the damage was done, and the logger said that he would never work in our neighborhood again. As I watched him leave, I thought of one of Dad's old sayings that had never quite made sense to me. For the first time in my life, I got it—I was so mad, I could have thrown my hat in the fire.

Following the logger experience, I hired a pulpwood crew, consisting of a father and two sons, to harvest the wood. They only worked three days and hauled a few loads, then quit. I had previous experience with pulpwood crews and was not surprised, but very disappointed. The trees had begun to rot and were not fit for pulpwood by then. I had to hire a firm with bulldozers to come in and clean up our land. None of the trees had touched or damaged our home, and homeowner's insurance will not cover downed trees that don't damage your home. The tree and land clearing cost us over five thousand dollars.

16

The Dumpling Lady

In 1985, my mother caught the entrepreneurial bug and started a new company. She created a business making dumplings in her home kitchen. These are the kind of dumplings that are used in making chicken and dumplings.

Mother's background in growing up on a farm in South Georgia, along with her long history of being a great southern cook, was the right mixture for creating a food business. Also, she had been a hospital dietitian. Sunday dinners at our family's dinner table regularly included chicken and dumplings.

She had also shared her dumplings at church dinners and other special events for many years. Mother was a great partner to my dad during his time as a minister. He spent many hours visiting with the sick and elderly, and Mother would frequently accompany him, usually taking along some food, particularly chicken and dumplings, which are universally recognized to have medicinal value (check with your grandmother on this claim). They were also awesome soul food.

During her many ministry visits with Dad, and on many other occasions, people would say things like, "Have you ever thought about selling your dumplings?" or, "I would buy those dumplings if you were to sell them."

One day, during a family Thanksgiving celebration, mother made chicken and dumplings and asked us kids and grandkids what we thought about her making and selling the dumplings. We were enthusiastic and encouraged her, but my dad was skeptical about the venture. He didn't believe that people would buy something as simple as dumplings.

In the spring of 1985, Mother started researching the business of making dumplings. She found a company from Florida that was already making them, and they were available locally. She bought a package and made chicken and dumplings. Disappointed by them and feeling that she could make a better-tasting product, she began experimenting and eventually got the recipe just the way she wanted it.

In continuing her research, Mother contacted the Georgia Department of Agriculture, which regulates this type of food production. They assisted her and suggested she start the business in her home to make sure that the venture would be successful. They helped her create the proper processing procedures, including meeting the regulations needed to operate the business.

Shortly thereafter, she started The Dumplin Shoppe out of her home kitchen. She ran a classified ad in the local paper, the *Jeff Davis Ledger*. Her advertisement stated, "Fresh or frozen dumplings for the busy housewife or househusband, call me." She listed her home phone number. Her telephone began to ring. She started the business with five pounds of flour and a dozen eggs. To facilitate customers picking up their dumpling orders, Dad placed a large, converted mailbox on the curb in front of their house. Customers would call and place an order for twelve ounces or a larger amount, and Mother would give them the price. She told them when the order would be placed in the old mailbox and to leave the money in the box. She never lost a penny on the transactions. Her first year's gross sales were sixteen thousand dollars.

The calls continued to come in, and Mother had to hire a person to help her on the morning shift and then had to hire someone on the afternoon shift. The traffic got so congested on the street that the police had to come and direct traffic. The police finally advised her that she needed to move her new company to a business address.

Dad, by this time, had created his own construction business, Jasper Hill and Son Construction. He rented a commercial lot on Highway 342 North in Hazlehurst and built Mother a building to house The Dumplin Shoppe. This worked for a little while, but the company outgrew that building quickly. Mother and Dad looked for a new location and found commercial property on West Jefferson Street in Hazlehurst and bought it. He then moved the building from Highway 342 to the new location. Dad added additional square footage as the business grew.

Mother kept hiring staff and eventually had nine women and one man working for her. The women were local, with lots of southern cooking experience, and knew how to roll out dumplings. The man was the truck driver, who delivered the dumplings to grocery stores.

The first large-chain grocery store to carry my mother's dumplings was the Kroger store in Dublin, Georgia. Randy Waters, store manager,

Mary Hill in The Dumplin Shoppe making dumplings

met with mother and asked her to cook chicken and dumplings for him. He loved them and stocked his store with The Dumplin Shoppe dumplings. I met and became friends with Randy many years later. He told me that he knew that she had a great product and that it would sell— and it did!

The front of the package had Mother's picture on it, along with the slogan, "Yes to Dumplings and No to Drugs" inside an oval-shaped sticker. Her motto was: Made Especially For You With Love.

Mother created the cooking directions for the chicken and dumplings and listed them on the back of the package. The directions were:

> *Place cut-up hen or fryer in a large pot, add water to cover, cook till tender. Remove chicken, remove skin and bone, bring broth to boil, drop dumplings one a time. After the last dumpling, stir very gently. Turn heat to low, cover, cook 30–35 minutes or until tender, stirring occasionally— GENTLY. Chicken may be added back to the dumplings. Serves 4–6 people.*

Also, on the back of the label, was the Golden Rule:

Therefore, all things whatsoever ye would that men should do to you, do ye even so to them: for this is the law and the prophets. *Matthew 7:12*

Starting up and operating the business was not easy. Mother ran into many issues. After she was up and running, many people were excited about her venture and wanted to learn more about it. They would come by her shop to meet her and ask questions. Mother was one of the most accommodating people you would ever meet. They would ask questions like, "How do you make them, and what are the ingredients?" Mother would take them into her kitchen area and show them how to make the dumplings and explain the entire process.

When I found out about these visits and questions, I explained to Mother that she should not share her trade secrets and details, because one of the visitors might steal her idea and start a company in competition with her. She said to me, "Son, you don't understand that these are people who truly want to meet me and just love the dumplings."

Very soon after many of these visits occurred, several newly formed companies started making dumplings. They tried to enter the grocery markets and undercut her prices. They were able to get into some smaller stores in the area. Fortunately, none were successful in the long run.

At one point, a food salesman who wanted to sell her dumplings to his customers contacted my mother. She was not working with any brokers or salespeople then. He made her several promises regarding great sales and profits if she worked with him. She did not have a UPC Code for the dumplings when she started. The wholesaler promised to get her the code, as well as start selling hundreds of cases of dumplings. He got the UPC Code for the dumplings put in his name. He ordered dozens of cases of dumplings, and he never picked them up. She had to scramble to get those sold because she didn't have much frozen storage space at the time. With all of this to deal with, Mother went through quite a learning curve on starting her dumpling business.

I still enjoy going into grocery stores and looking for the dumplings. If they don't have them, I request that they stock them. If they have them, I get the package out of the freezer and ask customers to look at Mother's picture on the package and then look at my face. I ask them as I hold up the package, "Do you see the likeness?" I do have a resemblance to my mother. Customers might think I am a crazy man. However, I do sell some dumplings using that technique.

Whenever I buy dumplings, I always asked the cashiers the same question about the resemblance. Many of them will say things like "no way"; "you are kidding me"; "let me see that picture again"; "let me see your driver's license"; "I have always wanted to meet a celebrity. Can I touch you?" Needless to say, I have had a lot of fun with the dumplings in grocery stores. I used to share my experiences with Mother, and she always enjoyed hearing about them.

One time, I stopped at an all-you-can-eat buffet restaurant in Hawkinsville, Georgia, for lunch. The buffet had chicken and dumplings, and I tried them. They were delicious, and I suspected that they were my mother's dumplings. I asked to speak with the cook. He came out, and I asked him if they were Mary Hill Dumplings. He asked me how I knew. "I have eaten many pounds of Mary Hill Dumplings in my life as she is my mother," I told him. He was excited to meet someone associated with Mary Hill Dumplings.

Sam, Mary Hill's traveling partner

Mother would visit grocery stores that carried her product and some that had not yet started. She would conduct cooking and tasting demonstrations. She traveled a wide area in south and middle Georgia, letting grocery shoppers taste her delicious product. She would cook the chicken and dumplings on-site and serve them along with a helping of southern hospitality. Customers always loved to meet her. She traveled alone most of the time during these cooking demonstrations. Occasionally, an employee or a grandchild would accompany her. On those days when no one was available to go with her, she took her assistant, Sam. Sam rode in the passenger seat and kept her company, but more importantly provided her safety and security.

Mother was the first commercial dumpling manufacturer in Georgia. She became known as The Dumpling Lady, a title she holds to this day. Her product was described by *Georgia Magazine,* in 1998, as the "Cadillac of Dumplings."

She sold her company in 1994, due to health issues, to Tim Callaway, who still operates the business today. Tim has added frozen biscuits to his product line. You can visit the company website at www.maryhill products.com.

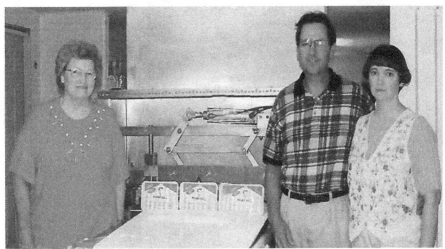

Mary Hill with the new owners - the Callaway's
* Photo Courtesy of Tim Callaway and Georgia Magazine

According to the latest figures, Mary Hill Dumplings, along with the newest products—Southern and Buttermilk biscuits—are now sold in eleven states. They are available in Walmart, Kroger, Publix, Piggly Wiggly, Harvey's, Ingles, and many other stores. If your local grocery store doesn't carry them, ask for the manager and request them.

Mary Hill, The Dumpling Lady, passed away on December 4, 2012, at the age of eighty. She made the front page of the *Jeff Davis Ledger* on Wednesday, December 12, 2012. The headline read, "The Dumpling Lady Now Rolls Flour in Heaven."

17

Heat Pump Marketing and HVAC Dealer Program

Our move to Atlanta in August 1981 saw my involvement at a new level with Georgia Power. The heat pump marketing and HVAC dealer program was my first significant development project for the company.

Though I had accepted the field engineer position back on June 25, the IBEW strike had delayed my arrival in Atlanta. I had to hit the ground running the moment I started.

Among my other responsibilities, I would be working closely with division personnel in implementing this new program. The department consisted of Vice President John Roberts, Bill Davidson, Jim Manley, Buddy Cromer, Dave Beavin, Diane Berry, Mary Alice Caldwell, Bantes Hodges, Doug Jones, Walter Lovett, Bill Starrs, Mike Wright, David Kee, Linda Smith, Emma Henry, and others. These people had a lot to do with my success, and I thank them.

This was a newly created position, and I had to come up with my specific job responsibilities, which included research, design, and implementation of these programs.

These were my keys to being successful:

- Research the most up-to-date heat pump data and learn all I could about the technical specifications and how to apply them in a new marketing program
- Use my extensive experience in sizing HVAC units but enhance my experience and become certified to teach the HVAC system sizing, design, and installation of the residential air duct system
- Involve Georgia Power marketing employees by seeking their input in what they wanted in a heat pump marketing program
- Seek input from HVAC manufacturers and dealers on their ideas, suggestions, barriers, and opportunities in marketing heat pumps, including how Georgia Power might assist them

- Investigate how other Georgia Power departments might assist the Residential Marketing Department in implementing a heat pump program
- Seek corporate approval and implement the Heat Pump Marketing and Heat Pump HVAC Dealer Program across the state of Georgia

Vice President Roberts called me to his office on my first day to give me my marching orders for developing and implementing the heat pump marketing and the HVAC dealer program. I will never forget what he said to me: "Jimmy, I want these programs to be designed so that I will never hear a complaint from a customer about the installation, operation, or comfort of their heat pump system."

"Yes, sir," I said. "That is certainly my goal. Some of my previous customers have experienced shoddy and improper installations, and I will make sure that we insist and verify that the systems are installed properly."

Everything I envisioned in the marketing program was built around my meeting with Vice President Roberts and his marching orders.

I spent a considerable amount of time researching the databases on heat pumps, primarily through the Air Conditioning, Heating, and Refrigeration Institute (AHRI), a trade association of manufacturers of air conditioning, heating, and commercial refrigeration equipment. They published a detailed listing of the manufacturers, available equipment with model numbers, and efficiency ratings.

I also had numerous meetings with the twelve HVAC wholesalers serving Georgia to seek their input on our marketing program. The wholesalers provided equipment to the hundreds of HVAC dealers across Georgia. They were very interested in working with us as we implemented the program.

Georgia Power had instituted a heat pump program back in the 1960s, and I was familiar with that program and its service warranty for residential customers. I was in charge of the Waycross District heat pump service program and used this experience to further advance my ideas on how to market the current, higher-efficiency generation of heat pumps.

Based on my research, I developed the major criteria that heat pumps must have a minimum of an 8.0 efficiency rating on cooling and 1.8 efficiency at 17°F on heating. Of course, dealers and customers could certainly buy units that were even more efficient, and that was encouraged. The higher the efficiency numbers, the more energy the customer would save, and the lower their power bill would be. Today's efficiency ratings are much higher.

The heat pump is one of the most efficient heating and cooling units on the market today. It can use the outside air or the earth as its source of heating or cooling. The electric heat pump helped the ultimate customer use their energy efficiently and balanced the load for the utility company— a win for all.

Having encountered dealers who were great, and others who lacked some expertise, I knew that training would have to be part of any heat pump marketing program.

Back when I had been in Americus, my awesome experience with Parker's Heating and Air Conditioning Company had taught me a lot. Mr. Roy Parker was a consummate and meticulous professional, who was one of the best HVAC dealers I have ever come across. His ideas were a major thread throughout my program design.

I had many personal experiences with customers who had high power bills that were directly related to sizing and installation issues. It was not that dealers did not want to install systems correctly, but in many cases, their employees did not have adequate training. These experiences led me to include training as a major component of the heat pump program.

I immediately enrolled in courses that would increase my technical expertise and certify me as an instructor in the design and installation of residential heating and air conditioning systems. This would allow me to teach these courses to Georgia Power employees, HVAC dealers and their employees, and others. These courses specifically related to Residential Load Calculation (Manual J) for residential winter and summer air conditioning as well as the Duct Design (Manual D) for residential winter and summer air conditioning and equipment selection. I taught about fifty of these courses across Georgia.

Based on my previous work experience in about 20 percent of Georgia's counties, I already had a good sense of some of the issues that needed to be addressed in our marketing program. Also, I traveled to every Georgia Power division office, and to some district offices, to seek counsel from marketing employees as well as HVAC dealers.

After I had finished gathering their input, I started the design process for developing the marketing program.

My draft plan was based on the following criteria:

- Having well-trained HVAC dealers/personnel on sizing, installation, and service of high-efficiency heat pumps
- Developing minimum efficiency ratings of heat pumps, as determined by a nationally recognized rating firm
- Dealer support for qualifying and participating dealers
- Enhanced training for company personnel who would be communicating to our customers the advantages of the high-efficiency heat pump

My next step was to seek input from the HVAC industry. My associate Doug Jones and I attended about sixty meetings with HVAC manufacturers, wholesalers, and dealers across the state of Georgia. These meetings took place for over a year as we invited ideas from the HVAC industry to help shape the final design of the marketing plan. A dealer council was created after the heat pump marketing program was implemented. The council was a way for dealers to provide Georgia Power with continuous input on the program.

I furthermore identified several departments within Georgia Power whose ideas and assistance I would solicit for implementation of the heat pump marketing plan.

Georgia Power had created, many years earlier, the Skills Development Center, a technical training facility for employees. It was located in central Georgia, on the grounds of a power generation plant.

Based on my observations and research, I knew it would be important to provide heat pump training opportunities for HVAC dealers and their technicians. After I learned about the existence of the Skills Development Center, I met several times with the manager of the Technical Training Division to learn more about their training capabilities, and we determined that they could provide the technical training that the HVAC dealers needed. Together with the skills development staff, we came up with a plan to implement specialized training.

The courses would be taught in a ten-thousand-square-foot facility where heat pumps, donated by twelve manufacturers, were installed. Each heat pump would be wired to allow instructors to create different electrical, refrigerant, and mechanical problems. The students would have to analyze the problem and explain how to repair the issue. No other HVAC training facility of this kind had ever been constructed.

The technical courses taught were electricity, solid-state controls, brazing and soldering, and heat pump service. Also, the skills center built a replica of a house to be used for demonstration purposes in the Manual J and Manual D training.

Using Manual J, each student was taught how to size the HVAC system for the house based on factors such as overall construction type, insulation, window- and door-construction, the orientation of the house, weather design criteria, and other factors. This data would lead to the size of the HVAC system.

Using Manual D, each student was taught how to use the data derived from the Manual J calculations for each room to design the air duct system. In addition to designing the duct system, the students had to install their designed system and measure the airflow to each room to verify their design. This process would ensure the homeowner would receive a quality and efficient heat pump system that produced year-round comfort and lower power bills.

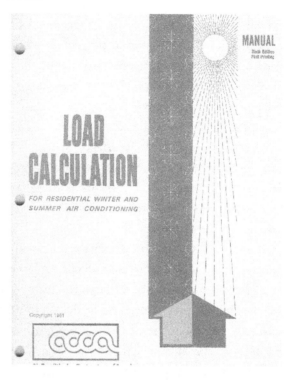

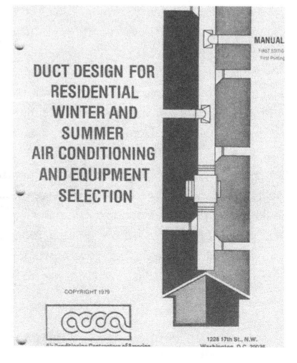

The HVAC technicians raved about the excellent training and outstanding instructors, and how beneficial the courses were to them. The HVAC dealers also expressed their appreciation for the training and how it helped their technicians improve their expertise and competence. In return, the dealer had very satisfied customers.

The technical training attracted the interest of HVAC manufacturers. Manufacturers sent staff to meet with me and visit our training facilities. Several media outlets ran stories on the program, including a major, nationwide HVAC magazine, as well as several Georgia newspapers.

The Center staff taught the HVAC courses from September to May of each year. For the remainder of the year, they taught Georgia Power personnel and Georgia technical school instructors.

The Skills Development Center was an important partner in our heat pump marketing program. The contributions of the Center leadership and staff were a key part of the program's success. Those team members included Billy Carver, Bill Nolan, Ben Forston, Darrell Howell, Glenn Williams, Bill Coombs, and others.

We needed to reach Georgia Power customers with the heat pump story. To that end, I worked with Bob Hughes, Georgia Power's advertising coordinator, who was a great partner in developing an advertising campaign to tell that story. Our plan included television, radio, and print advertising.

One of the challenges Bob and I faced was how to explain the workings of a heat pump in simple, non-technical, and appealing terms. The best non-technical way to explain the heat pump is that it is a highly efficient, year-round home heating and cooling system that runs on electricity. It is called a heat pump because it pumps or moves heat from where it is not needed to where it is needed. In winter, even if the temperature outside is below freezing, there is enough heat in the air to heat your home. The heat pump takes this heat and pumps it inside your home. In warmer months, the heat pump takes the hot, sticky heat that is inside your house and pumps it outside.

The challenge was to put this non-technical explanation into our heat pump advertising. In other words, how does the heat pump work? Well, we hired Steve Landesberg, from the *Barney Miller* TV series, to use these same principles to explain the heat pump operation in an advertisement. The ad won a **Silver Effie** Award for advertising effectiveness from the American Marketing Association.

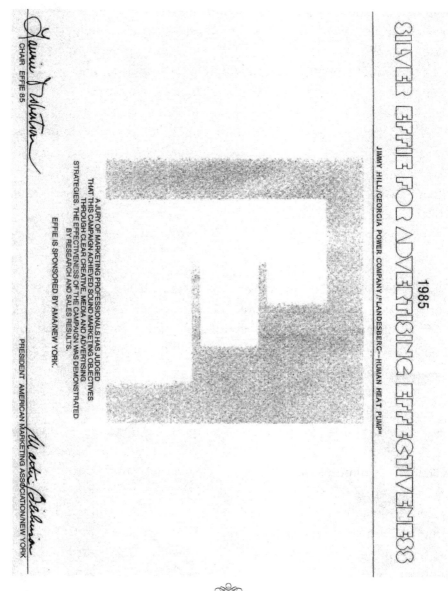

Part of my project required assistance from the Accounting Department. To help us track installations and make sure the HVAC dealers received credit for the install, a mechanism was needed for our marketing representatives to code a customer's file when they put in a new heat pump. We already had a heat pump code available in the customer's record. After further investigation, we determined that we could change the code, and as the files were scanned for updates overnight, the heat pump would be recorded. This procedure worked great and allowed us to capture installed heat pumps. I appreciated the accounting team's help in capturing the success of the heat pump program.

The day arrived for me to present the Heat Pump Marketing Plan to the Georgia Power Management Council. The council members were the senior leadership at Georgia Power. I had never made a presentation to a senior level group like this, and I was scared to death. I felt my career and livelihood depended on getting this plan approved.

My senior executive, Grady Baker, asked the first question: Why market heat pumps? I was thrown off track for a moment. The slide presentation I had prepared for the council assumed that question had already been answered and that they were ready to hear my plan. I am sure that I hesitated at that moment, but my manager, Jim Manley, came to the rescue and talked about the benefits to the ultimate customer and Georgia Power. I then moved into my presentation and successfully got through it. There were several questions, and I was able to answer them appropriately. My marketing plan was approved.

Jim Manley, Buddy Cromer, and Ray Spratlin, my managers at that time, arranged for my promotion to senior field engineer as soon as the council approved the plan. This was a great surprise and was much appreciated. Working on this project was a once-in-a-lifetime opportunity that was professionally very rewarding. Thanks to Jim Manley for promoting me to the corporate office and allowing me to work on this great project!

With approval for the marketing plan received, the next step was its implementation.

The key points of the implementation plan were:

- Setting robust requirements for the selection of high-efficiency heat pumps
- Training and education of HVAC dealers and their technicians in the sizing, design, and installation procedures of high-efficiency heat pumps through Georgia Power's Skills Development Center and at Georgia Power's expense
- Training and education of Georgia Power marketing staff through Georgia Power's Skills Development Center in the sizing, design, and installation procedures of high-efficiency heat pumps
- Rewards to the HVAC dealers for installing high-efficiency heat pumps, including cooperative advertising credits and free training for their employees
- Creating the Heat Pump Information Center that provided a toll-free number for customers to call with questions about their heat pumps. Information Center Staff was trained at the Skills Development Center on how to answer technical questions.

The Heat Pump Information Center was staffed by college students, who rotated shifts in managing the center. The students— Richard Joyce, Pamela Ware, Shannon Brown and Teresa Vigil—did an out-standing job answering calls and handling the administrative work associated with the Center.

Heat Pump Information Center
* Photo Courtesy of Georgia Power Company

The rewards to customers who installed high-efficiency heat pumps were lower power bills, quality installation, and knowing that their HVAC dealer was trained and qualified. This is all in addition to the excellent heating and cooling comfort a heat pump provides in the home. A further benefit has been that it is a great load-leveling demand technology for Georgia Power, allowing more efficient use of its power plants year-round.

Thousands of new high-efficiency heat pumps were installed in new and existing homes all over Georgia under this program. Hundreds of thousands of dollars were saved on electricity bills as a result.

The Georgia Power Heat Pump Marketing Plan was adopted, in part, by other electric utilities, which created the opportunity for customers not served by Georgia Power to have access to the high-efficiency heat pump and to lower power bills.

I was asked to go to North Dakota to make a speech at a conference about heat pumps. I should have known that something was up when I discovered that my boss and his boss and his boss and his boss were asked to go and declined. I was politely told to go and was not given a choice.

I arrived in Minot, North Dakota, on an overcast, snowy day in December. Did I mention that it was snowing? Saying that it was snowing does not do it justice—it looked like a blizzard to me. I did not know how far away the conference hotel was located, so I rented a car and left the airport. As soon as I pulled onto the main road leaving the airport, there was the hotel. I turned into the parking lot and stopped under the front canopy, right at the main door. Did I mention how cold it was? It was -7°F! And the wind was blowing with a wind chill of -52°F. It was the coldest weather I had ever experienced.

I locked the car and went inside the hotel to check-in. By the time I came back outside, several vehicles had parked behind me. I took out my car keys and discovered that the door would not unlock. I had often heard about frozen locks, but why did it have to happen right then? Here I was in a foreign land, and my car door lock had decided to freeze. After several attempts to unlock the door, I went around to the passenger side to see if I could unlock that door. No luck! I went back to the driver's side. I gave it another try. Nothing—I mean no movement, except maybe the key was trying to bend or break.

By this time, several people had gathered around me. They asked me if I was from around there and offered advice, such as heating the key with a cigarette lighter or a match, though no one had either. I became flustered and put the keys back in my pocket. I thought maybe if I removed my gloves that I could get a better grip on the door key. With my ungloved hand, I reached into my pocket again—and felt two sets of keys. The other set was to my vehicle sitting at the Atlanta airport. Both were General Motors key sets, each with two keys on the ring. The rings were identical.

I knew that if I confessed to the group about the mix-up, I would be very embarrassed and laughed at in this foreign land. I chose the only viable option: I announced to those assembled that as a kid, I had developed strong hands. I could lift and turn things that most people could not. I pulled out the correct set of keys and inserted the key in the door. I made a loud South Georgia grunting noise, turned the key with a quick move, and the door unlocked. I got a round of applause and heard words like "amazing," "unbelievable," and "wow!" I accepted those words with all of the humility that I could muster at that point.

I drove the rental vehicle to the nearest curb and parked it. As I started back toward the hotel entrance, I noticed an electrical outlet in front of where I had parked my car. Looking around, I realized they were in front of every car. Several of the vehicles had electrical drop cords running to the outlet. I was amazed to see so many electric vehicles. There were not many around in the early 1980s.

Then I heard a woman's voice: "You are not from around here, are you, Mister?" I turned to her and asked her how she knew.

"Come over here, by your car," she said. She then explained how and why you plug your vehicle into the electrical outlet. "Are you planning on leaving anytime this winter?" she asked. I told her I was leaving in two days, to which she replied, "Not if you don't plug your vehicle into this outlet to keep the engine warm." I found an extension cord and plugged it in.

The following afternoon, I spoke to a crowd of about two hundred people. I told the true story about my experience with the door locks. I also shared the story about being asked if I was from around here and plugging in the car, that I hadn't been aware that North Dakota had electric cars. My stories brought the house down. People were laughing until they cried.

That evening was the closing dinner of the conference, and they asked me if I would like to attend. Since a blizzard was going on outside, and the temperatures were below zero, I decided to attend the dinner. I was asked to sit at a table in the front of the room. I had the pleasure of dining with two older ladies, probably in their early eighties. As soon as I sat down, they told me that they had enjoyed my speech earlier in the day. I thanked them. Then one of the ladies said to me, in a whisper, "We don't have electric cars." I thanked them for educating me.

The vehicle did start the next day, and I was able to get out of Dodge— I mean North Dakota.

north dakota
power use council
DEDICATED TO SAFE AND EFFICIENT USE OF ELECTRICITY

January 6, 1986

Mr. Jimmy Hill
Georgia Power Company
333 Piedmont Avenue
Atlanta, GA 30308

Dear Jimmy:

On behalf of the North Dakota Power Use Council, it is my pleasure to
extend our appreciation and thanks for your great presentation at our 28th
annual meeting in Minot. You had the audience "in your hand" with your
presentation on Georgia Power's marketing efforts, not to mention your
humorous way of communicating. I had so many comments on your presentation,
and the part you played in the annual meeting program; you truly did a
good job.

I hope we have a chance to meet again sometime, perhaps in your neck of
the woods. We all enjoyed your company, and your presence with us in
Minot. Thanks again!

Have a Happy New Year!

Sincerely yours,

Bradley J. Schmidt, President
North Dakota Power Use Council

BJS:mm

18

Marketing Technical Support

Bill Davidson, former district manager in metro Atlanta, was promoted to vice president of Residential and Commercial Marketing in late spring of 1986. He led an effort to restructure the corporate marketing organization, of which I was a part.

Vice President Davidson talked to me about being a part of his new leadership team. I was interested, and he set up a confidential executive appraisal process for me with psychologist Dr. Tory Herring of Tanner, Leay, and Associates PC, of Birmingham, Alabama. As it turned out, Dr. Tanner and Dr. Herring had already completed an appraisal on me earlier in 1986 for another job. However, I had not seen the results or heard anything further about it.

The appraisal sent to Davidson covered the areas of motivation, intelligence, communication skills, temperament, social style, and leadership style. I will not bore you with the details, but he sent me a copy and attached a note that said, "I agree with this appraisal. I wish mine would be nearly as good."

Davidson asked me to assume the position of marketing applications manager on May 20, 1986. I moved across the twentieth floor from my five-foot-walled cubicle to a new office with a window. Donna Camp became my first-ever full-time secretary.

I was one of six marketing managers reporting to Vice President Davidson. The others were: J. F. Boyd, Marketing Administration; L. B. Cromer, Residential; T. D. Beavin, Existing Residential; J. L. Hood, Chain Accounts; and J. H. Brown, Commercial.

My job was to manage the Marketing Applications section in supplying technical and research data, sales program operations, and direct and indirect sales support to general office marketing managers and the divisions. This support helped the divisions analyze their markets and develop appropriate sales programs to increase their kWh (kilowatt-hour) sales.

The specific areas of my responsibility, company-wide, were outdoor lighting; commercial and residential heating, ventilation and air conditioning, heat pump and water heating; economic and financial analysis; codes, wiring, energy management systems, and interior lighting; electric cooking and food service; and HVAC dealer training.

My job required technical knowledge, which included an understanding of the following: residential and commercial HVAC; heat pumps and water heating; interior and exterior lighting design and engineering; electric cooking and food-service design, installation, and service. It also required familiarity with various codes (electrical, mechanical, and building) and with research techniques and sources, as well as a basic understanding of financial and economic analysis, and a thorough understanding of residential and commercial heat loss and heat gain techniques. All of these were skills that I had acquired in previous positions.

Management, leadership, and communication skills were also important requirements. I had a team of six professional staff: J. R. Smith, G. W. Thomas, J. M. Proffitt, R. L. Purvis, A. S. Rose, and E. D. Carswell. Donna Camp was my secretary.

There is an organizational chart, in this chapter, of the entire Commercial and Residential Marketing organization with specific listings for each manager's responsibilities and staff listing.

Due to extensive travel, I was assigned a company vehicle along with a designated parking space in the corporate garage.

Vice President Davidson's management team's first responsibility was to visit each of the division point towns and meet with all marketing personnel. This visit was to introduce the new organization and the team. We had meetings in Rome, Columbus, Valdosta, Macon, Augusta, Athens, and Atlanta, traveling as a group to each of these locations and sharing each of our department's goals and how we intended to work with each division.

My first order of business in Marketing Applications was to meet with my team members and discuss their specific responsibilities and our business plan for accomplishing their goals. Our department's expertise was wide-ranging and covered many technical areas. I expressed to my team that I wanted us to work together in providing great service to our clients.

We were a newly created department, and we had to feel our way forward in meeting our responsibilities. I had an open-door policy with my staff, and they could come to see me at any time. If they had a problem, I wanted to know about it and their proposed solution. I shared with them that I didn't believe in having a lot of meetings; I believed in getting results and staying focused on our goals. My personal goals were based on our department goals and on helping each of my staff when they needed my help.

I had been in my new position for eighty-one days when I received a call from Jack Talley, vice president of Economic Development. I had interviewed with Mr. Talley early in 1986 for the position of manager of the Agricultural Affairs Department. This was the job for which I had already gone through an extensive set of tests, a personal evaluation, and interviews with Dr. Tory Herring. However, not having heard anything more from Mr. Talley regarding the job, I had accepted the Marketing Applications position.

Vice President Talley's call was to offer me that agricultural affairs manager position, which would report to him. It was a higher-level position than I currently held, and I was very interested.

I went to speak to Senior Vice President John Hemby about my dilemma. "Jimmy, you have a great job, and you have a chance to get another great job," was his advice.

Gail and I prayed about it and considered it by putting together a list of pros and cons. The prayer and pros won. I accepted the job on August 9, 1986.

Those eighty-one days turned into the shortest time frame that I ever held a full-time job. I was looking forward to the Marketing Applications job, but I felt a calling to be involved in agriculture and rural Georgia. I knew that my background, education, and previous positions had prepared me for this new position.

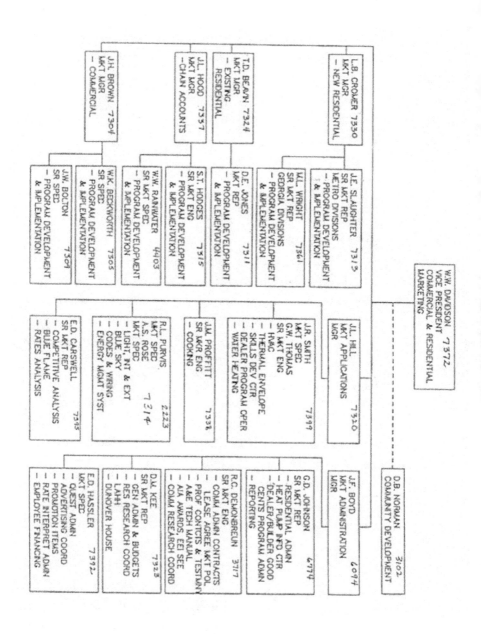

19

Agriculture and Agribusiness

The calendar was already full of events, meetings, and trips when I reported for my new position as manager of Agricultural Affairs on August 18, 1986. Mr. B. J. Sumner was the temporary contact at Georgia Power for the agricultural community before my arrival. He was contracted to work with me for several months to assist in my meeting and assimilating with agricultural leaders in Georgia.

On my first trip to South Georgia, Mr. Sumner was quizzing me on my knowledge of agriculture. As we passed a farm, he asked me the size of a galvanized washtub leaning against the barn. "Number 3," I said. He seemed almost surprised I knew the answer.

Further on down the road, there was a green tractor parked in a field. He asked, "What is the make and model of that tractor?"

"It's a John Deere model 4020, made from 1964 to 1972," I replied.

He nodded. "So, I guess you do know something about agriculture and rural Georgia." He never asked any more questions.

When I had interviewed for this position several months earlier, along with two other candidates, it had been a complex and lengthy hiring process. All three of us were agricultural engineers. We went through several interviews, tests, and meetings with Dr. Tory Herring, who was an industrial-organizational psychologist. Conducted over several weeks, the assessments involved psychological testing, social interaction, and several one-on-one interviews with Dr. Herring. This experience was unlike any other job interview that I had been involved in.

Since a lot of time had passed without my hearing anything more, I had assumed that they were not going to fill the job or that I was not a viable candidate. However, I discovered later that the delay in Georgia Power's hiring decision had been due to discussions about the job level.

There had been an agricultural affairs manager position for over forty years at Georgia Power, and when Mr. Olin Ginn retired, it was abolished.

About a month after Mr. Ginn's retirement, a group of agriculture and agribusiness leaders met with Georgia Power president Robert Scherer and asked that the job be reinstated. They were convinced that Georgia Power was an integral part of helping the agricultural industry grow and thrive in the state. Georgia Power was an early supporter of students in 4-H and FFA and many other agricultural organizations. Mr. Ginn and his staff were all agricultural engineers who had brought technical expertise and served as a liaison to the agricultural industry. The agricultural affairs management role provided a key interface with the industry on important energy matters and in other technical areas.

President Scherer thanked them and shared their thoughts with the company management team. It was decided to re-create the position. An evaluation was conducted to determine what level the job needed to be. As I learned later, the job was rated at a vice-presidential level; however, there was discussion in the management team that Georgia Power had too many vice presidents, and a stalemate developed. All of this was going on before, during, and after the interviews for the position. In the end, the job was created not at the vice-president level, but as a higher-level senior manager position.

The new job was based in the Georgia Power building at 270 Peachtree Street in downtown Atlanta and reported to Jack Talley, vice president of Economic Development. This position was one of three reports to Jack. The other two were Jim Martin, manager of the Economic Development Department, and Myles Smith, who managed the Community Development Department.

Jack's staff included David Norman, Judy Byrd, Margaret Schumacher, Jim Vaseff, Randy Clements, Kelly Craven, Allen Lockerman, Carol Shipley, Robin Gerald, Bill Hall, Mary Lee Poss, Roy Plott, Mary Beasley, George Dickens, Ed Houtz, Ed Holcombe, Jeff Mitchell, Kathy Butler, Jim Grissett, John Malone, Richard Johnson, Larry Moolenaar, Bob Oglesby, Lynn Pitts, Andy Andrews, George Allen, Bill Bryant, Carl Flowers, and Tommy Wade. Nettie Felder was Jack's administrative assistant and, as I did not have an assistant at that time, she also assisted me.

Photo Courtesy of Myles Smith

I was faced with the challenge of refining the vision, mission, and goals of the new department. Olin Ginn's time as agricultural affairs manager was before the extensive use of computers, and primarily paper files were used. Most of the paper files were long gone, and I had to re-create the department. Fortunately, Nettie had handled Olin's administrative paperwork, and she had some corporate history of the department. Her help was invaluable.

The Agricultural Affairs Department was to serve as a liaison for agriculture in Georgia and to build mutually beneficial relationships with the industry. We would seek ways to help the agricultural industry enhance its economic activity for its benefit and the benefit of the state. Agriculture was, and still is, the single largest industry in the state of Georgia.

In my new position, I was the official agricultural representative for Georgia Power and worked with Georgia's agricultural industry through various associations and organizations, including the state legislature, the state Department of Agriculture, colleges and universities, and other agriculture education groups. My efforts were directed toward promoting the growth of agribusiness and rural communities in Georgia.

The following is an excerpt from the Georgia Power press release announcing my promotion to manager of Agricultural Affairs:

> "Hill's educational background and work experience make him well qualified for his new duties," said Jack Talley, Georgia Power's vice president of Economic Development. "In his 18 years with the company, Jimmy has proven to be an innovative leader and now can apply his talents in this important area."
>
> In 1968, while a student at the University of Georgia, Hill started as a co-op student in Georgia Power's Residential and Rural Sales Department. He joined the company full-time in 1971, after graduating from the University of Georgia with a Bachelor of Science degree in agricultural engineering.
>
> Hill has held several positions in Georgia Power's Residential Sales Department and was recently responsible for the development and implementation of the company's heat pump marketing program. This program includes the nationally recognized training school for Georgia's heating and air conditioning dealers.

Hill is currently serving as the chairman of the American Society of Agricultural Engineers, Georgia Section, and has been a member since 1971.

Photo Courtesy of Georgia Power Company

In July 1987, less than a year into my role as manager of Agricultural Affairs, I received an offer to swap jobs with an employee from the South East Queensland Electricity Board, located in Nambour, Queensland, Australia.

The swap would be with a senior technical marketing and advisory officer. His responsibilities included: selling and promoting efficient utilization of electricity in the commercial, industrial, and rural sectors; designing electric hot water system applications; designing and advising on controlled environmental situations using electric energy for use by agricultural customers; designing and advising on all types of irrigation for agriculture; automatic and radio-controlled irrigation design and application; designing and advising on industrial heat applications; promoting a "good image" for the Board, and investigating energy-efficient methods for utilization of electric power. These job responsibilities and skills were certainly in my wheelhouse.

The exchange would involve a commitment for twelve months minimum and eighteen months maximum. The arrangement included the stipulation that families would accompany the employee as well. They would swap not only jobs but houses. Financial arrangements would be such that each family would neither lose nor profit financially by the exchange.

I told my family about the offer and that I might accept it. I was kidding about accepting the swap, but they were beyond excited. Both my children immediately searched the world map to find where Nambour was located. They found that it was a city north of Brisbane and eight miles from the Sunshine Coast and the Coral Sea. Even Gail seemed to be excited about the adventure.

I had thought that they might be somewhat excited but would not want to do the exchange. I was wrong. They all wanted to do it. However, since I had only been in my job for less than a year, I chose not to consider the job swap. They all got mad! To this day, I think they are still upset with me.

In my second year heading up Agricultural Affairs, I was able to hire Conda Ware as my administrative assistant. Over the next four years, I added three more staff members. Jeff Mitchell came on board first. He was a long-time Georgia Power employee and stayed for about one and a half years. Travis Henry called me one day, out of the blue, and asked me if I could meet with him. He was also a long-time Georgia Power employee, and I had worked with his wife, Emma, in the Marketing Department a few years earlier. During the meeting, he shared that he would like to work in my department if an opportunity arose. Not long afterward, a position opened up, and I called Travis. I hired him because of his agriculture background, skills, initiative, and willingness to work in the agriculture arena. Travis came on board as an assistant agribusiness representative in February 1990 and was a valuable addition to the team.

In 1991, due to the department's success and to the growing demand for our services, I received approval for another staff person. The person who applied was Charles Gillespie, another long-time Georgia Power employee, and agricultural engineer. Charles was a great candidate with an extensive agricultural and utility background. I hired him as a senior agribusiness engineer, and he became an awesome addition to the staff.

Agricultural Affairs Staff L-R: Jimmy Hill, Charles Gillespie,
Conda Ware and Travis Henry (Not pictured Garland Anderson)
Photo Courtesy of Georgia Power Company

Two years later, when I had the opportunity to add another senior agribusiness engineer, Garland Anderson, again a long-time Georgia Power employee, was brought to my attention. He had an agricultural background and was also an agricultural engineer. I hired Garland to cover the southern part of the state. He rounded out the staff of highly competent employees who would provide world-class service to Georgia agriculture and support Georgia Power efforts in the agricultural industry.

Agricultural Affairs had an extensive history with Georgia Power. The first employee of the Agriculture Division was L. W. Gray. He was an agricultural engineer and began working for Georgia Power in the 1930s. His work revolved around extending Georgia Power lines into rural areas and providing power and expertise specifically to farmers.

On March 1, 1945, Channing Cope was named the first manager of the Agriculture Division at Georgia Power. At one point, Cope had a popular farm show on an Atlanta radio station. He was the owner of the Yellow River Farm near Covington, Georgia. He was also a popular after-dinner speaker and addressed many agricultural organizations, farm groups, and other gatherings. Cope published a book titled *Front Porch Farming* in 1949. He was an early promoter of year-round livestock grazing.

Cope was an interesting man. He was president of the Georgia Kudzu Club, which had twenty thousand members. His kudzu promotion was based on the idea of the conservation of land; erosion control of agricultural land was a major concern at that time. The kudzu plant was claimed to halt erosion, rebuild the worst land, provide good grazing for livestock, and produce hay comparable to alfalfa. According to an advertisement that Cope ran in *The Atlanta Constitution,* in 1944, the members of the Kudzu Club of Georgia planted seventy thousand acres of land, and the 1945 goal was 100,000 acres. Kudzu roots or crowns sold for between ten and fourteen dollars per thousand, with five hundred crowns planting an acre of land. Kudzu planting was so successful that stories about kudzu ran in many national magazines, including *Time, Readers Digest, Country Book*, and *The Land.* Channing Cope received inquiries from almost every state and even from foreign countries. One might question the value of kudzu today since it has become a nuisance in many places.

Olin Ginn, an agricultural engineer, went to work at Georgia Power in 1945 and became a legend in his own time. He spent forty years with Georgia Power and managed the Agricultural Affairs Department for many years. He had a staff of agricultural engineers, including Bill Land, Robert Carpenter, Clabe Chapman, and J. C. Lumsden.

Ginn was the only company employee that I knew who had two company vehicles assigned to him. I learned this one day when Nettie Felder told me that the company garage needed my other vehicle for service. "My other vehicle?" I asked. Nettie explained that Ginn had another vehicle assigned to him for use in hauling equipment, displays, and other items for work-related assignments. She handed me the keys to the vehicle, and I went to the garage and found it. I immediately turned in the car to the garage personnel and told them that I no longer needed it. After further investigation, I learned that Ginn had received personal approval from the Georgia Power president to secure the second vehicle.

Ginn was active in farm electrification work and contributed to the design of electrical equipment and farm wiring methods. He was active in many agricultural organizations and served in leadership capacities in several of them. He was a charter member of the Georgia Agribusiness Council. His crowning civic achievement was being inducted into the Agricultural Hall of Fame at the University of Georgia in 1991. Ginn died on July 17, 1992, after retiring in 1985.

Agricultural engineers played a large role at Georgia Power over the years. In the late 1970s, the company employed eighty-one agricultural engineers in various positions within the company. We knew that many of us were employed at Georgia Power. However, we had never seen a list until it was published in 1981 by the Human Resources Department at the request of Mr. Ginn.

Mr. Ginn was the senior agricultural engineer in the company. By sharing the list, he wanted to thank all of us for helping to build a creditable reputation for the agricultural engineering profession at Georgia Power.

The following departments employed agricultural engineers: Energy Services, Operating, Power Generation, Agribusiness Development, Project Analysis, Safety and Health, Regulatory Affairs, Rate Analysis, District Management, Transmission, Substation, and Community Development.

The projects, assignments, or other agricultural development roles described below are examples of how the Agricultural Affairs Department was able to effect positive change for Georgia agriculture and Georgia Power.

One example was addressing rate tariffs for specific agricultural processing firms. One of my first visits to meet with agricultural customers occurred at a statewide meeting of agricultural processors related to a specific agricultural crop. I discovered, from the agenda of the meeting, their intent to discuss electrical rates and usage. They were specifically concerned about Georgia Power's rates and how they impacted their processing facilities. They were so concerned that they were contemplating hiring legal representation to investigate the issue. I immediately introduced myself to the organization's president and asked him to share with me some background on their concerns. After hearing what he had to say, I asked if he would allow me to work on the issue before they hired attorneys. He shared my offer with the organization, and they agreed to delay seeking legal representation.

I followed up on the issue with Georgia Power's Rate Department, which led to a committee being assigned to look into the matter and report back. I served on the committee, along with several company rate experts. The investigation resulted in a deep dive into usage patterns and the new technologies being used by the industry. The outcome was a revised rate structure that allowed the processors credit for their usage patterns and off-peak use of electricity. The organization's membership was very pleased with the results, which enabled them to avoid seeking legal remedies. This was a great example of using the expertise of the Agricultural Affairs Department in addressing an issue of vital importance to the agricultural processing industries and of working with Georgia Power departments to solve an issue.

Another key role for Agricultural Affairs was during the 1996 Summer Olympics in Atlanta. I describe this in more detail later in the book. Georgia Power was a major player in the securing of the 1996 Summer Olympics for Atlanta and in contributing to its success. It was the official power source for all the events and loaned employees to the Olympic Committee to assist with the implementation of the games.

Georgia Agriculture 1996 was a huge undertaking to familiarize Olympic visitors to Georgia and southern agriculture, put together by the

Georgia Agribusiness Council, Georgia Power's Agricultural Affairs Department, the University of Georgia, and many other companies and organizations.

Another promotional program the Agricultural Affairs Department was heavily involved in during the Olympics was Operation Legacy. Its purpose was to expose out-of-state corporate leaders to the value and benefits of expanding or locating their company in Georgia.

Close to my own heart, for all the training and mentoring I received, is the sponsorship of the **Georgia FFA Association** by Georgia Power. FFA is part of the agricultural education program of the Georgia Department of Education and has over 43,000 members in 347 chapters with more than 475 agricultural education teachers. Agriculture, agribusiness, forestry, and the food industry combine to make Georgia's largest single economic generator. This is why Georgia Power supports this youth program and has done so since FFA's inception in Georgia in the 1930s. Our Agricultural Affairs Department coordinated Georgia Power's support for the FFA program.

Another vocational organization supported by Georgia Power is the **Family, Career and Community Leaders of America (FCCLA)**, a nonprofit student organization that helps youth develop leadership and workplace skills to prepare for both college and careers through peer-to-peer education, community engagement, and the application of skills learned in the Family and Consumer Sciences (FCS) classroom. The FCCLA empowers students to balance career and family responsibilities, develop leadership skills, practice STEM skills, and build technical skills in FCS related careers. The company has been supporting FCCLA since its beginning in Georgia in the 1930s as the Future Homemakers of America (FHA).

The Food Processing Advisory Council (FoodPAC) was a collaboration between state government, universities, and private enterprises to address issues of concern from food processors and enhance their economic viability. Georgia universities have outstanding technical expertise in food processing. The council accepted joint proposals from university staff and private food processing companies to evaluate and propose solutions to specific food processor technical needs. Some funding by both parties was required to initiate the approval evaluation process. FoodPAC council members evaluated each proposal and made the final decision as to whether to fund the project.

I was one of the founders and the first chairman of FoodPAC. The organization was managed by a steering committee made up of food industry leaders. Areas of technical interest were workforce development, process and product competitiveness, and environmental and food safety. Each technical area was staffed by food industry leaders and university personnel.

FoodPAC was able to address many key issues and find solutions for the food processing industry during its tenure. Issues were related to improving food processing techniques, packaging and marketing, ingredient evaluation, food waste streams, and more.

The organization started in 1993 and was phased out about twenty years later.

On May 4, 1965, forty-eight members of the University of Georgia Agricultural Alumni Association met in Atlanta, Georgia, to discuss the possibility of forming an agribusiness council. The association formed an organizational committee to pursue the project.

The **Georgia Agribusiness Council (GAC)** was incorporated on January 17, 1966, in Atlanta. Several agribusiness leaders met and formed the council to bring a focus on agribusiness interests in Georgia. Georgia Power's Olin Ginn was one of the founders of the organization. Other leaders were: Frank E. Bailey, Redfern Foods Corp.; John R. Duncan, Southern Railway Systems; Bill Estes, Empire Pedigree Seed Company; Ed Fain, Colonial Stores Inc.; Clyde Greenway, Sears, Roebuck & Company; Joel B. Gunnels, Bank of Worth County; Elmo Hester, Georgia Farmer

Magazine; Harley Langdale, The Langdale Company; W. F. Mullen, Rome Plow Company; Homer Nichols, International Harvester Company; C. W. Paris, Cotton Producers Association; Ed Parker, Columbia Nitrogen Corporation; W. A. Sutton, Citizens & Southern National Bank; and Dr. Irvin Wofford, Southern Nitrogen Company Inc.

The GAC is the state's leading trade association for agribusiness. Its mission is: To Advance the Business of Agriculture through Economic Development, Environmental Stewardship, and Education to Enhance the Quality of Life for All Georgians. The specific objectives of the mission are: represent the agribusiness industry in the legislative and regulatory arenas; provide economic services to members; promote agribusiness development; build coalitions with the agricultural community; promote agricultural education through elementary, secondary, college, and adult programs; and educate the public about agribusiness issues.

The thirty-second and current chairman is Steve Crouch. Other chairmen, in order of service, were W. A. Sutton, W. C. Greenway, C. W. Paris, Hulan Hall, Fisher L. Barfoot, Olin Ginn, A. B. Carlan, Fred Greer Jr., Hugh Craig, Preston M. Collins, Lovick Corn, Garland Thompson, K. C. Williamson, Jerry Dempsey, Sam B. Hay Jr., J. Eugene Southerland, Jimmy L. Hill, E. Raybon Anderson, Jimmie Loftis, Delbert G. Shelton, Wayne Christian, William C. "Bill" Baisley, Joseph S. Tyson, Darvin Eason, Steven Woodruff, David Skinner, Ken Morrow, Merrill Folsom, and Jimmy Champion. Several chairmen served more than one term, as I did.

I was elected to the board of directors in 1987. In 1988, I was elected secretary of the board, and in 1989, vice-chair. I was then fortunate enough to be elected as the seventeenth chairman and served for two years, starting in 1990. My meteoric rise came about due to a couple of officers retiring and lack of availability of some other candidates; I was next in line.

The following people served under my leadership as chairman: vice-chairman, Bill Baisley; secretary, Raybon Anderson; treasurer, Billy Grimsley; past chairmen, Gene Sutherland and Sam Hay; and president, Gary Black. Directors serving were: James Lee Adams; J. B. Amos; Irving Bell; Bobby Boone; Neal Butler; Roy Chappell; Todd Clay; Charles Clotfelter; Lovick Corn; Dr. Joe Crane; Steve Crouch; Mort Ewing; Jim

Gillis; Darl Hinson; Russell Ivie; John Jenkins; Jimmie Loftis; Perry McCranie; Jim Newman; Jimmy Paul; Loyd Poitevint; Garland Thompson; Alvin White, Robert Wilkinson; and Chuck Williams. I have included more information on the Georgia Agribusiness Council during my period of involvement in the Appendix.

A major event each year for GAC was, and still is, the Harvest Celebration, held around Thanksgiving. The event features a four-course dinner, an outstanding performance by a well-known music artist, a silent auction, and a "Field of Dreams" raffle. Not only is it a major fundraiser, but it celebrates the end of the bountiful harvest season in Georgia. In the early years, we found old farm tractors, like the Ford 8N, and had them restored by the students at Abraham Baldwin Agricultural College to be auctioned off at the event.

Following my term as chairman of the Georgia Agribusiness Council board of directors, I stayed on as past chairman and then served as a director until 2013.

Georgia Agribusiness Council staff: Gary Black, Grace Adams and Chairman Hill
* Photo Courtesy of Georgia Agribusiness Council

GAC Chairman Hill with Gene Sutherland and Governor Joe Frank Harris
* Photo Courtesy of Georgia Agribusiness Council

Jimmy Hill and other GAC members with Speaker of the House Newt Gingrich
* Photo Courtesy of Speaker Newt Gingrich

Jimmy Hill on trip to US Congress in Washington, DC
* Photo Courtesy of Georgia Agribusiness Council

*Jimmy Hill and other GAC members meeting
with Secretary of Agriculture, Ed Madigan*
* Photo Courtesy of USDA

Jimmy Hill with Former Governor and US Secretary of Agriculture, Sonny Perdue

In search of other funding methods and wanting to provide another outstanding member service, the GAC board decided to evaluate the possibility of providing a self-funded worker's compensation program for members. The board appointed five members to a committee to investigate the idea and report back to the board. I was asked to accept an appointment to the committee and joined four other board members: Wayne Christian, Raybon Anderson, Steve Crouch, and Gene Sutherland. The committee had its first meeting in April 1992 to explore the idea. We met numerous times over the following nineteen months to research, investigate, and put together the worker's compensation package. I applaud the other four members of the committee for the perseverance and outstanding work done to bring the self-funded worker's compensation plan to completion.

On November 1, 1993, the Georgia Insurance Commissioner approved the formation of the **AgriTrust of Georgia Self-Insured Worker's Compensation Insurance Program**. The program is owned by its policyholder members and sponsored by the GAC. I served on the board until October 23, 1996.

AgriTrust of Georgia trustees refund excess premiums to qualified fund members each year. AgriTrust has been operating for twenty-nine years and has refunded dividends of over nine million dollars.

Georgia Agri-Leaders Forum Foundation (GALFF) was created in 1989, with a focus on providing leadership training and development for individuals working in agriculture, agribusiness, and forestry. GALFF aspired to create a program that fulfilled the mission of "developing individual leaders skilled in communication, educated in local, national and world affairs, familiar with the changing needs of our society, and prepared to meet the present and future challenges of our times."

I was one of five people who helped create the forum. The original idea for developing the training came from Louise Hill (no relation), who was working with the Georgia Farm Bureau Federation at the time. She was pursuing the idea of leadership training for Farm Bureau leaders and farmers. The first formal meeting to discuss the idea of a leadership training program was held in Randy Williams's office at the University of Georgia in 1989. My fellow attendees were Gary Black, Louise Hill, Don Rogers, and Randy Williams. As a result of this meeting, the process was begun for creating the leadership development program, which I describe later in the book.

One of the most interesting commissions I was asked to serve on was the **Georgia Aquaculture Development Commission,** which was created by the Georgia Legislature in 1987 under § 27-4-6 of the Georgia Code. I served from 1987 until 1989.

There were twenty members, appointed by various entities with an interest in developing the aquaculture industry in Georgia. My appointment was by the Georgia Aquaculture Association. Why did they select me? Because Agricultural Affairs had been involved with the industry for many years, specifically in assisting two companies trying to start catfish processing plants. Our department was generally known for assisting in agricultural economic development, and they wanted our expertise.

The commission was charged with making a thorough study of aquaculture and the potential for development and enhancement of aquaculture in the state. They were to "develop, distribute, and, from time to time, amend the aquaculture development plan for the State of Georgia to facilitate the establishment of growth of economically viable aquaculture enterprises in Georgia." Our role included assessing natural resources and evaluating species with potential for culture, identifying constraints to the development of aquaculture, making recommendations to remedy them, identifying roles of state and federal agencies in supporting the aquaculture industry, assessing physical and personnel resources, and more.

There is more information on the Georgia Aquaculture Commission in the Appendix.

In 1993, the Agricultural Affairs, Community Development, and Urban Affairs Departments were all scheduled to move into a new office space in a nearby building. Due to a mix-up, some of the space dedicated to our three departments was assigned to another company. While this was a setback at first, it required us to think outside of the box and to consider a relatively new concept called **telecommuting**.

After careful study and evaluation, we decided to use telecommuting to help us solve the lack of adequate office space in downtown Atlanta. This would allow our employees who traveled extensively across the state to work from a home office instead of driving into the center of Atlanta. These employees were on the road several days a week. Studies indicated that telecommuting would save fuel and emissions, increase employee satisfaction and productivity, and reduce the budget for office space.

A couple of other departments had previously used telecommuting, and we learned from them how to implement the program. We set up a framework of accountabilities for program participants. It included a binding contract that outlined ground rules, signed by the employee and manager. This included an inspection of each employee's home to assure that it had adequate space and a suitable location.

The company would provide each employee with a desk, chair, computer, printer, fax, statewide pager, cell phone, and a direct line to the Georgia Power headquarters office in Atlanta. Productivity rose for those participating in the program by about 20 percent. However, it took some getting used to the idea and to not being able to see fellow employees daily. Our three departments saved Georgia Power around $100,000 by the end of 1994.

I was one of the participants in the telecommuting process and was extremely pleased with how well it functioned for Georgia Power and our employees. Of special note: currently, in March 2020, we are in a state of emergency nationwide, dealing with the coronavirus pandemic. One of the recommendations is for employers to allow employees who can do so to work from home. I telecommuted from my home and worked many days in my home office. Maybe we were years ahead of the working-from-home trend.

The **Governor's Science and Technology Advisory Council** was created by Governor Zell Miller. In 1995, he charged the council with focusing on agriculture as part of its goal to continue to develop and refine a science and technology policy for the State of Georgia. I was one of twenty-two voting members appointed to the council from the field of agriculture, which included academics, research and development, and producers and consumers of technological resources.

Jimmy and Gail Hill talking with Governor Zell Miller
* Photo Courtesy of Governor Zell Miller

The other members were Carl Swearingen, Dr. Claudia R. Adkison, Mark Armentrout, William L. Brown, James Lee Adams, Dr. Larry Allen, Paul Brower, Dr. Gale Buchanan, Wayne Christian, Dr. Glenwood Hill, Dr. Marcia Jones, Dr. Lars G. Ljungdahl, Roy Noble, Marvin Singletary, Randy Swafford, Earl Crosby, Dr. Michael J. Kocurek, Laura Meadows, Frank R. Pidcock III, J. E. (Gene) Sutherland Jr., and J. Craig Wyvill.

Our role was to evaluate Georgia agriculture and focus on identifying twenty-first-century solutions to issues, using science and technology. Governor Miller also asked the council to prepare a strategy for using science and technology as a means of promoting the economic development of agriculture in the state. This involved identifying barriers to technology formation and commercialization, as well as preparing a strategy for marketing Georgia agriculture's strengths, as the state's largest industry, and to improve awareness of Georgia's technology identity in the national and international marketplace. It also involved advising the governor on the needs of the state's technology-based industries and the state's institutions of higher learning.

The council convened under the leadership of Chairman Carl Swearingen for seven working meetings in 1995 to develop an extensive, forty-five-page final report on the current situation and recommendations for the future. The report was presented to Governor Zell Miller on December 15, 1995.

The **Sunbelt Agricultural Exposition** had its beginnings on the campus of the Abraham Baldwin Agricultural College (ABAC) in 1964. It was initially for tractor and farm implement companies to show off their equipment to ABAC students. These same companies employed many ABAC students after graduation. The Expo eventually moved to Moultrie, Georgia, and now attracts thousands of visitors each year.

The mission of the Sunbelt Expo is to produce the premier farm show in the world, one that is conducive to trade and emphasizes information, education, and implementation of the latest agricultural technology, research, and equipment. It now has over twelve hundred exhibitors within the hundred-acre exhibitor site. There is a six-hundred-acre farm attached, where crops are grown and harvested each year. More than three hundred different seminars and demonstrations are offered over the three-day event in October of each year. At least twenty-two land grant colleges and universities from the southeastern United States attend and offer a variety of educational opportunities for Expo visitors. The economic output value of the Sunbelt Expo is over twenty million dollars to South Georgia.

Georgia Power was one of the first exhibitors, outside of the farm equipment dealers, to participate at Sunbelt Expo. The company had a small booth in the agribusiness area for many years. When I became manager of Agricultural Affairs, and as I began to realize that many of Georgia Power's farm, residential, and commercial customers attended the event, I decided to explore ways to enhance our presence at the Expo.

Our first expansion was to a thirty-foot by forty-foot tent, which was cooled by electric heat pumps. We used this setup for two years, and it worked well; however, we were swamped with visitors.

Electricity . . . The Energy For Agriculture
* Photo Courtesy of Sunbelt Expo

Working with the Georgia Electrification Council, we put together a team of various electric utilities in Georgia and came up with the idea of a huge tent to combine all the utilities under one area. The group consisted of Georgia Power, Georgia Electric Membership Cooperatives, Municipal Electrical Authority of Georgia, Georgia Electrification Council, and various other vendors, including heat pump dealers. We named the huge tent "Electricity. . . The Energy for Agriculture." It was eighty feet by four hundred feet.

Our exhibit was one of the largest tents at Expo, and with all the electrical equipment we had, including air conditioning, it required four

200-amp panels with special connections provided by the City of Moultrie. On many days, the exhibit was full of visitors. We finally had to get radios so that our staff could communicate with each other.

This collaborative effort increased our visitor numbers dramatically, and we were able to reach thousands more of our customers with energy conservation topics, electrical safety, and home comfort technologies. The electricity tent was one of the more popular and visited exhibits at Sunbelt and continued for several years after I left Georgia Power in the fall of 1996.

A popular draw was Miss Georgia, who performed her talents each day for the visitors. One year, while she was taking a break from performing in our exhibit, she asked me if I would show her around the Expo. She and I rode on a golf cart around the site. With only forty-five minutes before her next show, I was not able to stop at any of the exhibits. As we were traveling along, I heard someone shouting, "Hey, hey, hey!" I kept going because we were tight on time. The person behind us kept shouting even louder. Miss Georgia asked me if I would stop the cart, thinking it was probably one of her fans who wanted to say hello. I stopped, and the man caught up with us and said, "Jimmy Hill! How in the world are you? I haven't seen you in years!"

Miss Georgia looked at me with a smile on her face. As we set off again, she said, "I have never had that happen before. They always want to meet me."

I didn't say anything. She told the story when we got back to our exhibit.

In September 1990, while I was serving as Georgia Agribusiness Council chairman, I was asked by Gary Black, council president, to be a master of ceremonies at the Sunbelt Willie B. Withers Luncheon, which was to be held that year on Tuesday, October 16. As I understood it, this was a one-time-only responsibility for me. However, Ed White, who was executive director of Sunbelt at that time, asked me to emcee the luncheon again the following year. Following Ed's death in 1997, Chip Blalock was named executive director. Blalock asked me to stay on as emcee for the luncheon.

To make a long story short, I served in that role for twenty-seven years, retiring in 2017.

Serving as emcee at the luncheon was a very interesting and challenging experience. I had to make sure the event started on time and ended on time. When I first started emceeing, the luncheon ran from noon to nearly 2:00 p.m. This was of great concern to many attendees who were exhibitors and needed to get back to their exhibits. Ed and I worked hard to keep speakers within their allotted time frame and to keep the program moving along. During one lengthy luncheon, Tommy Irvin, Georgia Commissioner of Agriculture, made the comment: "Jimmy, you forgot to

Jimmy Hill presiding at the Sunbelt Agricultural Exposition Luncheon
* Photo Courtesy of Sunbelt Expo

introduce the justice of the peace from Hahira." Note, there is no justice of the peace in Hahira—but I got his point. I did have a long list of dignitaries to introduce that day. His comments gave me even more encouragement to continue to find ways to tighten up the timing. Blalock and I finally were able to shorten the program by forty-five minutes.

One particularly long, unscheduled speech occurred back in the 1990s. US senator from South Carolina, Strom Thurmond, had his staff ask me if he could speak. He was not on the schedule. I told them that I could give him five minutes but no more. His staff person agreed to the time frame. Senator Thurmond spoke for five minutes ... six ... seven; at ten minutes, he was still going strong. I asked his staff person to get him off the stage. "He generally speaks as long as he wants," was the reply. I knew that I was in trouble. Finally, as the senator took a breath, I eased to the podium and thanked him for being with us; he went back to his seat. I learned that day not to allow unscheduled speakers to have the podium.

As I was presiding, I would, from time to time, receive notes that I had forgotten to introduce someone in the audience. I quickly learned how much time such digressions could add to the program. It became a balancing act between keeping the program moving and introducing a non-scheduled guest.

Part of my preparation for my emcee duties was to prepare detailed notes to keep things on track and not overlook any part of the program. The event was generally hosted by Maule Air, in their hangar, which was located adjacent to the Sunbelt site. The weather conditions at Sunbelt, over the years, would always provide challenges. Each of the three days of the Expo could have completely different weather: the first day might be hot, the second day rainy, and the third day cold—and on any day, we could have strong winds. There was one particularly gusty day when I was emceeing the luncheon and the wind blew my papers off the podium. As I scrambled to retrieve them, I realized that they were not numbered. Trying not to panic, I worked quickly to organize my notes back into their proper order while attempting to act as if nothing had happened. I learned my lesson; after that, I numbered my papers and put them all in a three-ring binder.

Due to the untimely death of Bobby Batson, manager of national accounts with Swisher International, I was asked in 2007 to emcee the Swisher Sweets/Sunbelt Expo Southeastern Farmer of the Year Award Dinner. This dinner takes place on the Monday night before the start of Sunbelt each year.

I emceed both events until 2017. I never expected to serve as master of ceremonies at Sunbelt for so many years, especially when I think back to how I had feared public speaking as a young man in FFA. Mr. Claxton's advice back then had been to take every chance you have to face your fears. My years of emceeing at the Sunbelt Agricultural Exposition gave me plenty of chances to do that. I soon learned that keeping an event program on track required not only having carefully scripted notes but also being ready to make changes to those notes at a moment's notice. It was a rewarding and enjoyable experience and an honor to have a part in the Sunbelt Agricultural Exposition for so many years, including meeting the "best of the best" farmers in the ten southeastern states each year.

As manager of Agricultural Affairs, I had extensive involvement with the **University of Georgia's College of Agricultural and Environmental Sciences.** I also, of course, had a personal connection, having earned my bachelor's degree in agricultural engineering through the college.

In the early 1990s, I was elected to the board of directors of the Georgia 4-H Foundation and remained a member until late 1996. The foundation supports the programs, activities, and events of the Georgia 4-H program, which is a unit of the college. I was responsible for providing resources to the foundation. I spent time at the Rock Eagle 4-H Center, where Georgia Power had funded a lodging facility. Other centers included the Burton 4-H Center, Fortson 4-H Center, Georgia 4-H at Camp Jekyll, 4-H Tidelands Nature Center, and the Wahsega 4-H Center.

My family and I supported the remodeling of the auditorium at Rock Eagle. The project's fundraising effort was chaired by Senator Herman Talmadge. One of the seats in the auditorium has a plaque that reads *Jimmy, Gail, Chris, and Miranda Hill.*

The 4-H program in Georgia is very strong and impacts thousands of lives each year. I was a member of 4-H when I was in the fifth grade at T. G. Ritch Elementary School in Jesup. Both of my children participated in 4-H activities as well, as did Gail.

I was appointed to the College of Agricultural and Environmental Sciences Dean and Director Search Committee in 1991 by the president of the University of Georgia, Charles B. Knapp. Our committee recommended three candidates for the dean and director position. Ultimately, Dr. Gale Buchanan was hired and served for many years.

The following year, Dean Buchanan appointed me to serve on the College of Agricultural and Environmental Sciences Georgia Agricultural Experiment Stations Research Advisory Board. Our board addressed recommendations for consideration by the leaders of the three experiment stations in Georgia: College Station in Athens, Georgia Station in Griffin, and the Coastal Plain Station in Tifton. I served from 1992 until my term expired in 1996.

Over the years, I have had extensive involvement with the College of Agricultural and Environmental Sciences at UGA-Griffin. I assisted them in getting a retired bucket truck for use in the maintenance of the campus. I also interacted with many of their professors as I addressed issues facing Georgia agriculture and hosted many meetings with agricultural leaders on the Griffin campus.

I have had equally extensive involvement with professors and staff at the UGA-Tifton campus on issues facing South Georgia agriculture over the years and held many meetings there with various agricultural organizations.

Our department was always on the lookout for opportunities to benefit energy-related education in Georgia. We learned that Georgia Power was removing its huge array of solar panels that covered about two acres of the low-rise portion of the corporate office in downtown Atlanta. The solar panels had been in operation for many years and were due to be replaced. Travis Henry worked with the corporate office staff to secure the panels for us to offer to middle and high schools across the state of Georgia. He developed an installation protocol for teachers to follow so that they could install the panels and use them for solar education.

On Wednesday, August 11, 1993, the headline of the *Waycross Journal-Herald* read: "**Innovative Magnet School at Manor Given Approval.**"

Nobody had any idea how this news would impact the education of Ware County students, and only a very few people had any clue as to the amount of time and work that had been done during the year leading up to approval. The Ware Board of Education had voted to close the Manor Elementary School the year before. The school building had been constructed by WPA workers in 1936 for local students from first through eleventh grade.

From the time the closing of the school had been announced, the principal, a Manor, Georgia, native, had been trying to find a way to save the school and the Manor community; as in all small towns across South Georgia, everything revolved around the school, and the closing of a rural school has a major impact on the community. His idea was for a magnet school along the lines of the Chicago High School for Agricultural Sciences (CHSAS) in Illinois, and he had been working with Barry Deas on the concept. At the time, Barry was an agriculture teacher in the Ware County school system. He was also a graduate of the Georgia Agri-Leaders Forum Foundation (GALFF). I had known Barry for some time through agricultural education and as a member of the Georgia Young Farmers Association.

The first chance the two men had to meet on the idea was late one Sunday evening, around ten o'clock. They knew from the beginning that they would have to overcome local resistance and beat major odds to get school board approval to pull this off. Deas had developed a list of five major leaders in agriculture in Georgia who could be useful in recruiting state-wide support for the school. At this point, GALFF became a major player in the effort to form the new school. All five people on Deas's list were members of the GALFF board of directors. Deas was a member of the Charter Class of Agri-Leaders and had just returned from a weeklong agricultural tour in Florida with most of the people he had listed.

The first meeting to present the concept of a K–12 agricultural magnet school, along with the data from the Chicago High School for Agricultural Sciences, was held at the Georgia Cattlemen's Association headquarters in Macon, Georgia. Jim Loftis, director of Public Affairs with Gold Kist, and I, as manager of Agricultural Affairs at Georgia Power, were among those who attended the meeting.

It was agreed it would be desirable to visit the magnet school in Chicago. I arranged for Larry Barber, Barry Deas, Talmadge Booth, Clarence Billups, Gary Black, and I to make the one-day round trip on the Georgia Power company plane.

The magnet school concept had been created after the Chicago Board of Education decided to close one of its schools, which had over ten acres of excess land that had been leased to a local farmer. He produced vegetables and fruits for the residents around the school property. When the residents heard about the school closing, they were upset that the farmer was losing his lease and that they would not get fresh vegetables and fruits each year. The school principal proposed creating a magnet school for agriculture. The school board agreed, and the principal, along with his hand-selected teachers, created the Chicago High School for Agricultural Sciences.

CHSAS added one more class per day than other schools were offering. The student government was run by the FFA Chapter. The first year of operation led to seniors getting over one million dollars in scholarships. The school was so popular that it had to implement a lottery system for applications. Absenteeism at the magnet school was about one percent, which was much lower than other Chicago public schools. Students had to ride city buses to the school, some of them traveling two hours one way. The hallways were lined with FFA awards that had been won by the students. We met one student who had a special interest in aquaculture. His teacher had allowed him to have a small room with several large fish tanks for research on fish. The teacher told us that his student had developed a relationship with professors at Auburn University, who were helping him with his research, and that Auburn had already offered him a scholarship, even though he was only a sophomore.

Our Georgia group was impressed and inspired by what was an extremely innovative and successful high school.

After a year of promoting the magnet school concept, constructing curriculum, and securing resources, the time arrived to offer the opportunity for Ware County students to register to attend the magnet school. Deas and his team were hoping that enthusiasm was growing and that students and their parents would want to be a part of this new, innovative school.

On Tuesday, August 17, 1993, a week after its headline about the Manor Magnet School approval, the *Waycross Journal-Herald* ran a follow-up story: "Crowd Lines Up Overnight For Magnet School: Hundreds Waited Through the Night Sunday in Line to Apply for the School."

A Federal Magnet School Grant of $1.9 million, the most money per student in the history of the program, was acquired to hire specific teachers and staff for the first two years of the new school. Special thanks from the

Barry Deas and Jimmy Hill meeting about Magnet School

magnet school committee went to US Senators Sam Nunn and Paul Coverdell and US Congressman Jack Kingston for their support of the program.

The magnet school opened the following Monday, August 24, for K–10 students. Over the next two years, eleventh and twelfth grades were added. This made the Ware County School of Agricultural, Forestry, and Environmental Sciences (Ware Magnet) the only K–12 agriculture-based magnet in the United States.

The first graduating class, comprising seventeen seniors, was ranked seventeenth in academic achievement in the state. From that class of 1996 to the class of 2009, which had fifty seniors, the ranking went straight up. Ware Magnet was ranked the number four school in the state at that time, with a 99 percent graduation rate over all those years.

The school was designed for a good average student to get an outstanding education. The curriculum, starting in kindergarten, was based on agricultural and related fields and provided the opportunity to teach the practical application of mathematics, science, and technology at the highest levels. Even with a bare-bones budget, and despite many trials and tribulations, all students were provided with a top-notch education, with many receiving four-year scholarships to colleges across Georgia and in other states. Because of their deep understanding of the content of their classes, magnet students were often asked by their college professors where they had attended high school.

I am grateful to Barry Deas for providing many of the above details on the Ware County School of Agricultural, Forestry, and Environmental Sciences. Barry was tireless in the magnet school effort. Even during every Agri-Leaders Forum session, he would discuss the school and hand out materials to each presenter.

Barry shared the following as part of his recollections of this outstanding program: "There were many people who believed in and worked hard to support the K–12 agricultural magnet idea, including the Georgia Agri-Leaders Forum board of directors and the Charter Class. Others who were supportive were the Georgia Agribusiness Council, Gold Kist, and especially Georgia Power's Jimmy Hill, an absolute stellar supporter from day one! Thanks to these and many local leaders, but especially the parents, students, and dedicated teachers who made Ware Magnet a phenomenal educational success."

Barry is gracious in his praise and thanks, and I would like to add my appreciation and thanks to Barry. He was a major player and a leader in the creation of the magnet school.

There were many other entities with which the Agricultural Affairs Department was involved. The scope of these connections shows just how deeply the agricultural industry and Georgia Power connect in addressing agricultural economic development in Georgia.

ABAC, where I received my associate degree, serves rural and agricultural Georgia, as well as drawing students from around the world, as a place of higher learning for students majoring in agriculture and many other areas of academic study.

I was elected to serve as a board member of the ABAC Alumni Association in April 1988 and served for five years, during which I was elected vice president in 1990 and then, in 1991, president, after which I finished with a one-year term as past president.

In 1990, ABAC Alumni president Tommy Rollins appointed me to serve under DeNean Stafford, chairman of the ABAC Capital Campaign. Alex Kemp, Marolyn Mixon, and Tyron Spearman were also appointed as members of the campaign. I was also appointed to chair the long-range planning committee.

Our campaign goal was to raise $1.5 million for the college for the following purposes: $950,000 for student scholarships and financial assistance, $250,000 for equipment teaching resources, $100,000 for faculty development, and $200,000 for the library expansion and enhancement.

In 1991, during my term as president, our officer and director team included Susan Griffin, vice president, Tommy Rollins, past president, and the following directors: John Ellington, Susan Moss, Roby Murray, Jack Legg, Howard Turner, Ronnie Rollins, Jody Haley, Rick Bostelman, Yvonne Crawford, Mike Nations, D. Q. Harris, Harold Ragan, Wanda

Grogan, Randy Nichols, Alex Kemp, Susan West, Sarah Akins, Quay Allen, Jimmy Grubbs, Andrea Willis, Pattie Garett, Ron Jones, and Geneva Day.

I appointed Louise Hill to the executive committee. The board elected Ronnie Rollins to also serve on the executive committee. At the June 7, 1991, board meeting, Elaine Shellhouse Wright was elected to the board of directors.

Cecil Medders, Alabama Power Company agricultural engineer, and I jointly led the formation of a business planning model for Agribusiness in the American South on May 17–18, 1994. This meeting included Gary Black, president, Georgia Agribusiness Council, and Jack Buckner, executive director, Alabama Agribusiness Council, along with representatives from other agricultural organizations. The theme of the meeting was **Agribusiness: Changing the Paradigm of the American South.**

Four major issues were evaluated:

- Collaboration between southern agricultural states on marketing, promotion, and educating the public could provide a competitive advantage such as that now enjoyed by larger agricultural producing regions of the United States and the world

- Opportunities and threats from each southern state competing against each other for a market share of the global customer base

- How multi-state cooperation among agricultural organizations and agribusinesses, colleges and universities, state agencies, and private sector interests could offer more opportunities for growth for agriculture in the American South than the current level of competition seen among states at these levels

- The window of opportunity presented by the 1996 Summer Olympic Games being held in the American South could provide an excellent stage to showcase to the world the uniqueness and competitiveness of southern agriculture

One major result of this effort was the development of the "Showcase of Southern Agriculture: Georgia Agriculture 1996" exhibit at the 1996 Summer Olympic Games held in Atlanta, which I cover further in a separate chapter.

I joined the **American Society of Agricultural Engineers (ASAE)** in 1971 as I completed my senior year at the University of Georgia. At that time, ASAE was an international professional society devoted to agricultural engineering. It was founded in December 1907 at the University of Wisconsin-Madison and is now known as the American Society of Agricultural and Biological Engineers (ASABE).

My agricultural engineering degree was tremendously beneficial in allowing me to address technical and engineering issues for Georgia Power's agricultural and agribusiness customers. The ASAE was a great resource for information and expertise.

In 1991, I was elected as a technical director of the society's board of directors. Later I was elected director of the Mechanization, Marketing, and Technology Management Committee within the board of directors.

I also became active in the ASAE–Georgia Section in 1971. I became an officer in the late 1980s and was elected chairman in 1986 for one year. I was featured as the "Engineer of the Issue" in the December 1987 Georgia Section newsletter and was honored to be elected by my peers to receive the Georgia Section ASAE Engineer of the Year Award in 1991.

The **Atlanta Farmers Club** started in 1945 under the auspices of the Atlanta Chamber of Commerce. John Sibley was the first president. The purpose of the club was to develop closer relationships with others who were interested in promoting agriculture and agribusiness—Georgia's largest industry. The club sponsored the North Georgia Rural Community Development Program in cooperation with the Cooperative Extension

Service. They reached hundreds of communities building rural and urban relationships.

The club held a monthly luncheon program with guest speakers. It also sponsored field trips to points of agricultural interest. Sponsorships of cattle shows for 4-H and FFA members were provided, and the club was a host sponsor of the state 4-H Congress held in Atlanta each year.

Several Georgia Power Agricultural Affairs staff members served as presidents of the club over the years. Olin Ginn served in 1966, Lamar Wansley in 1967, and a member of my staff, Travis Henry, served in 1995. I served as director for two years ending in 2000.

This was a club that attracted the agricultural movers and shakers of North Georgia. Many key decisions affecting Georgia agriculture came out of relationships that were built as a result of club membership. Some prominent members included: Gary Black, now Georgia's Commissioner of Agriculture; Judge William Daniel, Fulton County; Wayne Dollar, president, Georgia Farm Bureau; Dr. Glenn Glover, economist, Gold Kist; Fred Greer, Agricultural Bank, C & S National Bank; Dr. Fred Harrison Jr., Fort Valley State University; Tommy Irvin, the previous Georgia Commissioner of Agriculture; Melvin Johnson, state director for agricultural education; William Moore, Georgia Milk Producers; State Representative Robert Ray; Dr. Robert Schulstad, University of Georgia College of Agricultural and Environmental Sciences; David Skinner, Georgia Development Authority; Robert Trulock, Dean Witter Reynolds; John Wilkinson, Georgia FFA; and Dr. Gene Younts, vice president, University of Georgia.

The **Electric Power Research Institute (EPRI)** is an independent organization that conducts research, development, and demonstration projects focused on electric energy for the benefit of the public in the United States and internationally. A component of EPRI was the Agriculture Technology Alliance (ATA), which had the same mission as EPRI but focused on agriculture, studying, evaluating, and conducting research projects.

I became a member of ATA when I joined Georgia Power's Agricultural Affairs Department. We evaluated several agriculture technologies and conducted scoping studies. These included agricultural research, irrigation, nitrate evaluation in groundwater and estuaries, animal waste issues, cotton production, handling and drying crops, soil testing and the internet, postharvest crop physiology, and soil science.

We held meetings, conducted field trips, and obtained input from experts to evaluate these issues. Many of the research topics were of interest to my agriculture and agribusiness customers at Georgia Power, and results were shared with our customers to enhance their business success.

Fort Valley State University is a public, historically black university located in Fort Valley, Georgia. It is one of the thirty-one colleges and universities that are part of the University System of Georgia.

I have had the pleasure of working with several professors at Fort Valley State University on agricultural projects over the years. Dr. Curtis Borne, professor of agricultural education, and I have worked together for many years on issues regarding agricultural education and the FFA program. I met Dr. Seyedmehdi Mobini, professor of veterinary medicine, in 2001, when he interviewed for selection in the 2002 class of the Georgia Agri-Leaders Forum. Dr. Mobini was selected and was an outstanding member of the 2002 class. He and I also worked together on several projects over the years.

The mission of the **Georgia Cattlemen's Association (GCA)** is "to unite and advance the cattle industry in Georgia through legislative representation, producer education, market development, and community events." GCA was established in 1961 and has over five thousand members.

The cattle industry in Georgia has a three-billion-dollar economic impact in Georgia. An interesting fact is that cattle are reared in every county in Georgia. The cattle producers have stewardship of over four million acres of land in Georgia.

I have worked with several GCA executive vice presidents, including Glenn Smith, Bobby Freeman, Jim Collins, Josh White, and Will Bentley. Dale Sandlin is the current executive vice president. I have enjoyed working with long-time employee Michele Creamer, who is the vice president of operations for GCA. Michele is from Hazlehurst, Georgia, where I finished high school.

I was at the dedication of the new GCA headquarters building in Macon in 1987. I worked with several presidents of the association, including Sam Hay, Harvey Lemmon, Gene Chambers, Mike Peed, Sam Payne, Bobby Miller, Newt Muse, Howard Jones, Mark Armentrout, Ralph Bridges, Lane Holton, Jim Goodman, Dr. Frank Thomas, Joe Duckworth, Betts Berry, Curly Cook, Chuck Sword, Robert Fountain, Jr., Louie Perry, Tim Dean, John Callaway, and Dr. Jim Strickland.

The **Georgia Egg Commission (GEC)** was formed in 1961 by a group of egg producers who saw a need for promotion, education, and research in the egg industry. The commission was one of the first of its kind to be created in Georgia.

The commission staff met with hundreds of thousands of consumers over the years, explaining the benefits of eggs. They ran thousands of advertisements, including on the radio, to reach egg consumers. They attended thousands of events to communicate the value of eggs in family diets, developing hundreds of recipes, and conducting research and educational programs to benefit the consumer and the commission's member farmers.

The budget of the GEC was funded by egg producers in Georgia. The refrigeration of eggs was not mandated before 1994. It was this commission that championed and led to the refrigeration of eggs in the United States. The GEC researched and determined that eggs should be refrigerated at 45°F to hold down bacteria and help guarantee freshness and quality. This recommendation was accepted by the United States Department of Agriculture on August 27, 1999, and the 45-degree storage temperature is now required for all eggs produced in the United States.

Every three years, Georgia egg producers were required to vote on whether to continue to fund and operate the commission. On April 30, 2013, the egg producers voted 7–5 to end the commission, and it ceased operation on June 30 that year.

Robert Howell was the executive director of the commission from its start in 1961. He shared with me that no other egg promotion has been undertaken in Georgia since the GEC was officially disbanded.

The **Georgia Electrification Council's (GEC)** mission was "to serve the electrical industry by combining the various capabilities of member organizations and various allies into coordinated activities to identify and provide educational and training opportunities."

I was elected to the board of directors in 1988. In 1990, I was asked to assume the role of vice-chairman of Governmental Affairs. At that time, many electrical industries and their allies had representatives on the board, including Billy Smith, Curtis Kingsley, Preston Johnson, Deforrest Parrott, Jay Gray, Lowry Gillespie, Roy Thomas, Jerry Boatwright, Linda Brock, Ray Watson, Lloyd Bird Jr., Keith Bass, Dr. Wayne Jordan, Dr. William Flatt, Dr. Dale Threadgill, Richard Cox, Mort Ewing, Bob Kesterton, Don Stokely, Forest Stacy, Stanley Hill, James Rayburn, Earl Woods, Earl Smith, and Olin Ginn. The staff included Cecil Beggs, Rita Hatcher, Katrina Claxton, Kim Drew, and Mark Thomas.

I also taught courses on heating and air conditioning as part of the curriculum offered by the council before, during, and after my service on the board of directors. I served on the board until late 1996.

The **Georgia Farm Bureau (GFB)** is the largest voluntary agricultural organization in Georgia. A non-governmental organization, it has around three hundred thousand member families and was formed in 1937 by fifty farmers. GFB has a strong grassroots network with 159 county farm bureau organizations. They provide all types of insurance, member discounts, and various communication tools to members. They also have a strong public policy department that works with regulatory and legislative organizations to communicate farmer issues.

I have worked with them over the years in addressing policy positions related to electricity production and tariffs that affect farmers. I attended every yearly convention to meet with Georgia Power farm customers to discuss issues of interest while I was the manager of Agricultural Affairs, starting in 1986 and until 1996.

The GFB presidents that I worked with included Bob Nash, Mort Ewing, Wayne Dollar, Zippy Duvall, and Gerald Long.

The **Georgia FFA Alumni Association** was formed to support the FFA agricultural education program in Georgia.

The purposes of the association are to:

- support and promote the FFA organization, activities, and agricultural education at local, state, and national levels
- provide a tie to the state FFA and assist agricultural education/FFA personnel to involve former members and others interested in supporting worthy activities
- promote greater knowledge of the agricultural industry and support education in agriculture
- promote and maintain an appreciation of the American free enterprise system
- promote the personal development of Georgia FFA members through our support of the Georgia FFA

In 1989, I became a life member of the association. I led the effort to develop its strategic plan in 1992. I was elected association president for the 1993–1994 term.

I joined this association to continue the support of state agricultural education by the Agricultural Affairs Department at Georgia Power. Our department had been a long-time sustaining supporter of the program.

With Georgia's largest economic engine being agriculture and agribusiness, supporting agricultural education was a way to ensure the industry's continued success in the future.

The **Georgia Young Farmers Association (GYFA)** was formed in 1971 as an extension of the state's agricultural education program, which had begun in 1951. Its purpose was to coordinate activities at the state level and to develop leadership in its members. The association has fifty-nine chapters and 5,705 members in Georgia.

The Agricultural Affairs Department coordinated with the GYFA in sponsoring an awards program to recognize the most outstanding young farm family in the state of Georgia.

The awards program:

- encouraged efficient management of land, labor, capital and electrical energy usage in farming
- developed leadership for moving agriculture forward in Georgia
- encouraged the farmer and family to become more involved in community service
- encouraged practices of sound environmental actions

Four farm families would compete for the award each year. GYFA and Georgia Power would host a judging tour to visit each of the farms. Georgia agricultural experts would do the judging. The winning family was presented with a cash award, a plaque, and a sign for their farm indicating they are being named the Outstanding Farm Family at the yearly GYFA State Convention.

Following my departure from my position as manager of Agricultural Affairs, the Georgia Development Authority picked up the sponsorship of the awards program.

I had the pleasure of working with Terrell Weeks after he was named executive director of the GYFA in the late 1980s. Terrell was a former agricultural education teacher and was the second director of the association. He met with an untimely death in an automobile accident on September 28, 2002, near Watkinsville, Georgia. GYFA created a scholarship in his name. The Terrell Weeks Memorial Scholarship has awarded a scholarship each year since 2003 to a deserving high school senior from a GYFA member family.

Leadership Georgia (LG) was created in 1971, with the first class conducted in 1972. Its primary purpose is to identify, train, and inspire a network of emerging young leaders, from twenty-five to forty-five years old. The young leaders are chosen for their desire and potential to work together for a better Georgia.

Dr. J. W. Fanning, Pat Pattillo, Jim Linetz Sr., and Rogers Wade were the program's founders, with Dr. Fanning serving as a guiding force. Though the training initially focused on just one person in the family, Dr. Fanning's wife, Cora Lee, insisted that the spouse or significant other be invited to attend as well. She also played a key role in the program in its early years.

Dr. Fanning described LG's purpose as being to prepare strong and effective leaders for the future development of Georgia. Those who participate are from every nook and cranny of Georgia, from the countryside and small towns to the big cities.

Gail and I were selected to participate in this year-long leadership program in 1990. We joined with about 120 people from across the state of Georgia who met five times during the year to address various issues affecting the state.

Our participation in LG started in January 1990:

- The first program kicked off at Unicoi State Park and Lodge in Helen, Georgia, on January 18–20. Its focus was "Brave Leadership for a Preferred Future," led by Bryan Bell.
- The second program was held in Thomasville, Georgia, on March 15–17. Ray Chadwick Jr. led the training weekend on

the topic of "Crime, Drugs, and Morality: Is the Damage Already Beyond Repair?"

- We met on St. Simons Island, Georgia, May 10–12, for our third program, "Of Neighbors and Neighborhoods, *Comprende?*" led by Merry Jo Whidby.
- The fourth was held in Dalton, Georgia, on September 6–8 with a focus on "What Then Education?" led by John Raudabaugh.
- Duane Harris led the fifth and final program, "Our Physical Environment: Who's in Control?" It was held in Warm Springs, Georgia, on November 15–17.

This was a great experience, meeting leaders from across Georgia and discussing issues facing our state. About three thousand leaders from across the state have participated in this program since its inception.

The **National Food and Energy Council (NFEC)** was formed in 1957 to serve the needs of 225 electric utilities by providing valuable information and technical support on topics related to production agriculture. The NFEC started with initial discussions in 1952. The first full-time executive manager, J. Turrel, was hired in 1962. He retired in 1976, and Ken McFate was hired as the new executive manager. In 1991, Richard Hiatt was hired as the executive manager. In 2008, the NFEC became the Rural Electricity Resource Council (RERC) under Hiatt's continued leadership.

My immediate supervisor, Jack Talley, vice president of Economic Development, served for several years on the NFEC board of directors. I represented him at NFEC board meetings when he was unable to attend, including in Washington, DC; Minneapolis, Minnesota; St. Louis, Missouri; Lexington, Kentucky; Des Moines, Iowa; Indianapolis, Indiana; Branson, Missouri; and Atlanta, Georgia.

The NFEC produced technical manuals that the Agricultural Affairs staff used extensively in working with our farmer customers and other agribusinesses. I spoke a couple of times at their annual meetings on my agricultural work in Georgia. The organization disbanded in 2016 due to several factors, including an inability to generate sufficient funds to operate the organization, a refocusing of priorities, and funding issues of member utilities.

With so many varied responsibilities, experiences, and interactions during my ten-year stint as manager of Agricultural Affairs, there were of course some interesting stories that happened along the way.

One time, eight of us who were traveling together on a GYFA judging tour stopped for the night at a motel in the northern part of Georgia. We unloaded our luggage, freshened up, and were about to head to dinner. This was one of those motels where every room door opens onto the walkway, and the wall is all glass, so if the curtains are open, you can see right into each room. The motel staff had, as usual, opened all the curtains in the rooms. As we gathered in the parking lot, we could see Alvin White sitting on his bed with his television remote control, clicking on channels. Unbeknownst to him, David Skinner, known as a prankster, had got his remote from his own room and was standing on the walkway, off to one side, where Alvin could not see him. As Alvin clicked the channel forward, David clicked it backward. Alvin clicked it forward again, and David clicked it backward. It got funnier the longer we watched, as Alvin shook his remote, trying to get the channel to move forward. We finally could not control ourselves and began to laugh helplessly at the sight of Alvin fuming and David enjoying his mischief.

Some other incidents from my time on the road that stand out in my memory follow below.

Several years ago, I was hosting the GYFA judging team, traveling all over the state in a van with five others as part of the selection process for the Outstanding Young Farm Family. We arrived one evening at our scheduled motel at around six o'clock. The motel sign had a bag over it and no visible name. I found out later that it had lost its franchise and had been purchased by another chain.

We threw our clothes into our rooms, went straight out to eat supper, and returned a couple of hours later.

Back in my room, I proceeded to unpack my clothes and toiletries. As I was about through, something on the floor caught my eye. It was moving … it was dark-looking … it was slithering along like a snake … it *was* a snake, heading toward the outside door of the room. The problem: the door was not open, and the snake was between me and the door. Thinking quickly, I jumped on the bed to go around the snake on the right. He, the snake—I am not sure it was a "he," but, for this story, it was a "he"—decided to take a ninety-degree turn to the left and went under the dresser.

I immediately went to the motel office and asked the lady at the counter for another room. She asked why. How do you tell someone that there is a snake in your room?

"There is a snake in my room," I said, in a low voice.

"What?"

I said again, in a louder voice, "There is a snake in my room."

She turned and spoke to a man seated at a desk in a small room behind her. "George," she said, "this man says there is a snake in his room."

"It would not surprise me," said George.

I got a key to another room that was six doors down. It took several trips to move all my belongings, as I had already unpacked most of them. I took the key to the snake room back to the front counter. As I returned to my new room, it dawned on me: I had not searched this room for snakes. Do you know how long it takes to search a room for snakes? It took about one hour of looking into every cranny and lifting every piece of furniture. I did not sleep well that night.

The moral of the story: if you come to your motel and it has a bag covering the motel name, keep driving.

I checked into a motel on the beach and found the door to my room open. Of course, I was concerned—my first thought was that someone was in there. I slowly and carefully entered the room. I called out, Is anyone here? No answer. I continued looking around the room. Nothing. No one was in the bathroom or on the patio. No clothes were in the closet.

I was still curious, so I called the front desk. The very nice lady suggested that the maid had probably not closed my door after she had cleaned the room. That sounded like a good explanation.

I went off to dinner. After I returned, I again searched the room and found nothing. I had a great night's sleep and woke refreshed the next day.

As I awoke, I realized that I had agreed to meet a friend for breakfast that morning. I looked at the clock and knew that if I were to meet him as agreed, I would have to hurry and get ready. And I mean hurry—I had to travel quite a distance to meet him for breakfast.

I jumped out of bed, headed into the bathroom, grabbed a washcloth, and proceeded to take a quick shower. After rinsing off, I opened the shower curtain and reached for the towel. It was not there. I realized, as I looked around, that the washcloth was the only item of linen in the bathroom.

As I pondered my situation, I got out of the shower and went to see if maybe the towels were in the bedroom somewhere. No towels were to be found anywhere. What could I do to dry off? I went back into the bathroom, thinking I could use a hairdryer. But there was no hairdryer to be found. I called the front desk, explained the situation, and asked that they bring me a bath towel. The clerk said that he could not leave the front desk unattended. It was 5:00 a.m., and he was the only person on duty. He suggested that I come and get a towel from the front desk. I explained again that I was naked and could not leave the room. He had no further suggestions for me.

I then had a thought: maybe I could dry off using the bedsheet. I lay down on the bed and rolled around. It was not working—the sheets were not absorbing the water. Then I pulled a sheet off the bed and wrapped myself up in it. Surely this would work. I learned a valuable lesson: bedsheets do not absorb water. All the sheet did was move the water around.

It was at this point that I thought about making the trip to the front desk. If I wrapped the sheet more securely around me, maybe I could make a dash over there and get a towel. I fashioned myself a makeshift toga, which looked ridiculous, but it was 5:00 a.m. and dark, and who would be out at that time of the morning? I peeped out the door of the room, and all I heard was quiet.

I then realized that in the time that I had been moving around wrapped in the sheet, I had begun to get drier. I gave up the idea of the trip to the front desk. I was dry enough that I could now get dressed. I made it on time for breakfast.

Moral of the story: if your motel door is open when you arrive, check to see if you have towels.

I was traveling on business in South Georgia. I spent the night at a Holiday Inn, which had a great buffet breakfast bar. The breakfast was the reason that I stayed at this hotel. They served the best cinnamon rolls: soft, fluffy, hot, and so delicious.

Well, let me get back to the story. I went down to breakfast at 6:00 a.m., sat down, and ordered coffee. I had a couple of sips and got a whiff of those famous cinnamon rolls. Making a beeline for the buffet bar, I took a few rolls and some other breakfast items, then returned to my table and started eating.

As I took another sip of coffee, I noticed this nice couple come in and sit about two tables to the north of me. They were served coffee, and they, too, went straight to the buffet. The man went back to their table after also loading up with cinnamon rolls and other assorted breakfast items.

His wife came around the corner from the buffet and came to my table. She pulled out the chair across from me and sat down. I watched her for a moment, trying to figure out what she was doing. She proceeded to unwrap her silverware from her napkin. She reached for the salt and pepper. By this time, I was speechless, watching this strange lady seated at my table, preparing to eat her breakfast.

Suddenly, I heard a voice: "Honey … Honey, I am over here." I looked up; it was her husband, calling her from their table. She looked at me, somewhat confused. She then mumbled a few words, got up, and went to join her husband.

I sat there for a few minutes, trying to figure out what had happened. I must admit that her husband and I resembled each other. He was about my size, and we both had silver hair. After they had finished eating, they came by my table and she apologized to me. She said that she had not been fully awake when they had come down to breakfast. Her husband smiled and shook his head as they left the restaurant.

The moral of the story: before eating breakfast in a restaurant, you had better be fully awake or you might utterly embarrass yourself by sitting down with a stranger.

I checked into a motel in South Georgia on a hot, muggy afternoon in July. I went to my room and deposited my clothes and set out to find a local "greasy spoon" for supper.

After eating, I went straight back to the room, hoping for a quiet and cool evening. I had turned the air conditioner on High Cool before going out, and sure enough, it was very cold and inviting when I got back. The motel king bed even looked comfortable after a long day on the road.

As I sat down on the edge of the bed to untie my shoes, I noticed a straight, black streak on the floor running from the outside door to under the lavatory sink. I didn't remember that black streak being there earlier. I looked closer and saw it was a line of black ants! I followed their trail to under the lavatory sink and discovered leftover fried chicken bones lying there. Most of the meat had been eaten off the bones, but there was enough left to attract a colony of ants.

The front desk clerk was not even surprised when I told her about the black ant colony that had invaded my room. She explained that the motel had hosted a family reunion over the weekend, and that probably explained the chicken bones in my room. I immediately asked for another room. She explained kindly but firmly that there was no other room to be had—they were sold out. She did offer to go spray the ants. I declined and asked to speak to the manager. After a few minutes of discussing the situation with the manager, who I had woken up at home, I was given another room.

The moral of the story: always check for chicken bones.

You just never know what or who you will find in your hotel room. My family and I were traveling to Florida and spent the first night in South Georgia at a Holiday Inn. I checked in and got our room key, and we headed to our room. Gail and the two kids were right behind me as I opened the door to the room. To my surprise, a woman was sitting in the middle of the bed, eating an apple. I apologized and started backing out. She said, "I will be out of here in a few minutes."

I told my family that we needed to get another room, and we headed back to the front desk. The lady at the check-in counter did not seem to be shocked by my story. I got another room.

On another occasion, I was headed to a southern Georgia city for a convention. I had a meeting that afternoon, so when I got to the hotel, I quickly checked in, then rushed up to my room and left my luggage. Gail was due to join me after the meeting. We met in the lobby when she arrived and headed up to the room together.

As I opened the door, I saw a lady in the room. Gail was right behind me.

"Hi, Jimmy! I guess we are rooming together at this convention," said the lady.

My mouth was wide open, but nothing came out. By this time, Gail had pushed me aside to see who this woman was. It was an awkward moment that seemed to last close to five minutes. But a moment later, a man walked out of the bathroom.

"Hello, Jimmy. It's good to see you," he said. "I guess the hotel must have been full and they are doubling us up."

As it turned out, I knew this couple from my ABAC days; they had been students there when I was, many years earlier. They had noticed my luggage and had thought they had a roommate. I told them I was sure the hotel had enough rooms, and Gail and I went back downstairs with our luggage to the front desk and explained the situation. They apologized and gave us another room immediately.

One time, I was due to attend a convention on the coast of Georgia, and I had reservations at the hotel where it was taking place. Unfortunately, I was late getting to the hotel and arrived around midnight. I was able to check in and headed to my room. I had driven six hours to get to the hotel and was extremely tired. I was so thankful that I was about to get some needed rest and sleep. This was an older hotel, and I had to climb stairs to reach my room, which was then at the very end of the hall. I inserted my key into the lock, and it would not work. I pulled it out and then tried again—no luck.

I retraced my steps back to the lobby and explained the key issue. The lady gave me another key. I trudged back up the stairs and along the hallway and tried the key. It worked!

As I pushed the door, it seemed as if something was blocking it. I finally got it open enough to stick my head in and see what the problem was. I could not believe what I saw: the entire plaster ceiling had collapsed and fallen on the bed, the floor, and everything else in the room. It took me a minute to understand the gravity (pun intended) of the situation.

I headed back downstairs to explain this unbelievable turn of events.

"You are probably not going to believe me," I said, "but my ceiling is on the bed and the floor of the room."

"Oh, I believe you. We have had that happen before," the lady said.

She gave me another room key, and I headed to the next adventure. Fortunately, I got an upgraded room that still had the ceiling intact. I told this story the next day at the convention and nobody believed me.

I was attending an agricultural convention in Columbus, Georgia, in the early 1990s. At 5:00 a.m., I was woken up by the fire alarm. I opened my door and looked out into the hall. There was no sign of a fire, and nobody else was in the hall. I called the front desk and asked if there was a fire in the hotel.

"We are trying to determine that right now," said the clerk.

I asked him to call me back when he found out; then I hung up the phone. My first thought after that was: is he going to remember to call

Jimmy Hill in Room 345 if he is dealing with a fire? I pulled some clothes on—it was below freezing outside—and headed for the exit. I had to descend the stairs from the third floor to exit the building. Several of my friends were leaving the building as well. We stood in the parking lot for about forty-five minutes before the all-clear was given. There was no fire.

When I returned home, I thought about what I had done. First of all, I should have exited the building immediately—no further discussion. Second, I should not have called the front desk and asked about the fire. The hotel staff would already have had their hands full. I decided to write to the hotel's corporate office and confess my sin of not exiting immediately. I also offered my opinion that their staff should have told me to exit immediately.

A reply came a few days later, thanking me for my letter. They agreed with both of my comments. They assured me they were reviewing all safety measures with their hotel staff.

The moral of this story is: get out of a building when the fire alarm goes off!

As I wrap up this chapter, I want to tell you about Jack Talley. Jack was a great manager, who allowed me and his other reports plenty of latitude in managing our departments. He would analyze everything that we requested from him and ask a lot of questions to make sure we knew what we were doing and what the likely outcome would be. I always kept him in the loop and asked for his wisdom as I tackled projects. He was an enthusiastic supporter of me and my department.

Jack's mentoring included making sure that I attended all appropriate Georgia Power management courses. He would suggest events or meetings that he thought I should attend that would benefit me professionally. He was someone who I could call on when making difficult decisions, as he would help me think through all the pros and cons.

He was a lover of boiled peanuts. In 1993, I found a supply of farm-fresh raw peanuts that made excellent boiled peanuts. Jack volunteered to go with me to South Georgia to help process and can them. He would often, over the years, brag about how good those peanuts were. He remained one of my best friends. He retired before me, but we always stayed in touch.

Jack was a jokester; he would do some hilarious things. Back in 1995, he and I attended a meeting in Nashville, Tennessee. We stayed at the Gaylord Opryland Resort and Convention Center. We were on our way to dinner one night, walking through the resort, and Jack noticed an auditorium on the right. He walked in and headed to the stage. The auditorium was about half full. I stood in the doorway, not knowing what he was about to do. He walked up to the stage and grabbed the microphone. What happened next was unbelievable and classic Jack Talley.

He was a man of many talents. He sang a country music song acapella, and the crowd rose to its feet and gave him a round of applause. Jack bowed, thanked them, and walked out. I was dying laughing. He walked past me, entered the hallway, and never said a word about that incident.

That same evening at dinner, he ordered a steak in the fancy, white-tablecloth restaurant. The waiter forgot to bring him a steak knife. Jack tried to get the waiter's attention but to no avail. Jack Talley was always prepared for any situation. He reached into his pocket and got out his trusty pocketknife, a bone-handled implement as big as any steak knife. People at the tables around us began to watch and whisper as he proceeded to work on his steak. Jack bragged about how he kept his knife sharp for any possible occasion.

Needless to say, Jack was a blast to be around. I sure miss our good times together.

Jack Talley and Jimmy Hill cooking Christmas breakfast for the staff
* Photo Courtesy of Georgia Power Company

20

Vidalia® Onions and Peanut Power

The Vidalia onion industry was started in 1931 by Mose Coleman in Toombs County, Georgia. Coleman ordered onion seed from a seed catalog that bragged on how great the onions tasted. He planted a one-half-acre plot as a trial and discovered that the onions he planted were sweet and not hot like most onions, the sweetness being due in part to the low sulfur soils in the area. Some people who bought Mose Coleman's onions said they were sweet as Coca-Cola. The "World's Sweetest Onion" was born on Coleman's farm that year.

Coleman sold all of his sweet onions, and the demand was larger than his supply. The next year, he grew more onions and sold out again. Area farmers started growing them, and they were being marketed outside of the Vidalia area. The Vidalia Piggly Wiggly grocery store started selling them, and they spread to other Piggly Wiggly stores in South Georgia. The demand for the onions rose even more. This was the start of the sweet Vidalia onion story.

The name "Vidalia" was given to the onions in the 1940s, when the State of Georgia built a farmers' market in the city of Vidalia, Georgia. Buyers began calling them "onions from Vidalia" or "Vidalia onions," and the name stuck. By the 1970s, production had reached six hundred acres. However, word continued to spread about the sweet onions, and by 1989, production had reached six thousand acres.

In 1965, I was in my senior year in high school and working part-time for the Piggly Wiggly grocery store in Hazlehurst, which is where I was introduced to the Vidalia onion. Our customers were buying them by the ten- and twenty-five-pound bags. Following my high school graduation, I worked at McLendon Grocery in Hazlehurst, and we sold hundreds of pounds of Vidalia onions that year. They were big sellers, and customers loved the sweet taste. I had no idea that almost a quarter-century later, I would become so involved with the Vidalia onion.

In 1870, Henry Harrison Grimes started farming in the South Georgia soil that would become Grimes Farm. The farm has been in continuous operation since then. In the 1980s, Grimes Farm was being operated by W. J. Grimes Jr., his wife, Bernice, his son Jimmy, and Jimmy's wife, Connie. They produced not only Vidalia onions but other vegetables as well. Grimes was always an innovator who was willing to try new ideas to increase production and profits. A mover and shaker in the onion industry, he spent time promoting and building the Vidalia onion industry, including serving as a leader on the Vidalia Onion Committee, which was the industry organization.

In the spring of 1988, I received a phone call from Mickey Harrelson, area manager with Georgia Power in McRae, Georgia. Harrelson asked me to meet with Mr. Grimes, who, he said, had an idea that he wanted to share with me that could change the Vidalia onion industry. Of course, this intrigued me, and I scheduled the visit without delay.

Vidalia Onions from Grimes Farms
* Photo Courtesy of Georgia Power Company

When I met with W. J. Grimes at his farm in Helena that spring, one of the first things I noticed was a picture on his office wall of the most awesome Vidalia onion that I had ever seen. It was large and juicy and looked as if it had just been harvested. Early in our conversation, I asked him what was so special about this onion. Grimes, at that point, opened his desk drawer and pulled out a Vidalia onion just like the one in the picture.

I was amazed. I knew that these special onions were harvested from the middle of April through June of each year and that they were a very perishable vegetable, only suitable for the fresh market for about eight weeks after harvest. When I asked him how he got this fresh Vidalia onion in the early spring of 1988, he responded, "Controlled Atmosphere Storage."

"Why isn't the industry using that technology?" I asked.

"Because we do not know how to do it. And that is why you're here today!" was his reply.

He had a gleam in his eye when he told me that the onion in his hand had been grown on his farm and that since June of the prior year, it had been stored on the Tifton campus of the University of Georgia using the Controlled Atmosphere (CA) Storage technology.

"I want you to help me figure out a way to store the onions commercially," he said.

This particular onion had been kept in a five-gallon bucket inside an insulated cooler using CA Storage. Grimes wanted to transfer a five-gallon technology to a large storage room, thus making it feasible to successfully store the onions and market them after the regular season had ended. By using this type of technology, and with effective marketing, millions of dollars could be added to farm revenue.

Following my meeting with W. J. Grimes, I began to research the issue and met with the UGA senior researcher, Dr. Doyle Smittle. I learned from him that this initial technology to store the Vidalia onion had been developed five years earlier and was being used to store apples. Dr. Smittle did not have the time or the technical expertise to move this research forward, as he was primarily focused on basic research.

For those technology geeks who are interested, I have listed the technical requirements to store the Vidalia onion in Controlled Atmosphere (CA) Storage as of 1989. These criteria, per USDA Handbook 66, are:

- An airtight and moisture-tight structure
- A well-insulated structure
- The storage temperature of 34 degrees Fahrenheit
- Forced-air distribution throughout the structure
- Relative humidity levels between 70% and 75%
- Oxygen level at 3%
- Carbon dioxide level at 5%
- Nitrogen at 92%

The above mixture of gases is not safe for humans to breathe but is perfect for the storage of Vidalia onions. Compare this to the normal atmosphere or air we breathe at 21% oxygen, 79% nitrogen, and .03% carbon dioxide.

As an interesting side note, I found information during my research for this book that a well-known southern gentleman had his way of storing Vidalia onions so they would keep longer. Lewis Grizzard, the great southern writer and humorist, wrote in a column for the *Atlanta Journal-Constitution* on August 12, 1988, that the best way to store the onions was to put them in pantyhose. Grizzard went on to explain that you cut off the top of the pantyhose and use the two leg portions to store the onions. Insert an onion, tie a knot above it, and keep adding onions with a knot between each one until you fill the pantyhose. Hang them in a cool place and enjoy them for months to come. I always knew that Grizzard was smart; he figured out the storage solution before the Vidalia onion experts did! I'll bet, though, that he would have preferred the CA Storage Vidalia onions over the pantyhose ones.

A group of Vidalia onion growers and others wanted to check out this CA technology. In other words, they wanted to see, touch, and kick the technology before investing in it. The apple industry had developed a similar process to store apples so that consumers could purchase them year-round. The onion growers wanted to visit a facility using this apple storage technology and see it for themselves.

W. J. Grimes asked me to put the trip together. Those traveling to Grand Rapids, Michigan, included Vidalia onion growers W. J. Grimes Jr., Jimmy Grimes, Anthony Cowart, Jim Cowart, Joseph Foss, Tony Foss, and Steve Roberson. Also, on the trip were Hank Barrett of Dusenbury and Alan Inc., Arnold Horton of Little Ocmulgee EMC, Ralph Rodgers of Merchants, and Citizens Bank, Dr. Doyle Smittle, and, with me from Georgia Power, my colleagues Mike Frassrand and Mickey Harrelson.

On the appointed day, I arrived at the Atlanta airport and was to meet five of the growers; I had their plane tickets. Remember, this was before the days of widespread use of cell phones. The five did not show up on time. I boarded the plane along with the rest of the group, thinking that the five growers would arrive momentarily. They did not! I deplaned and went to see if I could find them. I rushed to the main ticket counter at the front of the airport (this is a long way from the plane) and finally found the group to give them their tickets. We hurried to catch the airport train to get to our plane.

As we arrived at the gate, the plane was already backing up. I implored the agent on duty to stop it from leaving, but the plane kept moving, and we watched it taxi away from the gate.

Here is the situation: I had not yet given the other members of our group who were already on the plane the details of the trip. All they had were their tickets. In fact, for all they knew, I was on the flight with them. I could imagine their concern when they discovered that I was not on the plane.

This was not a direct flight to Grand Rapids, Michigan; there was a layover in Chicago. I went immediately to the ticket counter. The agent there responded quickly after I explained that six people who had no idea of where they were going, other than what was printed on their tickets, were on the plane that had just taken off. He put us on another airline, which had a plane leaving in ten minutes. I was relieved until I found out that our new flight was also not direct but had a stopover in Minneapolis-Saint Paul.

After boarding our flight, I asked an attendant if they could get a message to the other members of our party to let them know that we were a few minutes behind them but coming via a different route. I wanted them to wait without worry at our final destination. I was assured that they were given the message.

During our brief stopover in Minneapolis-Saint Paul airport, I tried to reach the other group at the Chicago airport to make sure that they had got my message but was unsuccessful.

When we finally got to Grand Rapids, I found the group wandering around the airport looking for me. My message had not gotten through to them. Only two of them had ever flown before, and the rest were rather shook-up because I was not there to provide details of the trip. Finally, I was able to get all of the growers together and explain what had happened.

The rest of the trip went without further problems. We visited two apple storage facilities in the Grand Rapids area. The HVAC equipment was very similar to what we planned to use for Vidalia onions. The major difference in storage was that the floor of the storage room was flooded with six inches of water to maintain the moisture level of the apples. The storage rooms were full of stored apples while we were there, so we could not go inside but saw what we needed to see. We had a productive visit, meeting with the apple growers and seeing the CA Storage technology in action.

The trip was successful; however, most of the Vidalia onion growers wanted the technology but were not willing to risk thousands of dollars in moving this new technology from a five-gallon bucket to a large storage room. W. J. Grimes was the only grower who was committed personally to fund the necessary research.

Grimes again asked me if I was willing to help him, and I assured him that I was as committed as he was to make it happen. This technology had the potential to make a tremendous positive increase in the economic value of the Vidalia onion industry.

After meeting with Mr. Grimes, I assembled a team of fellow engineers, and we mapped out a plan for adapting this CA Storage technology to a large storage room on Grimes's farm. Georgia Power engineers included Mike Frassrand and Mickey Harrelson. We were joined by Arnold Horton from the Little Ocmulgee Electric Membership Corporation, the EMC that supplied electricity to the farm.

Our team worked many hours with Lowell Flowers, a refrigeration expert, on fine-tuning the CA Storage technology. Flowers's firm provided the equipment to create an environment that would store the onions.

The Engineers - Jimmy Hill, Mike Frassrand and Mickey Harrelson
* Photo Courtesy of Georgia Power Company

Essentially, the CA environment put the onions to sleep: all chemical processes stopped, and the onions just sat there and stayed that way while in storage. Once removed from storage, the chemical processes started up again. However, the onions would still be in excellent, edible condition for some time. CA Storage would allow the growers to store some of their onion production from June until November or December. They would then be able to send their Vidalia onions to the market for Thanksgiving or Christmas, allowing consumers to enjoy sweet Vidalia onions during the holidays.

Grimes had started construction of an onion storage room that would hold 350,000 pounds just as soon as he decided to install CA Storage technology. The room was built inside an existing building, a packing shed. A key requirement was that it be airtight. No air could leave or enter the space during the CA Storage process. Conventional storage did not require the same airtightness.

During installation, the team discovered some of the technical issues were challenging and difficult. The primary issue was with adjusting the technology to work properly in the storage room. It took Mickey, Mike, and Arnold many hours of work to resolve the issues. The final challenge they faced was that air was leaking out of the storage room. After much investigation, the problem was determined to be with the door. The team tried several approaches to get the room to stay airtight, all to no avail. Leaks were still occurring around the door seal. An old technology that has been around since 1872 finally solved the problem: the door was sealed with Vaseline.

Probes were installed at intervals throughout the storage room as well as inside the four-by-four-by-three-foot bins in which the onions were stored. These probes were continuously monitored to make sure that the technology was working and that onion quality was maintained.

After W. J. Grimes committed to build the first CA Storage facility, word began getting out about this new technology. Some growers thought that the whole thing was a boondoggle and would lead to a storage room full of mushy, smelly, gooey onions. The three people who were convinced it would be a success (and who prayed for it) were W. J. Grimes, Jimmy Hill, and Grimes's banker!

Then word got out that the CA Storage technology was working. Grimes began getting calls from growers and other industry people who wanted to see this technology for themselves. It became evident that there would need to be an organized event to bring interested people in to witness the opening of the storage room.

Grimes asked me to help plan the event and to serve as the master of ceremonies. I agreed and immediately called Cindy Theiler, media relations coordinator for Georgia Power, who accepted the challenge and began researching and planning what would become a huge media event.

Recently, I asked Cindy, now retired from Georgia Power's corporate communication office, to send me her thoughts on this project she led so successfully twenty-four years ago. Here is her response:

Leading Georgia Power's communication efforts to help publicize and promote the extension of the Vidalia onions' life expectancy was a dream public relations project for me! I knew a lot was riding on this project's outcome for many entities, including the Vidalia onion farmers, the community and state, Georgia Power and other electric utility providers, and others.

Georgia Power's communication efforts would need to be very creative to entice members of the media to cover this story about the groundbreaking, controlled-atmosphere storage for onions. What better way to do this than to have an onion tasting for the media and other special guests on November 2, 1989, when the onions were initially removed from the storage at W. J. Grimes's farm in Helena, GA—just in time for the Thanksgiving Holiday.

Working with Jimmy Hill and others, Georgia Power's communication strategic plan included inviting various officials, including Georgia's then-Agricultural Commissioner Tommy Irvin, to speak at the event. Also, special invitations, press kits, a news release, photos, and video news releases were developed and distributed.

More than 80 media representatives were invited to the event that was held more than three hours south of Atlanta and about 20 attended, including a photographer from the *Atlanta Journal-Constitution* and representatives from six TV stations from Atlanta, Macon, and Savannah. As Irvin later personally told me, this was the most media he had ever seen at an event in South Georgia!

I developed and organized press kits, a Q & A sheet on the CA Storage, a Vidalia® onion fact sheet, a diagram depicting how the CA process works, Vidalia® onion recipes, black-and-white photos of the Grimes family and their onions, a map of the authorized growing region and new clips of earlier onion coverage. The press kits were given to the media on the day of the event.

Since some smaller publications might not have someone in attendance, Georgia Power produced black-and-white photos and mailed them to these publications for additional coverage. Georgia Power also developed and produced a 1:49 minute video news release for distribution to TV stations who could not attend.

In addition to witnessing this historic ribbon-cutting storage facility event that would positively change the life expectancy of the Vidalia® onion and the state's agricultural economy forever, about 250 persons—including the media reps—got to enjoy a great cookout of hamburgers and hot dogs as part of their taste test of the previously-stored onions from that year's harvest. All attendees also got to take home a brown-bagged onion as a souvenir!

On a personal note, the event was a professional achievement for me, as I won my first-ever Phoenix Award (first place) in the Georgia Chapter of Public Relations Society of America's annual awards competition in the marketing communication category for new services. Georgia Power's communications support of this project helped make this sweet-tasting onion story even sweeter!

I am grateful to Cindy for sharing her memories of this event.

I served as the master of ceremonies at the press conference. Other individuals attending and involved with this project were: Vidalia onion grower W. J. Grimes Jr.; Tommy Irvin, Georgia commissioner of agriculture; Hank Barrett, executive director, Vidalia Onion Committee; Dr. Doyle Smittle, researcher, and professor, University of Georgia; Arnold Horton, engineer, Little Ocmulgee Electric Membership Corporation; Dan Kamerman, community development specialist, National Rural Electric Cooperative Association; Dr. David Dilly, researcher, apple industry, Michigan State University; Mike Frassrand, marketing engineer, Georgia Power; Mickey Harrelson, operating superintendent, Georgia Power; Greg Sciullo, director of Publix Produce Operations, Jacksonville Division; and Lowell Flowers, refrigeration expert.

One of the more exciting moments, besides the greatly anticipated onion reveal and tasting, was the auctioning of a ten-pound box of the Vidalia onions. I served as the auctioneer and started the price off at $100. The bidding climbed steadily. Greg Sciullo had agreed ahead of time to buy the box at $1,000, in that Publix was getting all of the onions from this storage unit. However, another person bid the $1,000. The price moved to $1,100, and then to $1,200, and the final bid from Greg was $1,300. This was my first time as a newbie auctioneer, and I enjoyed it.

The storage room was opened up, and a forklift brought out one of the wooden boxes containing the onions. The crowd moved to the box, and everyone grabbed an onion and started peeling them. The comments around me were all enthusiastic: "These are just like the fresh ones from the spring crop"; "very tasty and delicious"; "sweet as a Georgia peach"; "This technology works!"; "awesome."

Commissioner Tommy Irvin and Jimmy Hill
* Photo Courtesy of Georgia Power Company

That day, skeptics of the new technology became believers! Several Vidalia onion growers were corralling Lowell Flowers, the refrigeration expert who installed the CA technology. They were asking lots of questions and expressing an interest in purchasing the technology.

In 1990, four more CA Storage facilities were built by Vidalia onion growers to take advantage of this new marketing idea. Two of the facilities were served by Georgia Power and the other two by the EMCs.

In discussion with W. J. Grimes and others in the Vidalia onion industry, the consensus was that the Vidalia onion needed protection for its name and a funding mechanism for research, marketing, and promotion. A Federal Marketing Order administered by the United States Department of Agriculture (USDA) seemed to be the perfect way to address these issues. The growers had been communicating with the USDA and with the Georgia Congressional Delegation for nearly two years on this matter.

Jimmy presenting Vidalia onions to US Secretary of Agriculture Clayton Yeutter
* Photo Courtesy of Secretary of Agriculture Clayton Yeutter

I traveled to Washington, DC, in early January 1989 with the Georgia Agribusiness Council's board of directors to visit with the USDA and the Georgia Congressional Delegation. We went to see Richard Lyng, who was then USDA secretary of agriculture under the Ronald Reagan administration. I met privately with Lyng to discuss the Federal Marketing Order, and he wrote me a letter, shortly thereafter, sharing the process for securing the order. He outlined the steps that had been taken so far and what still needed to be done, all of which I shared with W. J. Grimes.

On February 1, I traveled back to DC with five Vidalia onion growers and several other people to visit with Georgia's US Representative Lindsey Thomas and Georgia's US Senator Wyche Fowler. Traveling with me were Vidalia onion growers W. J. Grimes Jr., Randall Morris, Tommy Williams, R. E. Hendrix, and Delbert Bland. Jim Bridges from the Georgia Department of Agriculture was also on the trip.

The purpose of our visit was to bring to a close the discussion on the Federal Marketing Order and get it approved. We met first with Representative Thomas, First District of Georgia, which is where all of the Vidalia onions are grown. Shortly thereafter, we went to Senator Fowler's office to meet with him and with representatives from the USDA. Senator Fowler opened the meeting with a question for the USDA representatives: why hadn't this application for the Federal Marketing Order been approved? There were some blank stares, combined with some clearing of throats, but no answer from USDA. Senator Fowler said, in no uncertain terms, "I want this order processed and approved ASAP. Can you gentlemen get this done?" They answered in the affirmative. It was a brief meeting but very impactful. Shortly thereafter, the approval process was begun, and final approval of Federal Marketing Order No. 955 was given in late 1989.

W. J. Grimes and I were discussing the Vidalia onion industry one day, and I asked him how they recognized their grower members for outstanding service to the industry. When he said that they were not currently recognizing them in any way, I suggested to him that I would sponsor an outstanding grower of the year award if he felt that would be appropriate. He brought it up at the next board meeting of the Vidalia Onion Committee and called me later to say that the committee would be pleased if I would sponsor the award. The first Vidalia Onion Grower of the Year Award was presented in 1991 to Wade Usher, and the 1992 recipient was Adger Kicklighter.

Mr. W. J. Grimes Jr. was nominated and approved in 1990 to receive the National Food and Energy Council's (NFEC) Distinguished Service Award. The presentation took place on July 17, 1990, at the NFEC's annual meeting in Indianapolis, Indiana.

The Distinguished Service Award recognizes outstanding individuals whose contributions exemplify concern for the critical interdependence of food and energy supplies and the benefits derived from the marketing and efficient use of electricity in agriculture. This award recognized Mr. Grimes's innovative work in applying Controlled Atmosphere Storage technology to the storage of Vidalia onions. W. J. Grimes is known as the Father of CA Storage of Vidalia Onions.

Characterized as a hardworking marketing genius, Grimes was recognized for his foresight and fortitude in pursuing this technology for application to the Vidalia onion industry.

Arnold Horton, Little Ocmulgee EMC, and I made a presentation at the NFEC meeting entitled "Promoting Value-Added Agriculture: The Vidalia® Onion." We told the story of the Vidalia onions and how the CA Storage technology came about and was implemented.

The Vidalia® onion, by law, can only be grown in a strictly defined region of South Georgia. There are thirteen counties where the Vidalia® onion can be grown anywhere in the county: Emanuel, Candler, Treutlen, Bulloch, Wheeler, Montgomery, Evans, Tattnall, Toombs, Telfair, Jeff Davis, Appling, and Bacon. Portions of the following counties may also grow Vidalia® onions: Jenkins, Screven, Laurens, Dodge, Pierce, Wayne, and Long.

W. J. Grimes, far right, and others who worked on the
Vidalia Onion Federal Marketing Order meeting with Senator Wyche Fowler
* Photo Courtesy of Senator Wyche Fowler

The State of Georgia passed laws that protect the Vidalia® onion trademark and the legal framework for the industry. These laws make sure that if you see the Vidalia® onion logo anywhere in the world, with the registered trademark symbol, you can be sure it was grown in Georgia.

In January 2015, I unexpectedly received a call from the Vidalia Onion Committee. They had a photograph of the individuals who had traveled to Washington, DC, to meet with the USDA and the Georgia Congressional Delegation regarding the Federal Marketing Order. However, no one could identify me. Most of the committee leadership and staff were new and were not there back in 1989. Finally, someone was able to tell them who I was. They invited me and the others who went on that trip to attend their upcoming annual meeting in Vidalia, Georgia.

Jimmy and Gail Hill
* Photo Courtesy of Vidalia Onion Committee

On February 7, 2015, Gail and I attended the 2015 Annual Meeting of the Vidalia Onion Committee at the Vidalia Country Club. I was able to address the meeting and thank the committee for the recognition. This was twenty-five years after the Federal Marketing Order was approved.

Mr. Mickey Harrelson passed on September 2, 2014. He was a major player in the CA Storage application and worked tirelessly in fine-tuning the technology. Rest in peace, my friend and Georgia Power co-worker.

Mr. Arnold Horton passed on November 13, 2014. He was a major player in the CA Storage application as well and worked with our team in making the CA technology work for the Vidalia onion industry. May you rest in peace, my friend.

Before I move to the next topic, allow me to share one more thing: A few months after the media event, Mr. Grimes said to me, "Jimmy, I am glad that you believed that this CA Storage technology would work."

I said, "Me? I thought you believed that it would work."

We looked at each other and had a great laugh!

I am sad to report that Mr. W. J. Grimes Jr. passed on November 3, 2017. Rest in peace, my visionary and innovative friend. You are missed.

Needless to say, this project was successful and very beneficial to the growers and consumers of the delicious and sweet Vidalia onion. I am very proud and honored to have been a part of it.

Peanut Power

It all started in 1987 when Georgia Power Company (GPC) had a request from a major peanut sheller who was considering using peanut hulls for fuel in a small, on-site generating plant. The cost of building the plant was deemed not feasible after an economic evaluation.

The peanut sheller's request, however, led Rhett Ward, GPC industrial marketing engineer, to consider the possibility of burning peanut hulls in GPC's coal-fired generating plants. Ward contacted Glen Kinzly, GPC's system performance engineer, Power Generation Services, to inquire about the feasibility of burning peanut hulls. He also placed a call to me, as Georgia Power's manager of Agricultural Affairs, to discuss the issue.

I put a plan together to learn everything I could about peanut hulls. I wanted to know about the quantity, location, availability, costs, and other current uses of hulls. I decided to use an outside firm to query the peanut processors who shelled the peanuts and had to dispose of the hulls.

Photo Courtesy of Georgia Power Company

The 1987 survey produced the following information:

- Georgia grew 750,000 to 900,000 tons of peanuts on 695,000 acres.
- A great majority of the peanuts were grown in South Georgia.
- The United States grew 1,800,000 tons per year.
- Georgia grew 42–50 percent of the nation's total production.
- 30% of the peanut weight is the hull.
- Uses of the hull were for fuel, livestock feed, cat litter, fire logs, mulch, surplus (landfill).
- 30% or 59,460 tons per year of hulls were landfilled or given away.

It was determined that the 59,460 tons would be enough surplus to consider using them for power plant fuel.

A team was formed to continue exploring the Peanut Hull Project. This team was composed of representatives from various Georgia Power departments:

- Agricultural Affairs
- Division and District offices
- Industrial Marketing
- Power Generation
- Plant Mitchell management (the power plant that was initially going to conduct the experimental project)
- Fuel Services

Based on the evaluation of the concept and input from the Peanut Hull team, Georgia Power decided to conduct a test at Plant Mitchell in South Georgia. The idea of putting peanut hulls into the combustion chamber of a boiler that only burned coal was concerning, at the least. Would the peanut hulls damage the equipment? Would they burn as efficiently as the coal? Could we burn only peanut hulls, or could we mix the hulls with coal? Could we pulverize the peanut hulls as we did the coal?

It was finally decided to conduct a small test burn. A fifty-five-gallon bag of hulls was injected into the boiler. It was determined that the peanut hulls burned efficiently and without creating any issues. More tests were run, and everything was okay.

The team conducted an additional evaluation that led the team to determine that peanut hull costs were 40 cents per million British Thermal Units (BTUs) and coal costs were $1.80 per million BTUs. In simple terms, it takes about 1,500 tons of peanuts to produce the same energy as 1,000 tons of coal.

At those rates, every truckload of peanut hulls burned instead of coal would represent $400 in fuel cost savings to GPC customers. Actual fuel costs at GPC are passed on directly to customers with no added fees.

Coal was being brought to the plant by railcar and dumped on the ground. The coal was then being taken by a bulldozer to a conveyor belt and fed into a pulverizer. The pulverized coal (now a fine particle) was then being burned in the combustion chamber. During the project, the peanut hulls were hauled by truck to the plant and dumped onto the coal pile. Experiments led to 50 percent each of coal and peanut hulls being determined as the ideal mixture for combustion.

I have simplified this overall research and implementation process description, but many hours of work went into getting the project approvals and conducting the actual burn process. During the project, 3,045 tons of peanut hulls were burned, and they displaced 1,950 tons of coal. The resulting cost savings were passed directly on to customers via the fuel-cost portion of their bill.

We shared this story with the public during the Sunbelt Agricultural Exposition held in Moultrie, Georgia, in October 1988. I asked Mr. R. W. Scherer, president of Georgia Power, to hold a press conference on Tuesday, October 18, 1988, to share the results of the peanut hull project.

At the press conference, Mr. Scherer announced that he was pleased with the results so far and planned to continue the test project. He introduced Georgia's commissioner of agriculture, Tommy Irvin, who shared his thoughts on the project and endorsed the effort to use the peanut hull as a fuel of power plants.

Georgia Power concluded the research project but determined not to pursue the project any further at that time. The reasons included, but were not limited to: other uses being found for the excess hulls; the hulls' absorbing water during rain events on the coal pile, which required using heat to remove the moisture before the hull could be burned efficiently; and lack of storage facilities for the hulls at the plant.

Several other Georgia Power employees contributed to this project, and they include Jeff Mitchell, agricultural affairs representative; Robin Gerald, community development representative; Meg Reggie, media representative; Perry Bowen, Plant Mitchell manager; Sam Wills, Albany District marketing representative; Carl Donaldson, vice president, Power Generation; Sam Reagan, senior fuel specialist. Mr. Flint Harding, president, Stevens Industries, provided valuable assistance to the project, including the supply of peanut hulls.

William Coe, Georgia Power senior Plant Mitchell engineer, and I made a presentation entitled "Peanut Hulls for Power Plants" at the National Food and Energy Council Annual Meeting on July 27, 1988, in Lexington, Kentucky. We presented the research, testing, implementation, and evaluation phases of the project conducted by the Georgia Power team.

We closed the presentation by saying that we had shared, to the best of our ability, the *hull* truth and nothing but the *hull* truth. Yes, I know it was corny, but hey, this was an agricultural group.

21

1996 Summer Olympics

Georgia was selected to host the 1996 Summer Olympic Games at the close of the 1992 games in Barcelona, Spain. I can still hear Juan Antonio Samaranch, president of the International Olympic Committee, announcing that Atlanta had been chosen.

A small contingent of Atlanta leaders had decided to put a plan together to bid for the 1996 games. All odds had been that Athens, Greece, would host the 100th anniversary of the Olympic Games as they had hosted the 1896 games, but Atlanta lawyer Billy Payne did not get the message that Athens was destined to be the host. He and his team surprised the world with their successful bid.

Payne was a graduate of the University of Georgia and had been a starter on the football team. He was a unique individual with a strong, competitive spirit. In 1987, he had been asked to chair a campaign to raise $2.5 million for a new sanctuary for his church in Atlanta. He was successful in raising the money and basked in the success of this undertaking. The morning after being feted at the church's note-burning ceremony, Payne was at his law office in Atlanta, still on a high from the success of the fundraising campaign and ready to experience that feeling again. He started listing ideas on a legal pad. He made list after list and threw them in the trash can as he was not coming up with anything that excited him. Then it came to him—sports and community. The idea of the Olympic Games fit the bill. What about hosting the next Olympic Games in Atlanta and Georgia? He did not even know when the games were scheduled to take place.

Excited, Payne told his wife about his idea. She did not dare to question him or tell him it would be impossible. She suggested that he call his closest friend, who was very conservative; she was confident that he would talk Payne out of this crazy idea. Payne phoned him with the idea and said that he wanted a few friends who could write a fifty-thousand-dollar check to help get the process started. Without hesitation, his good friend said, "Let's do it." Thus began the journey to secure the 1996 Summer Olympics for Atlanta.

Payne and his team accomplished the impossible. The Olympic Games were held in Atlanta and at other Georgia locations, including Athens, Columbus, Conyers, Gainesville, Jonesboro, Savannah, Stone Mountain, and a few others. The 1996 Summer Olympics took place from July 19 until August 4, 1996. This was one of the greatest opportunities to showcase Georgia to the world in Payne's lifetime.

Gary Black and I discussed the possibility of involvement of agriculture and agribusiness in the 1996 Olympic Games. We had discussions with others in the agriculture and agribusiness community as well.

The first meeting to talk about that possibility took place on August 29, 1994, at the Georgia Farm Bureau headquarters building in Macon, Georgia. The meeting was conducted by Gary Black, Georgia Agribusiness Council, and Bob Ray, Georgia Farm Bureau.

Those attending in addition to Black and Ray were Jennifer Pinson-Harvey from the Atlanta Committee for the Olympic Games, Carey Campbell of Operation Legacy from the Georgia Power Company, Mac Holiday from the Governor's Economic Development Council, and Frank Spence of Eventmasters. Following the daylong meeting, seven top objectives were developed as follows:

- Create the Georgia Agriculture 1996 (GA AG 96) organization, office, and staff
- Develop an "Agricultural Media Guide" and information package
- Make an effort to be a Super Center Partner
- Create the GA AG 96 International Pavilion–Perry Ag Center
- Showcase Georgia agricultural products with a "Feed the Media" idea
- Lead package tours of Georgia to showcase agriculture and agribusiness

- Pursue international marketing opportunities for Georgia products
- Seek corporate sponsors for GA AG 96

The committee met four times in 1994, thirteen times in 1995, fifteen times in 1996, and a couple of times in 1997.

Research indicated that no other Olympic Games had included any involvement or activity connected to agriculture. This was a first-time event, so no previous experience could be studied. The GA AG 96 team created and implemented an amazing effort to expose the world to Georgia and southern agriculture.

GA AG 96 was a statewide consortium of commodity groups, agribusinesses, educational institutions, and the Georgia Department of Agriculture that came together to showcase Georgia agriculture to the world during the 1996 Summer Olympics.

GA AG 96 Board of Directors and Management

Mitch Head, chairman, Peanut Advisory Board, and Georgia Peanut Commission
Nancy Hanson, vice-chairperson, Georgia Egg Commission
Gary Black, secretary-treasurer, Georgia Agribusiness Council
Anne Young, coordinator, UGA College of Agricultural and Environmental Sciences
Danette Amstein, Georgia Beef Board
Paul Brower, Georgia Poultry Federation, and Gold Kist
Jim Loftis, Gold Kist
Denise Fallin Deal, Georgia Farm Bureau
Levi Glover, Fort Valley State College
Cheryl Hayn, Southeast. United Dairy Industry Association
Jimmy Hill, Georgia Power Company
Horace Hudson, UGA College of Agricultural and Environmental Sciences
Susan Hughes, UGA College of Agricultural and Environmental Sciences

Shirley Manchester, Vidalia Onion Committee
Lawton Mathews, Georgia Tobacco Commission
Neil Nichols, Georgia Tobacco Commission
Richey Seaton, Georgia Cotton Commission
Commissioner Tommy Irvin, Georgia Department of Agriculture
Lisa Ray, Georgia Department of Agriculture
Sherry Loudermilk, Georgia Green Industry
Jane Crocker, Georgia Pecan Growers
Kelly Scott, Georgia Ratite Council
Don Sims, Southwest Georgia Council on Economic Development
John Wells, Southern Foresters

In late October 1994, Gary Black and I went to visit with Dr. Gale Buchanan, dean and director of the College of Agricultural and Environmental Sciences at the University of Georgia. We asked him to loan our group Anne Ponder Young to coordinate GA AG 96. He consented, with Anne's agreement, to her assisting in coordinating our agricultural Olympic effort. On November 1, 1994, Anne Ponder Young

Anne Young and Kelly Scott
* Photo Courtesy of GA AG 96

assumed the coordinator role and was headquartered at the Georgia Agribusiness Council in Norcross, Georgia. This was one of the best decisions that we as a board made to ensure the success of GA AG 96.

GA AG 96 was incorporated as a 501(c)(4) non-profit organization and the articles of incorporation were approved on December 21, 1995.

Final decisions were made concerning participation in GA AG 96. It included a fee of ten thousand dollars, and that would allow a company or entity to fully participate in the planning and implementation of the effort.

The main groups who agreed to fund GA AG 96 were: DuPont USA, Fort Valley State University, Georgia Agribusiness Council, Georgia Apple Commission, Georgia Beef Board, Georgia Cotton Commission, Georgia Department of Agriculture, Georgia Egg Commission, Georgia Farm Bureau, Georgia Forestry Commission, Georgia Green Industry, Gold Kist, Georgia Peach Commission, Georgia Peanut Commission, Georgia Pecan Growers Association, Georgia Poultry Federation, Georgia Power Company, Georgia Ratite Council, Georgia Tobacco Commission, Southeastern Poultry and Egg Association, Southeastern Foresters, Southeast United Dairy Association, Southwest Georgia Council on Economic Development, University of Georgia College of Agricultural and Environmental Sciences, and the Vidalia Onion Committee.

Everything concerning the Olympic Games and the Centennial Olympic Park had to be approved either by the Atlanta Committee for the Olympic Games (ACOG) or by the World Congress Center, or both. The World Congress Center controlled the Olympic park area. All of our plans, ideas, designs, plants, colors, flags, structures and their footprints, electrical, plumbing, walkways, access to the park, and so forth were approved by these two organizations.

At our request, EDAW, an international landscape architecture, urban and environmental design firm, developed a skeleton plan for the park exhibit for presentation to the ACOG. We faced challenges, in that we were a voluntary group with few resources, at that point, to create, build, and operate an Olympic Games exhibit. Lindsay Thomas, a farmer and former US representative, joined ACOG as their legislative liaison. Thomas helped sell the idea to ACOG and specifically to Sherman Day and Billy Payne.

In the meantime, GA AG 96 explored plans to build the "American South Marketplace–Country Store and Farmers' Market" across from the State Capitol in Atlanta. This project moved along for a while until our event-coordinating company was not able to sign up enough vendors to make it viable, and we had to abandon it. We explored doing something next to the Coca-Cola Museum, which was then also across from the State Capitol, and that did not work out either. A decision was made to concentrate fully on building a facility in the Centennial Olympic Park in downtown Atlanta.

We contracted with The Hauseman Group to develop plans for the structure to be built in the Centennial Olympic Park. Their plans were based on building an agricultural barn with open sides. The original firm that was to construct the barn backed out. We only had six weeks to get the barn built, or we were not going to have an exhibit in the park. We frantically searched for another construction firm. Gary Black and I visited with a friend of ours who constructed buildings, and he said it could not be done in six weeks. We were extremely disappointed in his decision. We were getting desperate and running out of time to get the pavilion completed in time for the Olympics.

In the meantime, I had asked Travis Henry, a member of my staff in Agricultural Affairs, to be the GA AG 96 lead person heading up the construction of the barn. Henry was very experienced in construction and had great people skills. He found a construction company owned by Jimmy McDade. When Henry asked him if he could construct the building in six weeks, McDade accepted the challenge to build the facility on time and within budget. Jimmy McDade subcontracted with Genesis

Six Construction Company, and the barn was indeed built on time and on budget.

The exterior landscaping and planting of flowers was done by professors, staff, and volunteers from the University of Georgia College of Agricultural and Environmental Sciences. Familiar Georgia plants were added to the landscape, including aucuba, artemisia, butterfly bush, canna, chaste tree, coneflower, crape myrtle, crimson pygmy barberry, juniper, lantana, miscanthus, setcreasea, and wax-leaf ligustrum.

Committee assignments were made to facilitate the implementation of the work plan for the pavilion:

Video: Mitch Head, Bob Mueller
Volunteers: Horace Hudson, Karen Nikitopoullos
Marble hardscape: Nancy Baker Hanson
Displays, exhibits, and signage: Danette Amstein, Cheryl Hayn
Architectural and boardwalk: Jimmy Hill, John Wells, Glenn Smith
Travel, parking, and credentials: Gary Black, Marcus Evans
Uniforms: Kelly Scott, Shirley Manchester
Preview Week: Nancy Hanson
Animatronics: Anne Young, Cheryl Hayn
Planting: John Beasley, Levi Glover
Pictorial documentation: Robert Howell, Branch Carter
Media: Faith Peppers

Interior construction, including the laying of the wood floors, plumbing, and electrical work, was done by GA AG 96 board members and volunteers.

I worked on almost everything, including wiring. Charles Gillespie, another of my Agricultural Affairs staff members, and I wired the 200-amp electrical panel and all electrical circuits for lighting, visual, and audio equipment. Volunteers and board members from several organizations did the wiring of electrical outlets and lighting.

The pavilion approved by the GA AG 96 board of directors was a barn-like framework of wooden columns and beams with open sides and a metal top. It was four and a half stories tall, with four thousand square feet under the roof. The framework was fabricated using Parallam, an engineered

Glenn Smith, Jimmy Hill and Travis Henry
* Photo Courtesy of GA AG 96

Jim Loftis, Travis Henry, Jimmy Hill and Gary Black
* Photo Courtesy of GA AG 96

lumber product made by Weyerhaeuser that could be made in any size for any type of construction. Parallam is made from veneer strands, allowing each column and beam to become a high-grade structural member. The product has a great load and strength capacity.

The beams were made to our specifications and donated by Trus Joist MacMillan, a subsidiary of Weyerhaeuser. Parallam is an excellent building product and is still holding up the relocated pavilion today, twenty-four years later.

The centerpiece of the exhibit was a map of the state of Georgia made from Georgia marble. The marble hardscape remained in Centennial Olympic Park permanently after the Olympics.

GA AG 96 planted several plants and fruit trees around the outside of the pavilion. These crops included tobacco, Vidalia onions, peanuts, cotton, peach trees, apple trees, and pecan trees. We stationed volunteers at each of these areas to answer questions. Probably the most asked question was about peanuts. Visitors thought that peanuts grew on trees and not on a plant in the soil.

Construction of the GA AG 96 Pavilion
* Photo Courtesy of GA AG 96

Each of the organizations participating in GA AG 96 designed a storyboard to explain their role in Georgia agriculture. The boards were hung around the inside of the pavilion. The participating organizations also each provided a segment for the GA AG 96 video that played continuously from July 19 to August 4. The video provided an overview of Georgia agriculture.

ACOG was helping to commemorate the centenary of the modern Olympic Games. As part of this commemoration, they sold engraved bricks to line the numerous walkways throughout Centennial Olympic Park.

Each brick purchased was a thirty-five-dollar, tax-free, tax-deductible contribution to the committee. Purchasers could choose to have their brick engraved with a name, company name, birthdate, family name, or memorial name. Duplicate bricks were available for twenty-five dollars. Each brick purchased came with a keepsake certificate depicting the personalized brick engraving.

GA AG 96 committed to selling forty thousand bricks to be installed around the pavilion. A GA AG 96 Brick Committee was chaired by Susan Hughes, UGA College of Agricultural and Environmental Sciences. Serving with Susan were Nancy Baker Hanson, Gail Buckner, Denise Fallin Deal, Bo Ryles, and John Wilkinson. The Brick Committee set its detailed plan in motion on July 26, 1995, with specific goals for each month from August to December. The campaign concluded on December 19, 1995.

GA AG 96 also enlisted its board of directors, volunteers, 4-H clubs, FFA chapters, FHA-Hero chapters, Georgia Farm Bureau, Gold Kist, Georgia Egg Commission, UGA Agricultural Alumni Organization, Georgia Ratite Council, and many others to sell the bricks.

I do not have a total of the bricks sold, but I know it was substantial. I bought a brick for my family, listing it as "Jimmy, Gail, Chris, and Miranda Hill."

Georgia Agriculture 96 Pavilion

* Photo Courtesy of GA AG 96

Vice-Chairperson Nancy Hanson was in charge of the GA AG 96 Ribbon Cutting and Preview Party. The evening event was held on July 11, 1996.

Hanson's themed menu included heavy hors d'oeuvres, cheese, milk, Vidalia onion relish, and roasted peanuts.

Invitees included: GA AG 96 board of directors; ACOG management and staff; staff from the Governor's Office; legislative leaders; Bayer Corporation; Beers/Russel; Georgia Department of Agriculture; Georgia Department of Community Affairs; DuPont Ag Products; EDAW; Exhibits Plus; The Forestry Industry; Fort Valley State University; Georgia Agribusiness Council; Georgia Apple Commission; Georgia Beef Board/Cattlemen's/Cattlewomen; Georgia Cotton Commission; Georgia Egg Commission; Georgia Farm Bureau; Georgia Green Industry; Georgia Marble; Georgia Poultry Federation; Georgia Power; Georgia Ratite Council; Georgia Tobacco Commission; Georgia Tech Research Institute; Gold Kist; The Hauseman Group; McDade Construction; Mead Corporation; media organizations; Monsanto; peanut industry; Saul Nurseries; Southeastern Poultry and Egg Association; Southeast United Dairy Association; Southern Family Farms; Southwest Georgia Economic Development; Trus Joist MacMillan; University of Georgia; USDA; Vidalia Onion Committee. Many other guests also attended.

Governor Zell Miller and Gary Black
* Photo Courtesy of GA AG 96

Hanson and her team did a great job of organizing and implementing the ribbon cutting and the preview party.

Our GA AG 96 team had worked tremendously hard and had overcome many obstacles to get the pavilion ready for opening day on July 19, 1996. We were excited when the Centennial Olympic Park opened that morning and let visitors in. We were swamped with people from all over the world.

We had the pavilion ready with continuous videos playing that extolled the numerous crops, fruits, livestock, and other agricultural assets of Georgia. The planted vegetables, crops, and fruit trees were glistening with bright colors. Volunteers were ready for the thousands of questions from our world visitors. And we did get the questions. The animatronics were moving and talking and attracting large crowds. Everyone wanted to touch them. The atmosphere was electric with anticipation of eager minds wanting to know more about these mechatronic figures.

Our volunteers were dressed in their khaki pants or shorts, white shirts, and straw hats and were stationed at every major area within the pavilion. No significant problems developed during our first day and very few throughout the entire sixteen days.

Opening Day of the 1996 Olympics
* Photo Courtesy of GA AG 96

After all of the effort that had gone into building the pavilion, it was fun now to engage with the visitors and ask and answer questions. We met people from all walks of life and cultures. It was an awesome experience to be involved in such a great event.

Part of the GA AG 96 Team

* Photo Courtesy of GA AG 96

GA AG 96 had four animatronic displays built for the exhibit. Animatronics are built to look, feel, move, and act like real animals but are completely man-made. Joseph Hurt, Joseph Hurt Studio Inc., from Stone Mountain, Georgia, built the animatronics for us. His firm also built various types of characters for movies and museums over the years. The animatronics looked so real that many visitors were convinced that they were real animals.

Our life-size figures included chickens, a dairy cow, a beef cow, and an emu. They were individually sponsored by the organizations that represented these specific animal agriculture industries. The animatronics always had huge crowds around them and became so popular that we had

Beef Cow Animatronic

Emu Animatronic

Dairy Cow Animatronic

Chicken Animatronic

* Photos Courtesy of GA AG 96

to cordon them off because of all the touching by so many visitors; they had begun to look disheveled and worn. We finally had to station someone at each animatronic to maintain discipline.

As I was sitting next to the emu one day, a lady came up and wanted to know if she could take a photo of it. I said sure. The lady then addressed the bird: "Here, emu! Here, emu! Come this way, so I can get a picture." It moved its body from right to left and then left to right and bowed its head in front of the woman. She took her photo and left. I did not have the heart to tell her the emu was not real.

The dairy and the beef cow talked, as well as moving their heads and flicking their tails. It was amazing to see people respond to them. There was one day when I was stationed by the dairy cow, and a woman and her friend came in and marched right up to the cow and looked her over. The woman asked me, "Where did you get this dairy cow?"

I responded, "Stone Mountain, Georgia."

"There are no dairy cows in Stone Mountain," she said.

About this time, her friend said to her in a low voice, "That cow is not real." The woman's face turned red, and she rushed out of the exhibit.

"Is she okay?" I asked her friend.

"She milks three hundred dairy cows every day," was the reply.

That is an example of how lifelike and awesome these animatronic farm animals were. The milk cow's udder was so realistic that you could almost see milk coming from the teats.

The chicken animatronic exhibit was also a visitor favorite. The head and tail moved on the chickens, and they were very realistic. Japanese visitors seemed to enjoy the chickens and wanted to take their picture with them.

I was told by one of our volunteers that a man from an animal rights group came in one day to view the chickens. He informed her that he was going to report us to the authorities for cruel and unusual punishment of the creatures. She asked him why. He said it was because the chickens' feet were glued to the display. She encouraged him to report us. She informed him that we would have the chickens on display until the end of the Olympic Games. He left.

The most disruptive and horrible event during the Olympics occurred at approximately 1:20 a.m. on Saturday, July 27. A bomb went off inside the Centennial Olympic Park, the major gathering place for visitors and Olympic athletes. The park also hosted exhibits and venues of major Olympic sponsors, companies, and vendors.

One person was killed by the blast, and another died of a heart attack after rushing to the scene. The injured included 111 people who unfortunately were near the bomb blast. Several of our GA AG 96 staff members who were working that night assisted the wounded before the arrival of emergency services.

I was not there the night of the explosion but was due to work the following day. Five o'clock the next morning, I was about to leave the house when my home phone rang. It was my mother, asking me if I was okay. I said yes and asked her why she was asking me that question at five in the morning. She told me about the bomb. It was the first I had heard anything about it. "Turn your TV on," she said. I thanked her and immediately went to turn on the television. Of course, the park was closed that day, and I did not have to work.

Park security was extremely sophisticated before the bomb, but it was even stricter afterward. I parked at my office at the Georgia Power building, a block from the Centennial Olympic Park; every day, my vehicle was searched, and a dog sniffed around it for explosives. I had to wear a different color Olympic armband for each day I attended, as well as an Olympic badge, and anything I carried in was searched.

The investigation of the bomb incident lasted for over two years. The first person accused of the bomb was Richard Jewell, who was a member of the security team at the Olympics. He was eliminated as a suspect after three months. It took nearly two years for the actual suspect, Eric Rudolph, to be identified and charged with the bombing. Rudolph was finally arrested in North Carolina on May 31, 2003. He is serving four consecutive life sentences plus 120 years in prison.

The Centennial Olympic Park was reopened on Tuesday, July 30, with no further complications.

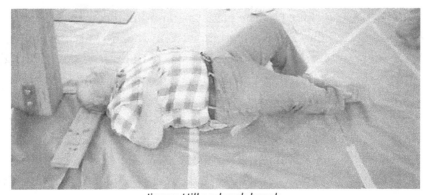

Jimmy Hill on lunch break

* Photo Courtesy of GA AG 96

Jimmy Hill and Danette Amstein

* Photo Courtesy of GA AG 96

Many volunteers from our sponsoring organizations came and donated hundreds and hundreds of hours to help construct the barn and assist during the entire event. GA AG 96 did not have the resources to hire a contractor to do the wiring, plumbing, inside carpenter work, masonry work, etc. These volunteers met the challenges by doing whatever it took to complete the exhibit. Many of us worked ten to twelve hours a day for over a month completing the pavilion before the opening day.

Many thanks to Travis Henry, Charlie Gillespie, and the late Garland Anderson for their hard work in supporting the GA AG 96 project as they represented the Agricultural Affairs Department exceedingly well.

Naming names is a perilous thing to do since I may miss some volunteer names. I will attempt to name as many as possible who contributed to this massive effort. If I have missed someone, please know that it was not intentional, but that lack of complete volunteer records and reliance on personal memory contributed to this oversight. This list does not include those people previously mentioned in this chapter.

Volunteers included: Don Koehler, Trish Alderman, Arthur Lanita, Brenda Patterson, Barbara McCarthy, Brenda Tuck, Carol Perry, Heather Hardy, Woody Shepard, Elizabeth Doyle, Butch Ferree, David Skinner, Patsy Aamoth, Merrill Folsom, Chi Thai, Elizabeth Odell, Bina Berry, David Rogers, Lillie Ward, Fred Harrison, Mark Latimore, Larry and Ruth Benyshek, Frank and Judy Connell, Dorthy Conteh, Johnny Crawford, Willie Jo Dowdy, Allison and Bryan Hubbel, Tim Ligon, Bobby and Gale Miller, Richard Morgan, Mark Risse, Donna Sims, Brenda Tuck, Carl and Cheryl Varnadoe, Jeff Alevy, Robert Brannen, Sharon Cassidy, Wayne Christian, Brian Dill, Jean Gable, Ronnie Gheesling, Elizabeth Hancock, Audrey Hardin, Susan Harrell, Louise Hill, Jan Holden, Ruth Jarrett, Chris Jones, Rosalyn Joseph, Lisa Kelly, Gil Landry, Joyce Latimer, Mary Ellen Lawson, Gal Lilja, Luanne Lohr, Marilyn Mansell, Sandra McDaniel, Sharon Omahen, Wayne Peavy, Carol Perry, Janie Rogers, Delbert Shelton, Albert Smith, Tony Tyson, Scott Utley, Leslic Wagner, Jerry Walker, Pat Wicken, John Ruter, Thomas Crocker, David Adams, Wayne Crawford, John Carter, and Bob Izlar.

I have included my work schedule for the GA AG 96 exhibit during the Olympic Games in the Appendix.

Jimmy answering questions about tobacco
* Photo Courtesy of GA AG 96

Jimmy Hill at GA AG 96 Pavilion

* Photo Courtesy of GA AG 96

For Heather Hardy, one of our volunteer staff members, working the GA AG 96 exhibit dramatically changed her life. Heather was an intern with the University of Georgia College of Agricultural and Environmental Sciences and was on duty during the last night of the Olympics. A man walked in just as the exhibit was about to close. She noticed him because he was alone, and many visitors were usually in groups. He asked Heather about the Vidalia onions that were on display near where she was standing. She explained that they were sweet onions, grown in South Georgia. As soon as they started talking, she noticed his accent. He was from Australia and had traveled over to tour America and to visit the 1996 Olympics. He introduced himself as Steve Leo.

Steve had a couple of other questions about the Vidalia onions, then told Heather that he would like to see a small town in Georgia. She immediately offered to give him a tour of her hometown of Madison, Georgia, the next day.

Steve left to attend the closing ceremonies with his Australian tour group. Heather had to work until the early hours of the morning, along with the rest of us, to secure the building and remove any valuables. We had to be out of Centennial Park by 6:00 a.m.

She spent the night with a friend near Atlanta and woke around noon the next day. Her friend reminded her of her commitment to meet Steve at three o'clock that afternoon. She had not remembered making the call, but at some time during the night, she had left him a phone message to meet her at the Decatur MARTA station at 3:00 p.m. She got dressed and drove to the station.

Steve did not arrive at three o'clock, and she began to wonder if he was not going to show up. She waited a while longer and then decided to leave. Just as she reached her car, she heard "Heather! Heather!" in his Australian accent.

The two of them drove to Madison, where they first looked around her father's farm, and then went on to her mother and stepfather's farm, finishing the visit there with an old-fashioned, southern, home-cooked dinner.

Heather took him back to Atlanta to meet up with his tour group. As he got out of the car, he said, "If you are ever in Australia, give me a call."

He telephoned her from several points along his journey home to Queensland.

When Steve arrived back in Brisbane, he had five letters waiting for him from a certain Georgia girl. This started a long-distance relationship that went on for two and a half years, including her spending three months in Australia, and his spending three months in Madison.

They knew that it was time to make their decision about getting married. He asked and she accepted his proposal. They celebrated their twenty-first wedding anniversary in June 2020. They are happily married and have two boys.

Heather credits the 1996 Olympics and Vidalia onions for this amazing journey!

The GA AG 96 was a great success, bringing together Georgia agricultural organizations and companies with a common goal of promoting Georgia and southern agriculture to the world. The GA AG 96 pavilion had over six hundred thousand visitors from all over the world, who had the opportunity to experience Georgia agriculture and southern hospitality!

On a personal note, Gail and I attended one Olympic sporting event together, and that was the artistic gymnastics competition at the Georgia Dome on the evening of July 28. I also attended the handball competition at the Georgia Dome on August 4.

Faith Peppers, who was with the UGA College of Agricultural and Environmental Sciences, was our media coordinator for GA AG 96. Faith led her team in putting together a Reporter's Notebook with facts and figures about Georgia agriculture. The notebook was shared with all media personnel and other interested parties. She connected with dozens of major farm publications and provided them with facts and contacts for their use in reporting on the Georgia agriculture Olympic efforts.

Faith handled all contact with the print, radio, and television news outlets. She worked months in advance, making sure the media had everything needed to cover agriculture during the Olympics. She arranged for tours and visits to farms, agribusinesses, and other sites for reporters from Holland, India, Sweden, and France.

She made other contacts with international media visitors from Sweden, Japan, India, Jamaica, Norway, Thailand, The Netherlands, Taiwan, Argentina, France, Brazil, Germany, and Russia.

Faith maintained logs of media reports, articles, and audio and video clips. She produced a weekly and a final report, listing clips for various print media. She also compiled reports on television video feeds.

She also conducted live interviews with visitors who came by the pavilion, which demonstrated how they enjoyed the pavilion and how much they learned about Georgia agriculture.

The media plan results for the exhibit were submitted to the South East Chapter of the National Agriculture Marketing Association (NAMA) and won "Best of NAMA for 1996" for Georgia Agriculture 96. Thanks to Faith Peppers for your hard work and for winning this award. She did an outstanding job of media coordination before, during, and after the Olympic Games.

The 1996 Olympic torch relay was a fifteen-thousand-mile, eighty-four-day journey across America. The torch came within a two-hour drive of 90 percent of the population of the United States. It was carried by runner, bicycle, nineteen-car train, horseback, canoe, steamboat, sailboat, and airplane. There were ten thousand torchbearers, who between them carried the torch from Olympia, Greece, to Atlanta, Georgia.

Norman Farm, located in Mitchell County, Georgia, was one of twenty farms in Georgia that donated hickory and pecan wood to be used to make the ceremonial torches. Greg Findley, district forester with the Georgia Forestry Commission, helped identify the trees that would yield the necessary eight-foot lengths of knot-free timber. The wood was processed in Athens, Milledgeville, and Newnan, Georgia. The final processing was done by a Louisville Slugger baseball bat factory.

The GA AG 96 pavilion closed on August 4, 1996, at midnight. All equipment, animatronics, displays, signs, etc. had to be removed from the site by 6:00 a.m. As you can imagine, the pavilion became a madhouse of volunteers and board members dismantling and removing everything from the site. We completed the work on time.

The next day, the flowers, plants, and other items were removed. The board of directors handled the sale of the television screens, audio equipment, displays, and other equipment. The animatronics were transferred to their respective industry representatives. It took several months to dispose of all the items.

Following the successful implementation of the GA AG 96 goal of showcasing Georgia and southern agriculture to the world, the organization filed for Intent to Dissolve on July 8, 1997. The approval for dissolution was received on September 4, 1997.

The GA AG 96 team raised over six hundred thousand dollars in cash; with in-kind donations, the total investment was over one million dollars. The commemorative bricks remained in the park, and you will find my name, along with thousands of other Georgians' names, on those bricks to this day.

The board authorized me to handle the process of selling and removing the pavilion following the conclusion of the Olympic Games. It had to be removed no later than September 10, 1996, as required by ACOG in our original contract with them.

I issued a request for bids on dismantling and removing the pavilion. The bid document was sent to several interested parties and to others who might have a need or desire to purchase the pavilion. I received proposals from four Georgia entities: Rockdale County; the City of Conyers; Cobb County (City of Kennesaw); and the University of Georgia Griffin Campus.

UGA's Griffin Campus had the top bid and was approved to receive the pavilion. Dr. Jerry Arkin, assistant dean of the Griffin Campus, facilitated the securing of funds to dismantle and remove the pavilion. We obtained approval from ACOG for an extension beyond September 10.

Dr. Arkin arranged to move the structure, but there were not sufficient funds at that point to re-erect it on campus. He and his staff continued fundraising and were able to raise the $250,000 needed to complete that final step in the fall of 1997.

It was decided to place the pavilion at the front of the UGA Griffin Campus, on the north side of Stuckey Auditorium, and to name it the "Naomi Chapman Woodroof Agricultural Pavilion." Mrs. Woodroof was a woman ahead of her time. She was the first female student to attend the College of Agriculture at the University of Idaho and the first woman to graduate from there. She was also one of the first two women to receive agricultural degrees in the United States. Also, she was the first woman scientist at the University of Georgia Griffin Campus, known then as the Georgia Experiment Station.

Naomi Chapman received her bachelor's degree and master's degree in plant pathology. At that time, jobs for women in the agricultural field were nearly nonexistent. After looking extensively for work, she found that the Georgia Experiment Station accepted women as faculty. She applied and was accepted for a job at the station. Chapman obtained a bank loan to fund her trip from Spokane, Washington, to Griffin, Georgia. She held several positions at the Experiment Station, eventually working with Dr. Guy Woodroof on a pecan project. They fell in love and married. Dr. Guy Woodroof was named the first president of Abraham Baldwin Agricultural College in 1933 and relocated to Tifton, Georgia. Mrs. Woodroof was hired to work at the Coastal Plain Experiment Station, also located in Tifton.

Naomi Chapman Woodroof was an unsung hero in plant pathology in the southern peanut belt. The newly re-erected pavilion was named in her honor to recognize her outstanding academic achievements and valuable research contributions to Georgia agriculture.

The opening ceremony for the Naomi Chapman Woodroof Agricultural Pavilion was held on Tuesday, October 21, 1997. Dr. Gale Buchanan, dean and director of the UGA College of Agricultural and Environmental Sciences, welcomed the attendees to the event. Speakers included the Honorable Gail M. Buckner, District 95, Georgia House of Representatives; Dr. Gerald F. Arkin, assistant dean, UGA College of

Agricultural and Environmental Sciences, Griffin Campus; Mr. Lindsey Thomas, president, Georgia Chamber of Commerce; and Mr. Mitch Head, chairman, Georgia Agriculture 1996.

The UGA Griffin Campus also conducted a commemorative brick sale to raise money for the re-erection of the pavilion. I bought a brick inscribed with "Jimmy & Gail Hill, GA AG 96." We were happy to support their campaign to secure the pavilion on their campus.

On September 13–15, 2001, the Georgia Agri-Leaders Forum Foundation (GALFF) hosted a study institute on the UGA Griffin Campus. I, in coordination with members of the original GA AG 96 board of directors, decided to include a five-year reunion event on September 13. We invited members of the GA AG 96 board and others to take part in the event, which was to be held in the Naomi Chapman Woodroof Agricultural Pavilion.

The reunion was kicked off by Dean Gale Buchanan, who shared his thoughts on the GA AG 96 project. Other speakers included Georgia commissioner of agriculture, Tommy Irvin; Gary Black, president, Georgia Agribusiness Council; Lindsay Thomas, president, Georgia Chamber of Commerce; Mitch Head, former president, GA AG 96; Anne Ponder Young, coordinator, GA AG 96; and Dr. Gerald Arkin, assistant dean, UGA College of Agricultural and Environmental Sciences, Griffin Campus. I was also honored to speak, in my role as executive director, GALFF, and GA AG 96 board member.

Speakers reminisced about the opportunities, challenges, barriers, more barriers, good luck, bad luck, and finally the awesome success at the end.

As soon as Atlanta was selected to host the Olympic Games, the governor of Georgia, in conjunction with several public and private entities, created a worldwide economic development program called **Operation Legacy**. Georgia Power Company was one of the program partners, along with the Governor's Development Council, Georgia Department of Industry, Trade and Tourism, Georgia Chamber of Commerce, Atlanta Chamber of

Commerce, NationsBank, and the Atlanta Committee for the Olympic Games.

Operation Legacy was designed to entice a select group of the world's leading investors, companies, and corporations to Atlanta and to acquaint them with the amazing economic opportunities that were developing in Georgia.

The program hosted several invitation-only, VIP tours of Atlanta and Georgia in the months leading up to the 1996 Atlanta Olympic Games. They would include special visits to Olympic venues, meetings with the leaders of the 1996 Olympic Games, VIP tours of businesses and technologies, as well as a recreational event of choice. While on the tour, guests would have opportunities to meet and discuss business with Georgia's corporate and economic development leaders. Georgia was one of the key states where business and investment opportunities abounded.

Olympic Tour Packages were designed for different business segments, and destinations selected accordingly:

- Plastics: Athens, Augusta, Clayton County, Macon, Rome, Savannah, Statesboro
- Agribusiness: Albany, Brunswick, Columbus, Dublin, Eatonton/Greensboro, Gainesville, Macon, Rome, Valdosta
- Business Info: Augusta, Cobb County, Henry County, Macon, North Fulton, County, Rome, Savannah
- Consultants: Brunswick, Dublin, Eatonton/Greensboro, Fayette County/Peachtree City, Savannah, Statesboro, Toccoa, Valdosta
- Electronics: Albany, Cartersville, Cobb County, Fayette County/Peachtree City, Gainesville, Macon, North Fulton, Savannah
- Chemical: Athens, Augusta, Cobb County, Macon, North Fulton, Savannah, Statesboro
- Automotive: Albany, Cartersville, Clayton County, Columbus, Henry County, Macon, Savannah, Toccoa

My involvement was of course in the agribusiness segment, for which we put together the following plan:

- Background: Agricultural products are Georgia's most significant exports. Changing societal work trends are increasing the need for additional food processing facilities.
- Strategy: Host an Operation Legacy Olympics tour of the Sunbelt Agricultural Exposition to showcase Georgia's agricultural and agribusiness industry strengths and show the ability of Georgia to handle the needs for increasing business expansion.
- Team: Building on the strengths of Georgia Power's Agricultural Affairs Department, led by manager Jimmy Hill, link the many and varied agribusiness associations, governmental service providers, and academic leadership at Georgia's key agribusiness institutions.
- Activity: Preceding the October 17–19, 1995, Sunbelt Expo, bring together CEOs of the food processing companies, equipment manufacturers, and export market targets for an Operation Legacy tour. The tour should focus on food marketing opportunities and take advantage of existing industries in identifying, inviting, and courting prospects. Seek to encourage strategic alliances for export opportunities. Use the state's best incentives in seeking expansions of Georgia operations and attracting sister divisions.

Georgia business and government leaders were a part of this pre-Olympic program designed to showcase the positive aspects of doing business in Georgia. The agribusiness tour segment of Operation Legacy took place on September 9–11, 1995. The VIP agribusiness corporate officers arrived in Atlanta on Friday, September 8, for an opportunity to experience southern hospitality with other agribusiness leaders from across the state.

On Saturday, September 9, events included an option of various recreational activities. The executives could choose from fishing at private lakes, golf, Stone Mountain tour, antique shopping, trapshooting and skeet shooting at South River, Atlanta History Center tour, or CNN Center and King Plow Arts Center tour.

My group of nine executives represented the poultry, candy, pork, food processing, and grocery industries. They chose to take the fishing expedition to Griffin. The private, stocked lakes did not disappoint. The executives caught some large, near-trophy fish and had a great time.

Saturday night involved attending the IX Diving World Cup Championship at the Aquatic Center at Georgia Tech. This was a new facility, built for the Olympic aquatic competitions. Following the Georgia Tech visit, the executives had dinner at the top of NationsBank Plaza, one of the tallest buildings in Atlanta. The group was also taken up to the roof for a fantastic city view.

On Monday morning September 11, Robert Ratliff, president of AGCO Corporation, addressed the group. Following breakfast, the executives traveled to various agribusiness-related companies across the state. I was the host for the group that traveled to Griffin.

As of June 1999, Operation Legacy overall was responsible for forty-two locations and expansions within Georgia, according to Lynn Pitts, economic development manager in charge of the Operation Legacy program. These new locations brought 6,671 jobs and $373 million in capital investment. For more information on Operation Legacy, please refer to the Appendix.

22

Georgia Agri-Leaders Forum

I was very fortunate and blessed to be involved in the creation, development, implementation, and management of the Georgia Agri-Leaders Forum. This chapter will take you from the idea of a leadership development program to its final implementation. It is a journey of exceptional commitment to a goal that led to changed lives.

Louise Hill—no relation—was the director of program development and education with the Georgia Farm Bureau Federation, located in Macon, and had been working on leadership issues in her role there. Louise graduated from Leadership Georgia in 1988. She had come out of that experience with the conviction that a leadership program was needed for agriculture. I graduated from Leadership Georgia in 1990 and had come away with the same conviction.

There were five of us, a "Gang of Five," who hung around together as we attended agriculture meetings across the state of Georgia. Louise and I were part of that group. The others were Gary Black, president of the Georgia Agribusiness Council, Don Rogers, Georgia Department of Agriculture, and Randy Williams, UGA Extension. Louise initiated the conversation within our group regarding leadership. After a few discussions, we came to believe that maybe we should take on the mantle of leadership and see if there was an appetite for those in agriculture to participate in a leadership development program.

The Gang of Five decided to meet in Athens, Georgia, at Randy Williams's office on the UGA campus. We met on the morning of Wednesday, October 25, 1989. As we discussed the idea of developing an agricultural leadership program, Louise shared that several states had already developed similar programs. The W. K. Kellogg Foundation had provided the seed money for them. However, she had learned Kellogg no longer offered this type of funding. A majority of the programs had been developed through land-grant colleges and university extension programs, and a couple of others as privately funded foundations.

Gary Black

Jimmy Hill

Louise Hill

Don Rogers

Randy Williams

The "Gang of Five"

We visited with Dr. Gale Buchanan, University of Georgia's dean and director of the College of Agricultural and Environmental Sciences. He was responsible for the extension service. Dean Buchanan shared that he would love to have the program but was concerned that pending budget cuts by the State of Georgia would leave the program in a perilous condition. As it turned out, he was right: severe budget cuts were coming for the next fiscal year. We regrouped to think about alternatives.

We had, in the meantime, been contacting leaders of agricultural organizations to determine if there was a perceived need for leadership training. The initial feedback was positive. The next move was to create a questionnaire to be sent to as many agricultural organizations, companies, and individuals as possible. The questionnaire was developed and mailed to about three hundred individuals and organizations. The responses were overall very positive. There seemed to be a consensus that an agricultural leadership program was needed and desired.

The Gang of Five developed a list of agricultural leaders and interested parties we would invite to a two-day session to discuss the idea of a leadership development program. The meeting was held in Macon, Georgia, on March 13–14, 1990, at the Twin Pines Facility, owned by the Macon Georgia Power employees.

First meeting of AG leaders to discuss forming a leadership program

I called the meeting of the Agricultural Leadership Forum Project Team to order at 1:00 p.m. on Tuesday, March 13. Dr. Dale Threadgill, chairman, and head of UGA's Department of Agricultural Engineering, was the meeting facilitator. Dr. Threadgill was an advisor to the Leadership Georgia program.

In addition to Dr. Threadgill and me, the following people attended the meeting:

Gary Black	Lyvia Lynch	Glenn Smith
Bill Brim	Laura Meadows	Jimmy Smith
Robert Dickey	Charles Norman	Larry Snipes
Tom Dyer	Winfred Owens	Oscar Strickland
John Gunter	Willie Paulk	Harry Stanley
Louise Hill	Ann Ravan	Garland Thompson
Terrell Hudson	Lisa Ray	Bill Verner
Buddy Leger	Jim Respess	Dr. Melvin Walker Jr.
John Leidner	Don Rogers	Terrell Weeks
Jim Loftis	Rep. Richard Royal	Alvin White
Dr. Harold Loyd	Dr. Keith Scearce	Dr. Randy Williams

Between them, the attendees represented interests in agribusiness, vegetables, peaches, pecans, watermelon, row crops, forestry, poultry, equine, beef, dairy, Georgia Farm Bureau, agricultural press, educational institutions (UGA, ABAC, Fort Valley), community development, chambers of commerce, Georgia Department of AG, legislative, banking, power companies (Georgia Power and EMCs), and the Georgia Young Farmers Association. This was an amazing grouping of people interested in developing leaders for their respective companies and organizations.

Dr. Threadgill presented the primary objectives of the meeting: to examine the need to establish an agricultural leadership forum, and, if there was a need, how it should be structured.

I presented the history leading up to this meeting, including the meetings of the Gang of Five in late 1989 and early 1990, and told those assembled that we would determine over the following two days if this idea had merit and support for moving forward.

Dr. Threadgill then spoke about Leadership Georgia. It is the oldest statewide leadership program in the country and in 1990 was already in its nineteenth year. It cuts across all professions and started from a nucleus group led by Dr. J. W. Fanning. The program is still thriving now, in 2020, and is non-partisan, with focuses on networking and education. Each graduate goes back into the community, gets involved, and makes a difference.

Louise Hill took us through the information on other leadership programs around the country, which had been mailed to each attendee ahead of the meeting. Mr. T. M. "Mort" Ewing, president of the Georgia Farm Bureau Federation, told the group that he was personally interested in the development of an agricultural leadership program and emphasized the Farm Bureau's commitment to this project.

The attendees were divided into groups to discuss the leadership needs of agriculture in Georgia. They were challenged to develop goals and a mission for the program. As each group reported their findings, there was very little divergence in their responses. All recognized the need for skills development and that the global aspect of agriculture needed to be incorporated into the leadership curriculum.

Dr. Threadgill shared that leadership existed in the state, but that there had been no coordinated effort. The program should develop leadership skills, not provide leadership. Individuals would be part of the program, not representing any specific commodity or advocacy group.

After supper, Dr. Oscar Strickland, from Alabama's agricultural leadership program, spoke to the group about the structure and success of their program. He strongly encouraged those gathered to pursue the establishment of a Georgia program.

On Wednesday morning, we all reconvened at 8:30 a.m. with Dr. Threadgill facilitating. The group was divided into five subgroups, and each was assigned a different topic: funding, name, and mission; structure; election processing; staffing and governance; and organizational structure.

After about an hour, the subgroups reported the results of their discussions to everyone.

Their findings were as follows:

- The mission statement should be "To provide a forum for developing individual leaders skilled in communications, educated in local, national and world affairs, familiar with the changing needs of our society, and prepared to meet the present and future challenges."
- The board of directors would be self-perpetuating and would come from a nominating committee from the board.
- Spouses would be involved in the interview process, the first meeting, and either the last meeting or a meeting structured with spouse involvement.
- One at-large participant from a non-agricultural field— media, for example—should be invited to participate in the program.
- A fifteen-member board of directors was recommended. The group asked that the Gang of Five be automatically placed on the board. The Gang of Five would recommend ten additional members for the board. This slate would be presented to the members of the Agricultural Leadership Forum Project, who would have the ability to nominate additional persons to the slate. The members would vote on the final ten.

Dr. J. W. Fanning, known as the Father of Leadership Georgia, spoke at lunch about the qualities of a leader. Dr. Fanning talked about the Ten Pillars of Leadership: Retain custody of value; Be willing to listen and hear; Have an ability to articulate the heartfelt concerns and desires of people; Dispense hope; Project foresightedness; Build knowledge with common sense; Maintain integrity of character; Show courage to think and act anew; Share oneself with others; Motivate people to act (source: https:// www.fanning.uga.edu/about/history).

The Gang of Five held several meetings to work on details of the Georgia Agri-Leaders Forum. The meetings were held on April 23, June 13, June 21, July 11–12, August 24, October 4, and November 30, 1990. At the July 12 meeting, the election of the remaining directors took place. The ten people elected as new directors were: James Lee Adams; Robert Dickey, Dr. Harold Loyd, Jim Loftis, Abit Massey, Ann Ravan Jones, James (Jim) Respess, Richard Royal, Terrell Weeks, and Alvin White. This group joined directors Gary Black, Louise Hill, Randy Williams, Don Rogers, and me.

The election of officers also took place at the July 12 meeting. I was elected president. Three vice presidents were elected: Jim Loftis, Ann Ravan Jones, and James "Jim" Respess. Robert Dickey was elected secretary-treasurer, and Gary Black was elected assistant secretary-treasurer.

The August 24 meeting addressed the structure of the program. It was decided that each session would be described as a study institute. Twelve study institutes were conducted over two years starting in March 1991.

At the November 30 meeting in Macon, at the Farmers' Market office building, I, as president, laid out the stark reality that no funds had been identified to start or operate the Forum. There should be an opportunity to solicit funds from agricultural companies and organizations as well as to charge a tuition fee. I challenged the directors to raise enough money to start the program and provide operating funds for the first year of the two-year program. Each director was asked to personally commit to raising eight thousand dollars, either by contributing personal funds or by securing the funds from companies, organizations, etc. There was complete silence in the room for what seemed like five minutes. Then I heard groans and comments like, "This may be impossible!" There was some serious discussion about this idea, but in the end, everyone committed to raising their allotted amount. To tell the truth, I was shocked that I had generated this crazy high number and that they bought it. I knew that we had to dream big to make the Georgia Agri-Leaders Forum come to life. We raised enough money to start and operate for the first year.

The Georgia Agri-Leaders Forum Foundation was a 501(c)(3) non-profit organization as determined by the IRS. The headquarters of the Forum was located in Grayson, Georgia, until 1999, when it moved to Dawsonville, Georgia. A fifteen-member board of directors set the direction and policy for the Foundation.

In January 1991, we sent out a packet of materials regarding the Forum to over three hundred people in Georgia agriculture. The start date for the first study institute was set for March 28, 1991.

Lynne Kernaghan, Susan Reynolds and Jimmy Hill

I started the search for an executive director to run the day-to-day operations of the Forum and was fortunate enough to locate Lynne Kernaghan from Macon, Georgia, who graciously accepted the position. Lynne worked out of her home in Macon. She and I created the duties and responsibilities as we went along. We could not afford to pay Lynne what she was worth, but she accepted the job anyway. She did an outstanding job and stayed with us through early 1994.

Our next executive director was Ester England, whom I hired in early 1994. Her son, Terry England, was a participant in the 1994 class. Ester also worked out of her home and served until mid-1998, when she took a position with the Georgia Agribusiness Council. Ester took the executive director's job to the next level and did an outstanding job.

I served as the first chairman of the board of directors until 1994. In 1995, I was elected to serve as the past chairman. I left the board in 1996, then came back as a director in 1997. In 1998, I was elected chairman of the selections committee, but resigned middle of that year to accept the position of executive director of the Forum. Gail also came on board as an assistant executive director. I served as executive director until the job title was changed to president and CEO, then continued in that role until I resigned in 2010.

Ester England and Jimmy Hill

The Forum implemented its mission through six study institutes. These institutes varied in length from two days to a week and focused on the following:

- What makes a leader?
- Policy and politics of agriculture, agribusiness, and forestry
- Developing successful communication skills

- Investigating the challenge of change and what technologies and new practices are on the horizon
- Traveling to another agriculture-intensive state to see what challenges and opportunities they have faced and how they have solved them
- How to put leadership skills and training to use for the benefit of Georgia agriculture

It is intuitively obvious how important it is to have trained and motivated leaders ready to assume leadership roles in Georgia. Many agricultural organizations and companies have struggled at times due to the lack of good leaders. One way to eliminate trial and error in selecting a good leader was to select someone who had graduated from the Forum.

How do we know Forum graduates have been successful in providing outstanding leadership? Listed below are thirty-five ways graduates have demonstrated their leadership skills:

- Two have written books
- One became the agricultural advisor to the governor
- One manages a twenty-five-thousand-acre plantation
- Three became Georgia state representatives
- One is president of a large agricultural chemical firm
- One became a student recruiter for a Georgia college
- Several ran and were elected to a county school board
- Several ran and were elected to a county commission
- Another was promoted to the head of a cotton marketing firm
- One became a district leader in UGA Extension
- Three became department heads at UGA College of Agricultural and Environmental Sciences
- Two were promoted to top ag lending positions in Georgia
- Two were selected as assistant state commissioners of agriculture
- One is starting a new company in the aquaculture industry

- One became the marketing manager at a large hunting and fishing preserve
- One started a new business in the beverage industry
- Another started a new business in the beef industry
- One became the head of the largest farm organization in Georgia
- Two serve on the State Advisory Board to FSA
- One was named the teacher of the year in his school system—he teaches agriculture
- One became the vice president of a large agricultural chemical firm
- Five became president of the Georgia Young Farmer Association
- Two were elected sheriff
- One was selected as the head of the Agricultural Education Department at the Georgia Department of Education
- One was promoted to a top leadership position in the College of Veterinary Medicine at UGA
- One became one of the world's top experts on avian influenza
- One was elected the president and CEO of a Georgia EMC
- Over fifteen graduates have been recognized as Farmer of the Year by various organizations
- Nearly four dozen are employed by UGA in extension, teaching, and research or other areas
- One was elected as a bank president
- One started a food company using Georgia agricultural products
- Another was named the curriculum director for agricultural education in Georgia
- One became the project manager of a soon-to-be-built corn ethanol plant
- Another was selected as the vice president of sales for a large, national poultry firm

- One became the administrator of the USDA Farm Service Agency in Washington, DC

Since 2012, this list of graduates and accomplishments has grown even more under UGA's Advancing Georgia's Leaders in Agriculture and Forestry program. One significant example is that graduate Zippy Duvall was elected the president of the American Farm Bureau located in Washington, DC.

Including the first graduating class in 1993, there were seventeen classes, with a total of 346 participants completing the requirements of graduation for Georgia Agri-leaders. A listing of the graduates can be found in the Appendix.

Numerous men and women served as officers and board members between the years of 1991 and 2010. These individuals committed the time and expertise in serving the Forum: James Lee Adams Jr., Dr. Scott Angle, Roger Austin, Gary Black, William Bowen, Paul Brower, Dr. Gale Buchanan, Bob Budd, Roebie Burriss, Dr. Tom Call, Wendell Cannon, Becky Carlson, Nancy Coleman, Cathy Cox, Gale Cutler, Dr. Fred Davison, Denise Deal, Robert Dickey III, Wayne Dollar, Dick Dowdy, Frances Edmunds, Chap Enfinger, Ed Faircloth, James Ford, Don Giles, Tammy Tate Gilland, Charles Gillespie, Horace Hamilton, Philipp von Hanstein, Will Harris, Jimmy Hill, Louise Hill, Clint Hood, Commissioner Tommy Irvin, Dot James, Ann Jones, Emory Jones, Dr. Bill Lambert, John Langdale, Paul Larson, Jimmy Lewis, Jimmie Loftis, Dr. Harold Loyd, Gene Maddux, F. Abit Massey, Steve McClam, Mary Alice McGee, Dr. Lee Myers, Steve Newton, Randy Nichols, Joyce Niggley, Ronnie Noble, Randy Nuckolls, Stephen Parrish, James L. Respess III, Tom Rodgers, J. Donald Rogers, Bobby Rowan, Richard Royal, Wes Shannon, Henrietta Singletary, Donnie Smith, Doris Smith, Glenn Smith, Jody Tyson Strickland, Bill Verner, Michael Volimer, Terrell Weeks, David Westmoreland, C. Alvin White, Dr. Ed White, Allen Whitehead, Collie Williams, Dr. W. Randy Williams and Gibbs Wilson.

Dr. Fred Davidson and Ester England

Institute One dealt with What Makes a Leader. Ron Hart and I were the instructors. Ron was a longtime employee of Georgia Power and worked in human resources. I met him back in the early 1980s while I was taking one of his courses on leadership. That course was based on a book by Stephen R. Covey entitled *The 7 Habits of Highly Effective People*. The premise of Covey's book is that a highly effective person will be a leader. In it are powerful lessons in personal change that could change the direction of your life. They changed mine.

Ron was a very effective instructor, who lived his life by the principles of the 7 Habits book. Back in the late 1980s, Ron started having some health issues. It was finally determined to be muscular dystrophy (MD). MD is a group of diseases that cause progressive weakness and loss of muscle mass. Treatments can help, but there is no cure. It began to affect Ron, and he was having trouble walking. He eventually navigated with crutches and several years later was confined to a wheelchair.

Ron Hart teaching at an Institute

I felt strongly that Ron would make a great instructor for the Georgia Agri-Leaders Forum. I asked him if he would assist us and teach the 7-Habits course. He agreed and taught for several years until MD made it very difficult for him to teach and to travel.

Ron's philosophy for teaching the 7-Habits book was to let the class members teach it. I found that to be an awesome and effective process, based on demonstrated class member experiences. Ron believed that if you internalized these concepts such that you could teach them, you would come to believe in them, and they would change your life.

One of the first things we did in this institute was to go around the room and learn about backgrounds, family, work, and anything else the participants wanted to share. This led to group bonding that helped to facilitate the teaching of the 7 Habits.

Covey indicates that if you practice and internalize the following, which he terms Habits, you will be an effective person and an effective leader: Be proactive; Begin with the end in mind; Put first things first; Think win-win; Seek first to understand, then to be understood; Synergize; Sharpen the saw.

The Agri-Leader participants were assigned to read the book before they came to the institute. They were divided into seven teams, and each team was assigned a Habit to teach. Each had about four hours at the beginning of the institute to prepare to teach their Habit and one and a half hours to teach it.

As each team member internalized their Habit, they would share how that Habit had or had not impacted their life. We had individuals who opened their hearts and shared raw experiences of their lives, and many tears were shed by everybody in the room. The participants became very emotional at times. I know, based on the opening-up and the raw emotion that was exhibited, that lives were changed in the sessions. Many participants shared their feelings immediately, and others did so at the end of the institute, during wrap-up. I received written notes after the institute sharing similar sentiments about the experience. To this day, I still hear from participants who say how this session changed not only their lives but the lives of their spouses and children.

At one of our graduation institutes, a spouse asked me what we had done to her husband. He was, she said, a changed man, who volunteered to help her with the housework and shared more of the workload around the home. He was kinder and more caring and loving! She said that she had noticed the change immediately after Institute One. I remember her spouse had one of those "aha" moments when he said, "I have got to go home and fix some things with my wife and family." I guess he did.

In studying and teaching the Habits, you are led to look inside your heart and mind to see if you are aligned with your personal mission and goals. One of the things that Covey teaches is to write your mission statement and, if applicable, your family's mission statement. This forces you to examine your life, and that is what led to many emotional experiences shared by class members.

This is the story class member Spencer Black shared with us about being involved in a vehicle crash with his girlfriend—who would later become his wife. He said that he was a very immature, borderline reckless, overconfident jerk before the accident.

They were traveling down Interstate 75 near Adel, Georgia, when the crash occurred. He did not know until later that a semi-truck had come across the median and hit his vehicle head-on. He did not remember seeing the truck. He did remember reaching to change the radio station and his girlfriend screaming at the top of her lungs. The next thing he recalled was waking up trapped in his vehicle, upside down. He believed that seatbelts, airbags, and the Grace of God were what saved them. He was pinned in and could not move. He looked across the seat, and his girlfriend was gone. Unbeknownst to him, she had crawled out through the back window of the vehicle and up the hill to the edge of the interstate before she collapsed. She suffered from a severe concussion and went into shock from the trauma. Before she blacked out, someone handed her a cell phone. She could not remember his parents' phone number or anyone else's other than her ex-roommate. She called her friend, who contacted the young man's parents. They rushed to the Valdosta hospital, where they assumed that their son and his girlfriend would be taken.

His girlfriend collapsed after making the call and was transported to the hospital in the first ambulance that arrived. He was unconscious most of the time. He learned later that it took the fire department forty-nine minutes to cut the truck apart and get him out. That did not include the nine minutes that it took for them to arrive. He did some additional damage to himself by trying to get out of the vehicle. He remembered before he came to, seeing a glimpse of Heaven … and it was wonderful.

Once they got him on the gurney, one of the EMTs said, "Son, God has a plan for you." The EMT said that he had not thought anybody in the vehicle could have survived this wreck after being hit by a semi-truck. Fifty-eight minutes after the accident, he was put in an ambulance and, fifteen minutes later, was wheeled into the hospital emergency room. His parents had been waiting for fifty minutes for his arrival. He was in such bad shape that his mother did not recognize him.

Over the next three months, he had to relearn how to walk and deal with two broken ribs, a fractured sternum, a broken hip, a torn diaphragm, a punctured lung, a missing spleen, a broken hand, a severe burn, and enough scars to gross out a fifth grader.

He learned, as a result of the accident, who he was going to marry, that he needed to get serious about his job, that he wanted a family—and that he knew God was real.

As he shared his story, there was not a dry eye in the room. He told us that this experience fundamentally changed him forever. He recovered fully from his injuries.

Many participants set personal goals at Institute One. One participant set himself a goal of losing weight. He was obese. Eight months later, he had lost over a hundred pounds. As you can imagine, he was overjoyed. At Institute Four, the weather had turned cold, and he did not have a jacket that would fit him. As we traveled to visit with State Representative Terry England, class of 1994, class members noticed the absence of a jacket. They purchased this young man a jacket from England's store to express their pride in his achievement.

I stressed at the beginning that the first thing they had to do after getting back home after each institute was to thank those who held the farm, the home, and the family together while they were away. The family made sacrifices so that they could attend each institute.

Sometimes, the first institute stirred a great desire for making significant changes in one's life. I cautioned participants to remember that their families were not a part of this emotional moment nor of the other events that had taken place at the institute, and not to move too fast in making changes. If the desire for change was strong enough, it would be there after everybody was on board. In other words, not to sell the farm, buy a new tractor, or start a new operation immediately. They should let the emotions and feelings soak in and see how they might fit into their own life and their family's lives.

Many times, participants would hang around after the institute, sharing their thoughts and emotions regarding what had happened during the sessions. Gail and I encouraged them to share by staying around until everyone had left. I can tell you from personal experience that lives were changed, and priorities were made as a result of this institute. Participants would write me letters afterward expressing their thanks for allowing them to be in the program and sharing what the experience had meant to them. Gail and I were touched and inspired by many of the participants. One attendee told me that it was like a revival meeting at church. It does not get any better than that!

The policy and the politics of agriculture, agribusiness, and forestry were the focus of **Institute Two**. This included studying the legislative process in Georgia. For example, what was the best way to communicate with your state representative or senator, and with state agencies? This institute got into the nuts and bolts of the legislative process. It is a proven fact that if you don't know your representative and senator personally, you may be missing out on having an impact on legislation that might affect you, your family, or your business.

We talked about how to be involved in the political process and how to share thoughts and ideas with your representative and senator. We spent time at the Georgia Capitol during the legislative session. We learned how bills are created and the process for moving a bill through the legislature. The committee structure is how each bill is vetted and enhancements are made if needed. We visited the House Agricultural Committee and were able to see the committee process at work. Later, each participant was encouraged to call their representative and senator and talk to them. The legislators want to hear from folks back home.

One of our class participants met his representative for the first time. As they chatted, the representative was enthusiastic to learn he was part of an agricultural leadership program and said his knowledge of agriculture was limited and he would love to have someone to provide him information on the topic. "Call me anytime!" said our class participant, pulling out his business card. That was a solid contact that produced results for the participant and the representative.

Three Georgia Agri-Leaders graduates were members of the House of Representatives at that time. We had a chance to talk with each of those men during our visit. They were Terry England, Jay Roberts, and Lynmore James. Sam Watson was later elected to serve in the House. One of Georgia Agri-Leaders Forum's original founding directors, Robert Dickey, is also a state representative.

We met various state elected officials during our visit to Atlanta. We met with governors, with the commissioner of agriculture Tommy Irvin, with secretaries of state Lewis Massey, Cathy Cox, and Karen Handel, and with other officials.

Institute Two also included understanding the policies and politics of dealing with the legislative branch at the federal level. We covered similar topics to those we had studied at the state level. We also spent time at the US Capitol during the legislative session, with the group split into teams based on who their representative was; of course, both senators serve the entire state. Each team visited their offices and met with them or their staff.

While in Washington, DC, we varied our visits to federal agencies over the years, though we generally visited the United States Department of Agriculture every time. On many occasions, we met personally with the secretary of agriculture. We met with the Environmental Working Group to learn what they were doing and how that impacted agriculture. One time we visited with the Mexican Embassy staff. We always had a meeting with the American Farm Bureau as well.

Arlington National Cemetery and the Tomb of the Unknown Soldier were on our itinerary every year. The changing of the guard at the Tomb of the Unknown Soldier was impressive, awe-inspiring, and patriotic. If you observe that ceremony and are not touched, you are probably dead. The visit always made me further appreciate the service and sacrifice given by our military veterans for our country.

One of the highlights of visiting Washington, DC, is seeing the nation's memorials and monuments. We would schedule time at night to visit these sites when they are illuminated and especially impressive. We visited the Lincoln Memorial, Jefferson Memorial, Washington Monument, FDR Memorial, Korean War Veterans Memorial, Vietnam Veterans Memorial Wall, World War II Memorial, and the US Marine Corps War Memorial depicting the iconic scene from Iwo Jima from 1945.

As you can imagine, some interesting things happened during some of the institutes. You are about to learn about some of them.

I always spent time at the end of the Atlanta portion of Institute Two sharing some valuable information about the upcoming trip to Washington, DC. Advice included such things as "if you don't have an ID card, you will not be going to Washington with us," and caution about "no guns, knives, bombs, hand grenades, explosives, etc." being permitted on board the plane. I explained how important it was to be on time in Washington. Each participant had a detailed agenda with the time and location of every meeting and event.

On one trip to Washington, DC, we had an interesting experience at the Atlanta airport. I was always the last of our party to board to make sure that everyone was on the plane. One young man told me that his ID was headed back to South Georgia. His brother had brought him to Atlanta and was on his way home again with the ID since he had seen no need for a driver's license in DC. I explained that he would not be able to board the plane. I spoke to the gate agent about our dilemma, and he suggested that we go to a place called The Travel Agency to get a temporary ID. We rushed to the location inside the airport. We learned that if someone verified the young man's identity and signed an affidavit to that effect, they would give him a temporary ID for the trip. The ID was issued, and we headed back to the departure gate.

As we got to the gate, I decided to ask him if he had any guns. He said, "No." I whispered a thank-you prayer.

Then I asked if he had any knives. "A small one and a large switchblade," he replied.

Oh Lord, help me, I thought.

"Let's see the knives," I said. He pulled them out, and one appeared to be big enough to skin and cut up a deer. I visited my favorite gate agent again.

"Around the corner is a place to purchase a box, and the knives can be mailed home," he told us.

Thank you, Lord! I was afraid to ask if he had any bombs or explosives since we were running out of time. We were the last two people on the plane and had a successful journey.

Another experience at the Atlanta airport involved Delta Air Lines. We were at the ticket counter to check in our luggage. The Delta representative noticed that our ticket numbers did not match the individuals' names on their system. I quickly took out my records, since I had bought the tickets through group travel. All things seemed to be okay on our end. All at once, there was a huge commotion coming from all the ticket counters. The Delta computers had hiccupped and slid a person's name forward one slot, causing every passenger name to be linked to the wrong ticket number. It took about twenty minutes for Delta to get the problem fixed. Fortunately, we had arrived early and did not miss our flight.

We were in Washington, DC, on another visit and had an appointment with a government official (the name will remain anonymous to protect the guilty). The official arrived in our meeting room along with an assistant, who set up a computer and video projector. The assistant put a compact disc into the computer and began the slide program as the government official started talking. The official was facing us and could not see the screen. The picture that came up first was of a naked woman.

Of course, our mouths flew open, and several people pointed at the screen. The official looked around and told her assistant to stop the presentation. He immediately ejected the disc, but the picture stayed on the screen. It took him a few seconds to realize that he had to cut the power to the projector to eliminate the picture. The official sent the assistant to get the correct disc. I was expecting her to offer an immediate apology and to express how embarrassed they were. Nope, the official just kept talking. I shared that story with one of our US senators. He asked me who it was, and I told him.

As I mentioned, I always stressed that participants needed to be on time for every event so that we could make our appointed rounds. One morning, as we were loading the bus, getting ready to travel to George Washington's Mount Vernon, I counted heads and we were missing one person. We waited an extra five minutes, and he did not show up. No one knew where he was. We left and traveled the thirty-eight miles to Mount Vernon. As we were about to get off the bus, the participant knocked on the bus door and got on. He had caught a cab and followed my instructions that if you miss the bus, your agenda has the details of the next event and to catch up any way you can. He did and was never late again.

On another of our visits to DC, we took the bus to the Jefferson Memorial, and everybody got off and was to return to the bus at an appointed hour. At the designated time, the bus was at the proper location, and participant David Yelton was not to be seen. Due to the massive crowds and buses, our bus had to leave, so we left David behind. However, I asked the bus driver to make a circle and return to see if we could find him. It took about twenty minutes to get back again. David was standing there looking pretty perturbed. He thought I had left him for good. I still think that he believes that I left him as a prank. Honestly, I did not, but it would have been a good prank.

As we were winding down our DC visit in 1999, we had a debriefing to talk about what we had learned, experienced, and enjoyed. One participant, Jay Roberts, told me that he had figured out what he wanted to do next in life. He immediately called his wife and said, "Honey, I am calling from Washington, DC, and I now know what I want to do. I am going to run for the Georgia House of Representatives." Roberts was elected and served six terms in the House.

One of the most interesting and funny episodes that occurred involved me. We were having dinner our last night in DC at Phillips Flagship Restaurant near the Potomac River. We left from our last visit to Capitol Hill and traveled by bus to the restaurant, where we had a great seafood meal. As we finished eating, I was going to pay for the meal and so I asked for the check, but the server had some trouble getting it for me. The group was getting restless, so I told them to go on to the bus and that I would join them shortly.

I went to the front of the restaurant to wait for the check. While I was standing there, a lady stepped up to me and asked, "Are you Vice President Dick Cheney?" I had never thought that I looked like Dick Cheney. I was dressed in my best suit and tie; I am somewhat bald and wore glasses like Cheney.

I don't know what came over me, but I said, "Yes, I am, but please don't say anything. I hardly ever get out without the Secret Service, but I wanted some fresh seafood tonight."

She said, "May I have your autograph?" "Sure," I said.

She grabbed a table napkin, and I scribbled a bunch of letters on the napkin and handed it to her.

She then said, "Would you do another one for my sister?"

I replied, why not, and repeated my "signature" on another napkin. She left with a huge smile on her face. I did too. I could not refuse her request because she was so excited to meet the vice president. Sorry, Vice President Cheney. I promise never to do that again.

Dr. John Kline was the guest speaker for **Institute Three**, which dealt with developing communication skills and interacting with the media. He was with the Air University at Maxwell Air Force Base in Alabama. Dr. Kline's background included earning his Bachelor of Science, Master of Science, and Ph.D. at Iowa State University. He spent time as a professor of communication at universities in New Mexico and Columbia, Missouri. Since 1975, he had been a professor, dean, educational advisor, and, finally, provost at Air University, which is the US Air and Space Forces Center for Professional Military Education in Montgomery, Alabama.

Kline has written books, including one titled *Speaking Effectively: A Guide for Air Force Speakers*. He was an energetic and interesting speaker. He covered the basics of speaking, including the following areas: preparing to talk, organizing the talk, supporting the talk; beginning and ending the talk, and presenting the talk.

Dr. Kline's method of teaching was to review the basic concepts and use examples. He would ask each participant to prepare a two-minute talk.

The individual would deliver the talk, and the class, along with Dr. Kline, would critique the speech. After everyone had their turn, he would ask each participant to again give the speech using the thoughts and ideas from the critique to improve it. This was an extremely effective way of teaching.

Following the speeches, Dr. Kline would teach a session on listening skills. He would use interesting examples to illustrate how people listen and do not listen, presenting scenarios for the class to evaluate.

Dr. John Kline

The final session of the institute revolved around interacting with the media. I brought in various media representatives from print and television news. They would present examples of good and bad ways of working with the media. The class participants were put on camera and were thrown some tough questions. This exercise was to give them experience in handling questions and providing comments to media representatives. Questions put to them were related to agriculture and specifically to their occupation. The sessions were taped and played back to the entire class, allowing participants to offer and receive constructive critique. It provided everyone with great training in how to answer questions appropriately and effectively.

Institute Four, which covered the challenges of change and new technology, included visits to the three University of Georgia campuses on a rotating basis. The main campus is in Athens, and the other two are in Griffin and Tifton. These visits allowed participants to see the multiplicity of interdisciplinary educational opportunities, research, and extension pro-

1994 Class meets with Former Senator Herman Talmadge

Former Senator Herman Talmadge with Terry England

grams. We would occasionally visit with various agricultural leaders during this institute.

The University of Georgia was the first of many land-grant universities in the nation. A land-grant university is an institution of higher education in the United States designated by a state to receive benefits of the Morrill Acts, passed by Congress. UGA was given federal land upon which to locate an institution of higher learning specifically for agriculture, science, military science, and engineering.

As part of Institute Four, participants had the opportunity to meet with UGA faculty, including scientists, academicians, and engineering professors, who would share their areas of expertise and talk about the programs, research, or extension areas that they worked in. Class participants could ask questions, pose ideas, and discuss issues of importance to them.

One participant several years ago learned about a technology that could impact his company. He worked with the professor, and they installed the technology in his company. The class participant said later that it might have been years before he had learned about the technology, were it not for Georgia Agri-Leaders. We would usually include a visit to an agricultural enterprise, company, farm, or other venues during this institute.

In 1992, I was serving on the board of directors of the Georgia Electrification Council. During our annual meeting, a presenter spoke about agriculture and space. He gave an interesting presentation on how the space program was beginning to take agriculture into outer space.

I decided to invite him to come and present at Institute Four in Athens, Georgia, in 1993. My daughter, Miranda, was a senior in high school at that time and was very interested in space; at one point in her youth, she wanted to be an astronaut. I invited her to sit in on his presentation. Afterward, he gave her a writing pen that could be used in space.

The speaker told the group about how astronauts grew tomatoes as big as basketballs in space, that they had to jettison some of the crops because there was not enough storage space in the shuttle. Ears of corn grew to eighteen inches long. He had slides that showed the tomatoes and corn in space.

He shared that in space the astronauts could mix hard metals into a soft, pliable product that shirts could be made from and which provided the same protection as a bulletproof vest. He had worked for NASA at one point, but he said he knew too much and that they were after him now. He claimed to be a top rocket scientist.

He also told us his wife worked as a drug researcher using space technology. He had worked, he said, with the world's top space scientists. He kept the class members glued to his every word and seemed to be too good to be true.

I had an out-of-state business meeting later that year, which happened to be taking place close to where he lived. I arrived early for the meeting and decided to make a detour to his town. I stopped in at the town hall and asked them if they knew this space expert who lived there. "You mean that crazy guy that lives over on … [I am not listing the address]?" they said. They told me he was not a rocket scientist, that he just went around giving talks on space. I asked about his wife—the drug researcher. She was a pharmacist at the local drug store, they said. I went to his address, expecting to find an office with a rocket in front of the building. No rocket—just a shotgun frame house on a residential street.

He had an amazing story and was a thought-provoking speaker. He could share some tales of things unknown and ideas that seemed farfetched. Was he a rocket scientist? I will let you draw your own conclusions.

Those who helped plan the curriculum for the Georgia Agri-Leaders Forum felt that the classes needed to visit other states to learn about their agriculture. **Institute Five** dealt with exactly that. We chose Florida because of its diversity and its various environmental issues, including water allotments. Florida has water districts that allot the amount of water that can be used for agriculture, home, and industry. Georgia was facing challenges with water, but nothing like Florida's challenges.

We always made a stop at Florida's Farm Bureau in Gainesville. Their staff would give us an update on Florida agriculture, including challenges, obstacles, and successes. We visited cattle operations, fern and greenery operations, citrus farms, vegetable growers, mining concerns, farm lenders, sugar cane farms, sugar processing operations, food technology operations, and horse and dairy farms.

Another topic that we studied was cooperatives. In Florida, they are common in the fern and greenery, citrus, and dairy businesses, as well as in the sugar growing and processing industries. A cooperative was started in Georgia, based, in part, on what we learned in Florida.

One of the beef cattle operations that we visited was owned by Leroy and Sharon Baldwin. Mr. Baldwin bought his first calf with earnings from his paper route when he was six years old. He bought his first registered Angus calf in 1947. I remember him telling me that he bought a one-third interest in the top Angus bull in the country and did not possess the bull. He got one-third of the sperm that enhanced his cattle herd then and now.

He had served in the US Army during the Korean War, from 1952 to 1955. After the war, he bought the first forty acres and created **Baldwin Angus Ranch**. The cattle ranch grew to more than six hundred

Mr. Leroy Baldwin, Angus Cattle Rancher

acres and has sold Certified Pure-Bred Angus Cattle to forty countries around the world and every state in this country. With Baldwin, it was God first, family second, and then country. His loving wife, Sharon, was his partner in the business and in life. His three children, fourteen grandchildren, and eleven great-grandchildren live on or near the ranch.

Leroy loved his family and his cattle. He also gave God credit for his success. He was a leader in developing and using solid husbandry techniques in cattle.

Baldwin invited our classes to go to his farm and meet him, his family, and his cattle. Our bus would take us all over his farm and pasture as Leroy gave us a tour. Leroy and Sharon would feed us Certified Angus Beef for dinner.

He had a sign on the edge of his field that backed up to Interstate 75 which said: "Beef—it's what vegetarians eat when they cheat."

We had a young lady in our class, one year, who was vegetarian. I suggested to her not to share that fact with Leroy. On the bus tour of his farm, he asked the question that I dreaded, "Is anyone here a vegetarian?" I prayed that she would not speak up. She did. We enjoyed a forty-five-minute lecture on how a body needs all of the benefits that come with eating beef. And Leroy knew his scientific facts and shared them on a moment's notice. We were late for dinner that evening.

One of his grandsons, who was maybe seven years old, said the blessing for the meal one night. I wish you could have heard it. It went something like this: "Lord Jesus, we thank you for these Georgia folks that came a long way to visit us today. Lord, I pray that you bless these Georgia folks as they continue their journey. Lord, bless this food for our bodies and your service. Amen!"

The visit to the Baldwin Angus Ranch was just as much about meeting Leroy and his family as it was about seeing his beef operation.

On our trips to Florida, we had the same driver for nine years in a row. His first year driving for us was challenging for me. He knew very little about agriculture and was soaking in all of the information. He would ask me questions as we traveled between appointments. He started attending the sessions with us and asking questions. At one stop, he asked every question that was asked. I finally had to ask him to allow my participants to ask questions first. He was a great guy and an awesome driver and finally got his questions answered, so no more issues.

However, one year he was not available. Our new bus driver was not friendly, cordial, or accommodating. I got the first experience of his not being helpful when we arrived at the Baldwin Angus Ranch. Leroy would always meet us as the bus pulled up to this barn, get on board, and take us on a tour of the farm. On this visit, he got on the bus as usual and told the driver where to go. The new driver said, "I am not taking my bus into the pasture." I explained that we had always done the driving tour, and it had never been a problem. He still insisted that he was not driving into the pasture. We missed the ranch tour that year. I called the bus company that evening and told them that I was firing the driver and to have me a replacement ready the next morning. They did, and we did not have any more problems.

There was never a dull moment on the trip, and the participants enjoyed pulling pranks on me. Every restaurant we ate at, they would tell the server, behind my back, that it was my birthday. At the end of the meal, I always got a dessert and had Happy Birthday sung to me. When the server learned that I was paying for the meal, he or she would inevitably comment that it was not fair, since it was my birthday, that I had to pay for the meal. I was given a complimentary dessert at every meal!

The pranking worked both ways. We spent the night at the Clewiston Inn in Clewiston, Florida, on one of many trips. A few of the participants decided to take in some of the local nightlife. I overheard one or two comments about it the next morning, so I decided to have some fun with them; I didn't know any particulars, but it was amazing what I could learn if I acted as if I knew something. I knew that they must have taken a cab because it was the only transportation option available to them. Over breakfast, I asked the group which of them had been out for the evening. Almost to a person, those involved looked directly at me. I didn't say anything. After a moment, they asked me if something was wrong. I said, "The sheriff called me last night and said that a cab driver dropped some people off at the Clewiston Inn and he didn't get full payment for the ride."

One class member looked at his buddies and said, "I paid my share—did you all?"

The conversation took on a life of its own. Then one of them turned to me and said, "Do you know the sheriff or are you kidding us?"

I told them that I had talked to him the previous year when another problem had arisen within our group.

As we were leaving town after breakfast, I noticed a sheriff's car behind the bus. I pointed it out to the class, telling them that I guessed the sheriff wanted to make sure we left town.

Institute Six was about putting leadership skills to work and was the final meeting of this class. Each participant had committed about twenty-five days to the program. We wanted this institute to be fun and challenging. "Farmer Brown" Jolene Brown was our keynote speaker. You can learn more about Jolene Brown at https://jolenebrown.com. She and her husband operate their farm in West Branch, Iowa. Jolene was my choice for our keynote speaker from day one and spoke at most of the last institutes. She brought authenticity, credibility, humor, and wisdom to every keynote and workshop that she led. She was our most popular and inspiring speaker every year. We laughed, cried, celebrated, and focused on what the future held for each other.

Jolene Brown

Other speakers talked about current issues that would be of interest to the class. Kent Wolfe, a market analyst from UGA's Center for Agribusiness and Economic Development, was a frequent speaker on the economic value of the agriculture economy in Georgia. J. Craig Scroggs, cooperative development specialist, USDA, Rural Development, spoke on how cooperatives play a major role in agriculture in Georgia and across the United States.

This institute was also intended as a celebration time for the participant and their spouse or significant other. We built in some extra time for them to enjoy Jekyll Island, Georgia.

One of the last things that I shared with the class was that they should go home and seek ways to apply their newly acquired leadership skills. They had been trained and prepared for greater leadership roles. I hoped that they would step forward when the need arose for them to lead. Their leadership might be needed in their family, business, community, state, or even at the national level.

The last session of the institute included the graduation ceremony. Each participant received a diploma, a wristwatch with the Georgia Agri-Leaders Forum logo on the face, and a class photo.

The Ron Hart Memorial Leadership Award was given to recognize an individual in the class who had demonstrated outstanding ability in applying the principles of leadership in both their personal and professional life dramatically and positively. The recipient was determined by a secret ballot by class participants following Institute Five. The award was started in 2003 and was given every year through 2009.

The Ron Hart Memorial Award winners were:
   2003: David Turner
   2004: Godwin Onohwosa
   2005: Jeff Glass
   2006: Bill Tollner
   2007: Chad Etheridge
   2008: Elliot Marsh
   2009: Rome Ethredge and Johnny Jones

USAID is a United States government organization considered to be the world's premier international development agency. The agency coordinated with the Georgia Agri-Leaders Forum in soliciting participants to help with short-term agricultural projects in other countries, usually for about three weeks. Several of our participants had the opportunity to work with USAID on projects related to agriculture and food security.

Delane Borron, class of 1993, volunteered to go to Poland on a three-week work project. He was then a field operations manager in the Northeast Georgia Poultry Division of Gold Kist. His company's newsletter, *The Gold Line,* published his description of the experience in their July 1993 issue, which he shared with us and I have summarized in part below.

Borron was assigned to assist Sylwester Gajewski, a Polish poultry producer and a senator in the Polish parliament and chairman of the Senate Agriculture Committee. When Poland had been under Communist rule, poultry producers had been very affluent. The government had manufactured and sold the feed at a set price. They had also purchased and marketed the chickens for a set price.

In 1989, Poland regained its sovereignty and became an independent country. At that time, Communism ended, and the business structure, along with all government-run feed manufacturers, disappeared. The poultry industry had a hard time adjusting.

Borron was able to assist Gajewski with knowledge about the workings of an integrated US poultry operation and to provide recommendations on how their industry could benefit from such a system.

While over there, he also had the chance to teach English at a Polish school. He said, "People from America are almost like celebrities in Poland because they admire us so much." He was asked for his autograph many times. Borron was also able to do some traveling; he visited Krakow, one of the oldest cities in Poland, and the notorious German WWII concentration camp at Auschwitz.

He enjoyed his work assignment but said that he was very glad to get back to the USA.

Another participant in the leadership program was Donnie Smith, who shared the following memories:

> One of the first persons that I met when I was selected to be a member of the Charter Class of Georgia Agri-Leaders Forum was Jimmy Hill. He encouraged and gave me, just a farm boy from Willacoochee, an opportunity to experience a rewarding and unforgettable leadership adventure. I thought that life began and ended at the Atkinson and Coffee county-line signs, but that line of thinking changed quickly as I began my experiences in Georgia Agri-leaders.
>
> In my second year of Georgia Agri-Leaders, I was excited to be selected by Volunteers Overseas Cooperative Assistance (VOCA) to go to Slovakia on a trip of a lifetime to aid farmers. My mission was to encourage and advise Slovakian farmers to abandon their old Communist customs and adapt to the USA free enterprise system.
>
> To prepare for the trip, I dug and harvested my peanut crop a few days early, and left my wife, Marilyn, and hired help with instructions to harvest the corn crop, plant cover crops, and run the farm while I was in Eastern Europe for almost three weeks. I thought I was prepared to only teach the Slovakian farmers, but I was the one who came home with many valuable life lessons.
>
> Before the journey began for my first international trip, I was briefed by the VOCA staff in Washington, DC. While there I agreed to hand-deliver a laptop to the VOCA Team in Eastern Europe. I was told it was safer to hand-deliver than to mail. As any good Georgia farm boy knows, it is always good to help when you can, so off I went on the trip of a lifetime with this extra laptop in my possession.
>
> After a trans-Atlantic night flight, I was met at the airport in Vienna, Austria, by my translator, Stefan Bajo, and our chauffeur. Stefan became my immediate friend and protector. Little did I know how our friendship would grow and how much he had prepared for this assignment. He later shared that he had a plan for my escape in case Slovakia was invaded while I was there. Stefan was a person that I learned to admire in my time with him. He worked tirelessly to be able to fully translate for and engage with his new English-speaking friend.

I learned soon how he protected me on my trip. We have remained close friends since this initial visit, and we have visited each other a few times since 1995.

One of my first difficult experiences was to cross the border by car from Austria to Slovakia. It was just Stefan and me making this trip. All was going well until the border guard opened my luggage and saw the laptop that I had agreed to deliver for VOCA. After many questions, the heavily armed guard asked me to turn on the laptop and show him what information I was bringing into their country. I had to confess, I didn't know how to turn on the laptop or what classified secret information it might contain. Fear reared its ugly head and took control! All the novels I read in my youth assured me I was involved in high spy espionage. I felt like a human carrier pigeon, taking information unknown to me. At that moment I felt I would never see my South Georgia farm again. I was sure Stefan thought he had been corralled into something illegal, but he hung tight with me, translating every stressful question and response along the way. After being detained at the border for over three hours, we finally were permitted into Slovakia without the laptop. To this day, I don't know if the laptop reached its destination or if I transported secret information.

We finally arrived just before dawn at my apartment. After being deprived of sleep for over thirty hours, I was ready for a shower and some much-needed sleep. After looking around the modest but clean 2-bedroom apartment, I asked Stefan who to contact if an emergency happened. One must remember this is 1995. There wasn't a phone in the apartment, and no one had smartphones. Stefan, seeing the fear in my eyes, agreed to stay in the extra bedroom for the night. Sleep never came that night. I remembered Jimmy Hill's last words to me, "Don't worry; it will be a life-changing experience—enjoy!" At this time, his words "life-changing" weren't reassuring, nor was "enjoyable."

After a few nights, I felt comfortable enough to stay by myself and told Stefan he was welcome to go back to his home. He kindly asked if he could continue to stay. I agreed, but when I asked why, he shared that he wanted to practice his English and learn more about the USA. It was the beginning of a lifelong friendship.

After settling into my apartment and realizing no one was coming after me for bringing spy information over on a laptop, I needed to focus on my mission on this trip. The first obstacle was overcoming the trust factor involving not only me but also the farmers. The farmers and I grew up in the 1950s and 1960s. I had been taught in school that Communism was bad, and one couldn't trust a Communist. My Slovakian farmers had been taught a similar message and that everyone in the USA was their enemy. I knew that without trust, nothing would be accomplished. The first few days I was there, I was getting blank, cold, steely eyed, uncooperative stares from my farmers.

One morning an idea came to me as I was meeting with one of my farmers, Stefan Juhas. Mr. Juhas was a high-ranking Communist officer in the former Slovakian army. That morning he showed me his Communist uniform with many war medals attached. I knew I had to assure him I was not a spy and that I was a farmer here to help. After shaking hands that morning, I asked for both of us to show the palms of our hands. I pointed to my calloused hands and to his calloused hands that showed both of us were genuinely hardworking farmers. We immediately looked straight into each other's eyes and he smiled as wide as the Grand Canyon. His eyes were now void of his normal Communist unemotional, cold steel, untrusting stare. We rubbed our calloused hands together. With open arms, he gave me a big bear hug and planted a kiss on each of my cheeks.

Instantly we could trust each other and have become lifetime friends. In 1996 Stefan Juhas was named the Slovakian farmer of the year, a very similar honor to the one I received when I was named Georgia Lancaster Sunbelt Expo Farmer of the Year.

One of the life lessons I learned from Juhas was to work hard but take time to relax. Saturday was his "holiday" for rest and relaxation. After advising and working straight for two weeks, he wanted me to be his guest and experience one of his monthly visits to a spa. The water for this spa is fed with cold, spring-fed mountain water containing the perfect mineral composition and healing properties. It was now gaining notoriety throughout Eastern Europe as one of the best spas. The management was happy I would be the first person from the USA to visit their spa. I agreed to go but insisted that my translator would be by my side at all times through this experience. After being issued a small towel, we were sent into a community dressing area. All was going as planned until my translator said he couldn't go any further, because his future mother-in-law was giving massages that day. I decided to trust and follow my farmer, Juhas. He was laughing, speaking to all in the spa, and to further confuse me, no one was paying any attention to him or other patrons as they were strutting around with only towels draped over their shoulders. He smiled, patted me on the backside, and urged me to follow his lead. I followed him to the spa, with only my boxer briefs and towel. As I was getting prepared to get into the spa tub, the young lady, who couldn't speak any English, made it clear in hand language that my boxer briefs weren't acceptable to be worn while getting the spa treatment. I decided to lose all my modesty and to experience the European Spa. I decided, when in Slovakia do as the Slovakians do. I must admit the spa experience taught me how to trust and relax. I fell asleep on the table during the hot oil massage.

I had won Juhas's trust. Now I needed to figure out a way to gain the trust of my other farmer, Andre Palkavoch. Early one morning, we were going to his farm where his hired hand was turning the fertile black organic filled topsoil (Breadbasket of Europe) with a bottom plow similar to the one I had used many times as a boy on Dad's farm. But for some reason, the plow wasn't turning the land level. I had a plan and asked if I could get on the tractor and turn land for a short time. After about an hour of plowing and constantly adjusting the top link and arms, the plow was turning the land as if it had been laser leveled. At that moment trust was found and Andre knew I wasn't a diplomat sent from Washington, but a farmer here to help.

Sometimes simple advice can make one an American hero. Andre grew white potatoes to sell in his store in town. One morning, he shared his farmer-grown marketing frustrations. He couldn't sell his potatoes before they began to rot. I suggested he put up a banner in the front window of his store advertising his potatoes 1/3 off through the weekend. No one in town was using window advertising. On

Monday, he came smiling and sharing that he had sold three times the potatoes he normally would sell that weekend and prevented future spoiled potatoes.

My three weeks of advising and learning was coming to an end. The night before I left for Georgia, about forty of my Slovakian friends entertained me with a sheep goulash dinner, including homemade bread, and homemade apricot brandy. The farewell party included festive Hungarian music, dancing, and gifts.

After many hugs and best wishes, my translator and driver were ready to take me to the airport. When we were about to get into the car, I noticed Stefan's grandmother running toward me. She had tears running down her cheeks and her arms outstretched toward me. During World War II, her husband was captured and sent to a POW concentration camp in Poland. Our USA troops rescued him from the freezing, inhumane camp. She had a lifetime wish to thank an American for saving her husband. I will never forget that hug. After the hug, she gave me a bag of homemade cookies and sandwiches so I wouldn't be hungry at the airport. Until Grandmother's death five years ago, she sent us hand-stitched beautiful needlepoint artwork.

When my plane touched down in the USA, I understood one wanting to kiss the ground and sing God Bless the USA.

All was good when I arrived home, thanks to Marilyn, our children Hugh and Mandy, my farm helpers, and our neighbors. In our home, one can see reminders of my visit. There is a huge oil painting of Germer, Slovakia, and many of Grandmother's needlepoint treasures throughout our home. Thanks, Slovakian friends and family, for all the good memories. I will never forget it!

When I first arrived in Slovakia, all I could see were the fresh scars of Communism and their beaten-down spirit, but when I left I saw a better future for my friends and, for me, a better understanding of our world. I realize that my circle of county line friends grew to include my Slovakian friends. There are great people everywhere, especially our hard-working farmers worldwide.

Now after almost 35 years, I can truthfully say that while I was sent to be the teacher, I was the student. When Jimmy Hill said it would be a life-changing experience, I think that was an under-statement, as this was indeed a life-changing event. It was probably not so much for Slovakian farmers as it was for me, just a small-town farmer from Willacoochee.

Thanks, Jimmy!

Donnie Smith wrote this specifically for my book. Thanks, Donnie, for sharing your awesome experience.

Georgia Agri-Leaders Forum was a member of the International Association of Programs for Agricultural Leadership (IAPAL). IAPAL is a consortium of fifty-seven leadership programs in the USA and several other countries. I attended several of their annual meetings during my time as the president and CEO of Georgia Agri-Leaders Forum.

However, before I attended any of the meetings, I met by phone with Joy Dunbar, the program director of RULE, the Pennsylvania Rural-Urban Leadership Program. She invited me to have breakfast with her while she was in Atlanta for a meeting. She was staying at a hotel just down the street from my office at Georgia Power. I was to meet her in the lobby and have breakfast there in the hotel.

Since I had never met her in person, I asked her how I would recognize her. She said, "I will be the lady in the red boots."

I showed up and started looking at every lady who came into the lobby, trying to spot the red boots. Finally, I saw the lady in red boots, and I knew it must be her. "Are you the lady in red boots that I am having breakfast with?" I asked, and she introduced herself.

We went into the restaurant, found a table for two, and ordered our breakfast. All of a sudden, she murmured something. I was not sure what she said, but it sounded like she said, "I want a hug." Since I had never met her before, I thought it quite strange that she would want a hug in the middle of breakfast. So I dismissed the idea and tried to think what might rhyme with hug ... mug, rug, bug, chug, snug, jug, tub, etc. Nothing seemed to fit the situation. She began to stand up, and I thought ... she did say hug. She came around the table, and we hugged. It seemed like a five-minute hug, but surely it was only seconds. After we hugged, she sat back down, and we finished our breakfast. I thanked her for breakfast and went back to my office.

As soon as I arrived back in my office, I picked up the phone (I did not have a cell phone at that time) and called Gail. "You are not going to believe what happened at breakfast," I said.

She knew I had a breakfast meeting planned for that morning. I gave her a blow-by-blow account of the hug. The thought had gone through my head that I had had a prank pulled on me and that someone would call Gail and tell her about my hug with the lady in the red boots.

About two years later, I went to my first IAPAL meeting. It was held in Rhode Island. I got there early and was keeping an eye open for the lady in the red boots. I did not see her as we sat down to start the meeting. Within moments, she came in the door. Her first move was to go around the table and hug everybody. Now I know why I got the hug. She was just a hugger.

Due to a lack of financial support and a waning economy, the Georgia Agri-Leaders Forum suspended operations in 2010.

In 2012, the University of Georgia began operating a rebranded version of the program called Advancing Georgia's Leaders in Agriculture and Forestry (AGL), with the first cohort graduating in 2014. You can learn more about this program at https://alec.caes.uga.edu/extension/advancing-georgia-leaders.html.

The AGL program, operated by an eighteen-member advisory board of agricultural leaders and a program director, is a partnership between the College of Agricultural and Environmental Sciences and the Warnell School of Forestry and Natural Resources.

23

End of My Career at Georgia Power Company

In my first two full-time positions at Georgia Power, working in residential marketing, I was helping customers increase the energy efficiency of their homes and lower their electric bills. I was able to do so by recommending that they increase the thermal values of their homes and install high-efficiency heat pumps.

My third position was at the corporate level, providing expertise and experience to marketing programs. This allowed the field staff to accomplish the same goals that I had in improving energy efficiency and lowering electric bills. The opportunity to apply what I had learned in the field at the corporate level and to assist customers and Georgia Power in mutually beneficial goals was awesome. I worked with some great men and women in the field, who implemented the marketing plans that I had developed. They were the true heroes of this effort as they touched customer lives on the local level all across the state of Georgia.

I found my last position, as manager of Agricultural Affairs, incredibly rewarding. In assisting the agricultural community in addressing their needs, I strove to serve my clients with the information, expertise, and action plans that helped that community, its organizations, and its companies excel. I spent most of my time traveling across the state of Georgia to meet with clients, address their issues, and find solutions to make Georgia agriculture a little bit better than when I had come on board. These efforts helped to grow the agricultural economy, create jobs, and create wealth for those Georgians who work in the agricultural industry. Georgia's agricultural economy in 2020 is valued at seventy-six billion dollars and accounts for 399,200 jobs. Georgia agriculture is the largest economic engine in the state. My efforts in this regard are covered in many of the preceding chapters.

As I think back on my entire career with Georgia Power, I am thankful for all of the projects, ideas, and activities that I was involved in, the most significant of which were the following:

- Participating in Georgia Power's Cooperative Learning Program. The Cooperative Learning Plan was beneficial to me and to Georgia Power. It allowed me to get valuable work experience and to earn money for my college tuition and expenses. It also allowed Georgia Power to assess my potential for employment after graduation.

- As a result of my cooperative learning experience, I was fortunate to meet and work with Roy Parker, the HVAC contractor in Americus, Georgia, whose commitment to providing his customers with the highest quality installation and service made such a lasting impression on me: Roy did it right! This experience helped me as I moved to the corporate office and was charged with developing a heat pump marketing program for Georgia Power. Everything that I learned from Roy was an integral part of that marketing program.

- One of the most significant learning experiences for me in my early career was the interaction that I had with a customer in the Waycross District regarding a residential heat pump installation. He was new to the area and was building a new home. I sold him on the idea of building a highly energy-efficient home under the Georgia Power Good Cents program. One aspect of that program was the installation of a properly sized high-efficiency heat pump. Neither the customer's builder nor the heat pump dealer agreed with my assessment of the size of the heat pump that should be installed, but the customer went with my recommendations, and he loved his home and the comfort provided by his heat pump. He was so pleased that he wrote a letter to Georgia Power president, Robert Scherer, who read the letter to the Georgia Public Service Commission. I had stood my ground, based on my convictions and my engineering background, and the outcome was a customer's unqualified satisfaction and my receiving commendations for my work.

- One of my most rewarding and challenging projects was the development of the Heat Pump Marketing Program and the Heating and Air Conditioning Dealer Program. I had the weight of the whole Residential Marketing Department at the corporate level, as well as district offices all over Georgia, on my back. I could not afford to fail. I used all of my engineering training, practical field experience, people skills, company talent, and prayer to tackle the project.

- Another exciting project was the Vidalia Onion Controlled Atmosphere (CA) Storage Project and Federal Marketing Order. The Vidalia onion storage technology provided a new market for Vidalia onion growers well beyond the normal season. It created a revolutionary change in the industry, adding millions of dollars to its revenues. My 1989 trips to Washington, DC, with a group of the Vidalia onion growers to meet with legislative leaders and the United States Department of Agriculture (USDA) to lobby for a Federal Marketing Order for Vidalia onions resulted in success. The Marketing Order provided the onion growers protection for the Vidalia onion name, as well as a funding mechanism for research, marketing, and promotion. The Vidalia onion industry saw this as a pivotal point in their history and honored those of us who went to Washington, DC, at their annual meeting in 2015, the twenty-fifth anniversary of the Marketing Order.

- Probably the largest and most complex project that I worked on was the 1996 Olympics and Georgia Agriculture 1996 project. Our team explored the idea of creating an agricultural presence at the 1996 Centennial Summer Olympic Games in Atlanta, Georgia. Since no other group had ever attempted this, we were breaking new ground (pun intended). In short, we decided to create an agricultural pavilion at the Centennial Olympic Park in downtown Atlanta to tell the Georgia agriculture story to the world during the Olympic Games. Over six hundred thousand Olympic visitors went through the pavilion during the event. Our team faced many obstacles and challenges, but eventually, the exhibit came together and was a great success.

- Creating and implementing the Georgia Agri-Leaders Forum Leadership Program was an interesting and rewarding project. We created a way for young and aspiring agricultural leaders to be trained and motivated for future leadership. I was fortunate enough to be one of the Gang of Five who put together a meeting of the movers and shakers in agriculture and developed the name, mission, and implementation steps for creating the leadership program. The first seventeen classes trained 346 men and women for greater leadership roles. Many of those graduates went on to provide leadership in many organizations, companies, and government services, including four who ultimately were elected to the Georgia Legislature.

My career started as a student engineer working with Georgia Power Company in their Cooperative Learning program. My last position was as manager of Agricultural Affairs. I can only say great things about Georgia Power and the awesome people that I worked with. Georgia Power's motto is "A Citizen Wherever We Serve." This motto was very evident in everything the company did. I also adopted it as my motto.

I learned, shortly following the conclusion of the 1996 Olympic Games in early August, that several Georgia Power departments were being reorganized. A meeting was called by our management, and we were told that our department was one of those being reorganized. They did not give us any details but said that those of us who qualified for an exit package would receive one before the reorganization announcements were made. I was one of those who qualified for that package, which, based on my years of service, was very generous. I also had the choice, if offered a new position, to accept the offer or to take the exit package. We were told that we would be called in one at a time and told of management's decision regarding our future.

I met with Ron Hart from human resources, who happened to be a good friend, and he explained my choices. My job and my department were being abolished. I was offered a position at two levels below my current position with a salary decrease to that level after one year. The new job was not involved in working with agriculture. My other choice was to take the severance package and leave Georgia Power's employment. I chose to take the package. My career ended with Georgia Power on September 4, 1996, at 11:00 a.m.

My career with them had spanned twenty-eight years, and it was an emotional roller-coaster ride as I left the building and realized that I was no longer an employee of the greatest company that I had ever worked for. Gail and I had prayed that we would be led to make the best decision for our family. To this day, I know it was the right decision. However, I truly do miss all of the awesome people that I worked with for so many years. I had great support during my tenure from my staff and from those I worked for. We were able to accomplish many projects that helped the State of Georgia's economic engine thrive. These projects benefited Georgia and Georgia Power.

I am very thankful for my career and for the exciting things that I got to do and the people I came to know. I am also proud of my accomplishments and feel that I made a substantial contribution to Georgia Power and, in the final ten years, to the agricultural industry in Georgia.

I received a thank-you note from Georgia Power president Bill Dahlberg that I treasure. I have included a copy of it in the Appendix.

During my tenure with Georgia Power, I attended numerous conferences and training courses and was the proud recipient of several awards and honors. Here is a selected list:

1974: University of Florida: Environmental Systems Conference on Residential Heating and Air Conditioning

1977: Georgia Power Manpower Development: Forty hours of Foundations of Management

1979: The Georgia Institute of Technology: Completed the Home Builders Energy Workshop conducted by the Engineering Experiment Station

1980: Air Conditioning Contractors of America: Certified to teach courses in the design and installation of residential heating and air conditioning systems—Manual D for duct design for residential winter and summer air conditioning and equipment selection

1980: Air Conditioning Contractors of America: Successful completion of subjects related to advanced load calculation and design of residential heating and air conditioning systems — Manual J for residential load calculation

1983: Completion of the Executive Speaker course for becoming an outstanding performer in the field of executive speaking

1983: Georgia Power Safety Achievement Award for fifteen years of service without an accident

1985: American Marketing Association: Silver EFFIE for Advertising Effectiveness for Jimmy Hill/Georgia Power/*Steve Landesberg–Human Heat Pump*

1987: Georgia Section, American Society of Agricultural Engineers: Engineer of the Issue in *ASAE News*

1987: Southern College: Grid Management School

1988: AGHON: Named Honorary Member, the highest honor a student in the College of Agriculture, School of Forest Resources, and College of Veterinary Medicine can attain at the University of Georgia

1989: Georgia Young Farmers Association: Named Honorary Member

1989: Completion of the Fair Employment Practice Workshop

1990: Honorary American Farmer Degree from the National FFA Organization

1990: Georgia Egg Commission: Golden Egg Award

1991: Georgia Section, American Society of Agricultural Engineers: Engineer of the Year

1991: Abraham Baldwin Agricultural College (ABAC): J. Lamar Branch Award for Outstanding Agricultural Leadership

1991: American Society of Agricultural Engineers: Elected as Technical Director on the ASAE board of directors

1992: Southern College: Managing Under a Business Unit Concept

1993: Southern College: Be the Benchmark

1993: Georgia Power Area Development Organization: Twenty-five years of service

1994: National Food and Energy Council: Distinguished Service Award

1994: Georgia Future Homemakers of America: Honorary Member

1995: Southern College (Southern Company): Advanced Student of the Business

1995–96: Food Processing Advisory Council: Recognized for valuable leadership and service to the Council and for serving as the first President

1995–96: Electric Power Research Institute/Agricultural Technology Alliance (ATA): Recognized for outstanding support of ATA and for serving as President

2011: Recognized for forty years of continuous membership in the American Society of Agricultural and Biological Engineers (ASABE)

2017: University of Georgia College of Agricultural and Environmental Sciences (CAES): UGA CAES Alumni Association Award of Excellence

2017: Sunbelt Expo: Recognition of twenty-seven years of service as Master of Ceremonies

2018: Abraham Baldwin Agricultural College (ABAC): Distinguished Alumnus Award

Chris Hill, Jimmy Hill and Miranda Hill Skonie at UGA CAES event
* Photo Courtesy of Laura Meadows

Jimmy Hill with his UGA CAES Alumni Association Award of Excellence
* Photo Courtesy of UGA - College of Agricultural and Environment Sciences

24

The Hill Group Inc. and The Ambassador

On September 4, 1996, I walked out of the Georgia Power Company corporate headquarters in Atlanta unemployed, a first in my career. I was forty-nine years old and had twenty-eight years of employment with Georgia Power. The first thing I did was to call Gail and tell her what had happened. Of course, we had discussed it before my meeting, and it had been a joint decision. On my way home, I went by the Georgia Agribusiness Council to share my news with them.

I woke up at 4:30 a.m. the next day and felt as if a heavy weight had been lifted from my shoulders. I woke Gail up to tell her about my idea to form The Hill Group. She always needs plenty of sleep and did not appreciate my waking her up at that hour. She reminded me that she had to go to work that morning and told me to tell her about it later. Oops! I should have known better than to wake her, but I was so excited.

Here is the letter she wrote to me that day:

September 5, 1996

Dear Jimmy,

Man, what a week. You know just when we thought that things were finally going to slow down, bang. I guess that is what makes life so much fun.

I just want you to know how very proud I am of you and the way you are handling all of this. I have decided that you are right—this could be and is the best thing that has ever happened to us financially. It is just up to us to figure out what to do with it now. It is very hard for me to concentrate on work with so many things running through my head, especially on a very slow, quiet day.

One thing that I always want you to remember is that you light up my life and give me the hope to carry on when all else fails. You are a very special person and I love you dearly.

Isn't life grand … you know today is the first day of the rest of your life. Everything is new and different today. Not many people get to start fresh and excited all over again at this point in their life. You are very special and most of Georgia knows you and your talents. This could be your chance to let your little light s-h-i-n-e for the entire world to see. Oh, yeah, if your new endeavors lead us all over the USA and the world to visit or to live, I am ready to go and I really can't wait.

As I have told you many times in our twenty-seven years, I will be happy wherever you are. I L-o-v-e you more than words could ever say. Thanks for loving me through the thick and the thinnest of thins.

Love, Gail

Since this was such a drastic change in our life, Gail and I decided that we needed to share in person with our parents the news about my leaving Georgia Power and our starting our own company. We traveled to Hazlehurst to see my parents and then on to Tifton to see Gail's. It seemed important to us to share this news, but it did not appear to rattle them as we had thought it might.

I had always felt the entrepreneurial spirit and wanted to work for myself one day. That day had arrived. We selected the name "The Hill Group." I started writing a business plan that day. Consulting work had always interested me, and I had done some as the manager of Agricultural Affairs at Georgia Power. People had approached me with various ideas related to agriculture and had asked for my advice. Some of the services that I had offered under Agricultural Affairs would still be needed in the agricultural arena.

I immediately began work on determining the legal structure of The Hill Group. After consultation with my accountant, The Hill Group Inc. (THG) was incorporated on October 9, 1996. I began to set up my home office as the headquarters for the company. I purchased a computer, printer, fax, and other office equipment, as well as a cell phone and a pager.

Gail and I developed the THG mission statement: To become a premier agribusiness consulting firm by providing our clients with world-class products and services.

My first work assignment was as a keynote speaker at the Habersham County Farm-City Week Kick-Off Breakfast. Gilbert Barrett of Barrett Farms and White County Farmers Exchange, and a Georgia Agri-Leaders Forum graduate, asked me to speak. Gail framed and hung the dollar bill in my office to commemorate the milestone of getting my first pay as a consultant. It still hangs there today.

EPRI's Agricultural Technology Alliance was an organization that I had been a member of while serving in my previous job. ATA asked me to work with them as a consultant in cooperation with electric utilities in the agricultural arena. I had served as chairman of the ATA just before leaving Georgia Power. I negotiated a contract with ATA and traveled to meetings and conferences for them about four times a year for a couple of years. Several agricultural organizations in Georgia asked me to do consulting work as well.

The list of products and services that we developed included: Business Development; Newsletter, Brochure, and Publications Development; Public and Legislative Affairs; Group Facilitation; Team Building; Leadership Development; Strategic Planning; Association Management; Motivational Speaking; Teaching; Project Work; Electricity and Energy Issues; Agricultural Issues, and others. Over the next few years, we provided all of these services to our clients.

I got so busy with clients that I needed help, and I asked Gail if she would quit her job and come to work with THG. She was working for Design Connection at the time, a cross-stitch design and publishing company. She quit that job and started working with THG on March 10, 1997. It was the best decision that we ever made. I know that I had some concerns, as she did, as to whether we could work together. We sat down together and listed our strengths and weaknesses. Gail's skillset fits quite nicely with my weaknesses, and my skillset fits her weaknesses. Gail and I are still working together successfully.

Listed below are clients for whom we provided specific consultation or facilitation:

American Society of Quality Associates, Valdosta, Georgia
Alabama Agriculture and Forestry Leaders Program
Berrien County Chamber of Commerce
Dawson County Chamber of Commerce
Economic Development Association of Alabama
Georgia Department of Education—In-Service Training
Georgia Cattlemen's Association
Georgia Cotton Women
Georgia Crop Improvement Association
Georgia DCT Coordinators Association
Georgia Department of Education—Agriculture Education
Georgia FFA/FHA Center
Georgia Native Plant Society
Georgia Pork Producers Association
Georgia Young Farmers Association
Group Funds Association
National Food and Energy Council
Secretary of State, Cathy Cox
Western Area Power Association
Georgia Women in Agriculture

For other clients, we have provided services for a more extended period, and in some cases project leadership:

Dothan Area Chamber of Commerce: I worked with the chamber's agriculture committee for over two years, primarily meeting once a month, to help them develop a strategy for improving their agricultural economy. The Dothan area had a lot of agricultural potential, including peanuts, cotton, corn, grains, soybeans, vegetables, and animal production.

Electric Power Research Institute/ATA: I served as the chairman of the Agriculture Technology Alliance in 1997. ATA evaluated several agriculture technologies and conducted scoping studies. These included agricultural research, irrigation, nitrate evaluation in groundwater and estuaries, animal waste issues, cotton production, handling and drying crops, soil testing and the internet, and postharvest crop physiology and soil science.

Meetings and field trips were held evaluating these issues, along with input from experts. Many of these issues were topics of interest to my agriculture and agribusiness customers in Georgia, and much of what I learned was shared with my consulting customers to enhance their business success.

Georgia Agri-Leaders Forum Foundation: GALFF was created in 1989 with a focus on providing leadership training and development for individuals working in agriculture, agribusiness, and forestry. GALFF trained 346 individuals in seventeen years. I was one of five people who helped with the original concept of the organization and was elected the first chairman of the organization.

Georgia Department of Education—Georgia Agricultural Education Workshop and In-Service Teacher Training: These sessions were for agriculture education teachers and addressed solving issues facing agriculture education in Georgia, seeking new paradigms for agricultural education, exploring new solutions, and developing a plan of action to implement changes.

Georgia Department of Education—Agricultural Education: Mr. Melvin Johnson, director of agricultural education, Georgia Department of Education, asked me to facilitate his direct reports and all of the agricultural education teachers across the state in addressing how to improve the agricultural education program in the state.

Johnson and I laid out a plan to meet his goal of improving the department's effectiveness. I conducted a series of facilitated meetings with his direct staff at the State FFA Camp, south of Covington, Georgia. We took the findings from those meetings, and we traveled all over Georgia, meeting with agricultural education teachers, and shared what was learned in this process. These facilitated meetings provided a blueprint for changes and enhancements for the program. I finalized the report for Johnson, and he proceeded to implement the plans for the department.

I felt very blessed to be able to be a part of this effort since the agricultural education program was extremely beneficial in my high school years and my career.

Family and Consumer Sciences Teachers Association (FACSTA): THG was selected to provide administrative services and lobbying services for FACSTA, which was an organization of family and consumer science teachers from across the state of Georgia. The vision of the association was to enable teachers to empower students with life skills to succeed as individuals and members of the family, community, and workplace.

Sunbelt Agricultural Exposition (SAE): My involvement with SAE goes back to the 1970s. At first, I was asked to assist Georgia Power in working at Sunbelt during its three-day run. When I became the manager of Agricultural Affairs, I became the Georgia Power main liaison with SAE. I helped ramp up Georgia Power's involvement with Sunbelt to provide a pathway for reaching the company's many agricultural and agribusiness customers.

I also became the master of ceremonies at the Willie B. Withers Sunbelt Luncheon and held that position for twenty-seven years.

Toombs-Montgomery County Chamber of Commerce: I was asked to submit a bid to provide services to the chamber, including the following: help create and facilitate an agriculture committee which would evaluate Toombs and Montgomery counties for their potential of increasing the agriculture economy; facilitate the development of a strategic plan that would address issues discovered in the process of inventorying and examining the agricultural assets in the counties; develop and write a guide to use in creating and operating a successful county agriculture and agribusiness committee, as required by the funding source for this project.

I submitted the winning bid and was hired to help facilitate and develop their three-pronged plan. I met monthly with the agriculture committee for nearly three years. The committee developed three priorities to work on, which were to improve the Vidalia Onion Museum, to identify and promote agritourism entities in the counties with a marketing campaign, and to work toward building an agricultural multipurpose building in Vidalia. They accomplished all of their goals and even received an award for their agritourism efforts.

The Halifax Group—Oak Hill Farms: I provided consultant services to The Halifax Group regarding food laws and policies in Georgia. I investigated potential new business opportunities and provided liaison services with the Georgia Department of Agriculture and the Georgia Department of Revenue.

University of Georgia College of Agricultural and Environmental Sciences: I provided group facilitation services for three departments at the college. The departments were reviewing their missions and seeking input from their faculty, staff, and clients.

USDA Rural Development–Georgia: I provided consulting services for drafting a Rural Development Plan for the State of Georgia. This involved working with Laura Meadows, state director of the USDA Rural Development Office, and her staff.

Cathy Cox, Secretary of State: I provided consulting services and group facilitation during a staff planning retreat for newly elected secretary of state, Cathy Cox. The retreat addressed issues of customer service and how the department would operate under Secretary Cox's administration.

The Hill Group has wholly or partly owned four companies:

Southern Festivals **newspaper**: THG purchased *Southern Festivals, The South's Festival Newspaper* on March 21, 2003. Gail had been providing editorial and other services to the previous owner for several years. The newspaper was a major vehicle for promoting festivals in Georgia. It sold advertising space to festivals and vendors to fund the newspaper production and was provided free of charge to state and local welcome centers in Georgia. Local tourism offices would also receive free copies. Subscriptions were sold on an individual basis. During the economic downturn in 2008, festivals cut out their advertising budgets, which negatively affected THG efforts to continue publishing the newspaper. THG decided to suspend publication operations of *Southern Festivals* newspaper.

GrowingGeorgia.com: In 2010, I was asked to join in creating, as a partner with three other people, an agricultural news internet site with daily e-mail publication of agricultural news. The GrowingGeorgia.com site has been providing agricultural news via e-mail since 2010. The company has merged with GrowingAmerica.com and covers agricultural news and issues, telling the story of the American farmer in all fifty states. I left the partnership in 2019.

Hill Group Photography: I started Hill Group Photography several years ago as I had multiple requests from people wanting to buy my photographs. I take primarily landscape photos and other scenes around the North Georgia Mountains.

Classy Southern Charm: Gail started this jewelry company about ten years ago. She designs and crafts semi-precious gemstones into awesome pieces of handmade jewelry.

I was in my home office early on the morning of Tuesday, September 11, 2001, when my son called me and asked if I knew what had just happened. He told me to turn on the TV. I will never forget those images of the planes hitting the twin towers.

I also will never forget the response by the American people. I saw raw patriotism being exhibited all around the United States. I hung the American Flag that day, and it has flown every day since (actually, I have had to replace it many times due to wear and tear). I was extremely saddened by that event and still am. However, I am heartened that we will never forget that day. Have you listened to all the names spoken of those who lost their lives? I have, and it is heartbreaking.

Can you imagine anyone who would not have known about that event within a few hours of its happening? Well, I know someone. It was Gail. She was in the hospital that morning with her mother, who was recovering from cancer surgery. Her mother was given bad news following surgery. Cancer had spread, and they were not able to remove it. She did not want the television on. The nurses chose not to tell Gail or her mother about what had happened in New York City.

After talking with Gail several times and realizing from our conversations that she knew nothing about the event, I finally asked her to leave the room so that I could tell her. How do you describe that unbelievable series of events to someone who had not seen it on TV nor even heard a word about it? At first, she did not believe it. Then she immediately asked, where are our children? I told her that our son was at work in Gainesville, Georgia, and our daughter, who was an intern with Delta Air Lines, was at work in Atlanta. Gail was extremely relieved, as you can imagine.

Our daughter, Miranda, had been scheduled to fly to New York on September 11, but the trip had been canceled the night before. As you may recall, shortly after the towers were hit and news of other events started coming through, all planes were ordered to land as a matter of urgency because, at that point, we did not know what was going on. Miranda would play an integral part in helping Delta that day as I explain in Chapter 27.

It is a day that I will never forget, as I was alone—just me and the TV. It was extremely frightening to think that the USA could be attacked like that. I hope and pray that it never happens again. God bless America!

Abraham Baldwin Agricultural College (ABAC) celebrated its centenary in 2008. I was attending homecoming in April and was asked by Rosalyn Ray Donaldson, my former English professor, if I had heard from Sverre Stub, who had been my first roommate when I started college at ABAC. I told her that the last time I had spoken to him, or heard from him, was in the late 1970s. She suggested that I try to find him and let her know of his whereabouts.

A quick Internet search found him immediately. He was the Norwegian Ambassador to Greece, married and with two children. We e-mailed and shared information about our current lives. It was great to hear from him and to learn about his life since ABAC.

Eight years later, in early April 2016, Sverre contacted me via e-mail to let me know that he was planning a trip to Georgia that fall. He had come to ABAC in 1966 on a Rotary Scholarship sponsored by the Rotary Clubs in Tifton, Waycross, and Brunswick, Georgia. He wanted, on this trip, to speak to each of the clubs and thank them for the scholarship that had allowed him to come to Georgia and ABAC, and he asked if I could assist him in making local arrangements. I was pleased to do so.

Sverre provided the dates, and I began setting things up for his visit. It took a couple of weeks to contact each one, but I was able to secure him a slot on the agenda of each of the club meetings. He also wanted to speak to the students at ABAC. I worked with Dr. David Bridges, president of ABAC, in arranging Sverre the opportunity to speak at two events on campus.

Gail and I decided to host him at our home in the North Georgia Mountains for the first couple of days. He would be able to get over the jet lag, and we could have some time to get reacquainted. During the two days he stayed with us, we had several interesting discussions regarding taxes, climate change, and politics. No blows were exchanged, and nobody was hurt. I did enjoy the discussions and learned of his perspective on the United States and the world.

I asked Sverre, one evening, what would be the appropriate way to introduce him. I suggested Sverre Stub from Norway. He said, "For you, Jimmy, 'The Honorable and Distinguished Ambassador Sverre Stub from Norway' would be appropriate." I was glad that he laughed after he said that because he was just Sverre Stub to me.

I had the pleasure of introducing him at several of his speaking engagements. These were my introductory comments:

It was 2:30 a.m. one day in early September 1966, when I met our speaker for the first time. I was dead asleep in my dorm room at ABAC. I woke up to find this lanky young man standing there looking at me. That started a fifty-year friendship. I took him to his first drive-in theater date and his first southern meal at my parents' home and many other firsts.

I surprised him one evening at ABAC with Norwegian sardines for a treat. I brought them into the dorm room and opened them. I knew that scent would bring back memories of home. He said, "What is that smell?"

I said, "The best sardines known to man, and they are from Norway."

He said, "Get those things out of here! I can't stand the smell. We don't eat sardines; we ship them to the US."

Ambassador Stub spent more than forty years in the Norwegian diplomatic service, including postings in The Hague (Netherlands), Washington, DC, Caracas (Venezuela), Geneva, and Paris. He concluded his service abroad as ambassador in Amman (Jordan), accredited to Baghdad (Iraq), and then in Athens (Greece), and accredited to Nicosia (Cyprus). While in Amman, he was a member of the Amman Cosmopolitan Rotary Club. He attended the Senior Course at the NATO Defense College in Rome, Italy.

His responsibilities in Oslo have included the position as Director of the Foreign Minister's Office and Political Adviser in the Norwegian Government. He has also been dealing with natural resource management, environment, energy, and climate change, as well as international security issues. His last responsibility was to coordinate Norway's chairmanship of the Barents Euro-Arctic Council. He retired in 2014 and is now president of the Group of Retired Ambassadors.

On July 1, 2016, Ambassador Stub became the president of the Oslo Rotary Club in Oslo, Norway. He has been active in a network called Grandparents for Climate Change. He loves cross-country skiing, mountain hiking, bicycling, and golf.

His wife, Anne Marie (also Norwegian), and he have been married since 1971. They have two sons and three grandchildren.

I accompanied Ambassador Stub for his talks at ABAC, the Tifton Rotary Club, and the Waycross Rotary Club. An ABAC official took him to Brunswick for his speech to the Brunswick Rotary Club. He also attended a Savannah Rotary Club meeting before heading back to Norway.

Just for the record, I never learned to say, "The Honorable and Distinguished Ambassador Sverre Stub."

Ambassador Sverre Stub and Jimmy Hill with ABAC Stallion in the background
* Photo Courtesy of ABAC

25

Farm Again - AgrAbility of Georgia

My involvement with Farm Again began when I was hired as a part-time Program Manager III at Farm Again–AgrAbility at the University of Georgia in 2015. Farm Again–AgrAbility in Georgia is a cooperative effort between the College of Agricultural and Environmental Sciences and the College of Family and Consumer Sciences. It is part of the National AgrAbility Project, which is associated with the United States Department of Agriculture and is funded through the Farm Bill passed by the US Congress.

The vision of AgrAbility is to enhance the quality of life for farmers, ranchers, and other agricultural workers with disabilities. The program is currently administered in twenty-eight states: Alaska, California, Colorado, Georgia, Idaho, Illinois, Indiana, Iowa, Kansas, Kentucky, Maine, Michigan, Missouri, Nebraska, New Mexico, North Carolina, Ohio, Pennsylvania, South Dakota, Tennessee, Texas, Utah, Vermont, Virginia, Washington, West Virginia, Wisconsin, and Wyoming.

This program helps farmers and ranchers with disabilities or chronic health conditions to continue farming or get back to farming. This is accomplished by using innovative technologies. Some of the disabling conditions in agriculture could be, but are not limited to, arthritis, hearing impairment, brain injury, disabling disease, spinal cord injury or paralysis, respiratory impairment, amputation, head injury, cerebral palsy, and back impairment.

Farm Again has had a booth at the Sunbelt Agricultural Exposition in Moultrie, Georgia, for many years, thanks to Expo executive director Chip Blalock. After my first year on board, we were able to secure a large outdoor exhibit area to bring in vendors that could demonstrate their technologies. Many exhibitors participate with Farm Again during the Sunbelt Expo. If you attend the Expo, which takes place annually in October, you can meet the Farm Again staff and see the technologies that are available for farmers and ranchers.

The Farm Again program has provided life-changing solutions for many farmers and ranchers over the years. Sometimes it is by putting extra steps or even a seat lift on a tractor so that the farmer can get onto the tractor independently. Many technologies and other types of help are available. If you are a Georgia farmer who needs some assistance to continue or get back to farming or know of a farmer who would benefit from the program, please contact Farm Again at www.farmagain.com, or you may call 877-524-6264. You can also check out their Facebook page at Farm Again Georgia.

If you live in another state, please contact the National AgrAbility Project at www.agrability.org or call 1-800-825-4264.

Working with Farm Again–AgrAbility in Georgia was one of the most rewarding jobs that I ever had. One example was our work with a farmer who had lost the use of his legs but had good upper body strength. Through technology, we were able to put him back in his tractor seat, with hand controls for him to resume farming. It was awesome and inspiring to see him regain his ability to farm. He had the biggest grin on his face that I have ever witnessed.

I thoroughly enjoyed my time with the Farm Again–AgrAbility in Georgia program. I made the difficult decision to resign in April 2018, after nearly three years, so that I could work full-time on writing this book.

26

My Parents – Rest of the Story

My college education began in the fall of 1966 at ABAC in Tifton, and that is when I left home—at age nineteen. After that, I worked or attended classes, or both, every summer, and did not return home other than for short visits.

Dad's ministry at Mount Pleasant Baptist Church was rewarding, including all of the demands of sermon preparation, outreach, counseling, administrative duties, visiting the sick, and working with the deacons.

Unfortunately, the church did not have the resources to pay him what he needed to support a family of six. He had to supplement his income with outside work. He found a regular, part-time job as a public-school bus driver. He would get up early in the morning to pick up the kids on his bus route and take them to school. All told, it took about three hours in the morning and then another three hours in the afternoon, when he took them all home. I found several dozen school photos of his bus kids in his files when he passed. Kids loved him, and he did them. He drove the bus for fifteen years.

Dad's garden kept him busy in spring and summer. He would also occasionally do handyman jobs for church members or others in the community.

The most heartbreaking event for our family was the drowning of my younger brother, Ricky. I do not know how Dad was able to function after losing Ricky. Well, yes, I do know. He put his trust and faith in his Savior Jesus Christ. We, as a family, saw amazing things happen in the lives of many church members and others after Ricky's death; it touched many people in so many different ways. Dad and Mom were the strongest people of faith that I have ever known.

In 1975, Dad and Mom decided to build themselves a home in preparation for their eventual retirement. They found a building lot in Hazlehurst, and Dad built the new house. It was a three-bedroom, two-bathroom ranch with a carport. Dad and Mom loved to fish, so Dad put in a fishing pond next to the house. They stocked the pond with catfish

Mary and Jasper Hill

and bream and spent many enjoyable hours fishing. Dad eventually built himself a pond house, complete with kitchen and dining room.

Due to many requests for his assistance as a handyman, Dad decided to form Jasper Hill & Son Contractors in 1980. My brother Jerry worked with him for many years. Dad's business card stated that he would build, remodel, and make additions to residential and commercial structures. He hired other help as needed and operated the business for approximately seventeen years.

Daddy loved to fish   *Daddy was a carpenter and built this cabinet*

Dad served as a pastor for over thirty-seven years. His pastorates, all in Georgia, included: Union Baptist Church, Wayne County; Midway Baptist Church, Wayne County; Little Creek Baptist Church, Wayne County; Mount Pleasant Baptist Church (thirteen years), Jeff Davis County; Oak Grove Baptist Church, Jeff Davis County; Oak View Baptist Church, Jeff Davis County; Spring Hill Baptist Church (thirteen years), Wheeler County; Sharon Baptist Church, Telfair County; Friendship Baptist Church, Wheeler County.

He retired twice, the second time being on September 29, 1997. Mom had developed serious medical issues that required him to take care of her full-time.

Numerous souls were saved under Dad's ministry as Preacher Hill. Also, three young men felt the call to the ministry under his preaching. They were Keith Yawn, Donnie Brown, and Charles Morgan.

Keith Yawn was approximately fourteen years old when Dad was his pastor. Here is Keith's story that he shared with me about my father's (and mother's) influence on his feeling the call to preach.

As a teenager, Keith developed a relationship with Preacher Hill, and he trusted his advice and counsel. After high school, Keith went on to

Preacher Jasper Hill

a nearby college and, during that time, felt the call to preach. He called Preacher Hill to discuss his decision and to seek his approval and guidance.

Keith and his parents, who were very close to Preacher Hill and Mary, were all invited to come to their home in Hazlehurst. Keith had a lot of questions about the ministry, and Preacher Hill had lots of answers, but more importantly, wisdom, to offer. After that meeting, Keith pursued his dream of becoming a pastor using this advice. Today, Reverend Keith Yawn is the pastor of Oakview Baptist Church in Hazlehurst. Preacher and Mary Hill joined the Oakview Baptist Church when they retired. Reverend Yawn told us he was honored to serve as their pastor for several years.

Friendship Baptist Church in Glenwood, Wheeler County, called my father to serve as their pastor, and he was there for four years. During that period of his ministering, two young men felt the calling of God to go into the ministry. Both men were ordained and are now serving as full-time pastors.

These pastors shared some of their insights and stories with me about Pastor (or Brother) Hill and Mrs. Mary, as they called them. Both of them told me how they loved my parents. They received advice and counsel from them both. Pastor Hill, they said, was like a rock in his steadfast belief in the Bible and in Jesus Christ, and he and Mrs. Mary lived their lives as Christians, demonstrating it in many ways. Their presence and love were experienced by all who came in contact with them.

Donnie Brown told me the story of his being saved in a briar patch after a troubling life. He was welcomed into the church by Brother Hill after his life-changing acceptance of Jesus as his personal savior. Brown was participating in a discipleship class at the church, and during that experience, he felt the call to preach. After he made his commitment to the ministry, he found Brother Hill to be a constant source of information, ideas, and resources for him. He provided Brown with books and advice that helped him to be more confident as a pastor and shepherd of his church.

Reverend Donnie Brown is the pastor at the Mt. Galilee Baptist Church in Telfair County, Georgia. He has been there for almost six years and is a bi-vocational pastor who also works for the local school system.

Charles (Chuck) Morgan has described how he accepted Christ as his savior in December 1995 under Pastor Hill's ministry and Mrs. Mary's loving influence. Their presence in his family's lives was beyond influential. His decision to preach was driven by his love of Christ and the desire to spread the gospel of Jesus Christ, and also by Pastor Hill's example.

After only three months of his new life, Chuck was asked by Pastor Hill to take charge of the youth program. He said he felt so unprepared for the challenge, but that Pastor Hill encouraged him to accept it. After a while, Chuck felt that he was not the person for the job, that he was not impacting the youth as he wanted. Pastor Hill told him to slow down, not to get in too big of a hurry, continue forward, and he would be successful. Chuck said that he owed his success with the youth group to that advice.

Pastor Hill, he said, was a great mentor for him as a young preacher. He learned a lot from him about preaching funerals, conducting a marriage ceremony, and other ministerial duties.

Chuck shared a story about Pastor Hill that happened one Sunday night. Following his sermon, Pastor Hill asked the congregation to support a project for the community. That would be a normal and routine thing for the pastor to request of the congregation. However, this particular evening, the church members balked and said that they did not support the request. Pastor Hill closed his Bible and said to the congregation, "If you will not follow my advice as your shepherd, then you don't need me as your pastor." His next words were, "Mary, let's go." They immediately walked out of the church, leaving the congregation in shock and disbelief.

At the Wednesday night prayer meeting service, the church members agreed to support the project and asked that Pastor Hill come back and be their pastor. He did. This is a great example of Pastor Hill's belief in himself and his mission. He said what he believed and did what he felt he needed to do.

Chuck also told me that when he first started pastoring, Mrs. Mary sat down with his children and told them never to do anything that would hurt their father's ministry. Neither he nor his children have ever forgotten those words of wisdom.

My father was certainly a charismatic person. Chuck recalls having dinner with his wife, Gloria, and Pastor Hill and Mrs. Mary at a local restaurant in Hazlehurst. After overhearing a single lady, seated nearby, telling her friend that she wished that she could find herself a husband, Pastor Hill stood up and banged on the table to get everybody's attention. He announced in a loud voice, "We have a single, good-looking, well-off lady here tonight, who is looking for a husband." Then, after a measured pause, "Any takers?"

The lady in question was incensed. She was so embarrassed she "would have killed" Pastor Hill had it not been for the crowd around them and her knowing it was against the law to kill someone … especially a preacher! This is another example of Brother Hill's oratory skill and of his unflinching ability to cut to the chase, no matter the subject or timing.

Another tale Chuck related took place following a Sunday morning service, when Pastor Hill and Mrs. Mary had returned home and were having lunch. The phone rang, and Pastor Hill got up to go and answer it. Mrs. Hill heard him say, "We will be through with lunch by the time you get here, and I will meet you in front of the house." When she questioned him about the call, he said, "A man is upset about my sermon this morning and is coming over to whup me."

Pastor Hill finished his lunch, took a folding chair to the front yard, and sat there waiting for the man to arrive. Fortunately, he never came. Pastor Hill had no fear in him and would meet any challenge head-on.

Chuck and his family would frequently visit with my parents on Friday evenings. On one Friday evening visit, Pastor Hill told Gloria that he would teach her how to fish. They walked over to the pond, and, using a new rod and reel that he had recently bought, he demonstrated a few times to Gloria how to throw the baited line into the pond. He then handed her the rod and reel to try for herself. On her first throw, the reel came off the rod and landed in the pond. "Gloria, you threw my new reel into the pond!" he exclaimed. She tried to apologize, but all Preacher Hill could say was, "You devil!" From that point on, Gloria's nickname was Devil. She reciprocated by calling him Old Goat. And it was not the Greatest-of-All-Time "goat."

Reverend Charles (Chuck) Morgan's first church was Alston Baptist Church in Montgomery County, Georgia. He is currently pastor at Macedonia Baptist Church in Telfair County, Georgia. He is also a bi-vocational pastor and works in the funeral business.

Dad loved to fish, and if he had to name a hobby, it would have been fishing. I mentioned to him one day about my memories of fishing in Gardi, and he said that he would like to go back there and fish again. I immediately volunteered to take him. I had a thirty-foot camper at that time, and we planned a camping and fishing trip to Gardi.

I picked him up in Hazlehurst, and we traveled to Gardi, setting up camp at Jackson's Pond on the Little Creek–Gardi Road, which was only a half-mile from our old home. Gardi Creek had several small tributaries that crisscrossed unincorporated Gardi. We traveled to where the creek ran under the River Road Bridge and fished under the bridge for about forty-five minutes, catching a few small catfish. From there we traveled down River Road to Union Baptist Church. We took a few minutes to visit the

Union Baptist Church cemetery, which is where my dad's parents and grandparents, as well as other relatives, are buried.

Alex Creek flows right behind the cemetery. It had been a prime fishing spot many years earlier, according to Dad, so we went down to the creek and sought out some promising locations. As we started to fish, I had this weird feeling that someone was watching us. I said something to Dad about it, and he said, "It feels spooky to me, too. Maybe ghosts are here." I do not 100 percent believe in ghosts, but it was one of the most freakish feelings I had ever experienced. I pulled out my camera and took some pictures. Dad claimed he could see a murky outline of someone in the background of the photographs. I still get the heebie-jeebies when I look at those pictures. We fished for a short time and caught a few more catfish, but we finally had enough of the weirdness that hung over the creek and made a quick departure. We had caught enough for a fish fry that evening back at the campground.

The next day, we went to visit Dad's brother Jim. We told him about our fishing expedition. He volunteered to take us out in his son Jay's boat on the Altamaha River. In Jesup, we picked up some bait and chicken scratch feed to attract the fish, then we headed to Paradise Park Landing on the Altamaha River. Jay's small johnboat had a 10 hp motor. We headed south on the river, looking for a good spot to fish. The Altamaha is relatively shallow during low rain periods, with a lot of sand bars. Navigating the river to avoid them was a challenge. Uncle Jim was the boat captain, as he had the most recent experience on the river. The water was unusually low, and suddenly Uncle Jim hit a sand bar; the boat stopped as if it had hit a wall. I was in the front and almost went over the bow. Dad landed on top of me, and Uncle Jim was holding onto the motor, so he was okay. We had to get out and heave the boat into deeper water. Finally, we arrived at our fishing spot and set the chicken scratch in the shallow water. We didn't catch a single fish. After about an hour, we headed back to Paradise Park Landing. It had been a great day for a boat ride, so it was worth it.

Some of my fondest memories of Dad were on my birthday. He would call and sing Happy Birthday to me on the phone. Dad was not a singer by any stretch of the imagination, though he was a far better singer than I am. But he was still bad. I probably inherited my inability to carry a tune from him.

When he called on my birthday, he would occasionally get hold of me, but most of the time I was at work or out and about. He would sing every verse of the song on my voice mail. I thought that it was fun for him, and I tolerated it. Yet, after his death, I sorely missed those calls. Oh, how I wish that I could hear him sing it again. I still have his and Mom's phone number on my cell phone. I can't seem to delete it. It seems, in some way, that if I deleted it, I would be deleting them. I can't explain it.

I grew up hearing my dad being called Mr. Hill or, at other times, Preacher Hill, Brother Hill, or Jack (his nickname). It was so strange when I became an adult and people started calling me Mr. Hill. I would immediately turn around to see if my dad was there. I still have the momentary feeling that I need to see if my dad is nearby when I hear "Mr. Hill." At what age do you become known by the same name as your dad?

On my sixtieth birthday, Dad called me and sang his usual Happy Birthday. After he finished singing, he asked me how it felt to be sixty years old. I told him that I felt fine, great, and awesome. I asked him, "How does it feel to be the father of a sixty-year-old man?" He thought for a moment but had no comeback.

Have you ever learned something about your parents that shocked you but really should not have? After my parents passed, I gathered up their files and brought them to my home. I went through them when I was preparing to write this book. I found a Valentine's Day card from my dad to my mom. It was your typical card. The message on the front of the card said, "Someone with your charming ways ..." and on the inside, it said, "... deserves the loveliest of days!" It was followed by the words "Happy Valentine's Day" and signed Jasper Hill.

As I opened the card, a folded note fell out. I opened it, and there was a hand-sketched caricature my dad had drawn of himself. Under his drawing were the words, "Mary Hill, will you go to bed with me?" I told my daughter about the card, and she thought it was hilarious.

Dad was not able to save much money for his retirement because none of the churches that he pastored offered any retirement plans. The Georgia Baptist Convention, the statewide organization that served Baptist churches in Georgia, had a retirement program that churches could contribute to for their ministers. However, small churches very rarely had any money beyond operational and salary expenses to contribute to the retirement fund (Georgia Baptist Annuity Board) for their ministers. Dad never held a job that had retirement benefits, other than his bus driving job through the local school system, and that was so small, based on his limited salary, that it only amounted to about one hundred dollars per month.

The Georgia Baptist Convention and GuideStone Financial Services (formerly the Annuity Board) did, from time to time, have donated monies that were available to retired ministers and their spouses. One such grant, entitled "Adopt an Annuitant," assisted Dad and Mom with certain

Jerry, Linda, Jimmy, Jasper and Mary at a family wedding

expenses over a specific time frame. It helped to pay for escalating healthcare and prescription costs and onetime unexpected expenses. This fund was a very valuable asset to them.

Mom sold her dumpling business and was able to have income from that sale for several years. As always, they found a way, with God's help, to live in their twilight years.

Dad and his brother, my Uncle Jim, were always playing jokes on each other. They had a friendly and sometimes quite competitive sibling rivalry. They were always fun to be around because of the bantering and bickering that occurred.

Dad, Mother, Gail, and I went to visit Uncle Jim after he became bedridden. Uncle Jim's wife, JoAnn, told us that Jim did not have long to live. He was in the bedroom next to the living room where we were sitting. Aunt JoAnn asked me if I would be a pallbearer, and I said, "Of course." I believe that Uncle Jim could hear us. He lived more than six months after our visit.

Uncle Jim passed on November 7, 2005, at the age of eighty-six. He served in the army during World War II and left the service as a sergeant. He was a member and deacon at the Gardi Baptist Church and belonged to the Millwrights Local Union #865 in Brunswick, Georgia.

Rinehart and Sons Funeral Home of Jesup, Georgia, was in charge of the arrangements. The viewing and visitation were scheduled for November 9 at 6:00 p.m. Gail and I took Dad and Mother to the funeral home that evening. As we were nearing the casket, I noticed Dad reach into his coat pocket and retrieve something. Knowing him as I did, I knew that he was up to something. As we reached the casket, I saw him place something next to Uncle Jim. I caught a glimpse of it, and it was a picture of President George W. Bush.

The backstory is that Uncle Jim was a staunch Democrat, also known as a Yellow Dog Democrat, which is a person who will vote for any Democrat on the ballot, regardless of their qualification. They will vote for a yellow dog before they will vote for a Republican. Dad was a staunch

Republican and proud of it. He and Uncle Jim had fierce arguments about politics. I asked Dad why he put the picture of President Bush into the casket. Dad said, "Let him explain that when he gets to Heaven." I guess Dad got the last word.

Reverend Dewitt R. Corbin was a personal friend of my dad and mom. He was my dad's pastor at one point. Later in life, he became a hospice chaplain. He was the hospice chaplain for my dad just before his death when Dad was in the Community Hospice House in Vidalia, Georgia.

Reverend Corbin wrote a book about his experiences as a hospice chaplain entitled *Walking With The Dying: Chronicles of a Hospice Chaplain*. This book is an excellent resource for the family of a person who is in hospice care or the last days of their life. I highly recommend it, as I know it was an invaluable resource for me as I dealt with the passing of Dad and Mom.

Near the end of the book, Reverend Corbin wrote about Dad and mentioned Mom as well. The section was entitled: "The Rebel Preacher." He gave me written permission to share the following from his book:

> The preacher arose, his demeanor was stern;
> He moved to the pulpit without a sound.
> With searching eyes, he looked all around;
> He pounded the pulpit and the sermon began.
>
> Preach! Preach, Brother Jasper, tell us all,
> Give us a message, oh so profound;
> Tell us of God's love that does yet abound,
> Speak of the Crucified One, let tears now fall.
>
> Brother Jasper preached; it was of salvation, I recall,
> For many that night, Jesus was found,
> Others, by conviction, were brought low to the ground,
> It was with power he preached, with love Jesus did call.

Reverend Jasper Hill was not your average preacher. True, he was a pulpit-pounding, hellfire-preaching, no-nonsense, King-James-Bible-only Southern Baptist pastor. But his defense of the infallibility of the Bible, and his insistence that the word "missionary" ought to be part of the name of every Baptist church, was unequaled. Brother Jasper had been known to challenge anyone who might tread on the basic tenets of the Christian faith as he saw it.

Brother Jasper was married to Mary Hill, who was the successful founder of Mary Hill Dumplings. Mary loved her preacher man but openly admitted that he did things in his way. She always smiled when she said this, and I imagine her tolerance for him probably was the primary factor in their long marriage.

As they both grew older and developed health problems, Mary sold her business, and Jasper retired from the pastorate. Having known them for many years, I was delighted when they started attending the church that I was pastoring. The thing was, it wasn't always easy being Brother Jasper's pastor. He and Mary always sat on the fourth pew to my left as I stood in the pulpit, so I had direct eye contact with him. From time to time, I would detect some concerns from Brother Jasper by a change in his countenance or demeanor. After the service was over, he would approach me and say, "Now tell me exactly what you meant when you said...." As a younger pastor, I enjoyed these conversations because both of us would learn something from the other.

When Brother Jasper's health deteriorated to the point where Mary could no longer care for him, he was admitted to a nursing home. I had long since left the pastorate for the chaplaincy. When Brother Jasper was admitted to hospice care, I was proud to be his chaplain. While he loved all of the hospice staff, he hated the nursing home environment and didn't always respond well to the nursing home staff. The word was that Brother Jasper was giving them hell. As his chaplain and longtime friend, I was asked to speak to him about those issues. I made a special visit to see if I could find out just where the problem was and to encourage him to be more cooperative with those who were trying to care for him.

When I asked Brother Jasper what was going on, he openly admitted that he had to, in his words, "straighten them out" a time or two. I teased him with the idea that if he didn't straighten out himself, I was going to bring in the big gorilla to look after him. He laughed and told me "bring on the monkey" and that he would straighten him out, too. Somehow a monkey worked its way into every visit that I made after that.

One day when I was visiting Mary at her home, she gave me a stuffed monkey she had bought in a novelty shop. She told me to secretly give it to Jasper. I was excited about the prospect of the gag, and I asked JaLayne Coleman, the volunteer coordinator at our office and favorite visitor of Jasper's, to meet me at the nursing home with her camera. She remained out of sight as I went into his room with the stuffed monkey hiding in a bag.

Brother Jasper seemed to be in an ill mood when I first arrived, but soon mellowed as we began to talk. I then became very serious and told him that I was tired of warning him about giving the nursing home staff trouble and that I had finally brought that monkey with me that I had threatened him with. I secretly laughed as he looked around the room trying to see the monkey.

"Jasper," I said, "This is a special monkey that belongs to the Monkey Mafia out of Miami. His boss is a big, mean gorilla, so you had better treat this monkey with respect."

By then, Brother Jasper was totally puzzled. I then pulled the stuffed monkey out of the bag and placed it on his chest. I quickly stepped back, not knowing if he would throw it at me or swing that big fist of his at my chin. At the same time, JaLayne had stepped in and was recording the entire event on camera.

I admit I was surprised and shocked when Brother Jasper began laughing. He reached for the monkey, and then held it close to his cheek and kissed it. From that day forward until his death, he kept that stuffed monkey at his side.

Brother Jasper was my dear friend. I loved that old preacher and still miss his fellowship to this day. He was known to have lived his life serving his God, and yes, as Mary said, he did it his way. And for that, everyone loved him.

Reverend Dewitt Corbin was a great preacher and an awesome hospice chaplain. I am glad that I got to know him through my parents. I thanked him for being a friend to my parents and for being there for them in their last days. His poem at the beginning of this section pretty well summed up my dad as a preacher as well as his Christian life.

Reverend Corbin signed my personal copy of *Walking With The Dying: Chronicles of a Hospice Chaplain* with the following: "Jimmy, your Mom and Dad were very special friends. May God bless you and your family, Dewitt R. Corbin."

I calculated that after preaching for thirty-seven years, Dad had preached a minimum of 3,868 sermons, not counting week-long revivals. I found two boxes full of his sermon notes. I may have all of his sermons, but I am not completely sure. I did notice that he preached some of the same sermons at all of the nine churches that he pastored. He put the date of each sermon and the church name on the back of his sermon notes. Dad did not write out his sermons but just wrote key points and scripture verses to remind him of his thoughts.

Listed below is one of his sermons:

Subject—The Virtuous Woman with Scripture from
Proverbs 31:10–19

1. Woman (Mary Magdalene) was first to the grave of Jesus—Matthew 28
2. A woman washed Jesus's feet with tears wiped from the hairs of her head—Luke 7:36-38
3. Jesus saw a woman passing by that had been sick for 18 years and call her to him and healed her—Luke 13:11-13
4. A woman of faith overcomes an unjust Judge—Luke 18
5. A woman had been sick for 12 years, she said to herself, If I may but touch the hem of Jesus's garment, I shall be healed—Matthew 9:20–22
6. A poor widow gave all she had to God—Mark 12:41–44
7. Who can find a virtuous woman in this day and time?

He preached a version of this Mother's Day sermon seven times between 1973 until 1993:

> Mount Pleasant Baptist Church on May 13, 1973, and May 11, 1975
>
> Oak View Baptist Church on May 16, 1977, and on May 14, 1978
>
> Spring Hill Baptist Church on May 8, 1985, and on April 15, 1990
>
> Friendship Baptist Church on May 9, 1993

Mother was having knee-replacement surgery, and she asked if Gail and I could come down from Tomahawk Mountain and help her and Dad. She would probably need help for about a week, she said. Gail and I were able to take our laptops and operate our business from their home. Dad had built a large dining room onto their home a few years earlier, and we made our offices there. We were managing the Georgia Agri-Leaders Forum and were getting ready for the Washington, DC, study institute.

I had quite a bit of computer work and a lot of phone calls to make and return to get the plans finalized for the institute. It was decided that I would go to the hospital in Tifton with Mother, and Gail would stay with Dad. He was not able to walk but had a motorized wheelchair that he could move around in and stay somewhat mobile. He was able to get in and out of the wheelchair for bathroom trips and to reach his favorite lounge chair.

Mom's surgery went well, and she was only in the hospital one night. We arrived back home the next day, and she was doing well with in-home physical therapy.

Dad did great while Mom and I were at the hospital. Gail responded to his needs, and he was pleasant. The night following my arrival back home with Mother, Dad woke us up at 3:30 a.m., screaming my name. I went into his room, just down the hall, and found him on the floor. He had attempted to get up and go to the bathroom. In getting out of bed, he had slipped and fallen on the floor. He had landed next to his wheelchair and had tried to move it by reaching for the joystick. As he touched the joystick, he caused the wheelchair to move forward and run over his foot. But he did not tell us about its running over his foot at that time. We finally got him up to the side of the bed, and he got in his wheelchair and went to the bathroom. Gail and I finally got him back into bed around 4:15 a.m.

At about 4:30 a.m., he was yelling my name again. We went to his room, and he said his foot was hurting. I uncovered his foot and found a nasty bruise. When I asked him about it, he told me about the chair running over it. Immediately, I got him out of bed and took him to the hospital emergency room about a half-mile away. This was a small hospital, and they had to call in a doctor to perform the x-rays. By 6:00 a.m., the doctor had established that there were no broken bones, and I took Dad home. We finally put a baby monitor in Dad's bedroom so that we could hear him and respond as needed.

Dad would get me up two or three times each night to go to the bathroom, or to adjust his bed, or if something in his room needed attention. I admit that I was tired after about three days of not getting much sleep. I asked Mother if she had to get up with him several times a night, and she said yes.

"How have you been doing that every night?" I asked her.

"I've had no choice," was her answer.

I had asked her continually about how she and Dad were doing, and she always told me that everything was okay. I was finding out that things were not okay.

Gail and I stayed at my parents' home for nearly three weeks, addressing all of the issues that we found. In consultation with Mother and my two siblings, we determined that Dad needed to have 24/7 care. Mother was not physically able to take care of herself and Dad.

We started researching nursing home care. My siblings, Mother, Gail, and I visited a nursing home in Glenwood, Georgia, unannounced, and felt that we had found a good place for Dad. It was about a thirty-minute drive for Mother one way. Unfortunately, Dad hated the place, and every day he woke up thinking about how he could escape. He hated any place that was not home. However, we were confident that he was receiving excellent care.

Mother gave Dad a cell phone so that he could communicate with her at any time. He called her ten to twenty times a day. He would tell her, "I am dying, and no one has checked on me in two days," or, "I am bleeding, and I can't get the nurses to come and check on me."

The last straw was when he called to tell her that he was really dying this time and that the nurses had quit coming to check on him. That call came at around dinner time, and Mother called the cell phone of the nursing home administrator and asked him if he had seen Dad. "I'm sitting here in the dining room having dinner with Jasper, Mrs. Mary, and he is doing fine," he said.

Mother shared her frustration with me about the phone calls. My suggestion, after asking her what she wanted me to do, was that we take his cell phone and that the nurses would call her if he needed anything.

Gail and I went to visit Dad on a Saturday morning, and I took the cell phone from his pajama pocket as he slept. I woke him, and we had a great visit. As I was leaving, I told him that I had taken his cell phone. He grabbed his pocket and said, "I want my cell phone, and I mean now."

I explained that he was calling Mother day and night and complaining about things that were not true. She needed her rest and could not run over to check on him every time he called. He was a hyped devil-preacher that day. Needless to say, he was furious with me. He said some things that he should not have said. However, he did eventually apologize.

Unfortunately, his health continued to decline, and Mother asked me to meet her at the local hospital just across the street from the nursing home one afternoon for us to speak to his doctor. I was the nearest for her to call on, as I happened to be working in South Georgia at the time. The doctor shared that we had two choices. We could send him to the hospital in Savannah or transfer him to hospice care. His care at the hospital would continue to keep him alive, but his medical conditions were worsening. I asked the doctor what the prognosis was for his recovery. He said that he was not going to get any better, but probably much worse with increasing pain.

I think Mother was mentally preparing for the inevitable hospice care situation. I called my siblings to update them. We had already discussed the possibility of hospice care. We all agreed that it was now time. I believe my mother was relieved with us all agreeing that this was best for him and her.

We arranged that day for Dad to be placed in the Community Hospice House in Vidalia, Georgia. The Community Hospice Company was owned by a family friend and was an excellent facility with awesome management and staff. After Dad was settled in, I visited with him, but he was asleep. I felt the need to say my goodbyes at that point. I am glad that I did because he died shortly after I returned home.

Mother already knew several of the hospice staff, as Dad had been placed in home hospice care before entering the nursing home. Of course, we already knew Reverend Dewitt Corbin, and Mom had met and become friends with JaLayne Coleman, the volunteer hospice coordinator. I met JaLayne and also became friends with her. She is an amazing person and does an awesome job in coordinating hospice care with the family. She is one of my heroes, and I stay in touch with her. Hospice care is a godsend to families that need assistance in caring for a loved one who is approaching death.

Jasper Hill was born on September 25, 1924 and died on August 14, 2010. His service was held at Elizabeth Baptist Church in Hazlehurst. The service was conducted by Reverend Keith Yawn, one of the young men who became a minister under Dad's influence. Jimmie Ryles, a local businessman and a great friend of Dad and Mom's, spoke at the funeral. My daughter, Miranda Faith Hill Skonie, also spoke at the service.

The pallbearers were my son, Chris Hill; my sister Linda's sons, Ricky and Michael Day; my brother Jerry's sons, Jerry Jr. and Chad Hill; and Jamie Sellers, the husband of Linda's daughter, Jennifer.

Dad was a hat person. He wore numerous hats and had quite a collection of them. He had a unique way of wearing his hats, tipped slightly

Daddy's pallbearers were five grandsons and the husband of a granddaughter.
Chris Hill, Jerry Hill Jr., Michael Day, Jamie Sellers Ricky Day, and Chad Hill

forward, with a tilt to the right. The pallbearers decided they would each wear one of Dad's hats, with his characteristic tilt, while carrying the casket to the church and to the cemetery. It was an awesome sight to witness. Mother was overjoyed they had chosen to do that in his honor.

My daughter, Miranda Skonie, gave the following eulogy:

> I'm Jimmy Hill's daughter, Jasper's granddaughter. Even though we saw it coming and were preparing for this day, I've learned nothing can really prepare you for it.
>
> When I was asked to speak today, I was a little hesitant. Over the years I haven't been able to spend as much time as I would have liked with Pa and Mema. But somehow, I still felt very close with Pa and still feel that way with Mema. There is a connection there that really isn't hard to explain. It's called family.
>
> I learned from an early age that Pa liked to pick on me. He used to always play this one trick on me. He would drink something out of this weird bottle and then a few minutes later his hair would be stiff and crispy. Now... I'm not sure what was in that bottle, but he said it caused his hair to get stiff. As a kid, I was gullible and couldn't figure

out what it was; I'm sure he probably ran back to the bathroom and sprayed hairspray on his hair. But it was always a little game with us.

When we did visit Mema and Pa, it seemed like that car ride was so long. I remember one time when I was older, old enough to drive; Dad asked me if I knew how to get to Mema and Pa's house. I said no, and he asked, "What would you do if something happened to your mom and me?" I paused and said, "Well … I can read a map!" Well, Dad, I managed to get here just fine on my own. I did have my brother, Chris, with me and a little help from a GPS, but I did manage to get here.

In many ways, I'm much like Pa, and I'm very proud of that fact. I inherited "The Hill Look." The Hill Look is a firm, direct look that gets the point across without words. I'm sure many of you in this room also inherited it and if you didn't, I'm sure you have seen it.

Something I also inherited is "The Hill Fit." A Hill Fit is used when you really want something done your way, you know … the RIGHT way. Again, if you didn't also inherit this trait, then you have witnessed it.

I have twin daughters who will be three in October, and one of them inherited both The Hill Look and The Hill Fit. Her name is Madeline, and her middle name is … yep, you guessed it, Hill. I guess we got that one right, huh?! She is already on her way to perfecting the Look and Fit. I think my husband, Patrick, and I are in trouble. But at the same time, I'm very proud.

So, when I heard the news about Pa, I cried, of course, and laughed at the memories. Then I said, "God, you're going to have your hands full with Jasper!"

Pa, you will be missed, but you will live on in memories, Looks, and Fits.

Jimmie and Arlene Ryles were good friends of my parents. Jimmie, who spoke at Dad's funeral and would eventually speak again at Mother's service, recently shared the following memories of them:

The first time I met Brother Jasper and Mary Hill was when their son, Ricky, drowned while Brother Hill was pastor at Mt. Pleasant Baptist

Church. Later on that year, I was at Philadelphia United Methodist Church for a benefit sing to raise money to build a social hall and I got to visit with Mary Hill. Mary Hill, Mildred Walker, and Ludine Claxton, as well as others, sang at that benefit sing. I sang a solo, one of the few times I had sung alone at that time.

After the benefit sing, Mrs. Mary asked me if I would be interested in singing with her and Mildred since Ludine had quit. I had never sung with a group before except congregational singing. I accepted her invitation. We practiced at my house once a week. Harmon and Cloteel Dawson joined the group. Harmon sang bass and later Willard O'Quinn joined the group to play the guitar. Mrs. Mildred Walker played the piano. After the group came together, we called ourselves "The Good News Quartet." When we practiced in our home, my four sons were young, and they would listen to the singing even after they had gone to bed. Some of them remember that and mentioned it recently.

My wife, Arlene, had been working on a teaching degree and when she finished her schooling, she decided to open a private kindergarten since two of the four sons were still at home. Mr. Hill built the kindergarten onto our existing house, and she ran the private kindergarten for two years before going to work at the public school. I addressed Brother Hill as Jasper, Preacher Hill, and Mr. Hill. My two younger boys put the different titles together and called him "Mr. Preacher Brother Hill."

Mrs. Hill meant a lot to me and I sometimes called her Mama Hill. She made me feel special as she once told me I reminded her of Ricky because he had sung with her and now, I was singing with her. We sang together for probably twenty-five years. We sang at local churches as well as some out-of-town engagements.

Brother Hill and Mrs. Hill were very special to me and Arlene. After he got very sick, I would visit them some Sunday afternoons. He laughed at me because I would go to sleep sitting in the chair during my visit. Sometimes he went to sleep as well. When Mrs. Hill needed help with him, she would call, and I'd go over to assist him. I tried to shave him once, and we both got to laughing because I was having a difficult time. I had never shaved anyone except myself.

Mrs. Hill could make you feel loved and good about yourself. She was a good pastor's wife. Mr. Hill served several churches as pastor in Hazlehurst and neighboring towns. They were well-liked and loved.

Jasper Hill was buried at the Hazlehurst Memorial Cemetery. The following verse was engraved on his Ledger (Cover): I have fought a good fight, I have finished my course, I have kept the faith. Scripture is from 2 Timothy 4:7.

These words were on the companion monument: "Jasper (Preacher) and Mary Louise Hill, married June 13, 1945." The names of their children are on the back of the monument: "Jimmy Leroy, Jerry Woodrow, Linda Jean, and Jasper Ricky."

This section is about Mary Louise Ryals Hill and is the hardest section of any chapter that I have written. I have so much deep love and admiration for my dad and mother that it is hard to put it into words. Mother was the kindest person that I have ever known. She commanded the utmost respect from her family, friends, and those who would become her friends. I have never heard anybody say or infer any ill will toward her.

Based on writing this book and deep diving into her life, I am still in awe of her as a person and as a Christian. She wrote the early beginnings of her life story that I used in the opening chapter of this book. She had not shared the fact that she had written about her early life with me or my siblings. I found the handwritten documents on a legal pad in her files. The lead pencil writings were faded, and I had to darken them on a photocopy machine to read some of the information. This was the first time that I had learned about some of the particulars of her early life. I cried as I read about some portions of that period of her life, particularly the old man coming to her home and taking her into the woods. I got angry and upset.

Mary Hill

After my dad passed, Mother told us siblings about the old man, but not in detail. She never told my dad as she was afraid of what he would do. I am thankful that she left us her early history because it so defines the trajectory for the rest of her life.

She exemplified the life of Christ in her life and in the way she interacted with others. She was an "extra" pastor next to my dad. He was rough and gruff, and she was kind and gentle. People would naturally gravitate to her. They would tell her things that they would not tell anybody else. She counseled hundreds, if not thousands, of people who came in contact with her.

If I know one thing in life, it was that she loved me and my siblings unconditionally. She was the encourager and the one who made sure that we knew what was important in life. There were times when I am sure we disappointed her, but she never gave up on us.

She loved Gail just as much as she did me. She had the same love for my siblings' spouses as well. They fell in love with her too.

Mother was an engaged partner with my dad in his ministry. She went with him on almost all of his visits to the homes of his church members as well as on hospital visits. She would take food to those members who had lost loved ones. She was a great comforter. She was the most forward-looking person and knew that your past did not define your future. She loved the unloved when even their families did not love them.

Mother retired after twenty-two years at the Jeff Davis Hospital. She ministered for those twenty-two years at the hospital, meeting patients' dietary and spiritual needs. She continued her ministry after retiring. Her hobbies included cooking, reading, sewing, and crafts.

JaLayne Coleman, a hospice coordinator and a friend of Mother's, said this to me about her: "Mary Hill is the only person that I have ever met who gave unconditional love all the time, no exceptions." Thank you, JaLayne, for sharing your beautiful words.

JaLayne also shared this quote from mother: "I wish every day was Sunday; Jasper is so loving and caring on Sundays."

David Miller, a longtime friend of mine, as well as of Mother's, also shared his thoughts on my mother's goodness. He said, "Your Mother's specialty was sharing love." David, thank you for sharing your kind words with me.

I found a document in Mother's files where she listed her children. The first four listed were her birth children: Jimmy Leroy Hill, Jerry Woodrow Hill, Linda Jean Hill, Jasper Ricky Hill. The rest of the list named her special children: Jim Girtman, Jimmie Ryles, Judy Ricketson Carter, Teresa Carver Grantham, Faye Bennett Graham, Lola Bennett Jamsky, Dale Kirkland, Jimmy Ricketson, Mary Sue Deffily, and Genethel Brewer.

I was looking up addresses and phone numbers of Mother's friends in her address book. I was taken aback at what I found, but not surprised when I thought about it. She had the phone number to the White House in Washington, DC. She called regularly to inform the president about things that he should be doing. Her address book contained the names and phone numbers of her two US senators, her US representative, her state senator and representative, the governor of Georgia, and many other officials. She wrote many letters expressing her concerns and how they should be handled.

After I got her a desktop computer, she was the community go-to person, helping her neighbors with social security and other issues that impacted the elderly. She helped one young man with health-care issues related to his military service. Her life was built around helping other people. She did an amazing job and touched everybody around her in one way or another.

As she progressed in life, my mother, who had finished eighth grade at Gardi School, realized that she needed to get additional education. She attended classes and was successful in passing the GED test. She was so excited to get the diploma.

Also, Mother took courses at Brewton Parker College, The University of Florida, and Georgia Southern College. The classes were focused on food technology, dietary management, and hospital food service requirements.

Mother joined and eventually served as president of the Hospital, Institution, and Educational Food Service Society (HIEFFS), a professional food service organization representing fifteen states. The organization has reorganized and is now known as the Association of Nutrition & Food Service Professionals, located in Saint Charles, Illinois.

Mother had a great love of gospel music and was one of the founders of The Good News Quartet. The quartet recorded an album titled *I Want to Thank Him* in the 1980s, in the studios of Prestige Productions in Birmingham, Alabama. The members of the quartet, at that time, were Cloteel Dawson, Mary Hill, Mildred Walker (who played piano), Harmon Dawson, Willard O'Quinn (bass guitar), and Jimmie Ryles. The album included the following songs: I Want to Thank Him; What a Lovely Name; When my Feet Touch the Streets of Gold; The Prodigal Son; Come Morning; Walking in the Sunshine; Is That Footsteps That I Hear; The Lighthouse; That Wonderful Country; Let the Church Roll On; Tell the

King I Accept His Invitation; I'm Standing on the Solid Rock. Also accompanying the quartet were Randy Wright on the organ, Ted Crabtree on steel, and Goldie Ashton on drums.

The Good News Quartet

Mother's favorite songs, which were sung at her funeral, were "It Will Be Worth It All," "I'll Fly Away," and "It Is Well With My Soul."

Mother was just as proficient in knowing the Bible and its teachings as Dad was. She had several favorite scriptures, including John 3:16 (King James Version): For God so loved the world, that he gave his only begotten Son, that whosoever believeth in him should not perish, but have everlasting life. Her other favorites were 1 Timothy 6:11–12; 2 Timothy 4:1–8; 1 Corinthians 15:1–4; 2 Corinthians 12:19; and Proverbs 17:22.

Ethel Sapp met Mother in 1963 when our family moved to Snipesville, Georgia. They immediately hit it off and became best friends. Ethel and her husband, JW, had been members at Mt. Pleasant Baptist Church for many years before our family arrived. Their daughter, Wanda, also became a family friend.

Ethel, a nursing assistant, worked at the Jeff Davis Hospital for twenty-nine and a half years. This was during the time that Mother was the dietary manager at the hospital. Years later they both attended Elizabeth Baptist Church.

Almost every time I visited with Mother and Dad … Ethel was there. She and Mother were almost inseparable, like sisters. When I talked to Mother on the phone, she had just seen, talked to, or was about to see Ethel. I don't think that I have ever witnessed two friends who were any closer.

Following my dad's death, Ethel was over at the house offering comfort and doing anything to ease our pain. She, along with many others, brought food to our home that would feed an army. At one meal, we had plenty of meat and vegetables, but no bread. I went into the kitchen and saw Ethel making homemade biscuits. I had eaten her biscuits before and knew they were awesome. I eased over to her at the kitchen counter as she was making the biscuits and whispered, "Ethel, you are going to have to show me how to make these biscuits."

She leaned over and whispered in my ear, "Formula L."

"What did you say?" I asked.

"Formula L," she said. "They have it at Harvey's grocery store here in Hazlehurst."

After I got back home, I found Formula L Biscuit Mix by searching the Internet. It is a complete biscuit mix with golden shortening flakes made by Southern Biscuit. I thought all along that Ethel's biscuits were her recipe from her grandmother or great aunt. She asked me not to share her secret. I promised, but Ethel is now in Heaven with mother, and I am sure it is okay to share her biscuit recipe. She said, "Just follow the directions, including adding buttermilk."

Ethel died on March 13, 2018, at the age of eighty-eight. She was buried in the Hazlehurst Memorial Cemetery in Hazlehurst. Thank you, Ethel, for being Mother's best friend and confidante.

I found in Mother's files a letter and a note that she had saved because they meant so much to her. I contacted the authors, and they permitted me to share them. The first is from **Hanna and Johnny Rogers.**

January 8, 2011

(Great) Aunt Mary,

We were so glad to get your letter! Trust me it brightened our day! We also enjoyed our visit. We were hoping to come back this weekend, but Johnny got put on call. But that's ok; the Lord will send us that way soon.

And don't worry, if there is one thing that I have had to learn, that is you will never get anywhere in life if you don't work hard for it. I am very headstrong about what I want. I try to make the best out of what I can. Johnny and I may not have everything we want, but trust me, we have everything we need.

And I was so glad to hear that you will pray for me … please do. It almost made me want to bust out in tears because for the last seven or eight months, I was really starting to think that no one cared about me anymore. And even with you not knowing me, it touched me to know someone still cares as much as you. I just can't tell you how much just sitting and talking with you lightened up my day. We left your house with smiles on our faces and joy to know you all care. It means a lot to me to know that with Johnny I did do something right. I am so glad you all approve of him. This is something my mother couldn't even say to me.

But none the less you all filled us with laughter, and we loved it. We will have to come over and sit and talk again real soon. We love you, Hanna and Johnny

P.S. Hope you had a wonderful New Year!

The second is a thank-you card from **Judy Ricketson Carter:**

Mr. and Mrs. Hill,

You are wondering why I am writing you a Thank You card. I just want you both to know that you were two of the few people in my life that had faith in me and I know you said many prayers for me in years past. You loved me no matter what and never gave up on me. Going through having Jammie at 15 and cancer at 29 and lots of other things, I could not even touch on how it made me strong in my faith. I thank God for putting people like you in my life. There will always be a special place in my heart for you both. Please pray that God can use my life as a witness for him and that I may do what he is leading me to do. Pray that I can always do whatever I set out to do for him willingly. For that is my only goal. I love you both very much. I will see you Sunday. Love, Judy

Mother sent thousands of cards and notes, not only to her children and grandchildren but to friends and acquaintances alike.

This is a letter that she sent me on my fiftieth birthday:

Dear Jimmy,

On July 10, 1947, God sent us a little baby boy. This was a very special event because you were our firstborn. I was too young to be a mother; I didn't know a thing about caring for or raising a baby. I know this now, but I didn't know it at the time. I'm sure that I made mistakes, blunders, and boo-boos. Please forgive me.

In spite of all the boo-boos I made, you have done well. You have excelled in everything you set out to do and we are proud of all your accomplishments. God has richly blessed you and your family. He has blessed you with a wonderful wife and two wonderful children. You can be, and I know you are, proud of all of them. I am too.

May God continue to bless you on this your special day. May you have the best birthday ever. May God bless you with good health, lots of love, happiness, and peace.

I love you very much,

Mama

On October 21, 1988, Gail and I received a note from Mother, just a few weeks after we had spent nearly three weeks with her and Dad following her knee-replacement surgery. In the first paragraph of the note she said, "I appreciate the computer you have given me, and I can't wait to use it." She finished the note as follows: "Jimmy, I am so blessed to have a grown son who will still stay with me in the hospital. Many mothers don't have this opportunity. Thank you so much. Love you all, Mama."

My mother always sent me the greatest birthday cards. I never asked her about it, but she must have spent an inordinate amount of time selecting birthday cards. They always were very meaningful, and she would underline key words and write little notes to me. I have saved those cards. You know, nobody loves you like your mother. On those days when things are not going so well, I can pull out one of those cards and everything seems better.

When my Dad turned seventy, we had a big party for him, and it began a tradition: he had a big birthday party every year after that, and he would receive money as gifts. Mother always had quieter celebrations, and as a child, she had never had any birthday parties at all. So, my siblings and I decided for her eightieth birthday to give her a surprise party and to ask attendees to give her money.

I also sent a request to the White House Greetings Office to recognize Mother on that special birthday. I asked if they would do our family the honor of sending Mother a greeting from the president for this milestone in her life. They did, and we received it in time to present it to her at the party.

We surprised Mother with her birthday celebration on the day she turned eighty, February 4, 2012, at the Elizabeth Baptist Church Fellowship Hall. Over eighty friends and family members were in attendance, with some traveling from as far away as Maryland and Illinois.

My siblings and I had begun planning the event in November 2011, all the while maintaining secrecy. The fellowship hall was decorated with birthday banners and table runners. Guests wore birthday hats during the two-hour event and were treated to ice cream, mixed nuts, chips, and punch. The celebration was topped off by the bringing out of two birthday cakes, covered in candles, and the presentation of a birthday scrapbook full of letters and cards from family and friends.

Linda, Jimmy and Jerry with Mother at her 80th Birthday Party

Mother's family and friends contributed nearly $2,500 for her birthday. She was beyond ecstatic.

I wrote Mother this letter on her eightieth birthday:

February 4, 2012

Dear Mother,

It is your 80th birthday! Can you believe it? Where has the time gone? It seems just like last week that we were in Gardi, Georgia, living in the tar paper shack that you and Dad built. I can barely remember the shack, but I do have fond memories of those days in Gardi.

I remember Dad going to work and you staying home with us. I remember the good times of you allowing me to play in the woods and the creek. I remember playing cowboys and Indians almost every day. I remember the stick horse and the BB gun. I remember the sandy dirt road and how we played hard all day and had no problem sleeping at night. I remember the great meals that you prepared for us like oatmeal for breakfast (I still love it); dried beans, rice, and ketchup (I love that too!), and other assorted country meals.

I remember our first black-and-white TV and watching the Ed Sullivan Show. I remember my first experience with education and that you had to travel to school and get me to go into the first-grade classroom. I was extremely upset that they had closed the Gardi School before I had a chance to be officially enrolled there. Attending the Gardi School was my first big goal in life, and it was taken away from me. I remember you consoling me and telling me that everything was going to be okay.

I remember that we did not have a lot of material possessions, but you made up for it with love, compassion, and care. When times were tough. we didn't know about it because you always had that smile and upbeat attitude. I remember when you would make our clothes. We thought we were so special in that you put our initials on our shirts. I think the clothing manufacturers stole that idea from you. Now they put their names on clothes instead of people's names.

I am so proud to call you my mother. You still seem so upbeat and happy when I talk to you. And I know that there were times you could not have felt that, but it never showed.

You always ask what I am doing that particular day or week. You always ask about Gail, Chris, and Miranda and now the grandkids. You always seem to relish knowing what we are all doing and experiencing. True love and caring!

You are an inspiration to not only me, my family, but to all of those who know you. You have created an unbelievable legacy for all of us to aspire to reach. Your dumpling business amazes all of us who know you. You have impacted thousands of lives as a result of starting and operating that business. I know that you have encouraged hundreds of people to pursue their dreams as a result of your success.

Your love of people and your unselfishness have made an impact on all of us—family and friends. Your faithfulness in serving the Lord is beyond question. Your life has been a shining light on the hill that all of us admire.

When people ask the question—what have you done with your life? Your answer does not need words ... your life and your actions speak louder than words. I only hope to aspire to be the kind of person that you are and to have an impact on people like you have had during these 80 years. I love you so much!

What are we going to do for your 100th Birthday?

Your oldest son, Jimmy

Mother's death was totally unexpected. Gail and I had visited with her during the Thanksgiving holidays in November 2012. We arrived at Mother's house on Wednesday, November 21, and stayed with her until Sunday afternoon, November 25. Due to various circumstances, we were the only family members with Mother on Thanksgiving Day. We prepared a meal of turkey, dressing, and all of the sides. It was a great weekend, and she was doing great. Since Dad had passed, she had seemed to recover her strength and was busy with friends and doing all the things that she had wanted to do for a long time.

Mother mentioned that she had a colonoscopy scheduled for Monday, November 26, at the Tift Regional Medical Center in Tifton. My sister, Linda, was picking Mother up and taking her to the hospital and would be with her during the procedure. Linda called me on Monday, after the procedure, and told me that the doctor had punched a hole in Mother's colon and that they had to do emergency surgery to save her life. A major problem was that she had multiple medical issues and was not a good candidate for surgery. I thought the colonoscopy was for some recent medical issues. I found out, after the fact, that the procedure was a routine colonoscopy. At her age, eighty, I was not sure that she should have had the procedure. My sister said that Mother was under sedation and had not woken up after the procedure. I asked her to keep me informed.

On Wednesday, November 28, Linda called and said that Mother was not doing well and that I needed to come to Tifton. Gail and I packed and left almost immediately. When we arrived in Tifton, Mother was not any better. There was a man in the room with her who I did not know. He came over and shook my hand and said that he was Mother's doctor. I didn't know until he left that he was the doctor who had performed the colonoscopy.

Over the next six days, she did not improve and continually got worse. By Tuesday, December 4, it became obvious that she was not going to survive. Mother had signed a Do Not Resuscitate (DNR) order, and it was up to me and my siblings to carry out her wishes.

My brother Jerry and his wife Glenda were in the room on that fateful morning, visiting with Mother. Jerry sat in a chair by her bed and held her hand. As he was sitting there in silence, he heard a voice, "Jer-ree, it is going to be okay."

He quickly turned to see who was in the room … there was no one there except Glenda. He said, "Glenda did you hear that?"

"What?" she said.

My brother knew that voice. It was an old friend of many years—an African American preacher. The preacher had always called him Jer-ree. However, he was not in the room. Jerry stood up and took a moment to ponder what he had heard. He had always received great spiritual advice from his preacher friend. They had met many years earlier when Jerry was working for a building contractor in Douglas, Georgia. They had become fast friends as he helped his preacher friend with a church construction project. The preacher had been to Jerry's home on many occasions. Jerry knew his friend was a godly man, and he had shared his spiritual wisdom with Jerry many times. Jerry always felt rejuvenated after a visit or phone call with him.

Jerry and Glenda, along with Linda and her husband, Jerry, were with Gail and me in the room when the doctor came in to talk with us about removing our mother from life support. Mother's pastor, Reverend Keith Yawn, was in the room with us and led us in prayer.

Disconnecting Mother from life support was the single hardest decision that we siblings had to make in our lives. Just a few days earlier, Mother had been so happy and feeling good. I was extremely excited for her as she seemed to be doing so well.

As we were standing in the hospital ICU room, machines were beeping, lights were flashing, and the monitors were showing squiggly lines. Just before the removal of life support, Jerry said that he could not stay as the life support was removed. He and Glenda left. I promised to call him when Mother had passed.

I will never forget when the doctor and nurse removed the life support hoses and cables from Mother. The machines quit instantly, and the noise was silenced. The quietness was heartrending. I have never experienced anything like that.

The doctor explained that Mother would probably open her eyes for a few moments before she quit breathing and her heart stopped. She did wake up and look around the room, and I felt she looked directly at me with no smile ... just a blank look. After looking around, she closed her eyes, and her breathing slowed down. Her heart eventually stopped. The doctor announced her time of death at 3:05 p.m. on December 4, 2012. It seemed as if the whole world stopped for that moment in time.

I felt like my heart had been ripped out of my chest. I could not say a word. I had tears flowing down my cheeks. It seemed like an hour before she passed, but I am sure it was just minutes. As she passed, Linda and I and our spouses could not move for a few minutes as we were taking in what had just transpired. It was so hard to believe that she was gone. I called Jerry on his cell phone to let him know that Mother had passed.

Mother had multiple health issues, and we knew that instantly she was relieved of those issues and was joining Dad in Heaven. We also knew that she would now be "The Dumpling Lady" in Heaven.

Mother's service was held on Friday, December 7, 2012, at Elizabeth Baptist Church in Hazlehurst. Her service was conducted by Reverend Keith Yawn and Jimmie Ryles. Grandsons Ricky Day and Jerry Hill Jr. spoke as well.

She was buried next to Dad in the Hazlehurst Memorial Cemetery in Hazlehurst, Georgia. She requested the following verse be placed in the funeral program:

Let not your heart be troubled: ye believe in God, believe in me. In my Father's house are many mansions: if it were not so, I would have told you. I go to prepare a place for you. And if I go and prepare a place for you, I will come again, and receive you unto myself; that where I am, there ye may be also. John 14:1–3

Mother had three living children, eight grandchildren, twenty-two great-grandchildren, and recently one great-great-grandchild was added.

27

The Jimmy and Gail Hill Family

Brenda Gail Hobbs Hill and I have had a wonderful life together. I described earlier how we met and eventually married. Gail has been a wife, lover, mother, partner, inspirer, medic, neighborhood mother, contributor, supporter, calmer, counselor, mentor, engineer, and an all-around female "MacGyver." In the 1980s and 1990s, my job required that I travel a lot, and Gail had to manage things at home. She was always able to handle the whole kit and caboodle, anything and everything that was thrown at her and the kids.

I am so proud to call her my wife and partner. She is my counselor and mentor. She is the one who will keep me straight if I have a crazy idea or am about to step off a cliff. Many times, I will argue with her but, in the long run, she is almost always right. I cannot imagine my life without her

Jimmy and Gail celebrating 50th Anniversary

all of these years. We celebrated our fifty-first wedding anniversary in 2020.

Over the years, I have shared with her and with many people that the awards that I have received, in many cases, should have been given to her. She doesn't particularly like to be in the spotlight, but when she is, she is awesome. At one of our Georgia Agri-Leaders Forum institutes, I called on Gail to make some comments. Her words inspired me and the class members.

Gail and I formed The Hill Group Inc. in 1996. She joined the firm full-time in 1997 to help me with the growing business opportunities we were afforded. Again, Gail was a full partner in helping to manage and operate the firm. She traveled all over the country with me as we worked with various organizations and companies. We were a little unsure at first if we could work together, but, at Gail's suggestion, found the right way to blend our strengths and weaknesses and were able to create an excellent workflow plan.

During our years of managing the Georgia Agri-Leaders Forum, Gail was also a mentor and counselor to the hundreds of men and women who came through the leadership program. We received many thank-you letters from class members, and they always thanked Gail for her warm and inviting demeanor. Many letters came in thanking her for mentoring them and for making the leadership program so inspirational in their lives.

Gail was also the lead person in buying and managing the *Southern Festivals* newspaper. She was the editor and publisher, and the one who made the monthly publication happen, while I provided her with input and support and was the newspaper's sales manager.

She is also a consummate graphic artist and designer. During her years with THG, she taught herself over twenty computer programs. She did all of the work in designing, writing, and publishing the *Southern Festivals* newspaper.

Gail helped start the *Troup County News* in the west Georgia community of LaGrange. The paper started as a one-sheet, front-and-back, weekly news update, and it eventually became a thrice-weekly newspaper, with twenty-four to thirty-two pages, and the official newspaper for Troup County. Gail was the paper's graphic artist and designer. She also mentored the owner and publisher.

A few years later, Gail was recruited to work for the Forsyth County Sheriff's office. She was in the Crime Scene Evidence Department for about three years and was then offered a position in the Human Resources Department, which she eventually headed up, handling all of the paperwork in recruiting and hiring of civilians and sworn officers. She retired in 2018.

Gail has always been able to do whatever is needed in any area in which she has worked. One of her amazing talents is the ability to take any troubling situation and turn it around. Not only that, but she excels in providing great customer service and building rapport with fellow employees.

She now designs and creates jewelry using semi-precious gemstones. Gail also loves to bring vintage jewelry back to life, reimagining it in new designs and applications.

Below is a photo of Gail's family from years ago. Gail's Daddy was a hard-working farmer/home builder and her Mama was always by his side. She was a wonderful cook and I loved to tease her constantly.

Gail's Family: Wendell, Ruth (deceased) Gwen, Gail and Kay in her Mama's kitchen

I retired in 2018, as well, and we are now enjoying our retirement on Tomahawk Mountain. However, our focus right now is writing and publishing this book.

Gail and I have two children and six grandchildren. There were two things that we drilled into our kids: to get a good education and to develop a good work ethic. Each of them had jobs at various times that taught them about doing hard—and sometimes unappealing—work. For example, when Gail worked for a firm in Grayson that needed janitorial service for the office, she hired our children for the work, starting with Chris. Each weekend he had to clean, dust, and vacuum the office, including cleaning the bathrooms. Of course, he didn't particularly like the bathroom duty, but he did it. Chris also worked for Pizza Hut as a pizza maker. He brought home some awesome pizzas that he made. When Chris became a pizza maker, Miranda took over the cleaning duties at Gail's office. I believe this helped them to appreciate that working hard to earn compensation gives you a greater understanding of the free enterprise system. Also, no work is beneath you, no matter who you are.

Chris was a wrestler in high school. He was always asked to wrestle one level above his regular weight class. Many times, he was up against a kid who might weigh twenty, thirty, or more pounds above his class. One of the amazing things about Chris was his lack of fear when it came to wrestling one of the biggest kids on the other team. I never saw him hesitate when entering the ring, even though there was a good chance that he would be beaten. I was so proud of him, and I believe that experience of facing a giant and not being afraid has served him well in life.

For his graduation gift, Chris requested a "new" vehicle. Gail and I agreed to help him get one. I told him to do his research to find what he wanted. After a few months of due diligence, he decided on a 1965 Mustang. I almost croaked in thinking about what one might cost. However, I challenged him to find one.

Both Chris and Miranda were given the choice of where we would take our family summer vacation before they became a high school senior. They both chose Maine. During these trips, to eliminate discussion of who could stop the journey and when, we adopted a rule that any of us could stop the vehicle at any location.

In Maine, Chris chose to stop at a garage sale. He found a wheel cover for a 1965 Ford Mustang, and that was the beginning of his Mustang. After the summer was over, he started his senior year looking for a Mustang. He told me one evening that he had found one in Dahlonega, Georgia. He and I called and made an appointment to see the vehicle. The man selling the car was a retired teacher. Chris drove the car, and we decided to buy it. The man showed us a receipt indicating where the engine had been rebuilt. We felt pretty confident about the mechanical side of the car. The interior needed some repair, and the heater was not working, but with my background of having helped my dad fix vehicles, we chose to buy the car and to tackle it as a father and son project.

Chris Hill on Graduation Day with his 1965 Mustang

After a couple of weeks of our working on the Mustang, Chris cranked it one day, and the exhaust was smoking excessively. I took it to a mechanic, who analyzed the problem: the rings were gone in the engine. I had the seller's invoice, which showed the car had new rings installed and a complete engine overhaul before we bought it. We had to spend hundreds of dollars to replace the rings and other components because the engine had never been touched inside.

Our mechanic did a great job, and the car ran well. Chris and I replaced the inside door panels and floor carpet and installed a new radio, which was just like the old AM radio but with the addition of FM. We found the problem with the heater: the hot water line that ran to the inside heater coil had been kinked, preventing water from flowing through. We straightened the hose and had warm air inside the vehicle. The next job was to get the car painted. Chris decided to paint it the same color, which was dark blue. The inside was white, and with the refinished blue bodywork, the '65 Mustang looked awesome. We finished the car in time for his senior prom and graduation.

Chris had been accepted to the University of Georgia College of Agricultural and Environmental Sciences and was heading there in the fall of 1990. During his first year there, his science and math courses were proving to be a real challenge. He was beginning to feel that his veterinarian career was not going to happen. UGA decided to suspend his studies for a while.

Gail and I decided that he should attend Abraham Baldwin Agricultural College in Tifton, Georgia, and return to UGA later. He attended ABAC for five quarters and then headed back to UGA.

Chris had always liked to write but had never given serious thought to it as a career. He now decided to move in that direction. While at ABAC, he became the executive editor of the school newspaper, *The Stallion*, and was a correspondent for the *Tifton Gazette*. He also worked as a disc jockey with the campus radio station. It seemed as if the communication field might be his wheelhouse. Chris was making great grades at ABAC, including being on the dean's list. Rachel, his longtime girlfriend, also attended ABAC during the time he was there.

Chris returned to UGA and graduated in 1994 with a Bachelor of Science in agriculture, majoring in agricultural communications and with a minor in agribusiness. Rachel also left ABAC to attend the University of

Georgia and earned a Bachelor of Science in Education, with a specialization in corporate health promotion and behavior.

During Chris's college years, he interned over the summer breaks, first with the Georgia Department of Agriculture, in their Communications Department, and then with Georgia Power Company, also in the Communications Department.

After graduation, he moved back home for a while as he searched for a job and a career. His first job was with *Through the Green*, a trade publication for the Georgia Golf Course Superintendents Association. His next job was as an editor of medical evaluations for NHP Partners. Chris also worked as a production assistant for the *Atlanta Journal-Constitution* for just under a year.

His first full-time career position was with Poultry & Egg News Inc. in Gainesville, Georgia, where he worked for over two years. Chris was the production coordinator responsible for page layout and design of the company's three publications. He was also responsible for the design of special supplements to the publications.

His next move was to AGCO Corporation in Duluth, Georgia, as a communication specialist in the Marketing Communications Department. He stayed with them for almost a year, providing support to the day-to-day management and activities for the advertising and public relations of more than a dozen of the company's agricultural brands. He was also responsible for writing and disseminating news releases, working with the internal creative department on the development of advertising materials and product literature, and assisting with media relations.

Chris's next position was back to Poultry & Egg News for three and a half years. He was named the editor of *Poultry Times* and its related publications, *Poultry and Egg Marketing* and *Guide to Poultry Associations*.

After dating for several years, Chris and Rachel became engaged. Christopher Jimmy Hill and Rachel Manley were married on November 18, 1995. They moved into an apartment in Gwinnett County, Georgia, and ultimately purchased a home in Lawrenceville, Georgia.

In 2005, Chris accepted a job with Time Inc. Southern Progress, which published *Southern Living Magazine* in Birmingham, Alabama. Southern Living had a subsidiary that published magazines for other companies, such as Lowe's. For over five years, Chris was responsible for writing, editing, and publishing the Lowe's *Creative Ideas* magazine.

He had gained a lot of experience in publishing the magazine for Lowe's and decided to become a contract writer, editor, illustrator, and wood craftsman, providing writing, editing, and publishing services for the woodworking industry. He also did work for the HGTV and DIY websites. He still, occasionally, takes on contract work.

Chris worked from 2015–2017 as a senior editor of *Equipment World Magazine* with Randall-Reilly in Tuscaloosa, Alabama. He covered the road construction industry, including equipment and national policy, and was a finalist for numerous writing awards. He made several international

William, Ben, Jon, Chris and Rachel Hill

trips including a ten-day adventure in China, where he attended an equipment trade show and visited the headquarters, training center, and manufacturing facilities of a large Chinese construction equipment manufacturer.

His current position is with *Progressive Farmer* magazine. He was named managing editor of the magazine in 2017. He oversees the day-to-day editing and production of fourteen issues of *Progressive Farmer* annually. Also, he covers the off-road vehicle and truck industries and manages a staff of seven, including senior editors and production managers.

Chris and Rachel live in Alabama, along with their three boys, William, Ben, and Jon. Rachel works at a public library.

Gail and I are known as Nana and Papa to all of our grandchildren. We shared some fun times with the Hill boys, and I am glad that we recorded some of these events and tales.

In December 2006, we traveled to Alabama to visit with our son and his family for Christmas. Our grandsons were as excited to see their Nana and Papa as we were to see them. William was seven, Ben was five, and Jon was three. All three boys were so well-behaved and polite. In the middle of Christmas dinner, Ben suddenly said, "Mom and Dad, thank you for a great Christmas meal!" These boys were trained to say, "Yes, sir," and "No, sir," and, following a meal, "May I be excused from the table?" I know that I am bragging, but how many children can and will say those things? Their mother, Rachel, is the one that we owe so much to for their upbringing. She is such a great mother and has the patience of Job in teaching these boys.

We all attended church on Christmas Eve night and had a great time. We got to experience the real reason for the season—Jesus Christ. Ben sat between Papa and Nana for most of the service. His first question to me was, "When do we get to light the candle?" We had been handed a candle for use during the last part of the service. He could not wait, nor could I, but we did. It was good to be in God's house for this special event.

The pastor of the church conducted a children's sermon during the service. All of the children in the church went down to the front and sat around him. He showed them a Christmas package that was damaged, with the inside contents broken. He talked about how our lives can be broken and damaged, but that Jesus can repair them. He kept shaking the package, and the sound of the broken pieces got louder and louder. The children urged him to open the package. Of course, his intent had not been to open it but to use it as part of his sermon. The chants started, and they got louder and louder: "Open the present, open the present!" Even I wanted him to open it! The pastor momentarily lost control of the situation but regained it quickly. A word of advice to that pastor—never let a child take over the sermon, or you are in real trouble.

Christmas morning arrived, and we got to experience the excitement of the boys coming downstairs and seeing what Santa Claus had brought them. If you haven't done this lately, you need to do it. It will bring you a renewed spirit of life and serve as a reminder of why grandparents enjoy grandchildren so much. The look in the children's eyes as they experience this event is awesome.

Gail and I enjoyed the time that we got to spend with our grandboys and could not wait until the next time. It had brought back such wonderful memories of Christmases when Chris and Miranda were small. Had it already been twenty-five years? How time does fly when you are having fun!

We decided, in late June 2007, to invite the two older grandboys to spend a week with us. William was almost eight years old, and Ben was six.

We traveled on a Monday morning, June 25, to pick up the boys at their other grandparents' home, about an hour and a half from us. We were instructed to pick them up at exactly 9:00 a.m. When we got there, the boys were standing on the driveway with their luggage in hand and ready to go. Their dad and mother said that they had been ready to go for about a week. We loaded their luggage in our vehicle, and they said their goodbyes.

Lunchtime came as we were nearing our home in the North Georgia mountains. The boys saw the Golden Arches. Our lunch at McDonald's was defined by overturned drinks, dropped napkins, catsup faces, and wonderful hamburgers.

We arrived home to find our two canines waiting for us. Bear, the Corgi-Pomeranian mix, met us at the door, followed by Ree (Anniversa-ree), the Shih Tzu-Poodle mix. The dogs and the boys played together all week. I am not sure who was more tired every night, but all slept well.

We awoke early on Tuesday, as we did every day, with the boys piling into bed with us. Nana had a doctor's appointment in Cumming. We got the grandboys ready and headed to Cumming. They did not like the doctor's office. I kept them occupied while Nana went in for her appointment. Those two boys could talk the ears off an elephant. But I survived.

We made a stop at the pet store on the way home. Every pet in the store had to be visited, as well as those on the way in and on the way out of the store. We almost brought pets home with us but were able to withstand the pressure and say no.

The rest of the day was spent playing and answering questions. Nana prepared a great meal that the boys liked, and soon it was 8:30 p.m., bedtime. Wow, how quiet it was!

Wednesday was spent playing with toys and answering more of their questions. I have a collection of small-scale tractors, and the boys loved to play with them on every visit to our home. Only one of the tractors was battery-powered, and two boys wanted to operate it. I threatened to cut it in half but finally got them to take turns. I told them all about my knife collection. Each knife had a history, and we spent an hour talking about those knives. The boys were so interested that we did the knife-history lesson twice. We again played with the toy tractors ... and then again (we played lots of tractor games).

I assigned William a special project: he was to take a hammer and pound back in the nails that had come loose on our two decks. I gave him a few minutes of training, and he went to work. He did a great job. I gave Ben a project to work on as well. Both boys earned allowances for the week. Bedtime came again, and it was so quiet.

The boys crawled into our bed around six o'clock on Thursday morning, and the day started. We had promised to take them to see their great-grandparents in South Georgia. We loaded the vehicle with toys, food, car seats, water, and many, many questions and headed south.

We decided to take the boys to Lane Packing Company, which is about five miles off Interstate 75, below Macon. Lane Packing Company is a multifaceted facility where you can buy peaches, peach ice cream, peach preserves, peach candy, peach bread, and just about anything peach. They also have a restaurant. We bought some peaches to share with family and neighbors. Of course, we had to partake of the delicious peach ice cream.

We traveled on to Hazlehurst and visited with my parents. Nana cooked supper for all of us that evening. The boys had a great time and had plenty of questions for their great-grandparents. After dinner, we drove to Tifton to spend the night. What an experience! Trying to get two boys bathed, dressed, and to bed was what I would call an extreme challenge. We finally accomplished the impossible and got them to sleep before 11:00 p.m.

The next morning, we awoke early, as usual, and got ready to go pond fishing. We had promised William and Ben that we would take them fishing in their great-grandfather's fishpond, just outside of Tifton. The boys had been excited ever since we had purchased the worms, the day before. We arrived at their great-grandfather's farm and immediately headed for the pond, which was just behind the house. It took a few minutes to get the poles ready and baited. We started fishing. Ben fished for about five minutes and reached his tolerance level, or should I say his patience limit. William was a serious fisherman. He stuck with it, and yes, he hung his line a few times. However, he caught the most fish for the day. We decided to put the fish back in the pond to catch another day. Then they got to ride with their great-grandfather on his lawnmower. Another great day of grandparenting!

We set off for home after lunch. On our way back, we saw a sign on the interstate for Cordele Farmers' Market. We decided to stop and see what we could find and left with a box of tomatoes, several cantaloupes, and two watermelons.

As we were driving north on the interstate, Ben pulled something from behind the front seat and said, "Papa, I found a picket sign." I looked in the rearview mirror and saw that he was holding a funeral home fan that we had put in the vehicle at some point. As I was watching him, he turned the fan around—the face of Jesus was on the back. "Papa, it's a Jesus picket sign," he said.

"How do you know that is a picket sign?" I asked him.

"I have seen them on TV."

I nearly ran off the road laughing.

We went back by way of Lane Packing Company to make another ice cream stop. That peach ice cream was exceptionally good. When we arrived home late that evening, everybody was worn to a frazzle. Bedtime could not come soon enough.

As I had been thinking, during the week before their visit, about what the boys and I could do together, I had seen an article on Facebook about a book entitled *The Dangerous Book for Boys*. I had decided that I needed to order the book. Amazon had delivered it on Tuesday; however, I could never find time to read it. I did scan it after they left and resolved to use it for future visits with the boys. It was full of important facts and other valuable information: how to hunt and cook a rabbit; marbles; the seven wonders of the ancient world; how to play stickball or build a treehouse; fishing; how spies communicate with codes and ciphers; girls; how to call turkeys and construct turkey traps. The book included these and many more interesting facts that boys must know before reaching manhood.

I happened to have a turkey call that I had bought many years earlier, and on Saturday I found it and explained how it worked; the boys went onto our deck and called turkeys for hours. William had an idea to construct a turkey snare. He went around to the side of our house and placed the snare. Unfortunately, he never caught a turkey.

As I looked through my workshop, trying to find things the boys could do, I found two toolboxes. One was my first toolbox, which I had bought at the age of eighteen. The other I had purchased when I was twenty-one. I told William and Ben that if they helped me clean up the toolboxes, they could each keep one. They worked hard and were rewarded with a toolbox each. I also bought them each a screwdriver set and a pair of pliers as starter tools.

Sunday came. After early breakfast, the boys did their packing. We were due to meet their parents and their younger brother, Jon, for lunch in Douglasville, Georgia, which was about halfway between our homes. They were so excited to see their parents. This was the longest time they had spent away from home.

Nana and I traveled home discussing what a great week we had experienced!

One final note—if you want to learn about marbles, and other important issues in life, get the book *The Dangerous Book for Boys* by Conn and Hal Iggulden. It is a great read and excellent for teaching grandchildren about what we did in the old days.

Since Jon was the youngest, he didn't accompany us early on in our adventures with his two older brothers, but we loved hearing about his antics. Chris told us a story about Jon complaining about being bored one day. Chris told him to dig a hole in the backyard, and he would not be bored. Jon started digging the hole and kept digging until it was nearly as deep as he was tall. When Chris asked him how much deeper he was going to dig the hole, Jon said, "I don't know, but maybe to the other side of the earth." His dad told him to fill the hole up, as he was concerned about the sides caving in. Jon filled up his newly dug hole, and when he had finished, declared that he was still bored.

He seems to have overcome his boredom over recent years. Jon is a skillful artist and can draw anything and take any item and figure out how to use it artistically. He also loves the outdoors, as well as hiking and fishing. There is a creek near his home in Alabama, and he spends a lot of time there, which reminds me of another time we had the Hill boys with us, but this time all three of them.

In November 2015, Gail and I decided to invite the Hill boys for a four-day, after-Christmas vacation trip to South Georgia. William was fifteen, Ben was thirteen, and Jon was eleven years old. We picked them up in Lawrenceville, at their other grandparents' home, on Sunday morning, December 27. When we arrived, they were standing in the driveway with their bags packed, and they were excited.

We were headed to a cabin located on a farm owned by a friend. We drove straight to South Georgia and arrived there around 4:00 p.m. A winding, rutted, dirt road led to the cabin. It was very secluded and quiet, set on a huge lake, which looked promising for fishing.

The cabin was very nicely furnished, with two bedrooms, one of which had four bunk beds to accommodate the boys. We had with us all the food and supplies that we would need for the four days, with the expectation that we would catch fish for a meal or two.

Adjacent to the cabin was a large, screened-in area for outdoor dining, and there was a full kitchen of appliances. Several kinds of grills and smokers were available for us to use.

Right behind was a space that was designed for target practice, and there was a nearby forested area, where the boys loved exploring and seeing the wildlife.

I had brought along guns, ammo, and fishing gear for us all. I can tell you they used all three every day while we were there.

We would fish in the morning and do some target practice in the early afternoon; then the boys would go exploring in the forest in the late afternoon. Everybody caught fish almost every day. One morning, William caught a small redbreast. I asked him to save the little fish and called the other two boys over to give them a spontaneous fishing lesson. I told the three of them a fishing commandment that had been passed down through the Hill clan for many years—big fish eat little fish.

I hooked the small fish through the upper body and cast him toward the center of the lake. He made a loud splash, and five seconds later came a bigger splash: a largemouth bass had swallowed the little fish. It was a fight for about six or seven minutes until I got her ashore. I had hoped my big-fish-eat-little-fish lesson would teach the boys the concept, but it took me by surprise when it happened so fast. They were astonished and excited. I found a set of portable deer scales and weighed the bass. Deer scales are not very accurate at low weights, but she was over ten pounds and about twenty-two inches long. We took pictures and put her back into the lake to be caught another day.

Target practice was something the boys had never done. I taught them gun safety and supervised every shot that they made. I think Ben turned into the best marksman. The targets were steel plates hanging from a wooden structure across the lake. Ben would hit them almost every time with my semi-automatic .22 rifle.

Taking a trip like this with our grandsons was awesome. They live in Alabama, and we don't get to see them as often as we would like, so this gave us quality time together with the three of them. I gave them a large bag of the spent brass shells to take home as a memory of our time together.

On Wednesday morning, December 30, we left the cabin and headed in the direction of Alabama. Their dad met us about halfway, in Columbus, Georgia, for a bite to eat. Following lunch, they headed home, and we traveled back to North Georgia.

Our daughter, Miranda, was on the drill team in high school. She stayed busy with drill team practice, attending all of the sports games, and serving on the high school student council.

Yet already as a small child, she was fascinated with astronauts and space. She expressed an interest in flying when she was just three years old. Our family was on vacation in Washington, DC, and we were visiting the Smithsonian National Air and Space Museum. Miranda asked me to put her in one of the planes that were hanging from the ceiling of the museum. I did my best to explain that no one was allowed in those planes, as they were of historical significance. The historical significance did not mean anything to her at that point. She wanted on the plane. As I recall, that was the first time that I learned of her keen interest in aviation, as she exclaimed, "Well, someday I will!"

Her interest continued to build. She remembers, as a fourth grader, seeing the space flight tragedy that occurred on January 28, 1986, when the American Space Shuttle Challenger exploded seventy-three seconds after liftoff. She watched the explosion on television and heard the announcement that all seven astronauts had died. She and Chris were out of school that day due to a teacher workday. Gail received a call from Chris, who said, "Mom, you have to come home. Something is wrong with Miranda." Miranda seemed to be in shock for a couple of days.

We all assumed that she would lose interest in space after the tragedy, but she was convinced that one day maybe she could figure out what went wrong. She told us and her classmates at school that the astronauts had died doing what they loved and that was most important.

Miranda attended a week at the Space Academy in Huntsville, Alabama, while in high school. That experience furthered her interest in being an astronaut.

She started working part-time to earn money to take flying lessons. She found an instructor at Stone Mountain Airport, adjacent to Stone Mountain in DeKalb County, Georgia. It was there that she made her solo flight and earned her pilot's license several years later. She worked at the airport fueling planes and managing the front desk. She also worked at a Rockin' Robin's Diner and at a Famous Footwear store to earn money for her flight lessons. She was determined to pay for her pilot's license herself. And she did.

Miranda taking her solo flight at Stone Mountain Airport

For her high school graduation, Miranda received a vehicle as Chris had. I promised her my Isuzu pickup truck with a stick shift in the floor. She had a never driven a stick shift, so that presented some issues. After a harrowing experience in heavy traffic while crossing a busy four-lane road, we bought her a Chevrolet Cavalier.

Miranda attended two years at the University of Alabama–Huntsville (UAH) studying to be a mechanical aerospace engineer, which was the path most aspiring astronauts followed. However, the mechanical engineering experience led her to realize that what she really wanted to do was to fly planes.

After two years at UAH, she decided to continue her education at Southern Illinois University–Carbondale (SIUC). SIUC was nationally known for its aviation program. She decided to seek a degree in aviation flight and management. While earning her undergraduate degree, she served as a co-captain of The Flying Salukis, SIU's precision flying team. She went on to earn the honor of being named the "nation's top female collegiate pilot" and led her team to a fourth-place finish in the United States.

While at the university, she worked for the SIU airport, fueling airplanes, and in the weather station, advising student pilots on local weather conditions.

After earning her associate degree in aviation flight and then her Bachelor of Science in aviation management in 2001, she was selected as the top intern with Delta Air Lines in Atlanta in the fall of 2001. Right at the start of her internship, she was on duty with Delta during the terrorist attacks on September 11, 2001 (9/11). Following the attacks, the Federal Aviation Administration (FAA) issued an immediate order to redirect every plane in the air to the nearest airport and to ground all planes across the USA. She assisted in arranging hotel accommodations for the flight crews.

The commercial aviation industry shutdown after 9/11 lasted for four days; it then took years to fully recover. As a result, airlines furloughed thousands of pilots and other employees for an extended period. Delta would usually hire their top intern, but as a result of 9/11, they did not offer Miranda a job. She left Delta shortly after that and had to rethink her priorities for what was next in her life. She finally decided to return to

SIUC and earn her flight instructor certificate, to teach ground and flight classes for students. She taught for several years and became a coach for the Flying Salukis student team. Under her and the other instructors' leadership, they produced the next "top female collegiate pilot" two years later.

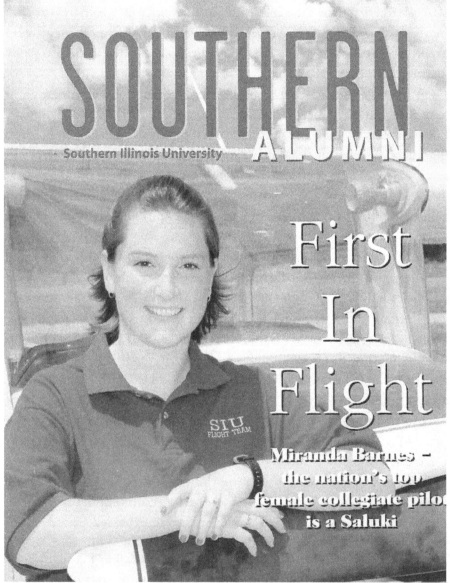

SOUTHERN

Southern Illinois University   ALUMNI

First In Flight

Miranda Barnes – the nation's top female collegiate pilot is a Saluki

Photo courtesy of Southern Alumni-SIU Alumni Association

During her teaching experience, she was able to earn her Master of Science in workforce education and development in 2005. While teaching, she also met her future husband, Pat. He was transferred to her class by another flight instructor who had far more students than Miranda. She and Pat became good friends. As she was telling Gail about Pat, she said, "He flew in under my radar screen." Pat earned his associate degree in aviation flight at SIUC in 2005 and became a part-time flight instructor while completing his Bachelor of Science in aviation management.

After leaving SIUC, Miranda was hired as an assistant chief flight instructor at the Leesburg Executive Airport (LEA) in Leesburg, Virginia. Shortly afterward, she facilitated hiring Pat as a flight instructor at LEA. As a means of earning some extra income, Miranda interviewed with and was hired by the Aircraft Owners and Pilots Association (AOPA). The association has over 500,000 members. She initially assisted in manning their Pilot Information Center, which was a resource for pilot members, providing answers to questions on aviation protocols and other information. Her last full-time job was working for the Air Safety Institute within AOPA.

Miranda Faith Hill and Patrick Thomas Skonie were married on June 11, 2006, at 4:30 p.m. at the SIU Airport. The wedding ceremony was conducted inside the airport with a backdrop of runways and three airplanes. The following day, Pat and Miranda flew in a four-seat Diamond BA-40 airplane back to Leesburg, Virginia, their home at the time.

Shortly thereafter, Pat decided that he was going to pursue a career as an air traffic controller. Miranda and Pat moved to an apartment in Minneapolis. He enrolled in a one-year course, taught at the Minneapolis Community and Technical College in Minneapolis, Minnesota, which led to an associate degree in applied science in air traffic control. The following spring, Miranda found out that she was pregnant and was going to have twins. After graduation, Pat applied to and was hired by the FAA. His next requirement was to attend the FAA Academy in Oklahoma City, Oklahoma.

Miranda called us on Friday night, October 19, 2007, and talked to us about how uncomfortable she was. She did not think she could make it to the twins' projected birth date of December 26. At two o'clock the next morning, Pat called us to say that she was in the hospital and was going to be moved to another hospital that was capable of handling multiple births. He called back at 5:00 a.m. They were at the next hospital, and things had quieted down somewhat. We talked to Miranda at about 11:00 a.m. Then Gail said (and I quote), "I am going to Minnesota!"

I was unable to go with her due to work responsibilities, but I knew my role right then was to get the arrangements made for her to travel to Minneapolis. It was a Saturday, just before noon, and I was on the Internet trying to find a seat on a same-day flight. Finding a plane seat on a weekend was not easy. There were only two flights to Minneapolis that day, and one had already left. I was able to get her a ticket for the 6:00 p.m. flight.

Gail had to pack for a trip of unknown length. She was washing, packing, and worrying. I was working on the logistics of getting her to the airport in time and was counting down the minutes. We live about one and a half hours from the airport, depending on traffic. I kept reminding her that we had to go.

Finally, we got on the road, and everything went great for the first thirty-five minutes. Then it started—traffic delays, one after another. Then came an accident ... then another accident. Time was slipping away. Traffic congestion was horrible, even though it should have been fine on a Saturday afternoon. We arrived at the Atlanta airport at 5:20 p.m.

I screeched the vehicle to a halt in front of the skycap area. Gail jumped out, and I unloaded her luggage (all one hundred and fifty pounds—at least it seemed like it). She rushed to the skycap, and he told her that she would not make the 6:00 p.m. flight. I was having to stay in the vehicle (due to homeland security regulations) and was waiting to make sure she made the flight.

Gail was frantic but determined. I could only hear part of what she was saying as she emotionally and insistently spoke to the skycap about why she could not miss that plane.

As I was trying to listen and see whether she would make the flight, I heard a loud knock on my driver's side window. The policeman did not even listen to my version of what was happening. He just said, "Move on," and, two seconds later, "Move on now." Of course, I moved on. I found a way to circle back by the skycap zone to check on Gail. She was gone. I was able to reach her on her cell phone. She said that the skycap was so moved by her explanation of why she had to catch the flight that he told her, "I am going to get you on that flight."

I continued circling and waiting to hear from Gail. She called just a few minutes later to say: "They're closing the door on the plane, and I have to turn off my cell phone." I felt a huge sense of relief that she had made it.

Gail got to Minneapolis in good time before the girls were born. Although about two months premature, they were healthy and required only a minimal hospital stay of about thirty days. They were very small—about three pounds. Gail spent three weeks in Minneapolis after their birth. The twins were named Emma Regan Skonie and Madeline (Mimi) Hill Skonie. Emma was born one minute before Mimi.

Since Pat still had to attend three months of further training in Oklahoma, we all decided that it would be easiest if Miranda and the twins moved in temporarily with us, and we quickly issued the invitation. They stayed with us for those three months.

During this time, Pat was given a choice of five states for his air traffic controller assignment after his training was completed. Georgia and Illinois (his home state) were on the list. Nothing was open in Georgia, so he decided on Illinois. The location happened to be not far from where he grew up.

He and Miranda both started researching the housing market on the western side of Chicago, close to where he would be working. They selected seventeen houses to look at, and Gail, Miranda, and the twins flew up to Chicago to meet with Pat to view the homes and choose one of them. They chose a townhouse in Yorkville.

As soon as Pat finished his training in Oklahoma City, he drove to Georgia and came to our home in the mountains for a few days before the family traveled to Chicago and their new home.

A few years later, a baby boy joined the Skonie family. Jackson Patrick Skonie was welcomed by the twins, and they loved him dearly.

Pat and Miranda had to enclose an open area upstairs in the townhouse to create a bedroom for Jack. After a few years, they looked for a new home closer to Pat's work and found a house in Batavia, Illinois.

Miranda opened a bakery business in Geneva, Illinois, which she sold a few years later. She is now a part-time baker at home, as well as a full-time homemaker, and is helping her kids with their remote learning at home during COVID-19.

Pat is an air traffic controller in an FAA Center in Illinois. His spare time is spent with Miranda and the three kids.

One of the fun things that I started with the twins when they were very young was pretending not to know my colors. For example, I would mention that Emma had on a beautiful red shirt when, in fact, it would be blue. Emma would say, "Papa this is not red, it is blue." I would insist that it was red.

I would then say to Mimi, "Mimi, you have on a beautiful yellow shirt."

Mimi would say, "No, Papa, this is a green shirt." Again, I would insist that it was yellow.

This drove the girls crazy. I would say the same thing the next day or the next time that I saw them. The girls would say, almost in unison, "Papa, you don't know your colors."

"Yes, I know my colors," I would reply.

The girls would tell Nana that Papa did not know his colors, and she would agree with them.

It got to be routine for us to have this conversation every time that we got together. Finally, the twins came up with a solution. One of them would show me a color, and the other would sit on my lap and whisper the correct color in my ear. I would still choose the incorrect color. The girls would then swap places and repeat the procedure. This continued for years.

There was an occasion when the girls were coming for a visit to our home in the North Georgia Mountains. As they got out of the car upon arrival, they shouted out, "Papa, we are going to teach you the colors in our color school." I could not wait. Emma drew several ladies in multicolored clothing on a sheet of paper. She would point to a color, and I would deliberately get it wrong. Mimi would correct me by naming the correct color. Mimi took her turn in picking a color and asking me to identify the color. Again, I would choose the wrong color. Emma took over the teaching again, and Mimi crawled in my lap and would whisper the correct color as it was pointed out by Emma.

We had so much fun with this color game, but as they got older; they figured out that Papa was teasing them. It sure was fun while it lasted.

I also started telling the girls stories when they were very young. Storytelling became a routine that the girls requested each time we got together. My strategy was to select a picture, item, toy, or something in the room around which I would make up a story. They would sit in my lap and listen. It was hard for me not to laugh as I made up the fantastic stories. As soon as I finished, they would ask me to repeat it. That was a problem: I made the stories so fantastic that I could not remember the details. So, I would say instead, "Have I ever told you girls the story about the bear?"

"No," they would reply. And I would then make up a story about a bear.

When I ran out of subjects, I would ask them to tell me a story instead. Emma would always start her stories with, "On a dark and stormy night." The twins' tales were, without fail, interesting and enjoyable. After every story they told, I would ask them questions about it, and they would share great answers. We had a wonderful time storytelling together.

One morning, during breakfast at their home in Illinois, when the girls were young and becoming inquisitive, Emma had a question for her mom: "How does God know what I like to eat when I get to Heaven?"

Miranda sent this to me in a text and wrote, "How do you respond to this question?" I texted her back: "God knows everything, and he even knows the number of hairs on their heads." Miranda texted back: "They are now counting the hairs on their heads, which will keep them busy for a while."

Miranda, Pat, Mimi, Emma and Jack Skonie

Now they are older, Emma and Mimi are still busy and still telling stories, but of a different kind, creating YouTube channels around their interests. Emma's is based on her love of crafting, which is mainly making bracelets from beads. In working with Gail, who crafts jewelry among other things, Emma fell in love with all things crafty. Mimi's channel is based on her love of baking. She got her love of baking from Gail and from her mother, Miranda. I am amazed by what they produce and by the quality of their videos.

Their brother, Jack, recently created a YouTube channel on his gaming expertise. Jack is one of those young technology experts. I can only imagine what life holds for this young man. As he is the youngest of Miranda's children, we haven't been able to spend as much time with him as we would have liked. He is an experienced gamer and is so fast in his movements that my head spins. I could watch him for hours as he plays— he is so animated in his reactions and far more fun to watch than what is happening on the screen. He is also a card-playing machine. He loves to play, but more importantly, he loves to win. He stayed with Gail and me a couple of summers ago, and we played all kinds of card games. In his early years, he could put puzzles together quicker than I have ever seen for a young child.

Chris and Rachel and Miranda and Pat have raised wonderful children. We are such proud parents and grandparents. They have been taught: to ask to be excused from the dining table, to clear the dishes, help cook, and to do chores.

Despite their living some distance away, we have been lucky to spend time with them. Our grandchildren are now growing up quickly and leaving childhood behind. Still, we look forward to telling more stories, having more adventures, and sharing and making more memories together.

28

Life on Tomahawk Mountain

Gail and I decided, after I left Georgia Power and we started The Hill Group, we could now live wherever we wanted. We both fell in love with the mountains after we moved to Grayson, Georgia, in 1981. As we started working on our personal mission statements and laying out plans for our future, two shared goals emerged: we wanted to make a positive difference for those around us, and we wanted to move to the mountains.

Georgia Agri-Leaders Forum allowed us to address our mission of making a positive difference in the lives of the participants in the Forum. We started thinking about how we would be able to move to the mountains.

I shared with my friend Nancy Hanson of the Georgia Egg Commission our desire to live in the mountains. She and her husband, Bobby Hanson, already lived in the mountains of North Georgia. Bobby was a personality on an Atlanta radio station and used the alias Ludlow Porch on his show. I am referring to him as Ludlow for this book. Nancy invited us to join them for Sunday dinner at their mountain home.

We traveled to Tomahawk Mountain on Sunday, September 14, 1997. The dirt and gravel road leading to the Hansons' house had winding curves and steep inclines. They lived about 0.6 miles off the main road. To the left, as we drove up, was an amazing view of the North Georgia Mountains and the valleys below. On the right side of the road, a high, tree-covered bank of rock and dirt rose upward to the sky. The views took our breath away.

We were greeted at the door by Nancy and Ludlow, who warmly welcomed us in. All along the rear of the house, windows overlooked a panorama of mountains and valleys. We stood there and just took in the view—we were mesmerized. Nancy said, "Dinner is ready. You-all can gaze at the view during and after dinner." The meal was delicious, but I could not take my eyes off the view.

Nancy and Ludlow were wonderful hosts. He was an award-winning radio host, author of seventeen books, and a great storyteller. This was my first time meeting him, but I had listened to him for years on radio stations in Atlanta. He was first on Ring Radio WRNG and eventually had a three-hour daily show on WSB Radio. Ludlow was a trivia expert and humorist and could talk about any subject with anybody. His fans looked forward to his humor and comments about the silliness of life. His show, which was called the Funseekers Radio Network, was eventually syndicated to over sixty stations across the southeastern United States.

I loved spending time with Ludlow because he kept me constantly laughing. Unfortunately, he passed away after health complications on February 11, 2011. His memorial service was held at Big Canoe Chapel in Jasper, Georgia. Gail and I attended the service. One of Ludlow's final requests was to have all of his friends attend a dinner following the service. The food was provided by none other than the world-renowned Varsity Restaurant in Atlanta.

One of the things that Ludlow was known for was playing jokes on his audience. His antics were well-known, and he wrote about them in his books, many of which had hilarious titles, such as *There's Nothing Neat About Seeing Your Feet: The Life and Times of a Fat American* and *Can I Just Do It Till I Need Glasses?: And Other Lies Grown-Ups Told You.* His last book was a collaboration with Emory Jones titled *Zipping Through Georgia … on a Goat-Powered Time Machine with Ludlow Porch and a Parrot Named Pete.*

I remember one of the first things that Ludlow told me about Tomahawk Mountain. He said that when he turned onto the road that led up the mountain, he felt his toes "un-scrunch." I now know what that means. It is another world on Tomahawk Mountain, where you can let go, relax, and unwind. Rest in peace, my friend Ludlow Porch.

Mountain Rainbow

Nancy took us on a quick tour of Tomahawk Mountain. We became more enthused as she showed us around. There was only one road on top of the mountain, with over a dozen homes and several vacant lots. Just about all of the undeveloped lots were owned by people who already lived there. Gail and I saw one lot that we both liked. Nancy told us it was not for sale, but I asked her for the name of the person who owned it anyway. We left Nancy and Ludlow that Sunday after a memorable and generously hosted visit, hoping that Tomahawk Mountain might be our new home in the mountains.

I called the gentleman who owned the lot the next day and inquired about buying it. He went into a long rant about how he had searched for years to find the lot and was planning on building a home there in the future. I listened and responded with, "I want to buy the lot."

"It is not for sale," he told me.

I called him back a few days later and told him again that I still wanted to buy the lot. To make a long story short, he finally agreed to sell, and we bought the lot.

On October 1, 1997, Gail and I came to Tomahawk Mountain to look at what would soon be our property. We met one of the neighbors, Mr. Len Foote, a longtime resident on the mountain and retired firefighter and deputy sheriff. "That view of the valley and mountains changes every five minutes because of the sun and clouds," he said to Gail. He had been observing the changing view for forty years. Unfortunately, Mr. Foote died a few years later.

We closed on the lot on October 10, 1997. Gail and I started thinking about what kind of home we were going to build. We studied house plans for months and could not find a plan that we both liked. The only choice was to draw something up ourselves. Gail was an excellent designer, and I had taken drafting in college, including drawing house plans. We combined our talents and started putting our ideas on paper. I cannot tell you how many plans we started on then scrapped. Finally, Gail found a computer-aided design (CAD) program, which got us on track. It took us about a year before we were comfortable with the plans.

In the meantime, we had been searching for a builder. We wanted somebody with experience in building on top of a mountain that involved extreme sloping on the backside of the home. Finally, we found someone who had built many mountain homes and decided he would fit our needs perfectly. We obtained a construction loan at the bank and signed a contract with him.

The builder started on our home in the early fall of 1998. Rain and icy conditions were a constant issue during construction. Then at one point, in early January, Sheetrock was in short supply, and we had to stop construction for six weeks until it arrived. Once it came and was installed, we got back on schedule. The rest of the work moved pretty fast, and the house was finally finished. We received our certificate of occupancy on May 20, 1999. It had taken nearly eight months to complete the home.

Gail and I started moving in on May 21. We hired a contract mover for the large items and boxed and moved most of our small items ourselves with our Chevy Tahoe and a trailer.

The Hill's home better known as "The Gathering Place"
Photo Courtesy EJS Aerial Photography

The development of Tomahawk Mountain began in the early 1960s. A building contractor bought the land and created a road across the top of Tomahawk Mountain. The road had just enough room on each side for a home site. For many years, the entrance was locked, and only residents had keys. Eventually, as more lots were sold and cabins and homes were built, the entrance lock was removed. The first water supply was spring-fed. The spring is still working today, but we don't use it presently. After a while, a well was drilled and water piped to each home as requested.

I know that wherever one lives, there are probably interesting neighbors with intriguing backgrounds and stories. That is no less true on Tomahawk Mountain. To maintain the privacy of Tomahawk Mountain residents, I will not be naming or identifying those who currently live here. You have already met Ludlow and Nancy, and Mr. Foote. They no longer live on the mountain.

Another neighbor, who became a close friend, was George. He lived two doors down from us, on the same side of the mountain. His view and our view from the back of our lots were known as the long view, which overlooked a wide valley with mountains beyond. The view from the other side of the street was of a narrow valley and close-up mountains and was known as the short view. George was retired and was a military veteran.

Snow on the Mountains

George loved to eat, and we invited him to our house many times for a meal. We also would give him part of every cake, pie, or any kind of dessert that we made. I would call him and say, "Meet me halfway between our homes. I have something for you." He loved fried fruit pies. One day, we bought blueberries and peaches to make Gail's delicious fried pies. We invited him over, and he ate pies until I thought he would collapse. They were just like his mama cooked, he told us. He also baked the best chocolate pie that we had ever eaten. He would make his chocolate pies every year at Thanksgiving and bring us one.

George moved away a few years ago to be closer to his family and medical care. I still miss him, and we talk occasionally.

We have had many occupations represented among our full- and part-time residents on the mountain over the years, from artists and teachers, doctors and lawyers, a forester and a talk-show host, railroad and postal employees, a restaurant owner, a publisher, an Indian chief, and many more. Okay … maybe not an Indian chief. Tomahawk Mountain got its name from a bird's-eye view of the mountain.

One part-time resident was Dr. Ferrol Sams. He and his wife, Helen, were both medical doctors and had owned property on Tomahawk Mountain for many, many years. Unfortunately, both have now passed on.

Dr. Sams was a great gentleman and friend to everybody on the mountain. Sambo, as he liked to be called, was a humorist of the finest sort. The room would light up when he entered. We were at one of our homeowners' association annual meetings one time, and he announced to the room that he was going to sit by Gail when the meeting started. Everyone, including me, looked at him when he said it. "Gail always laughs at my jokes," he said. And she did.

At another annual meeting, which was held at our home, Sambo was coming up my walkway toting an ice chest. I saw him coming, so I walked to the door and, just as he grabbed the door handle, I quickly pulled the door open. He flew horizontally into the foyer about three feet off the floor. Fortunately, I caught him before he landed. I was also glad that he had put the ice chest down before reaching for the door handle. If he hadn't, things could have gone badly with Sambo, the ice chest, and me all in the mix.

He thought it was funny, and we laughed at every annual meeting about that incident.

Sambo told us about an experience he and Helen had when they were on vacation in Europe. They were walking down a city street and came upon a young woman playing an air guitar. He was fascinated by her "guitar-playing" ability and her agility. But as he got closer, he became distracted by her belly button, which he saw was red and infected. Being a medical doctor and always prepared to assist anyone who needed help, he stopped to inspect it.

"Do you know that you have an infection in your navel?" he asked the girl. "That ring in your navel has caused an infection. You need to have it seen right away." She looked at him without saying a word and continued playing the air guitar.

Helen said, "Sambo, let's go!" He followed her, shaking his head.

In addition to Sambo's being a doctor, he was a best-selling novelist. He wrote *Run with the Horsemen, The Whisper of the River, Epiphany,* and *Down Town,* to mention just a few.

He referred to Tomahawk Mountain in his books as it was his favorite place in the world. I sure do miss Sambo and Helen. They were fine people. Gail misses his stories and his great sense of humor.

Snowy mountain road to our home

I guess the founder could have incorporated Tomahawk Mountain and created a city. However, that is what we were trying to escape from—the city. The closest thing that we have to any kind of organized effort is our homeowners' association.

The association meets once a year, and we conclude the meeting with dinner, where everyone brings their favorite dish. What a great way to get to know each other and share our mountain stories.

Gail and I attended our first meeting on September 18, 1998. Before we knew what had happened, Gail was elected secretary and treasurer of the association. It was supposed to be for a one-year term, but as it turned out, she served for nine years.

The other officer roles were chairman, vice-chairman, water commissioner, and road commissioner. At the September 2000 meeting, I was elected to serve as chairman. I eventually served for eight years. At the end of our terms in 2008, Gail and I both declined to serve again. It was time for other homeowners to step up and serve.

The road that leads into Tomahawk Mountain (our only road in the community) originally had a clay surface, and rain or snow would make it almost impassable. We worked with the county in trying to get them to keep it maintained, but they told us that it was not their property. Old association records indicated otherwise. The association hired a lawyer to investigate the records and it was determined that the county did indeed own the road. They took over responsibility for its upkeep, thank goodness, and we now have a hard surface covered with crush and run gravel. It serves our needs very well.

As I mentioned, the water supply on Tomahawk Mountain started with just a spring, and then a deep well was added. As the years went on, and there was more development, the water supply became an issue. During times of drought, we had to supplement the supply by using the spring, which required a lot of work to maintain.

One year during the fall, a person bought a lot on the mountain and went to talk with county authorities about hooking into our water system. The homeowners' association was notified that we were already past the maximum number of hookups allowed by law. This notification brought in state officials. I was chairman of the association at the time and started dealing with this issue, first hiring a lawyer and a professional engineer to determine our way forward. After long meetings and various reviews of water laws, we were permitted to split our water system into two systems. However, they had to be completely separate from each other. This meant we had to drill a second deep well.

Association leadership had several meetings with members to explain the issue and talk about solutions. The members voted to drill the additional deep well (1,000 feet deep) and to install water piping to create two separate systems. Due to financial constraints, the association had to assess each homeowner a fee to pay for this additional well and the associated work. We had some funds built up in the treasury but needed the fee to complete the installation. The monies were collected, and the water system update was completed. This solved our water supply issues—hopefully for many years.

Life on Tomahawk Mountain has provided many stories for us to share with family and friends over the years. Our eclectic collection of neighbors has made mountain life fun and sometimes surprising.

Before we moved in, a resident and his wife came by one day when we were at our homesite. They asked if they could look inside the house. We said sure and invited them in. We were still in the construction stage, but it was safe to walk through. The man's wife said, "Honey, this is about the size of our chalet in Switzerland."

He said, "We don't have a chalet in Switzerland."

She said, "Well, if we did, this is about the size it would be." I am shaking my head in amazement. She then said, "Well, it is about the size of our daughter's house."

"Our daughter's house is a small condo, and this is a large ranch with a basement," he said. She didn't respond.

On another occasion, after we had been living on the mountain for some time, our doorbell rang at about ten o'clock one night. I should explain that nobody rings doorbells on Tomahawk Mountain at 10:00 p.m., or indeed at any other time, without calling ahead. I have a door phone, which rings when the doorbell button is pressed. When I answered the phone, a man's voice said, "Don't you have a Ford vehicle?"

"Who is this?" I asked. He identified himself as a neighbor. I said, "No, I don't have a Ford vehicle, why do you ask?"

"I've locked myself out of my Ford," he explained, "and I've been told that there are only four different keys to Fords. I was hoping someone had a key that might open my car door."

How do you respond to that? I went to the door and invited him in. He would have called AAA, he said, but he did not have a phone at the house, and his cell phone and his AAA card were both inside the locked vehicle. I was a AAA member, so I went to find him the number, and he called them.

I could only hear my neighbor's side of the conversation. It went something like this: "Hello, this is Willie. I'm locked out of my car—it's a Ford—and I need someone to come and unlock it. [pause] Yes, you did unlock my car yesterday, but I was in metro Atlanta at that time. Now I'm at my mountain home."

He started to give directions to Tomahawk Mountain. This was of course before the widespread use of GPS. After he completed the call, he went back to his house to wait. About an hour later, my phone rang. It was AAA. They asked to speak to my neighbor. I explained that he was at his home and did not have a home phone. The caller told me he was with roadside assistance; he could not find the location of my neighbor's home. By then it must have been close to midnight. I asked him where he was. After a moment of listening to him, I realized that my neighbor had given him the wrong directions from his location. I gave him the correct information and went to bed. Wow! What a night on Tomahawk Mountain!

This same neighbor drove by my house a few weeks later and stopped to talk for a minute. There was a strong odor of gasoline coming from his vehicle, and I asked him if he had a gas leak.

"I have been smelling gas all day," he admitted. I asked him to unlatch his hood. When I lifted the hood, I saw gasoline spewing from a broken hose. I quickly told him to shut the engine off. He responded that he'd had the gas leak for some time, that it was not a big deal. Lord, I prayed his vehicle would not catch on fire.

Among our other interesting neighbors, we had one who was retired, and who we often saw drive to the end of the road and back, apparently just for something to do. He sometimes went back and forth several times a day. Another man in the neighborhood was deathly afraid of snakes, and his neighbor took a stick and mischievously drew snake tracks on the road, on both sides of the man's house. The snake-fearing neighbor would not leave his house until the snake tracks were gone.

Of course, there are some snakes you do not want to get close to on the mountain. I was coming home one day from work in the summer, and a copperhead was in the middle of the road. He was at least thirty-six inches long, which is about as big as they get. I did not have a gun with me, so I called my neighbor. He was just getting out of the shower, and it took a few minutes for him to arrive. He shot at the snake several times and missed every time, unloading his gun into the ground around it. The copperhead was lying very still. I guess it figured out that it was safe. Another neighbor then brought a gun, and it too was fired until it no longer had ammunition. The snake finally slithered off into the woods unharmed. I teased my veteran neighbor about his snake-shooting episode.

We found out, soon after we moved into our Tomahawk Mountain home, that we needed to be bear-aware, especially in spring and summer.

Black bear on Tomahawk Mountain

It took several months to build our home, and during that time we had many contractors, sub-contractors, and others working there. They all had keys so they could get into the house and finish their work. It seemed, as the completion neared, the contractors and sub-contractors needed more keys. It occurred to me that I would need to be sure to get all those keys back when the house was completed.

About a month after we moved in, Gail and I were picking blueberries together with our neighbor at his place, which was about two hundred feet away from our house. It was dusk as we finished harvesting the berries. We were about to walk back home when I noticed something in the middle of the road. It was a bear. He was very large—I would estimate maybe 350 pounds and standing about seven feet tall. I say estimate, because you cannot get close enough to a bear to measure or weigh him.

Being new to the area and certainly unaccustomed to dealing with bears, we immediately stopped in our tracks, trying to decide what to do. My neighbor reassured us, saying, "The bear will probably disappear when you head toward him." The word "probably" bothered me. What if he didn't disappear? What if he charged me? What would I do?

At this point, I need to clarify that Gail and I were about the same distance from our front door as the bear was, approaching from the other direction. We decided that we would chance it and cautiously proceed. As we moved toward him and home, he moved toward our front door. We sped up a bit, and he sped up a bit. We still felt that we could reach the front door before he could. By the time we reached the door, the bear was right there as well. Gail was immediately behind me.

I was so keyed up (no pun intended) that I had forgotten that we had locked the front door. I reached into my right front pocket to get my keys. As I reached for the keys, the bear appeared to reach for his keys. I knew right then that we had too many keys to our home floating around on the mountain.

At this point you might ask yourself, is this story true? Well, this is how I remember it. Maybe the bear wasn't reaching for his keys. Maybe he was scratching his fleas or his bug bites; it sure looked like he was going for keys. By the way, we made it safely into the house.

My next-door neighbor called me one Saturday afternoon and told me that a bear was in my front yard. I had my camera on a table next to the front door. I grabbed the camera and headed out the door to get a photograph of the bear. Just as I stepped out and closed the door, the bear and I were almost face-to-face. I saw my life flash before me. I made the quickest turnaround and retreat into my house that has ever been recorded.

Well, nobody saw it or recorded it, but trust me, it was fast. I learned a lesson that day, and that was to peep outside before opening the door.

Teenager black bear roaming around on the mountain

I had another encounter one night, at around eleven o'clock, when I was taking out our dog, Bear (so named because she had looked like a cute teddy bear as a puppy), for her last call of the evening. As we left the house, I noticed some movement across the street at my neighbor's house. He was not home at the time. I heard a loud grunt. I knew that sound; it was a bear. Quickly, I got our "Bear" back in the house. I then fetched my one million lumens portable light and went back outside. Well, outside might be stretching it a bit—I was standing in my doorway with one foot outside and one foot inside. I shined the light across the street. All of a sudden, I saw it. The bear was sitting on his hindquarters, eating corn. My neighbor had planted a small corn patch in his side yard. He and his son were planning on harvesting the corn in a few days.

I wanted to save the corn for my neighbor and his son, so I decided to see if I could scare the bear off. I made a loud, grunting noise in his direction. He responded with a loud, grunting noise of his own. However, he did not move—he just sat there and ate the corn, one cob at a time. I became a little braver. I went outside on my walkway, but still within a short, sprinting distance of my front door. I decided to try the grunt sequence again, except louder and with some enthusiasm. He responded with an even louder grunting noise. This emboldened me further. I thought that if I grunted even louder and gave the impression of moving toward him, that he would leave. I did, and he didn't leave. He sat there calmly eating the corn.

Now, I was not about to give up. I again made the loud, grunting noise and acted as if I was going across the street to attack him. This time, he responded by grabbing a nearby ten-foot-high oak tree and shaking it vigorously at me. I looked around for a tree that I could shake. No tree. However, I did find, next to me in the flower garden, some tall daylilies. I grabbed several of those around the top and shook them at the bear and again made a roaring, grunting noise. He again responded. He almost pulled that ten-foot oak tree out of the ground and gave an ear-piercing sound that convinced me that he was staying and finishing the corn. At that point, I let him. I discovered the next morning that he had consumed most of my neighbor's crop.

The bears come during spring and summer to look for food on the mountain. However, it is not advisable to feed them human food. They like it too much and will not go back to eating berries, fruit, roots, worms, etc. (their normal food supply) once they have tasted what humans eat. One neighbor started feeding her bear peanut butter—in the jar, with the lid removed. He loved it, but one day she forgot to put it out for him. He climbed up her deck to the top railing and looked inside her living room for his peanut butter. She was sitting there, reading a book.

There are bear caves on both sides of Tomahawk Mountain. Black bears don't fully hibernate like grizzly bears but do sleep a lot in the winter. When spring comes, they are hungry. The bears will, at certain times of the year, destroy bird feeders just to get to the birdseed. They seek them out in the spring, before the blackberries ripen, and in the fall before the acorns are ready. So, we know, during those times, to bring in the bird feeders so that they are not demolished—like the first ones we put out before we knew any better.

Springtime is when the bears tend to wander into metro Atlanta, as well. When you see news about a bear being captured in the metro area, that bear is brought to a site within a few miles of our home, and we generally see them in a day or two. However, we do live in a remote area that backs up to a state wildlife management area.

Bears have a terrific sense of smell and can detect food up to three miles away. We cannot leave food or garbage outside, as the bears will come running. We freeze our discarded food so that they cannot smell it. They are very determined animals and will even go inside a home. One of my neighbors and his wife left a cake on the dining room table and a jar of pickles on the kitchen counter one afternoon while they took a short walk. When they came back, the cake and pickles were gone. It was obvious that the bear had torn through the screen door and (fortunately) exited via the same door.

One night, at about ten o'clock, my phone rang; it was our neighbor, George. He said, "Jimmy, there is a bear on my screen porch." My first inclination was to wonder what he thought I might be able to do about it. However, he was a retired senior citizen who lived alone, and he was calling for help in dealing with a bear. I knew that I had to help him.

I called out to Gail that I would be gone for a few minutes to deal with a bear.

"What?" she said.

I yelled, "I will be back soon."

I got into my Chevy Suburban and headed down the street. As I turned into George's yard, I spotted the bear on the screen porch. He was tearing apart something metal and was angry. As my headlamps shined on him, he turned and ran full speed through the screen door toward me. Fortunately,

I had not gotten out of my vehicle at that point. He made a right turn and went down the backside of the mountain.

I got out of my vehicle and saw that George had come out of his home and onto the screen porch. I went through the opening where the screen door had been. George was still shaking. He told me he had heard a noise on his porch and opened the door to find himself face-to-face with the bear, which was ripping apart a galvanized trash can to reach the birdseed that was stored inside. George had chained the lid to the trash can and locked it. The bear had ripped the can apart as if it were cardboard. He had eaten some of the birdseed before I arrived.

As George had opened his door, his dog had run out. He was more worried about his dog than the bear. Fortunately, the bear did not see the dog. There was a few hundred dollars' worth of damage to the screen porch. He thanked me for coming and helping with the bear. All I did was scare him off with my vehicle lights.

Fortunately, I have never heard of anyone on Tomahawk Mountain being attacked by a bear. We see them frequently during the spring and summer. They will generally keep their distance from humans. The only situations to avoid are getting between them and a food source or getting too close to their cubs.

As I mentioned earlier, I am an amateur photographer. In addition to taking landscapes, I do like to photograph wildlife. Back nearly twenty-one years ago, when we first moved to the mountain, I spotted a mother bear with triplets across the road from our home. They were eating not-quite-ripe pears. I grabbed my 35 mm camera to try to capture the family group while they were eating. Needless to say, I was quite a distance away, and I was using my telephoto lens. As I was adjusting the lens, it made a clicking noise. The bears disappeared before I could get the shot. However, I have taken many bear photographs over the years. One of my best photos was of a teenage bear near the top of a plum tree. I had my camera set just right, and then I whistled. The bear spread the branches apart, and I got the shot.

I have installed a trail camera, and I now get photos of wildlife visiting our front yard. We have three deer that frequent the front yard several times a week. I have many photos of bears roaming our yard in spring and summer. We have a lot of turkeys, and occasionally we get visits from bobcats, coyotes, raccoons, opossums, and other wildlife.

The weather can be interesting on Tomahawk Mountain. We can have three to seven snows a year, from a trace to twelve inches. The first winter after we bought our lot, there was a twelve-inch snowfall. Many times, Tomahawk Mountain and the three or four mountains around us will be the only places in our county that receive any accumulation of snow.

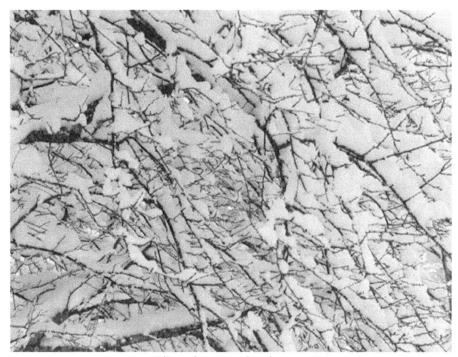

Blizzard on Tomahawk Mountain

We also get our share of ice storms. Fortunately, they don't happen too often. The worst one was in 2000. We were out of power for nearly two weeks. Since then, we have installed an auxiliary generator so that we can have power during emergencies.

Gail and Jimmy Hill at home for Christmas

Ice on Amicalola Falls. Photo taken on a 7-degree day.

Snow covered trees on Tomahawk Mountain

Home Sweet Home

One thing that all residents of Tomahawk Mountain would agree on is the awesome view of the valleys and mountains from our decks.

As Mr. Foote pointed out, every day the valleys and mountains look slightly different. As the clouds and sun move, the view is constantly changing. I have been on Tomahawk Mountain for twenty-one years, and I still see things every day that I have never seen.

We enjoy all types of birds, but the Hummingbirds are our favorites

On July 4, we have the best vantage point to view Independence Day celebrations. From our deck, we have seen as many as twenty-five different firework displays going on, all across the horizon.

One of the most gorgeous sights from our property is Amicalola Falls. The 729-foot-high waterfall is the tallest east of the Mississippi River. Words cannot describe that view.

We can also see Amicalola Falls Park Lodge. The dining room in the lodge has a wall of floor-to-ceiling windows facing our home, with gorgeous views, including Tomahawk Mountain and our house. Our first year on the mountain—it was late May and around 8:30 p.m. I noticed what looked like a fire at the park lodge. I was about ready to dial 9-1-1. I got out my spotting scope to take a closer look and realized what I had seen was the setting sun mirrored in the lodge windows. The reflection was so bright that it had completely obscured the rest of the lodge. It looked like a fireball. It was an awesome sight to behold. We look forward each spring to catching a glimpse of the ball of fire.

Aunt Red was an aunt on my mother's side of the family. Her real name was Edna Juanita Ryals Kerr Carr. However, I always knew her as Aunt Red. I thought her real name was Aunt Red until I was grown. She had been called that forever. She had a reddish complexion and bright red hair. She was asked one day why she was known as Aunt Red. She answered, "It is better than Aunt Gray." I have to agree.

Aunt Red

Aunt Red was born in South Georgia but moved north to Pennsylvania, where she spent most of her adult life. She came down to Georgia in June 2001 for a Ryals family reunion in Gardi. Aunt Lorraine (Aunt Red's sister) took her back to the Savannah airport for her trip home to Pittsburgh, Pennsylvania. On the way to the airport, Aunt Red asked Aunt Lorraine to find her a place to live in Georgia. She wanted to come home. Aunt Lorraine agreed but thought to herself that her sister would probably forget all about it when she got back home. The next day, Aunt Red called her and asked if she had found her a place yet. Aunt Lorraine got busy and searched the areas around Statesboro and Jesup. She called my mother, Mary, and asked her to help look for somewhere. To make a long story short, they finally found the perfect place; she moved back to Georgia in August of 2001 and located in Metter, Georgia. And we all know that "everything is better in Metter." Of course, Aunt Red said, "Where I am, everything is better anyway."

I didn't get to know Aunt Red well until she moved back to Georgia in 2001. I can truly say that she brought us joy and happiness, as I hope we did her. She had a keen sense of humor. She always described everything that happened to her as if it were the first time it had ever happened. She would say about an event, "That's the first time that I have ever done that." Or she would say, "It's the first time that I have ever seen that blue of a sky." She had a lot of firsts. You would believe her, based on how enthusiastically she said it.

Aunt Red saw humor and beauty in everything. She was the life of the party. She had the greatest laugh—I could listen to her laugh all day. I would say humorous things just to get her to laugh. She was always so positive and upbeat. She and I discussed, just two weeks before her passing, how life is too short to have people around you who drag you down. She told me that we all needed to surround ourselves with positive, uplifting people. What a great lesson for all of us!

Several years ago, Aunt Red, along with my parents, came to visit Gail and me at our home on Tomahawk Mountain. She was so excited about the trip. I traveled to South Georgia and picked them up for the five-hour journey. Aunt Red could not wait until we got to the mountains. She said this was her first vacation—another first. She would sit for hours and look at the mountains and valleys from our deck. Every meal that Gail cooked, Aunt Red would say that it was the first time that she had eaten that dish, or it was the best that she had ever eaten.

Aunt Red, who was single, met our single neighbor, George, and they immediately hit it off. She was prodding him about giving her a goodbye kiss after he had dinner with us one night. George placed a whopping wet kiss on her cheek. You should have seen her blush! It may have been the only time that I have ever seen Aunt Red blush. With her red complexion and red hair, it was hard to tell when she was blushing.

She told me before her passing that the visit to our mountaintop home was close to being in heaven. I was visiting her in a medical facility at that time. "When you get out of here," I said, "we will go to the mountain again." Well, she didn't make it back to Tomahawk Mountain, but she has gone on to the heavenly mountain. Aunt Red passed on May 30, 2007. May you rest in peace as you live forever in our hearts!

I have to agree with Aunt Red: it is almost heaven on earth here on Tomahawk Mountain, where fresh air abounds, and the views are awe-inspiring. The mountain is an awesome location to view constellations, meteors, galaxies, space station flyovers, and the great, expansive sky. And did I mention the quietness? Whenever friends and family are visiting, I always ask them the same question around dusk, as we sit on the deck: "Do you hear that?"

They respond with "I don't hear anything."

"Exactly," I say. "Nothing but quiet … isn't it great!"

Gail and I have loved every minute of living on Tomahawk Mountain. Our South Georgia friends and relatives ask frequently, "Why don't you move back to South Georgia?" I will let this book and this chapter answer that question.

As I finish writing this chapter, early on Friday morning, May 1, 2020, Gail and I are on our deck and about to enjoy a cup of coffee, some breakfast, and another awesome sunrise on Tomahawk Mountain. I make an outstanding fried egg and cheese breakfast sandwich.

The sun rises at 6:46 a.m. with a flood of rays across the valley beneath us. There is not a cloud in the sky. All we can hear are birds chirping and the trees swaying in the light breeze. Gail looks at me and says, "What a great morning to be alive on Tomahawk Mountain." I nod in agreement.

Sunrise on Tomahawk Mountain

29

They Inspired Me

Don't judge each day by the harvest you reap but by the seeds you plant.

Robert Louis Stevenson

What a blessing and privilege it is to share my life journey with my family, friends, and you.

This writing project has been an eye-opener for me—an opportunity to explore my own life and to learn more about the lives of others who have influenced me, even before my birth. It has helped me realize just how many people have inspired me along the way, some of them to an extraordinary extent, shaping the direction I have taken, from a country boy in rural South Georgia to a blessed retirement with the love of my life here on Tomahawk Mountain. Also, over and again, I have witnessed the importance of faith in my life and theirs.

The people and groups listed below are those who especially inspired me during my life journey. There are hundreds more, who are mentioned in this book, who touched my life as well.

Gail Hobbs Hill: Gail came into my life at Zion Hope Baptist Church on a Sunday evening in 1968. I knew then, deep down, that she was the love of my life and was going to be my wife. She has been all of that and so much more. She is my love, rock, partner, companion, fact-checker, and one of the smartest women I know. She puts others first in her life and has raised two great children. I still depend heavily on her expertise and counsel. She has been on my journey, right beside me always, and I thank the Lord for her. She inspires me every day.

Jasper and Mary Hill: As I get older, and hopefully wiser, I have begun to appreciate my parents even more. In writing this book, I had time to relive and ponder my life and theirs. Dad was the one who provided strict discipline, and Mother was the loving, protecting, and calming influence in my life when I was growing up, and even when I became an adult. They both played a huge role in my life. They also played a large role in the life of every person they had contact with. Dad's influence as a pastor, and Mother's role as an entrepreneur and godly woman, changed many lives, including mine. They inspired me in the totality of their life and influence.

Caryl Shanklin: Caryl was the one person I remember standing out as a leader in our community, in his role as Gardi's postmaster and general store proprietor, and as a man of faith who lived a godly life. I credit him for helping to convince my dad to go to church. Shanklin's life was a shining light in Gardi. I know he helped my family in a time of great need, and I am sure he touched other lives as well. After talking with his son, Gus, I am more inspired by Caryl and his impact on Gardi. I hope and pray that I can impact lives in even just a fraction of the way he did.

Fred Bennett: Fred was our landlord at the Lambert Bennett place. Lambert Bennet was Fred's father. The Bennett family had lived in the home many years earlier. Fred was more than a landlord. He was a farmer, railroad engineer, land surveyor, full-service gas station owner, and entrepreneur. I was impressed by his work ethic and his entrepreneurial spirit. I worked for him, driving a tractor on the Lambert Bennett place. He would give me specific assignments, and I would get them done. Fred hired me later to work in his land-surveying company, as well as at his gas station. He inspired me by demonstrating that hard work and commitment would lead to success in life.

Merle Cockfield: Mrs. Cockfield was my tenth-grade English teacher at Wayne County High School. I was having trouble in English grammar and was worried about my grades since I was moving to a new location that summer. I knew that if I did not pass English, I would be taking tenth-grade English in the eleventh grade at my new high school. She sat me down and tutored me so that I could pass the class, and in so doing, she set me on the road to success. I appreciated all she did for me as an inspiring teacher.

B. H. Claxton: Mr. Claxton is high on my list of individuals who greatly impacted my life. He was my agriculture teacher, mentor, and encourager. He instilled in me a desire to succeed in whatever I chose to do. He encouraged me to go to college. I am not sure how my life would have gone had he not mentored me. He would never take credit for his success as a teacher. But I know he changed my life and many others as well. He still does inspire me to live a life of service to others.

While writing this last chapter, I learned that Mr. Claxton passed away on April 26, 2020. I have an empty feeling in my soul as I have now lost a great man and mentor in my life. I miss him greatly already. He will continue to inspire me even though he is no longer on this earth.

Ricky Hill: My brother Ricky came along nine years after I was born. He was a unique soul, who was loved by everybody who knew him. He had an aura about him that made him glow with purpose, direction, and a godly presence. He could sing and play the piano and was a songwriter, as well. He dedicated his life to Christ and demonstrated Christ-like love for his family and friends. He is still, to this day, making a difference in lives. He has inspired me to be a better person each day.

Dr. J. Clyde Driggers: Dr. Driggers was the president of Abraham Baldwin Agricultural College (ABAC) when I attended. He was one of the friendliest, most down-to-earth, easily approachable individuals I have ever met. He would invite me to go see him in his office and talk about my future. He encouraged me to continue my educational pursuits. I supported his vision to build the Chapel of All Faiths on the ABAC campus and helped to raise money for the project. He believed that no matter the obstacles, you could achieve great success if you never gave up and worked hard. His book *It Took A Miracle*, about building the chapel, is as inspiring as he was. Thank you, Dr. Driggers, for your positive influence on my life.

Roy Parker: Roy was a heating and cooling dealer in Americus, Georgia. He was a great mentor to me as I was just getting into my early career with Georgia Power. He taught me many technical aspects of installing HVAC, but more importantly, he was a man compelled by his Christian faith. He lived a life of faith and service to mankind. Roy inspired me as I was developing marketing and technical programs at Georgia Power later in my career. His influence is still with me today. Thanks for your inspiring actions that impacted a young man early in his career.

Marshall Timberlake: Marshall hired me as a residential marketing engineer at Georgia Power and was my first full-time supervisor in Columbus, Georgia. He was a longtime employee, who had worked for a small electric utility in middle Georgia before going to Georgia Power. He worked his way up the ladder and became a supervisor in marketing. He guided me as a young employee on work attitudes, time management, and effectiveness in customer service. He scheduled training for me in other departments so that I could see how they interacted, which made me more effective with customers. He was even-tempered and was an inspiration to me as I became a supervisor later in my career.

Martha Ruth Hill Whatley: Martha Ruth (no relation) was a co-worker of mine in Columbus. She initially worked on kitchen and lighting design for customers who were building new homes. She was later a co-worker of mine in the Residential Marketing Department. We traveled together many times working on customer electrical and HVAC needs. She is one of the most positive people I have ever known. Her attitude and spirit are infectious. She still inspires me as I face challenges and opportunities in my life. Thank you, Martha Ruth, for your inspiration and friendship.

Jim Manley: Jim graduated a few years ahead of me at the University of Georgia. He and I both received our undergraduate degrees in agricultural engineering. When Jim was promoted to manager of Residential Marketing, he asked me to go to Atlanta to head up a marketing effort for the electric heat pump. I was also asked to develop an HVAC dealer program to run in conjunction with the electric heat pump program. Jim could have chosen any one of a hundred Georgia Power employees to take on this challenge, but he chose me. I am forever grateful for his confidence and belief in my skills to head up this effort. He was a great manager and an inspiring leader. He was a manager who gave me my challenge and said, "Get it done, and let me know if you need anything." Thanks, Jim, for your inspiring leadership, confidence, and support.

Bill Davidson: Bill was named vice president of marketing at the corporate office of Georgia Power. He was the first vice president I reported to directly. I did not know Bill before he went into the corporate office, but I knew that he had extensive leadership experience in the Atlanta area with Georgia Power. He chose me as one of his new managers when he reorganized the Corporate Marketing Department. I am grateful for Bill's confidence in my ability to take on that challenge. Bill was easy-going, likable, and approachable. He listened and was fun to work for. He inspired me by his approach to leadership and how he tackled problems and issues.

Bill Dahlberg: Bill was an inspiring individual, who had been with Georgia Power since his teens. He had worked his way up the ladder the hard way hard work. He was named senior vice president of marketing, and I had the pleasure of working for him. On one of his first days in the new position, he called several of us managers to his office and asked us, "What impediments are keeping you from accomplishing your job?" I had never had a person at his level ask me such a question. As soon as I told him my issue (I can't share what it was due to trade secrets), he asked me who could solve the issue. I told him. I thought he was making notes and would deal with this later, but he straightaway wheeled around in his desk chair, picked up the phone, and called that person. He didn't beat around the bush; he asked, "Why can't we solve this problem?" I was blown away by his actions that day. He immediately became a hero to me and still is. Bill inspired me to move forward and address whatever issue is an obstacle. He also would send me a thank-you note every time I received a commendation or some other recognition. It was a pleasure working for him. Thanks, Bill, for your inspiring leadership.

Dr. Tory Herring: Dr. Herring was an industrial-organizational psychologist. I mentioned earlier his role in my being selected as the manager of Agricultural Affairs. He was the most interesting individual, who could dig deep into my soul. His methodology was thought-provoking and as intensive a hiring process as I had ever witnessed. It was also very personally rewarding to know that I had been selected for the position after this extensive process. He asked some very tough but fair questions. His scenarios were challenging and required deep thought. He and I became good friends after my hiring. I used his services in selecting individuals for a non-profit where I served as chairman. Dr. Herring was inspiring in his work ethic and in how he managed the process of selecting individuals for job positions.

Jack Talley: Jack was the most multitalented individual I have ever met or worked for. He was brilliant and perceptive. He was able to catch my vision of what I was trying to do with the Agricultural Affairs Department and boil it down into a few words. He was one of the most supportive vice presidents that I ever worked with at Georgia Power. He was also loaded with great ideas and implementation plans. He gave me my marching orders after we had discussed them and said, "Go! And if you need me, call me." He helped me accomplish many things in my job as the manager of Agricultural Affairs. He was one of the most inspiring individuals I ever worked with.

Unfortunately, Jack passed away on Friday, May 1, 2020. I had the opportunity to visit with him on Friday, March 13. He was in good spirits but told me that his systems were shutting down. I knew that he would not be with us much longer. I thanked him for his support and friendship as I left. I already miss my boss and friend. May you rest in peace.

Gary Black: I met Gary Black shortly after I was named manager of Agricultural Affairs. He visited me one day in my office in the late 1980s. He had developed a box of agricultural products for use by companies as gifts. I did not buy any of his products, but I did buy into what he was selling—himself. As time went on, we became good friends. I was appointed to the Georgia Agribusiness Council (GAC) board of directors' selection committee for a new executive director of GAC. Gary sailed through the selection process and became the number one candidate. We hired Gary, and he served for twenty-seven years. Gary ran for and won the position as Georgia's Commissioner of Agriculture in 2010 and is serving his third four-year term. He is an outstanding leader with bold ideas, great vision, and servant leadership qualities, and is also a man of faith. Gary inspired me in so many ways as we worked together when I was chairman of the GAC and afterward.

Louise Hill: Louise Hill (no relation) was the director of program development and education for the Georgia Farm Bureau Federation when we first met. I could tell then that she was a quiet leader with a lot of ideas. She started working on leadership issues for the Georgia Farm Bureau and mentioned her project to several of us who worked in agriculture. She was the spark that helped create the Gang of Five mentioned in Chapter 22. She inspired me to take a keen interest in leadership development. It was through Louise's inspiration that we created the Georgia Agri-Leaders Forum. I dedicated over twenty-one years to the Forum as a result.

Louise asked multiple leaders in Georgia agriculture to write me a letter congratulating me on the successful launch and implementation of the Forum. I call it the Book of Letters. In addition, she wrote a personal thank-you letter which was the most awesome letter that I have ever received. A copy is in the Appendix.

I shall treasure these expressions of gratitude forever. The men and women who wrote the letters are also inspiring to me as I progress along my leadership journey. Thank you, Louise, for facilitating my Book of Letters. Names of the leaders who wrote letters are listed in the Appendix.

Dr. Fred Davison: How cool is it to become personal friends with the man who signed your college diploma! Yes, Dr. Davison signed my diploma from UGA. He believed in our vision of the Georgia Agri-Leaders Forum and joined our board of directors. He was a great, visionary man, who ultimately became the Forum's chairman. He helped us take it to the next level. Also, he was a down-to-earth, approachable, and awesome individual. Just sitting and listening to him talk was a blessing. Thank you for your inspiring leadership, which still invigorates me to this day.

Larry Windham: Larry Windham is the owner of Windham Greenhouses and was a 2000 Agri-Leaders Forum graduate. Larry came on the board of directors of the Forum and eventually served as chairman. He was a very insightful and practical individual and a great leader. He led us during the time of the economic slump in the 2000s. Larry gave of himself and his personal resources to make sure the Forum was successful. Larry, you didn't have to make the tremendous commitment that you made, but you did it anyway. I appreciate what you did, and it inspired me that day to do even more to be a better leader. Thank you, for all you did for the Forum and me personally.

Cathy Cox: Cathy Cox became my friend many years ago through our mutual friend, Louise Hill. Cathy has an outstanding civic and political record of serving Georgia. She is currently the dean of Walter F. George School of Law at Mercer University in Macon, Georgia. I met her when she was a state representative from the Bainbridge, Georgia, area. She is a member of the Democratic Party, a former secretary of state, and was a candidate for governor of Georgia in 2006. She served as the twenty-first president of Young Harris College in Young Harris, Georgia. She attended

ABAC after I did and earned an associate degree in agriculture, then went on to UGA and earned a journalism degree. Following UGA, she graduated magna cum laude from Mercer University with a law degree. During my consulting practice, I conducted a training session for Cathy's key staff from the Secretary of State's Office shortly after her election. I observed how Cathy instilled in her staff the concepts of excelling in customer service in state government. I knew right then that she was a great leader who would do even greater things in the Secretary of State's Office. She instituted new customer service objectives and met her goal of being the best customer service operation in state government. Her record of leadership and accomplishment are unequaled in state government and the educational arena. She has inspired me as I have watched her reach her goals and make this state a better place to live. Thank you, Cathy, for your life of service and dedication to all of Georgia.

Georgia Agri-Leaders Forum Founding Directors and All Board of Director Members: These men and women are the best of the best, and I am proud to have served with them. Please find their names in Chapter 22.

Ron Hart: Ron Hart was a co-worker of mine at Georgia Power for many years. Ron was in the Training and Human Resources Department at Georgia Power. I attended several of his classes over the years. One class, in particular, I really enjoyed; it changed my life in so many ways. It was based on a book by Stephen Covey entitled *The 7 Habits of Highly Effective People*. The principles in the book came alive for me during Ron's teaching. Unfortunately, Ron developed Muscular Dystrophy (MD) in his mid-fifties. His symptoms started with some difficulty with walking and quickly after that required him to use crutches and eventually an electric wheelchair. These challenges never appeared to faze Ron in his work or his personal life. He was one of the most positive individuals I have ever known. He said that MD did not define his life, that only he could do that. He chose to move forward and live life to the fullest.

Ron planted a garden every spring. He had to crawl on the ground to prepare the soil and plant the seeds. He tended the garden and harvested the vegetables in summer. He decided that he and his wife would go camping. Ron bought a tent and set it up in his backyard at least twenty times to work out all of the kinks before they went on that camping trip. He tried to maintain a lifestyle that he was accustomed to, no matter the challenges.

I attended a management session at a lodge in North Georgia that Ron facilitated for Georgia Power. We shared a bedroom in the lodge. All bedrooms were upstairs. He climbed the stairs with his crutches, which took about fifteen minutes. It took him about an hour to get ready for bed and about two hours to get ready in the morning. He was always the first person in the session in the morning and the last to leave in the evening. Again, he chose to do what it took to take care of his responsibilities.

After I left Georgia Power and directed the Georgia Agri-Leaders Forum, I knew that I wanted Ron to teach *The 7 Habits of Highly Effective People* to each class. He taught for me for several years, and his teaching techniques and his strong witness of not letting adversity affect his life changed many lives. Thank you, Ron, for your inspiration and encouragement. You certainly made a difference in my life and many others. Ron passed on April 16, 2002. Rest in peace, my friend.

Dr. John Kline: I met Dr. Kline at one of our first institutes at Georgia Agri-Leaders Forum. He taught a session on speaking and listening. He had written a book entitled *Speaking Effectively* while teaching for the Air Force, and he gave each institute class member a copy. I have read many books on speaking and given thousands of speeches; I found his book to be a most valuable resource. Dr. Kline retired as a civilian with the Air Force and accepted a teaching position at Troy University in Alabama. I asked him to continue teaching his session on speaking and listening for the Georgia Agri-Leaders Forum after I took over the Forum leadership.

Dr. Kline is a masterful teacher and speaker. He is a servant leader who impacted my classes and all of those with whom he came into contact. He is a man of faith as well. Several years ago, Dr. Kline's wife, Ann, developed Alzheimer's disease. She is now in a facility near their home in Montgomery, Alabama. Dr. Kline has been traveling for about thirty minutes each way to visit Ann for at least three hours every day. They have continued an amazing, lifelong love affair that is heartwarming to observe. However, during the current COVID-19 pandemic, Dr. Kline is not allowed in the facility to see Ann. Fortunately; she is in a first-floor room with a window. He goes to the screen window and talks to her, and they sing their favorite spiritual songs together each day. Their loving, daily singing together was in the local and national news in March 2020. Google "man sings to his wife daily through her nursing home window," and you will be blessed.

I have never witnessed a stronger or more loving relationship than they have for each other. Thank you, Dr. Kline, for inspiring me through your unconditional love of Ann as an example for all who are in loving relationships.

Jolene Brown: Jolene is an inspiring advocate for the people in agriculture who feed, clothe, and fuel the world. She is an awesome speaker, writer, and teacher and conducts keynote speeches for conferences, meetings, and seminars. Jolene has made it her life's mission to help farmers and ranchers share their stories with the wider world. She is an expert on growing and fixing farm businesses and transitioning them to the next generation. She uses humor and fascinating stories, as well as her insights, to bring home her point.

I was fortunate enough to have Jolene speak to almost every Georgia Agri-Leaders Forum class until we suspended the program in 2010. She was the most highly rated of all of our speakers. Jolene is a Certified Speaking Professional and has been inducted into the National Speakers Association's Council of Peers Award for Excellence (CPAE) Speaker Hall of Fame. She has written two books, *Holy Crap! I Married a Farmer!* and *Sometimes You Need More Than a 2x4!* She has also produced a DVD and workbook set, entitled *The Top 10 Mistakes that Break Up a Family Business!* Jolene's website is https://jolenebrown.com.

I highly recommend her as an engaging and inspiring speaker for your agricultural organization. Thank you, Jolene, for inspiring me with your success as a speaker and a leader in agriculture for nearly thirty years.

Georgia Agri-Leaders Forum Graduates (1991–2010): I am inspired by each of the graduates of the Forum. They have assumed many leadership roles on the local, state, and national level since graduation. These leadership roles are exactly what our founders hoped that the graduates would assume. They are inspired, engaged, and knowledgeable leaders, ready to assume leadership roles. Please see the list of graduates in the Appendix.

W. J. Grimes Jr.: W. J. Grimes Jr. was the Vidalia onion farmer who was a leader and visionary in helping move the Vidalia onion industry forward by leaps and bounds. His work in adapting the Controlled Atmosphere storage for onions was historic. He was the kind of guy you like to hang around because he was inspiring and down-to-earth. He certainly inspired me as I worked with him on the Vidalia onion project. He could analyze a situation and quickly develop a solution, and it was usually right. He treated people fairly and honestly.

Bernice, W. J.'s wife, was the love of his life. He adored her. W. J.'s eyes sparkled when he was around Bernice. I have never observed a more caring husband. W. J.'s love for Bernice was breathtaking and a great example of true and enduring love.

My life is richer for having known and worked with W. J. Grimes Jr., He passed on November 3, 2017. Rest in peace, my friend.

Leroy Baldwin: Leroy and Sharon Baldwin and their family operate the Baldwin Angus Ranch near Ocala, Florida. Leroy started his vision of raising cattle at the tender age of six. He was possessed with the drive to succeed as a rancher even though he did not come from a ranching family. He started a newspaper route and invested his earnings by buying cattle. He was a self-made man of incredible drive and humility. He used the word "we" when describing his success, and the "we" was his family and the Lord. He was a man of faith and lived it every day. He was amazingly focused on being the best Black Angus rancher in the country—may be in the world. He did sell Angus cattle all over the world. He was inspiring as he talked about the cattle and his wife and family. He inspired me as we visited his ranch every year as part of the Georgia Agri-Leaders Forum. Leroy passed on December 23, 2016. His family still runs Baldwin Angus Ranch. May you rest in peace, my friend.

Zippy Duvall: Zippy Duvall was an outstanding participant in the 1996 class of Georgia Agri-Leaders Forum. I was impressed with Zippy's demeanor and presence during the yearlong class. He was a dairy farmer when I first met him but has since shifted to hay, beef cattle, and raising broilers. Zippy served on the Georgia Farm Bureau Federation (GFBF) board of directors for many years, including as its president for nine years. He was elected president of the American Farm Bureau Federation in 2016 and is still serving in that position.

Zippy is a very likable and approachable leader. One of his greatest assets is his ability to build relationships with others. That skill has served him well as AFBF president. He is a family man and a man of faith. His leadership skills and accomplishments are inspiring to me, as well as to many others.

Rebecca Brightwell: Becky is the Associate Director of the UGA Institute on Human Development and Disability. She is also the co-director of Farm Again–AgrAbility of Georgia. I worked for Becky for nearly three years before I retired. Working with Farm Again was probably one of the most rewarding projects that I have ever been involved in. Helping farmers overcome health-related obstacles that had prevented them from farming and being part of the solution that enabled them to farm again was awesome. Becky was the driving force, along with Dr. Glen Rains, the other co-director. Becky is one of the hardest working; most dedicated and focused people I have ever known. She has positively impacted many farm families' lives. Thanks, Becky, for allowing me to work in and be a part of the Farm Again program. And thank you, for inspiring me and others to make a difference for those around us.

Tracy Rackensperger: Tracy and I met when I went to work with UGA in the Farm Again–AgrAbility of Georgia program. Tracy's mode of transportation is a wheelchair. However, she is not confined in any way. She loves to go waterskiing, snowboarding, fishing, hiking, climbing rock walls, and anything else that might be available. She lives life to the fullest.

Oh, by the way, she earned her doctorate at UGA, where she teaches in the Institute on Human Development and Disability. She is an amazing lady who focuses on what she can do, as opposed to what she cannot do. I believe there are no limits to what she can accomplish. Thank you, Tracy … for inspiring me every day.

Kyle Haney: Kyle and I met at the UGA College of Engineering as I was seeking senior student engineers to work on a project for Farm Again. Kyle and three other engineers designed an engineering solution for hooking up three-point-hitch agricultural equipment to farm tractors without the farmer having to leave the tractor seat. He and his team came up with a great design, which he was selected to present at the Annual Meeting of the National AgrAbility Project held in Portland, Maine, in March 2018.

Kyle received his undergraduate degree in mechanical engineering in late 2018. He was the most focused student engineer I worked with over my nearly three years with Farm Again. He had a great affinity for assisting farmers with disabilities, having grown up helping his grandfather on the farm. Rebecca Brightwell asked me if I thought we could attract Kyle to work for Farm Again. I was confident he would make a great employee— he had told me previously that he would love to work on providing solutions to challenges faced by farmers with disabilities. I also knew, however, that engineers coming out of school could draw a hefty salary. But based on Rebecca's interest and Kyle's expression of wanting to serve farmers, I recommended that she approach him.

Kyle accepted the position and has been a great addition to the Farm Again project. Kyle inspired me by staying focused on how he could serve farmers and by giving up a potentially higher salary in other engineering career paths. Thanks, Kyle, for your dedication and commitment to serving Georgia farmers.

JaLayne Coleman: I met JaLayne several years ago when our family was dealing with my dad's health issues. She helped us find a facility that could provide the care that Dad needed. She became a family friend to all of us and particularly a friend to my mother. JaLayne was a volunteer coordinator at Community Hospice in Vidalia, Georgia. She helped us to get Dad into the Community Hospice House during his final days.

JaLayne is a dedicated individual who makes sure family needs are taken care of during the most trying time in a family's life … the impending death of a family member. She was calling and visiting with my mother throughout the time Dad was under hospice care. I was very inspired by her work, dedication, and people skills. JaLayne leaves no stone unturned in relieving the pressure from a family during its time of greatest stress. She acts as if you and your family are her only responsibility. I can't say enough about JaLayne and her service to families losing loved ones. Thank you, JaLayne, for everything you did for our family and for all the other families you serve. You are awesome and inspiring!

Garland Thompson: I met Garland in 1986 when I joined the board of directors of the Georgia Agribusiness Council. Garland was from Douglas, Georgia, where he worked for a local bank. He was one of the most civic-minded individuals that I have ever met. Everything he did was based on how it could help others or the community as a whole. He was quiet and unassuming and did not seek credit for anything that he was involved in. He played a major role in economic development in South Georgia for many years. Garland served on several state-wide boards that positively impacted the entire state of Georgia. He was a role model in service to others and, as such, an inspiration to me.

Garland also was one of the people who inspired me to write this book. He wrote about his grandchildren, and his book, *Precious Gems*, led in part to me writing about my life, family, and career, and about those who, like him, inspired me along my journey.

Appendix

Chapter 1   Spring 1944 - Gardi, Georgia

A majority of this chapter came from a document that Mother handwrote, in pencil, about her early life. The document was found in her files following her death.

Chapter 2   Boyhood Days in Gardi

Early Gardi history information was summarized from a book titled *Miscellany of Wayne County,* published by Margaret Coleman Jordan, Jesup Sentinel, May 1976 1st printing. Every effort was made to contact Jordan was unsuccessful.

The Turpentine Industry information was summarized with permission from *The Illustrated History of the Naval Stores (Turpentine) Industry* by Pete Gerrell in 1998. The SYP (Southern Yellow Pine) Publishing Company published the book. SYP gave permission to publish the information.

The information regarding the Rayonier cellulose plant in Jesup, Georgia came from the Rayonier Advanced Materials public website at https://rayonieram.com.

The bicycle tour information came from Richard Jackson, a lifelong resident of Gardi, and my memories.

The history of the Honey House was provided by Troy Fore Jr., and he gave permission to publish the information.

Caryl Shanklin's history was provided by his son, Gus, who spent over an hour with me talking about his dad and memories of Gardi. Gus gave permission to publish the information.

Envelope and one of the letters that were sent to Mother while she was in the hospital:

Chapter 4   Faith Brings a Turning Point

Some of the background for this chapter came from my parents' files and documents found after their deaths.

Chapter 7   Selective Service and the Vietnam War

The Vietnam War information came from various Internet sources. The information about the Selective Service came from my files and The National Personnel Records Center in St. Louis, Missouri.

Chapter 8   FFA and Its Transformative Impact

The FFA definition and emblem came from www.ffa.org.

Listed below is the schedule of functions that I attended during my year as a state FFA officer. All were in Georgia, except the National Convention, which was in Kansas City, Kansas:

State FFA Officer Training	August 18–21, 1965	Macon
Area Agriculture Teachers meeting	September 14, 1965	Swainsboro
National FFA Convention	October 11–17, 1965	Kansas City
State FFA Rally–Jeff Davis FFA Outstanding Chapter Award	October 21, 1965	Macon
Patterson FHA-FFA Banquet	December 7, 1965	Patterson
Norman Gay Day Parliamentary Procedure Demonstration	January 6, 1966 February 9, 1966	Sylvester Reidsville
Hazlehurst Lions Club	February 15, 1966	Hazlehurst
Jeff Davis County Farm Bureau Meeting	February 17, 1966	Hazlehurst
FFA Parent and Son Banquet	February 23, 1966	Springfield
FFA Parent and Son Banquet	March 11, 1966	Baxley
FFA Parent and Son Banquet	March 15, 1966	Almo
Jeff Davis County Farm Bureau Meeting	March 17, 1966	Hazlehurst
FFA/FHA Banquet	March 24, 1966	Hazlehurst
Jeff Davis FFA Mother-Father-Son Banquet	March 31, 1966	Millen

Wayne County		
FFA Parent and Son Banquet	April 1, 1966	Jesup
FFA Area II Public Speaking and Livestock Judging	April 4, 1966	Reidsville
Guide Posts for Better Living	April 22, 1966	Alma
Glennville FFA Parents' Night	April 26, 1966	Glennville
Jeff Davis Vocational Industrial Club	April 28, 1966	Hazlehurst
Millen Dairy Festival	April 29, 1966	Millen
County Institute–FFA Banquet	April 29, 1966	Twin City
Glenn Academy FFA Banquet	May 6, 1966	Brunswick
FFA Area II Annual Rally	May 7, 1966	Jekyll Island
Toombs Central FFA Banquet	May 12, 1966	Lyons
State FFA Officer Goodwill Tour	June 13–17, 1966	Atlanta
State FFA Convention	July 10–16, 1966	Atlanta
FFA Area II Annual Rally	May 13, 1967	Jekyll Island
Lions-Kiwanis-Rotary Banquet	May 7, 1968	Hazlehurst

(Honoring Albert Wildes, 1967–68 State FFA President)

Listed below is the press coverage in print, television, and radio that I received while representing the FFA. Several of these opportunities allowed me to gain valuable experience in public speaking and the ability to think on my feet. This experience served me well in all phases of my career.

"Jimmy Hill wins State FFA Vice Presidency." *Jeff Davis County Ledger*, July 22, 1965, Hazlehurst, Georgia.

"FFA Horizons Are Wide, Young Denton Leader Says." by Harold Joiner, Farm Editor *Atlanta Journal and Atlanta Constitution*, Sunday, August 29, 1965, Atlanta, Georgia. (See article below.)

The Atlanta Journal
THE ATLANTA CONSTITUTION

Farm

HAROLD JOINER, Farm Editor

42   SUNDAY, AUGUST 29, 1965

STUDIED PARLIAMENTARY LAW

FFA Horizons Are Wide, Young Denton Leader Says

EDITOR'S NOTE: This is another in a series of articles on the newly elected state officers of the Georgia Association of Future Farmers of America.

DENTON—A young Jeff Davis High School graduate hopes to spread the idea that Future Farmers are students of more than just farming and forestry.

For Jimmy L. Hill, 18, this will be an easier task than it might have been because he is a vice president of the state association and will be speaking about FFA to many groups.

"It is thought by many that the FFA is only interested in farming, forestry and such, but this is completely wrong," he said. "I have studied parliamentary law in FFA which has helped me immensely in conducting a meeting."

PLANNING for a career as

JIMMY HILL
Preacher's Son in FFA

an agricultural engineer, Jimmy will attend Abraham Baldwin Agricultural College at Tifton and the University of Georgia after his year of service to FFA.

He has been assistant secretary and assistant reporter of his local chapter before last year being elected secretary. He has won soil and water management awards, was public speaking winner in the chapter for two years, winning third place in the area the first time and second place the next year.

A BETA CLUB member, Jimmy was a member of the guidance council during his high school days.

The son of Rev. and Mrs. Jasper Hill, Jimmy has been active in his church work. He was general superintendent of his Sunday school for two years after serving as assistant superintendent for a year.

Jimmy says the FFA is "the greatest farm youth organization in the world" and says he knows because of his many years of membership in the organization.

WVOH Radio Station interview; February 24, 1966, Hazlehurst, Georgia
WTOC-TV interview; February 26, 1966, Savannah, Georgia

"Farmers Must Feed World, FFA is Told." Front page story by Jimmy Hill, Georgia FFA vice president: *The Baxley News–Banner*, March 17, 1966, Baxley, Georgia.

"Glennville FFA Chapter Parents' Night is Huge Success, Jimmy Hill, State Vice President Main Speaker." Front page headline in the *Tattnall Journal*, April 28, 1966, Glennville, Georgia. I received a note from agriculture teacher W. C. Childs, who wrote, "Jimmy, you sure made a big hit down here. Thought you might like to have this section of the paper."

Chapter 9   ABAC Days and Bean-Harvesting Summers

ABAC history information came from www.abac.edu

ABAC classmates, professors, instructors, and staff listings came from my college records, ABAC yearbook, and from my memories. Classmates included: Barbara Allen, Gail Aultman, Daniel Avery, Margaret Barksdale, William Boone, Gary Bullock, Danny Brooks, Shirley Colston, Mike Galloway, Rhonwyn Dawson, Oscar Dean, Lee DeLoach, Leo Espinoja, Gary Farmer, Nada Fincher, Neal Ganzel, Marvin Giddens, John Godbee, Sandra Golden, Thomas Graham, Farrest Griffin, Kenneth Hall, Donnie Hand, Alex Hardy, David Harrell, Betsy Harris, Lee Harrison, Scott Hart, Yolonda Hires, William Hutchins, Renza Israel, Gary Jackson, Bess Kendrick, Mike Kerr, Ann Lofton, Larry Maddox, Alvin Manning, Nadine Morgan, John Page, Sandra Pate, Harry Reed, James Reid, Patty Rogers, Lora Lee Shroeder, Jay Shaw, Carol Southerland, Donald Spencer, Charles Stewart, Donald Stodghill, Virginia Thomas, Ralph Underwood, Nancy Waller, Sammy Ward, Rhonwyn Waters, Donald Watson, Donald Wilder, and Loma Young. They were among the 1800+ students who attended ABAC in the 1967 and 1968 academic years.

ABAC's administration, professors, instructors, and staff had a very positive impact on my life. They included President J. Clyde Driggers, Worth Bridges (dean of men), Paul Gaines (registrar), Miss Rosalyn Ray, Ron Jones, Baldwin Davis, Marshall Guill, Martin Sibbett, Joe Day, Sidney Smith, Frank Thomas, James Griner, James Rowe, Hugh McTeer, Jessie Chambliss, Miss Rosemary Johnson, Norman Hill, Tom Cordell, Jimmy Grubbs, Nathan Dyer, Ray Walker, Linnie Stansell, and Hilda "Ma" Goodman.

Chapel of All Faiths: The chapel information came from my memories and from Dr. Driggers's book titled *It Took A Miracle*.

Like Father, Like Son: ABAC is Special.

Like Father, Like Son: ABAC is Special

Father's Point of View . . .

We have fond memories about our experiences as students at ABAC. I shall never forget that day twenty-six years ago when I drove to Tifton to visit the campus for the first time. I got lost out beyond Tifton on Highway 82. A kind lady very graciously gave me correct directions when she saw my frustration at being lost. I was a happy kid once I saw the sign "ABRAHAM BALDWIN AGRICULTURAL COLLEGE".

I had two great years at ABAC. I made many friends some of whom are still my best friends. Classes were tough (I was in Agricultural Engineering) but the instructors were very, very patient with me. I do not know exactly how, but they let this old country boy graduate. I certainly attribute any success that I have had, in part, to the excellent educational experience at ABAC. You may ask, "why is he rambling on about his experiences at ABAC?" My reason for remembering so many things that happened is that my son, Chris, is now a student at ABAC. His first years was not Georgia's number one junior college. He spent some time at Georgia's number one senior college (that is the University of Georgia for those Georgia Tech fans or others who might by chance read this newspaper).

Chris and I have had several interesting discussions about ABAC. He has found a home in the same dorm where I began my college career. His advisor is a faculty member who I came to know and respect while at ABAC. In these discussions, my mind began to wander back to the good old days. I sure do miss those great times.

What does all this have to do with you as alumni and the ABAC Alumni Association? Please share the ABAC story every chance you get! Encourage young adults you know or come in contact with to consider ABAC in their educational plans. The ABAC today can offer those same great experiences that you and I so fondly remember. I know ABAC made a difference in my life and many of you have shared similar experiences. Become involved by supporting your Alumni Association or maybe you can help someone financially by contributions to the ABAC Foundation. You can change lives be becoming involved today.

Jimmy Hill   **Chris Hill**

Editor's Note: Jimmy Hill is the president of the ABAC Alumni Association and wrote this as his president's column for this publication. Chris Hill, Jimmy&son, is a sophomore journalism major and wrote this as his column for the student newspaper. Neither knew what the other had written. The editors of this paper saw the similarities and found them amusing and thought that you would, too.

ABAC Today

ABAC *Today* is published semi-annually by the Abraham Baldwin Agricultural College Office of Development and Alumni Relations. Third class postage is paid at Tifton, Georgia.

Harold J. Loyd
President

Melvin Merrill
Director of Development

Nancy Coleman
Director of Alumni Relations
& Executive Editor

Cindy Jones
Editor

Office of Development & Alumni Relations
Box 13, ABAC Station
Tifton, GA 31794-2693
Telephone (912) 386-3265

Son;s Point of View . . .

I had my doubts. I had my fears. I *was* confused about coming to this small college that I heard so much about, but knew so very little of. I thought I would never walk through these hallways. As we all can see, I am here.

In retrospect, I do have regrets. I regret that I did not come here first before attending four quarters at the University of Georgia. My father cam here-and then went to the university. I, of course, took the reverse route. As an 18-year-old, the last thing I wanted to do was what my father suggested or even what he had done himself. I admit I often made fun of ABAC. "An agricultural college? What? Me?!?!" This disrespect stemmed from my ignorance. I never would focus my attention upon what my father said about this school.

Now that I am here, I have a totally new prospective. I now see what my father sees. I have one of the same teachers he did, and I am staying in the same dorm that he did.

At ABAC I see tradition and respect stronger than any other college that I have witnessed or heard of. I see mighty bonds in the faculty and administration. These could not be broken by years or calamities. I understand why my father raves about ABAC so, and why he works hard in contributing to the progress of the school as the president of the ABAC Alumni Association.

At the University of Georgia and other like schools, one is just a number - another face in the crowd. Teachers do not care like they do here. At ABAC, a student is a real person, not just another sheep being herded through the educational process.

As a student, I want to speak out to my peers. Make the most of ABAC that you can. Use your mind and actually think! Don't just sit and wait for your education to be spoon fed to you. We only get one chance.

Chapter 11   My Brother Ricky Hill

The information on Ricky's education came from his report cards and one of his teachers, Mrs. Jimmie Nell Tate.

A copy of Ricky's school newspaper, *Jacket Junk*, was found in my mother's files upon her death. The newspaper pages are shown below:

JACKET JUNK 10¢

VOL. 1   MAY 15, 1970   NO. 8

STUDENTS SADDENED oooo

HE WON NO MEDALS, BUT WINNING HEARTS IS BETTER.....TO RICKY HILL.

He is gone, we know not where
Probably to that place up there.

His tone was soft, his way was kind,
People like him are hard to find.

His soul was pure, his heart was true,
Each day he lived was adventure new.

He went swimming we know not why
But it won't help anything if we cry.

His friends were few, his admirers many,
People envied him quite a plenty.

In time his memory will grow dim,
But I think we'll always remember him.

BY: MELINDA FARRIS

Death, be not proud, though some have
          called thee
Mighty and dreadful, for thou art not
          so;
For those, whom thou think'st thou
          dost overthrow,
Die not, poor Death, nor yet canst
          thou kill me.
From rest and sleep, which but thy
          pictures be,
Much pleasure, then from thee much
          more, must flow,
And soonest our best men with thee
          do go,
Rest of their bones, and soul's delivery.
Thou art slave to fate, chance, kings,
          and desperate men,
And dost with poison, war, and sickness
          dwell.
And poppy, or charms, can make us
          sleep as well,
And better than thy stroke. Why
          swell'st thou then?
One short sleep past, we wake eternally,
And Death shall be no more; Death,
          thou shalt die.
          (JOHN DONNE)

The students and faculty of Jeff Davis Junior High School were saddened at the death of an eighth grade friend.

Jasper Ricky Hill, 14, of Route 1, Denton, drowned Monday while swimming at a water hole near his home.

Surviving are his parents, the Rev. and Mrs. Jasper Hill of Denton; a sister, Miss Linda Hill of Denton; two brothers, Jimmy Hill of Athens and Spec. 4 Jerry Hill, U. S. Army, Vietnam; his grandmother, Mrs. L. W. Strickland of Jesup, and several aunts and uncles.

Ricky is at Miles Funeral Home.

Death has nothing terrible which life has not made so. A faithful Christian life in this world is the best preparation for the next. (Tryon Edwards).

We understand death for the first time when he puts his hand upon one whom we love. (Mad. De Stael).

We picture death as coming to destroy; let us rather picture Christ as coming to save. We think of death as ending; let us rather think of life as beginning, and that more abundantly. We think of losing; let us think of gaining. We think of parting, let us think of meeting. We think of going away; let us think of arriving. And as the voice of death whispers "You must go from eath," let us hear the voice of Christ saying, "You are but coming to Me!" (N. Macleod).

Death is the golden key that opens the palace of eternity. (Milton).

Is death the last sleep? No, it is the last and final awakening. (Walter Scott)

There is no better armor against the shafts of death than to be busied in God's service. (Fuller).

Each departed friend is a magnet that attracts us to the next world. (Richter).

GONE ....BUT NOT FORGOTTEN.

in Memory of ... Ricky Hill

R - is for rightousness his
    heart possessed.
I - is for instinct for the
    right life, the best.
C - is for cheerfulness that
    he showed every day.
K - is for kindness he gave
    along the way.
Y - is for the yielding in which
    he gave to Christ.

BY: Mary Beth Sams
    Betty Ann Ray

H - is for the happiness in
    which he shared with
    others.
I - is for the illness in
    which long years he
    suffered.
L - if for the laughter
    which rang throughout
    the day.
L - is for the love he showe
    to all that came his way

A FINAL TRIBUTE TO RICKY HILL

He lived a life of happiness as everyone
could see.
He never said an unkind word to you, his
friends, or me.

He always tried to do his best at
everything he'd do
His laughter touched the hearts of all,
especially me and you.

Everyone respected him as he respected
them,
His heart reached out to everyone, he
truly was a gem.

BY: Raylene Morris

I'LL REMEMBER RICKY HILL

He was the kind of guy who never had a
care,
His kindness he showed to everybody
everywhere.
He would have given you the shirt off
his back,
Or anything else that you might happen to
lack.
In church he sang with a deep glowing
voice,
And to God he would always happily
rejoice.
The many good things about him we will
remember and share,
Dear Lord, why is it the good people that
you can't seem to spare?

BY: Chris Casenelli

- - - - - - - - - - - - - - - - - - - -

Chapter 14   Waycross Georgia – It's a Girl

Below is the letter from Bob Williams:

BOB WILLIAMS FORD, INC.

U. S. Highway 84 - 213 E. Dame Ave.   Telephone (912) 487-5393
HOMERVILLE, GEORGIA 31634

June 23, 1979

Mr. Robert Scherer
Ga. Power Co.
P.O. Box 4545
Atlanta, Ga. 30302

Dear Mr. Scherer,

I am writing this letter in regard to one of your Energy Service employees
from the Waycross, Ga. district.

I met Jimmy Hill on Dec. 1, 1978, while in the process of getting started
to build a new house. Mr. Hill asked if he might borrow a set of my plans
to see if I could qualify for the Georgia Power Good Cents Home. Program.
His calculations showed that my home would meet the Good Cents standards
with a few changes.

One recommendation of Mr. Hill's that I was skeptical of at first, was the
size of the cooling unit. He recommended approximately a 2 and ½ ton unit.
I already had a recommendation from an air-conditioning dealer for a 4 ton
unit. I have an engineering background, so I asked Mr. Hill to explain why
the differences in the recommended air conditioner size. He explained about
heat transfer, R-value of insulation, and about how a heat gain is calculated.
I told him I wanted to qualify for the Good Cents Program including the smaller air conditioner to lower my energy bills.

After we agreed upon the size air conditioner, Mr. Hill explained the efficiency of air conditioning units. I told him that I wanted the highest efficiency available. He showed me a Carrier unit with a 10.6 E.E.R. I called my
air conditioning dealer and told him about this 10.6 E.E.R. unit. The dealer
said this particular unit was not available. Not satisfied with this information I called Mr. Hill and he checked with the distributor. No less than
seventeen units were available. I was beginning to realize that Jimmy was
knowledgeable and concerned about providing me with factual information.

Jimmy and I met many times during the next few months, he continued to give
me extremely good advice on a variety of ways to save energy in my home while
under construction.

Jimmy Hill has shown me that he is a professional, knowledgeable, and concerned individual that cares about the people he serves. I congratulate Georgia
Power on having such an individual as Jimmy Hill to work with customers in the
important area of energy conservation.

In closing, I hope this letter will help you to realize the capabilities of
this man, and may possibly prompt you to present Mr. Hill with an Accommodation
Letter, which he most definitely deserves.

Thank You,

Below is the letter from President Robert Scherer:

Georgia Power Company
270 Peachtree Street
Post Office Box 4545
Atlanta, Georgia 30302
Telephone 404-522-6060

R. W. Scherer
President

the southern electric system

July 9, 1979

Mr. Jimmy Hill
Energy Services
WAYCROSS DISTRICT

Dear Jimmy:

It is extremely gratifying for me to receive
letters such as the one from Bob Williams praising
one of our employees. Let me add my appreciation to
his for a job well done. It is this type of professionalism that our Company most needs and is most
appreciative of.

Once again, thanks for your fine efforts.

Sincerely,

R. W. Scherer

nch
Enclosure
cc: Mr. Rodney E. Moore
     Mr. John Roberts

Chapter 16   The Dumpling Lady

All of the information from this chapter came from Mother's files, my files,
and my memories.

Chapter 19   Agriculture and Agribusiness

The brief history of Agricultural Affairs came from old brochures, documents, a copy of an old advertisement, Olin Ginn conversations, and my memories.

All organization information, unless otherwise indicated, came from my files and memories.

Georgia Agribusiness Council documents came from GAC board meeting minutes and my files.

The continuation of the Georgia Agribusiness Council section, Chapter 19, is found below:

Charlie Crowder, executive director of GAC, retired in 1987. I served on the selection committee in 1988 that selected Dr. Tal DuVall to serve as the next executive director. DuVall resigned in 1989, and I served as chair of the next selection committee; we chose Gary Black as the next executive director. The board voted to change the title of the executive position to President. Gary Black served from 1989 to 2010. The board selected Bryan Tolar as the next president in 2011, and he served until 2018. Will Bentley was selected as the next president of GAC in November 2018. Will is currently in his second year of service to GAC.

In 1989, the GAC had 315 members, and in 2019 the membership had grown to over 1,100. During my time serving as chairman, we faced the challenges of how to grow membership and of providing services to our members. I urged our board to think outside of the fence row and figure out a way to move forward or we might lose the organization. I hosted a board retreat, in the early spring of 1990, to discuss the issues facing GAC. I presented the findings of the five-year strategic plan from the spring meeting to the board at our regular meeting on Monday, May 7, 1990, held at the Holiday Inn Airport-North in Atlanta. The board approved the report as the official five-year strategic plan for GAC. Further discussion led by Sam Hay was to move forward with hiring a membership recruiter.

The two staff members we had at that time were already very busy and did not have time for a dedicated focus on membership.

At the GAC winter board meeting, held on January 22, 1990, I brought up for discussion the idea of revisiting the GAC mission statement and developing long-range strategic plans. I suggested that we conduct a two-day board retreat to be held in Macon. The board approved the idea.

The board met on April 24–25, 1990, in Macon at the Twin Pines facility owned by Georgia Power employees. The mission statement was refined, and a draft five-year strategic plan was developed during the two-day meeting.

The next board meeting took place on May 7, 1990. The five-year strategic plan was discussed and adopted by the board. The board conducted other routine business at this meeting as well.

The next board meeting took place on Wednesday, August 8, 1990, at Abraham Baldwin Agricultural College in Tifton, Georgia. I presided at the meeting, and we addressed several issues, one being the proposal to hire a new staff person. This person would handle member relations, issue development, program development, and the Harvest Ball. After much discussion, my challenge to the board was that we needed to dedicate some of our Council savings account to hire the new staff member as soon as possible to get the ball rolling on increasing our membership. This move should increase our membership and allow for additional funds for the Council. I asked for a motion to authorize the executive committee to put together a proposal to work out the details on hiring the new staff person. Director Garland Thompson made the motion, and it was seconded by director Chuck Williams. The meeting was adjourned.

The 1991 winter board meeting of GAC took place at the Ramada Inn Capitol in Atlanta on Tuesday, January 29. After routine business was handled, I introduced Grace Adams as the new vice president of information for GAC. Grace made a presentation of her goals and objectives. She was working on having a member representing every county in Georgia. She had already started her membership recruitment program. She asked each director to submit to her three referrals for membership, and she would contact them. Grace implemented her plans, and they made a significant positive impact on the Council's membership and financial condition.

The next board meeting took place on May 6, 1991. Along with routine business, the board revisited the five-year plan. The board decided to revise the plan and approved a three-year plan with much more detailed objectives.

The three-year (1991–1994) plan had the following objectives:

Objective one: Represent agribusiness interests in the legislative arena
- Conduct legislative breakfast
- Conduct legislative seminar
- Conduct board member "Legislative Day" at the Georgia Capitol and conduct a board trip to Washington, DC
- Conduct an annual meeting for members
- Develop federal issues handbook for Georgia House and Senate Agriculture Committee members
- Track state and national legislation and agribusiness issues through board actions, broker information, and committee resources
- Highlight legislative accomplishments in GAC publications including the *Agribusiness Edition* and the *Predicate*

Objective Two: Educate the public on agribusiness issues
- Publish the *Predicate* newsletter monthly and send to congressional offices and agricultural media
- Sponsor FFA Star Agribusiness Award
- Establish lines of communication with various consumer interest groups
- Subscribe to various consumer group publications
- Conduct media relations conference
- Develop college/university intern co-op program
- Serve as program providers and sponsors of 4-H Camp, Natural Resource Workshop, etc.

- Serve on the Agriculture in the Classroom task force
- Conduct the Harvest Ball (celebration)
- Conduct GAC annual meeting
- Serve on the American Cancer Society State Nutrition Committee
- Co-sponsor the Georgia Agricultural Congress
- Conduct civic club presentations
- Serve as liaison with other agricultural groups
- Publish *Agribusiness Edition* at least twice yearly
- Upon request, develop management training seminars for agribusiness companies and organizations
- Conduct workshops with health-related organizations to promote wholesomeness of our food supply
- Sponsor Sunbelt luncheon and breakfast
- Publish Sunbelt exhibitor newsletter
- Sponsor All Georgia Products Dinner for the Georgia Association of Broadcasters and the Georgia Press Association
- Organize a committee to survey plans for a Georgia Food Festival

Objective Three: Promote agribusiness development

- Conduct AG-PLAN (Planning Leadership for Agriculture Now) program
- Enhance networking with the development community
- Develop an information system for Georgia agribusiness products and services
- Assist in conducting the Georgia Agri-Leaders Forum
- Cooperatively develop agribusiness brochure with the Georgia Department of Industry, Trade, and Tourism and Georgia Industrial Developers Association (GIDA)
- Provide agribusiness data on request from communities and business
- Actively serve on GIDA agribusiness committee

- Manage and implement the GAC Harvest Ball
- Upon request assist in organizing Chamber of Commerce Agribusiness Committees

One of the more important services that GAC offered was its legislative involvement. Gary Black was the Council's registered lobbyist. He was at the State Capitol every day during the legislative session to monitor any legislative activity that might impact Georgia agribusiness. Black sent out a weekly report to GAC members outlining bills that could impact their companies along with information on who to contact to express their concerns, opinions, or thanks.

GAC trips to Washington, DC, were a valuable way for board members to communicate directly with the Georgia congressional delegation. I participated in all of the trips from 1987 to 1996. Our board delegation would generally consist of ten to twelve board members and occasionally GAC agribusiness members. We would set up appointments over two days and generally spend one night in Washington.

The GAC sponsored the County Agribusiness Development and Leadership Recognition Program. Counties were encouraged to enter the program to spotlight their agribusiness activities and enhance their agribusiness economic development. Five counties were selected each year and were visited by a group of judges to evaluate their program. The best overall county agribusiness program was recognized as the best County Agribusiness Development and Leadership Recognition Program in the state of Georgia.

Georgia Aquaculture Development Commission (GADC)

The GADC members were Armand Marcaurelle, Tom Crow, Senator Harold Ragan, Alton Moultrie, Representative Henry Reaves, Harold Fallin, Mike Gennings, Jimmy Hill, Dr. Georgia Lewis, Wayne Balkcom, Dr. Ken Semmens, Walter Stephens, Paul Williams, Wayne Dollar, Don McGough, Michael Spencer, Dr. Loren Nichols, Commissioner Tommy Irvin, Frank Giles, and Andy Truan. I assigned Travis Henry to assist the

Commission in its work. The Commission met over an extended period to develop the plan.

The authors of the plan included Dr. Gary Burtle, Dr. Ronnie Gilbert, Dr. George Lewis, Dr. James L. Shelton, Dr. Mac Rawson, all from the University of Georgia. Michael Spencer with the Georgia Department of Natural Resources was an author. The report was typed by Mrs. Betty Smith. Travis Henry of Georgia Power assisted in getting the report printed.

Actions recommended by the Commission were:

- Implement a coordinated educational effort to educate lenders, producers, potential investors, and financial regulators about the industry
- Recommend that lending institutions employ specialists with the experience to fully evaluate aquaculture loan proposals and existing loans
- Recommend the employment of qualified appraisers with experience and training to assess the value of equipment and improvements used in aquaculture
- The Georgia Department of Natural Resources to produce a list of aquatic producers and their products for use by marketers and buyers
- Working with the Georgia Department of Agriculture, the aquaculturists will ensure only safe, wholesome food products enter markets. This includes self-imposed evaluation of products for compliance with generally accepted production practices
- The Georgia Department of Natural Resources will set guidelines for permitting exotic species and genetically altered animals and will share this information with the industry
- The Georgia Department of Agriculture and the Georgia Department of Natural Resources should take a more active

role in promoting the state's aquaculture industry, which could have a positive impact on rural economic development

- The Georgia Department of Industry and Trade (now known as the Georgia Department of Economic Development) should help promote the industry by recruiting aquaculture businesses to the state
- The UGA Cooperative Extension Service's Aquaculture and Fisheries Program should increase its staff, programs, and resources available to the aquaculture industry
- Recommend that the Southern Appalachian Fisheries Research and Extension Center (Cohutta, Georgia) add a professional staff member in a joint appointment with the Warnell School of Forest Resources to direct research and extension programs at the Center
- Recommend the UGA Tifton Campus enhance the aquaculture facilities, including research ponds and a wet laboratory/hatchery building
- A Georgia Aquaculture Commodity Commission needs to be established and administered by the Georgia Department of Agriculture. The Commission could be supported by a "feed check-off" program, pending approval by the state's aquaculture producers. This would allow for funds to assist in promotion, market development, and research.

Chapter 21   1996 Summer Olympics

My work schedule at the 1996 Olympics under the GA AG 96 Project. It was a very similar schedule to that of many other volunteers.

Saturday, July 13	9:00 a.m.–10:00 p.m.
Sunday, July 14	Noon–10:00 p.m.
Monday, July 15	Noon–9:00 p.m.
Tuesday, July 16	6:00 p.m.–midnight
Wednesday, July 17	Noon–6:00 p.m.
Thursday, July 18	6:00 p.m.–11:00 p.m.

Friday, July 19	5:00 pm.–2:00 a.m.
Saturday, July 20	Pavilion Supervisor
Sunday, July 21	4:00 p.m.–2:00 a.m.
Monday, July 22	4:00 p.m.–2:00 a.m.
Tuesday, July 23	Off
Wednesday, July 24	Pavilion Supervisor
Thursday, July 25	4:00 p.m.–2:00 a.m.
Friday, July 26	Off
Saturday, July 27	6:00 a.m.–4:00 p.m. (Bomb Explosion— did not work)
Sunday, July 28	Park closed
Monday, July 29	Park closed
Tuesday, July 30	Park re-opened, 4:00 p.m.–2:00 a.m.
Wednesday, July 31	Off
Thursday, August 1	4:00 p.m.–2:00 a.m.
Friday, August 2	4:00 p.m.–2:00 a.m.
Saturday, August 3	Pavilion Supervisor
Sunday, August 4	4:00 p.m.–midnight. Park closed. Olympic Games concluded.
Midnight–6:00 a.m.	Remove equipment and close down the pavilion.

Operation Legacy details from Chapter 21 are listed below:

On Sunday morning, the executives took a tour of the Olympic Stadium and Athletes' Village. Lunch was at the Ritz-Carlton with special guest Charles Wang, EVP, CP Group. At 2:00 p.m., a business session was held with moderator Dr. Gale Buchanan, College of Agricultural and Environmental Sciences, University of Georgia. Panelists included Rob Saglio, president, Avian Farms Inc.; Doug Cagle, chairman, Cagle's Inc.; and Rusty Griffin, president, Griffin Corporation. Following the panel discussion, Georgia Power president and CEO Bill Dahlberg spoke to the group.

On Sunday evening, the executives experienced the Legacy Celebration, a gala event that celebrated the Olympic Games. Billy Payne, president and CEO of the Atlanta Committee for the Olympic Games, spoke at the event.

Monday, September 11, the agribusiness executives left for a tour to Griffin. I, along with Gary Black, president, Georgia Agribusiness Council, and David Dykes, food industry engineer, Georgia Power Company, hosted and transported the group to the University of Georgia Griffin Campus.

Dr. Gerald Arkin, director, UGA Griffin Campus, welcomed the executives to the campus and gave a summary of the campus mission. The focus of the tour was on food science. Dr. Mike Doyle, director, Center for Food Safety and Quality Enhancement, gave an overview of the Center. He led the group to labs where faculty presented their areas of expertise. Dr. Dick Phillips and Dr. Anna Resurreccion discussed food product development and consumer testing. Dr. Manjeet Chinnan talked about his work with edible films for food products. Dr. Larry Beauchat discussed food safety in general and specifically how the Center was addressing industry needs. Dr. Steve Kreshovich talked about his work in the introduction of new agricultural plants. Dr. Stan Prussia, Dr. John Astleford Jr., and Dr. Yen-Con Hung discussed their work on determining the ripeness of fruit and vegetables with a laser puff device. The final speaker of the day was Dr. Ronny Duncan, who described the world-class turfgrass research conducted on the campus and at the UGA Tifton Campus. Georgia is the world leader in turfgrass research and production.

Monday evening, the executives and their spouses attended a reception and dinner at the Governor's Mansion with the Honorable Zell Miller, Governor, State of Georgia. Governor Miller spoke about Georgia and its reputation as a great place to do business. He emphasized Georgia's population growth, natural resources, Atlanta Airport, trained workforce, and Georgia's business-friendly approach to doing business.

Tuesday, September 12, the agribusiness executives were treated to a buffet breakfast before they headed home. They were shuttled by our team to their departure locations.

Chapter 22   Georgia Agri-Leaders Forum

17 Classes and 346 graduates are listed below:

Georgia Agri-Leaders Forum Graduates from 1993 - 2010

Grace Adams Stewart
Parrish Akins
Merett Alexander
Titus Andrews
Bruce Applewhite
Wil Arnett
Roger Austin
William Bagwell, Jr.
John Allen Bailey
Sandy Baldwin
Keith Barber
Gilbert Barrett
Danny Bennett
John Bernard
Keith Bertrand
Reuben Beverly
John Cary Bittick
Carter Black
Dennis Black
Spencer Black
Beth Bland
Graydon Bobo
Bill Boone
Delane Borron
William Bowen, Jr.
Jimmy Bradley
Bennie Branch
Roger Branch
Andi Branstetter
Chip Bridges
Kathy Brooks
Steve Brown
James Buck
Bob Budd
David Buntin
Tony Burnes
Al Burns
Roebie Burriss, III
Henry Burton, Jr.
Len Cagle
Art Cain
Debbie Cannon

Jennifer Cannon
Wendell Cannon
Louie Canova
Becky Carlson
Tim Carroll
Joy Carter
Mark Causey
Steve Chambers
Les Charles
Jimmy Clements
Nancy Coleman
Thomas Coleman, Jr.
Jim Colson
Forrest Connelly
Eddie Cook
Butch Copelan
Larry Copeland
Joanna Craven
Dominick Crea
Bert Crosson
Ali Csinos
Be-Atrice Cunningham
Caryn Curry
Gale Cutler
Thomas Daniels
Guy Daughtrey
Jeremy Davis
Jim Davis
Roger Davis
Maurice Dayton
Denise Deal
Frank Dean
Barry Deas
Earl Denham
Bruce Dillard
Dick Dowdy
Dennis Duncan
Paul Dutter
Zippy Duvall
Edward Ealy
Frances Edmunds
Chuck Ellis

Francois Elvinger
Chap Enfinger
Ester England
Terry England
Kim Erwin
Chad Etheridge
Rome Ethredge
David Evans
Jed Evans
Mack Evans
Ed Faircloth, Jr.
David Ferrell
Bobby Ferris
Juli Fields
Tim Flanders
Merrill Folsom
Jake Ford
James Ford
Rodney Fowler
Dory Franklin
Nancy Fussell
Linda Gambrell
Joe Garner
Roderick Gilbert
Donald Giles
Tammy Gilland
Larry Gillespie
Charles Gillespie, Jr.
Jeff Glass
Greg Glover
Brad Godwin
Justin Goodroe
Jim Graham
Timothy Grey
Keith Griffin
Dan Groscost
Chris Groskreutz
Fredrick Hall
Gregg Hall
Marc Hand
John Harrell
Mike Harris

Rusty Harris
Will Harris
Jeffrey Harvey
Larry Hawkins
Travis Henry
Cynthia Hernandez
Henry Hibbs
Jimmy Hill
Robin Hill
Murray Hines, II
April Hobbs
Stephanie Hollifield
Clint Hood
Kristi Hughes
Brent James
Dot James
Lynmore James
Sam James
Daniel Johnson
Bob Jones
Johnny Jones
Katrina Jones
Ross Kendrick
David King
Diana King
Mark King
Holli Kuykendall
Curt Lacy
Mike Lacy
Smitty Lamb
Zeke Lambert
Gil Landry, Jr.
Chris Langone
Lannie Lanier
George Larsen, II
Paul Larson
Teresa Lasseter
Keith Lassiter
Ben Lastly
Orville Lindstrom
Kim Lowe
Sharon Lucas

Georgia Agri-Leaders Forum Graduates from 1993 - 2010

Jerry Lupo
Livia Lynch
Gene Maddux
Blane Marable
Brian Marlowe
Elliott Marsh, Jr.
Lamar Martin
Todd Massey
Randy Mayfield
Alan McAllister
Hal McCallum
Steve McClam
Kenneth McEntire
Mary Alice McGee
Norman McGlohon
Eddie McGriff
Eddie McKie
Rusty McLeod
Tim McMillan
Jeff McPhail
Mark McWhorter
Roosevelt McWilliams
Earl Merritt
Keith Mickler
Molly Miller
Doris Miller-Liebl
Billy Mills
Kevin Mitcham
Brad Mitchell
Mehdi Mobini
J. Michael Moore
Chris Morgan
Steve Morgan
Steve Morgan
Candy Morris
Jason Morris
Megan Morris
Sid Mullis
Todd Mullis
Ken Murphree
Matt Murphy
Lee Myers
Chris Nail

Brian Nash
Brice Nelson, Jr.
Scott NeSmith
Terry Niblett
Randy Nichols
Ronnie Noble
Ricky North
Richard Oliver
Godwin Onohwosa
Jason Parker
Corey Parr
Steve Parrish
Mary Ann Parsons
Chris Paulk
Mark Paulk
Wesley Paulk
Jason Peake
Mark Peele
Deborah Pennington
Dana Perkins
Sammy Perkins
Calvin Perry
Lee Petigout
Paul Petigout
Don Phillips
Jon Pierson
Jimmy Pierson, Jr.
George Ponder
Paul Poole
Ralph Powell
Greg Price
Judy Purdy
Susan Ragan
Scotty Raines
Mack Rainey
Bob Ray, Jr.
Jody Redding
Dean Reese
Bruce Rentz
John Ricketts
Alex Riko
Brian Rivers
Cal Roach

Jay Roberts
Darrell Ross
Ken Rountree
Keith Rucker
Tim Savelle
Barbara Saxton
Jimmy Scott
Corine Sellers
Wes Shannon
Patricia Simmons
Earleen Sizemore
Billy Skaggs
Bobby Smith
Donnie Smith
Doris Smith
Kristin Smith
Tas Smith
Tony Smith
Ed Snoddy
April Sorrow
Wes Sparks
Tommy Stalvey
Velinda Stanley
Vince Stanley
Forrest Stegelin
Jean Steiner
Jody Strickland
Tim Strickland
Christopher Stripling
Shirley Stripling
Dale Stutchman
David Swayne
Tony Tate
Jeff Taylor
Stephen Taylor, Jr.
Todd Teasley
Julie Thames
Donnie Thomas
Harry Thompson
Melvin Thompson
Mid Thorne, III
Lynn Thornhill
Ed Thornton

Ed Tolbert
Bill Tollner
Clint Truman
Billy Turk
David Turner
Travis Turnquist
Chuck Tyson
John Uesseler
Marc van Iersel
Danny Vaughn
James A. Vaughn
Philipp von Hanstein
Bonnie Walker
John Walker
Glen Walters
John Walters
Russ Walters
Ellen Warren
Kenny Waters
Randy Waters
Jay Watrous
Sam Watson
Joe West
Terry Whigham
Allen Whitehead
Dick Whitlock
Collie Williams
Mike Williams
Rodney Williams
Gibbs Wilson
Larry Windham
Troy Windham
Jason Womack
Beth Wood
Carla Wood
Katie Woodall
James Woodard
Steve Woodham
Derick Wooten
Vann Wooten
David Yelton
Anne Young
Chris Young

Chapter 23   End of My Career at Georgia Power Company

Georgia Power President Bill Dahlberg's thank-you note:

*P*reston Arkwright, Georgia Power's first president coined the slogan "A Citizen Wherever We Serve" more than 60 years ago, in response to accusations that the power company looked after s own interests, not the interests of the community. He said, "We have come here to stay; and solely from ou wn interests it is up to us, as to no one else in Georgia, to do all we can to build up the territory we serve. We ant to be considered a citizen wherever we serve."

May 30, 1991

Dear Jimmy,

Once again, I would like to congratulate you on some very special achievements. It's an honor to be recognized once, but I believe you're trying to set a new record in the awards department.

But all levity aside, I am very proud of your achievements, and I am glad to see that such prestigious organizations have recognized your outstanding character and contributions.

Thank you for your service to the company, to your profession, and to the state. Again, congratulations on your honors, and best of luck as you begin your new duties with the American Society of Agricultural Engineers.

Sincerely,

A.W. Dahlberg

Chapter 25   Farm Again - AgrAbility of Georgia

Additional information was found at www.farmagain.com and www.agrability.org

Chapter 26   My Parents – Rest of the Story

All information for this chapter came from Dad and Mother's files, my files, and memories unless otherwise identified.

Thanks to Reverend Keith Yawn, Reverend Donnie Brown, and Reverend Charles Morgan for their valuable input in this chapter.

Thanks to Reverend Dewitt R. Corbin for his permission to print the section from his book titled *The Rebel Preacher*.

Chapter 28   Life on Tomahawk Mountain

Ludlow Porch's information and book titles were approved for publication by his wife, Nancy Hanson.

Information on Dr. Ferrell Sams and his book titles approved for publication by his son, Fletcher Sams.

Chapter 29   They Inspired Me

The names of the leaders who wrote letters included in the Book of Letters referred to in Chapter 29 are listed below:

GALFF Directors: Dr. Fred C. Davison, retired, president of the University of Georgia; Louise Hill, Georgia Farm Bureau, director, Program Development and Education; Dr. Harold J. Loyd, president, ABAC; Stephen M. Newton, executive vice president, Forest Farmers Association; J. Donald Rogers, assistant commissioner, Georgia Department of Agriculture; David L. Westmoreland, deputy director, Georgia Forestry Commission; L. Edward White, director, Sunbelt

Agricultural Exposition; Randy Williams, National Program leader, USDA; Lynne M. Kernaghan, regional coordinator, Georgia Health Decisions; Graydon Bobo, charter class, Georgia Agri-Leaders Forum; Delane Borron, field operations manager, Gold Kist; Ed Faircloth Jr., Agricultural Investment Management; Tammy Tate Gilland, director, Annual Giving, UGA; Charles Gillespie, charter class, Georgia Agri-Leaders Forum; Lamar Martin, Tift County Extension director, UGA; Doris M. Miller, DVM, UGA College of Veterinary Medicine; Chris Nail, editor/publisher, *Georgia Country Life*; Susan Ragan, class of 2005, Georgia Agri-Leaders Forum; Bob Ray, legislative representative, Georgia Farm Bureau; Donnie Smith, farmer, charter class, Georgia Agri-Leaders Forum; Velinda Stanley, charter class, Georgia Agri-Leaders Forum.

Members of the Georgia Agri-Leaders Forum, class of 1994, who wrote letters: Grace Adams; Parrish Akins; Roger Austin; Lee Brooks; J. Wendell Cannon; Caryn Curry; Terry England; James W. Ford; Don Giles; Larry Gillespie; Keith Griffin; Will Harris III; Travis Henry; Dot James; Mike Lacy; Eddie McGriff; Eugene M. Maddox; D. Scott NeSmith; Doris Smith; Jody Tyson Strickland; Julie Thames; William N. Turk; James A. Vaughn; Dick Whitlock; Dr. Joe West; and Ester England.

A special letter from Louise Hill:

Georgia Farm Bureau Federation

P. O. BOX 7068 • 1620 BASS ROAD AT I-75
MACON, GEORGIA 31298
912-474-8411

November 30, 1994

Mr. Jimmy Hill
Past Chairman of the Board
Georgia Agri-Leaders Forum
c/o Georgia Power Company
P. O. Box 459
Grayson, Georgia 30221

Dear Jimmy:

You have made dreams come true during the past six years. In 1989 when
we met in Athens in Randy Williams's office, an agricultural leadership
program for Georgia was simply a dream in a few minds. Because of your
unselfish commitment and leadership, we are now graduating the 2nd class
of the Georgia Agri-Leaders Forum. All of this would not have happened
without Jimmy Hill!

Your courage in leadership and willingness to step forward makes a major
difference in so many areas. Thank you for all that you do.

The most important thing to me is because of the last 6 years, I am very
honored to say Jimmy and Gail Hill are my friends. You are very special
people! Thank you for sharing your talents, wisdom, and kindness. I
especially appreciate Gail's patience in all those times I get referred
to as Mrs. Jimmy Hill. I am certainly not that, but I will claim to be
your adopted sister at any point.

All of this added together means, I look forward to every opportunity to
plan and plot with you! Here's to many more of those times.

With warmest regards,

Louise Hill, Director
Program Development & Education

LH/mfp

About the Author

Jimmy L. Hill grew up on the dusty, sandy dirt roads of deep South Georgia. He spent his early years working in the tobacco fields and doing other farm work. Working for entrepreneur Fred Bennett as a farmhand, land surveyor, and gas station attendant came a bit later. Jimmy had the entrepreneurial spirit at heart from an early age, starting with selling Grit newspapers.

Jimmy's first writing experience was at the age of 17 for his high school newspaper. He wrote numerous technical and procedure manuals for his first full-time employer - Georgia Power Company. As a member of Georgia Power's speaker's bureau, a senior manager, and an agricultural engineer, he gave hundreds of talks and presentations all over Georgia and in other states across the country.

As an engineer, he makes no apology for his minutiae of *details* in describing his life journey. He inherited his storytelling skills from his Dad. Jimmy's life work has been recognized by receiving numerous awards and honors. Also, he received outstanding alumni awards from Abraham Baldwin Agricultural College and the College of Agricultural and Environmental Sciences at the University of Georgia. Also, he won a Silver Effie Award from the American Marketing Association for advertising effectiveness.

Jimmy deep dives into his life history and identifies those who inspired him on his journey. In the last chapter of the book, he summarizes how each of these people impacted his life. He is now retired and lives with his wife, Gail, and their dog Amicalola (Lola) on Tomahawk Mountain in North Georgia. They have two children and six grandchildren.

Printed in the USA
CPSIA information can be obtained
at www.ICGtesting.com
LVHW051047300823
756590LV00001B/12